THE
PATHFINDER

The publishers will be pleased to send, upon request, an illustrated folder setting forth the purpose and scope of THE MODERN LIBRARY, *and listing each volume in the series. Every reader of books will find titles he has been looking for, handsomely printed, in definitive editions, and at an unusually low price.*

THE PATHFINDER

OR, THE INLAND SEA

BY

JAMES FENIMORE COOPER

INTRODUCTION BY NORMAN HOLMES PEARSON

"Here the heart
May give a useful lesson to the head,
And Learning wiser grow without his books."

COWPER

THE MODERN LIBRARY · NEW YORK

Library of Congress Catalog Card Number: 52 9772

Random House IS THE PUBLISHER OF *The Modern Library*

BENNETT A. CERF · DONALD S. KLOPFER · ROBERT K. HAAS

Manufactured in the United States of America

By H. Wolff

PREFACE

THE plan of this tale suggested itself to the writer many years since, though the details are altogether of recent invention. The idea of associating seamen and savages in incidents that might be supposed characteristic of the Great Lakes having been mentioned to a Publisher, the latter obtained something like a pledge from the Author to carry out the design at some future day, which pledge is now tardily and imperfectly redeemed.

The reader may recognize an old friend under new circumstances in the principal character of this legend. If the exhibition made of this old acquaintance, in the novel circumstances in which he now appears, should be found not to lessen his favor with the Public, it will be a source of extreme gratification to the writer, since he has an interest in the individual in question that falls little short of reality. It is not an easy task, however, to introduce the same character in four separate works, and to maintain the peculiarities that are indispensable to identity, without incurring a risk of fatiguing the reader with sameness; and the present experiment has been so long delayed quite as much from doubts of its success as from any other cause. In this, as in every other undertaking, it must be the "end" that will "crown the work."

The Indian character has so little variety that it has been my object to avoid dwelling on it too much on the present occasion; its association with the sailor, too, it is feared, will be found to have more novelty than interest.

It may strike the novice as an anachronism to place vessels on Ontario in the middle of the eighteenth century; but in this particular facts will fully bear out all the license of the fiction. Although the precise vessels mentioned in these pages may never have existed on that water or anywhere else, others so nearly resembling them are known to have navigated that inland sea, even at a period much earlier than the one just mentioned, as to form a sufficient authority for their introduction into a work of fiction. It is a fact not generally remembered, however well known it may be, that there are isolated spots along the line of the great lakes that date as settlements as far back as many of the older American towns, and which were the seats of a species of civilization long before the greater portion of even the older States was rescued from the wilderness.

Ontario in our own times has been the scene of important naval evolutions. Fleets have manœuvred on those waters, which, half a century ago, were as deserted as waters well can be; and the day is not distant when the whole of that vast range of lakes will become the seat of empire, and fraught with all the interests of human society. A passing glimpse, even though it be in a work of fiction, of what that vast region so lately was, may help to make up the sum of knowledge by which alone a just appreciation can be formed of the wonderful means by which Providence is clearing the way for the advancement of civilization across the whole American continent.

INTRODUCTION

by NORMAN HOLMES PEARSON

James Fenimore Cooper could never make up his mind whether *The Pathfinder* or *The Prairie* was his finest story; but he was as satisfied as others would be after him that if anything "is at all to outlast himself, it is, unquestionably, the series of 'The Leatherstocking Tales,' " of which both novels were a part. Having begun the panoramic series almost casually, perhaps as Faulkner was to undertake his (descendent) epic of Yoknapatawpha, Cooper was deliberately to fill in the bare spots, much also as Faulkner was to tidy up his saga of the South by the writing of intervening episodes. In each case what emerged was a use for history, in terms of the people and the nature of a region. In order of their fictional chronology—the dates of their publication indicated within parentheses—Cooper's completed series ran: *The Deerslayer* (1841); *The Last of the Mohicans* (1826); *The Pathfinder* (1840); *The Pioneers* (1823); and *The Prairie* (1827).

Among the figures who moved across the frontier of an emerging West, Cooper may be said to have drawn barely a few realized characters (in the fullest sense of subtleties of delineation), but he created a hero. He created also a landscape. Cooper's particular talents found their way through slapdash into their fullest expression in the mythical concept of the supremely skilled and deservedly lucky frontier hunter and guide, and in the depiction of the great expanses of unbroken American forests and the rolling waters within. When Mark Twain was to laugh at Deerslayer, he remembered everything except Cooper's genius.

Others recognized the genius. Victor Hugo, looking back from the 1880's, declared that, outside of France, Cooper was the greatest novelist of the century. Washington Irving, having finished reading *The Pathfinder*, declared: "They may say what they will of Cooper: the man who wrote this book is not only a great man, but a good man." Balzac, who knew a novel when he saw one, wrote in a review of *The Pathfinder* in the *Revue Parisienne:* "Leatherstocking is a statue, a magnificent moral hermaphrodite, born of the savage state and of civilization, who will live as long as literatures last. I do not know that the extraordinary work of Walter Scott furnishes a creation as grandiose as that of this hero of the savannas and the forests." Speaking of Cooper's landscapes in the book, Balzac continued: "This is the school that literary landscape painters ought to study; all the secrets of the art are here. This magic prose not only shows to the mind the river, its banks, the forests and their trees, but it succeeds in giving us a sense of both the slightest circumstances and the combined whole." Elsewhere he called *The Pathfinder* "a masterpiece."

And so *The Pathfinder* is, within its kind. Cooper had discovered the "matter of America," and in leading the native novel out from creaking Gothic hallways into the open air, he set up an easel on which he could represent the life of nature. What Bryant experimented with in poetry, Cooper achieved in prose. Seldom was he more successful than in *The Pathfinder*. He drew what his eyes knew. The rocky stream of the Oswego which leads characters and readers to the banks of Lake Ontario and the heart of the story was the general scene of his childhood. The particularities of Lake Ontario were the profit of his young manhood.

Having "left" Yale in his third year there, at the age of sixteen, to ship before the mast in 1806, he was in 1808 commissioned as midshipman, and after a brief tour of duty at sea served in the American "fresh-water navy" on Lake Ontario where a brig was being built for use against the British in Canada. There was no naval action, but there was the spirit of it, and there was travel. He sailed the lake. He went as far as the Thousand Islands and to Niagara. His eyes were on the frontier. In *The Pathfinder* it is not simply that the spirited navigation of Jasper Western is without broken twigs and has verisimilitude as well as verve, but that the landscape on every side has freshness as well as truth.

What Cooper's eyes had seen for the first time, Cooper's readers were to see for the first time through his novel. It was as much of a discovery for the seaboard population of America as it had been for Cap, the salt-water sailor of his romance, and as it was for the Europeans. The frontier landscape of the Great Lakes region was vanishing in 1840. "In a word," Cooper wrote in a preface to *The Pathfinder*, "though the scenes of this book are believed to have once been as nearly accurate as is required by the laws which govern fiction, they are so no longer. Oswego is a large and thriving town; Toronto and Kingston, on the other side of the lake, compete with it; while Buffalo, Detroit, Cleveland, Milwaukee, and Chicago, on the upper lakes, to say nothing of a hundred places of lesser note, are fast advancing to the level of commercial places of great local importance." In our own day Cooper's landscape has disappeared, and his pages become all the more valuable. They preserve the memory of fertility and innocence in the American scene.

The combination of lake and land, of skipper and guide, gives to *The Pathfinder* a unique concentration of Cooper's recognized talents. But nowhere more clearly than in *The Pathfinder* do we find the recognition on Cooper's part of what he felt to be a basic pattern to the myth of American tradition which the Leatherstocking tales contrive. The average reader may look simply for picaresque adventure in the episodes of Natty Bumppo, but Cooper tried to see beyond the exploits into an understanding of what pattern of values they represented at their best. What he recognized was a system of chivalry. What he presented was a code. As Faulkner was to fictionalize a code for the Southern planter, more deeply engrained in nature than Cabell's code had been for Poictesme, Cooper was to point out in the conduct of his hero and those about him the example of a natural and democratic scheme of values.

In adapting to the American scene the historical devices of Scott, Cooper did considerably more than people the landscape with Scott's figures. In part he was granting tribute to Scott; in greater part he was paying homage to the American past and its felt analogies. In terms of Cooper's philosophy of history, "the Westward movement of the agricultural frontier" was, as Henry Nash Smith has observed, "a unique process which seems to turn time backward in the New World and to make American history an inverted image of that of Europe. According to this scheme of interpretation, the new communities springing up in the West represent stages of society equivalent to conditions that prevailed in Europe in the remote past."

Cooper's use of the shooting-match in *The Pathfinder* is an example of his understanding of equivalents. As a form of frontier competition it was not Cooper's romantic invention. As turkey-shoot in the South, or shooting tossed coins in the Far West, it was and would be an inevitable comparison of skills in a dominant frontier mode. But Cooper saw it, not without relevance, in analogy to the joust or tournament of mediaeval knights. "A passage of arms," the fictional commandant of the Oswego garrison called it, himself knightly. The preparations were made in that spirit of translating the past. The women of the frontier court were assembled on an overlooking platform, the lesser-skilled knights were eliminated in preliminary contests, only the three suitors for the hand of the lady were left. Pathfinder's chivalry relinquished the token victory to Jasper, but when Mabel gives Pathfinder the silver brooch for his hunting shirt we know by the favor that she too is chivalrous.

Only by a firm sense of the innate decorum with which Pathfinder adheres to his code, and the tension that exists between the values and the violation of them by certain others, is one able to understand the significance of Cooper's democratic myth of the frontier ideal. Natty Bumppo was more than a virgin prince. "His motions, being natural, were graceful; and, being calm and regulated, they gave him an air of dignity that associated well with the idea that was so prevalent of his services and peculiar merits." The values of his code were explicit. He was faithful, morally modest, naturally good, fearless, prudent, had "a natural discrimination that appeared to set education at defiance," was possessed of "a beautiful and unerring sense of justice," was capable of the ultimate virtue of renunciation, and altogether was "a fair example of what a just-minded and pure man might be." The villains of the myth were those who, like Muir, consciously violated such values; the comics, those who, like Cap, unconsciously violated their decorum. The ideal was pre-lapsarian ("a sort of type of what Adam might have been supposed to be before the fall"); the fallen were tempted by the equivalents of the double-Louis which rolled from the dead body of the treacherous quartermaster. The Pathfinder did not dive for the coins spilling across the cabin floor, or across an increasingly commercial nation.

Natty Bumppo was a Rousseau-like primitive with American skills; the natural forests which kept him clean and could cleanse others were an invigorated Lake Country. But more important even than these aspects which inform *The Pathfinder* was the sense that the American tradition of breaking wildernesses was not one of anarchy and brute force or mere daring. It was given dignity by the decorum and the values inherent in nature itself and natural men, made explicit and articulate in a code of chivalry for those who should cherish the example in succeeding periods of history.

In *The Pathfinder* Natty Bumppo does not, after all, find new paths in the forest for the travelers, nor Jasper Western (the young manhood of the region) follow a new course to the fortressed island. They had been there before. But for readers of a novel who are willing to understand the dimensions of Cooper's fiction, they are pathfinders for those who without example and guidance might lose themselves and their values in an urban morass.

Yale University
August, 1952

THE PATHFINDER

CHAPTER I

The turf shall be my fragrant shrine;
My temple, Lord! that arch of thine;
My censer's breath the mountain airs,
And silent thoughts my only prayers.   MOORE

THE sublimity connected with vastness is familiar to every
eye. The most abstruse, the most far-reaching, perhaps the
most chastened of the poet's thoughts, crowd on the imagination as he gazes into the depths of the illimitable void. The expanse of the ocean is seldom seen by the novice with indifference;
and the mind, even in the obscurity of night, finds a parallel to
that grandeur, which seems inseparable from images that the
senses cannot compass. With feelings akin to this admiration
and awe—the offspring of sublimity—were the different characters with which the action of this tale must open, gazing on
the scene before them. Four persons in all—two of each sex—
they had managed to ascend a pile of trees, that had been uptorn by a tempest, to catch a view of the objects that surrounded them. It is still the practice of the country to call these
spots wind-rows. By letting in the light of heaven upon the dark
and damp recesses cf the wood, they form a sort of oases in the
solemn obscurity of the virgin forests of America. The particular
wind-row of which we are writing lay on the brow of a gentle
acclivity; and, though small, it had opened the way for an extensive view to those who might occupy its upper margin, a
rare occurrence to the traveller in the woods. Philosophy has
not yet determined the nature of the power that so often lays
desolate spots of this description; some ascribing it to the
whirlwinds which produce waterspouts on the ocean, while
others again impute it to sudden and violent passages of streams
of the electric fluid; but the effects in the woods are familiar to
all. On the upper margin of the opening, the viewless influence

3

had piled tree on tree, in such a manner as had not only enabled the two males of the party to ascend to an elevation of some thirty feet above the level of the earth, but, with a little care and encouragement, to induce their more timid companions to accompany them. The vast trunks which had been broken and driven by the force of the gust lay blended like jackstraws; while their branches, still exhaling the fragrance of withering leaves, were interlaced in a manner to afford sufficient support to the hands. One tree had been completely uprooted, and its lower end, filled with earth, had been cast uppermost, in a way to supply a sort of staging for the four adventurers, when they had gained the desired distance from the ground.

The reader is to anticipate none of the appliances of people of condition in the description of the personal appearances of the group in question. They were all wayfarers in the wilderness; and had they not been, neither their previous habits, nor their actual social positions, would have accustomed them to many of the luxuries of rank. Two of the party, indeed, a male and female, belonged to the native owners of the soil, being Indians of the well-known tribe of the Tuscaroras; while their companions were—a man, who bore about him the peculiarities of one who had passed his days on the ocean, and was, too, in a station little, if any, above that of a common mariner; and his female associate, who was a maiden of a class in no great degree superior to his own; though her youth, sweetness of countenance, and a modest, but spirited mien, lent that character of intellect and refinement which adds so much to the charm of beauty in the sex. On the present occasion, her full blue eye reflected the feeling of sublimity that the scene excited, and her pleasant face was beaming with the pensive expression with which all deep emotions, even though they bring the most grateful pleasure, shadow the countenances of the ingenuous and thoughtful.

And truly the scene was of a nature deeply to impress the imagination of the beholder. Towards the west, in which direction the faces of the party were turned, the eye ranged over an ocean of leaves, glorious and rich in the varied and lively verdure of a generous vegetation, and shaded by the luxuriant tints which belong to the forty-second degree of latitude. The elm with its graceful and weeping top, the rich varieties of the maple, most of the noble oaks of the American forest, with the broad-leaved linden known in the parlance of the country as the basswood, mingled their uppermost branches, forming one broad and seemingly interminable carpet of foliage, which stretched away towards the setting sun, until it bounded the horizon, by blending with the clouds, as the waves and the sky meet at the base of the vault of heaven. Here and there, by some accident of the tempests, or by a caprice of nature, a trifling opening among these giant members of the forest permitted an inferior tree to struggle upward toward the light, and to lift its modest head nearly to a level with the surrounding surface of verdure. Of this class were the birch, a tree of some account in regions less favored, the quivering aspen, various generous nut-woods, and divers others which resembled the ignoble and vulgar, thrown by circumstances into the presence of the stately and great. Here and there, too, the tall straight trunk of the pine pierced the vast field, rising high above it, like some grand monument reared by art on a plain of leaves.

It was the vastness of the view, the nearly unbroken surface of verdure, that contained the principle of grandeur. The beauty was to be traced in the delicate tints, relieved by gradations of light and shade; while the solemn repose induced the feeling allied to awe.

"Uncle," said the wondering, but pleased girl, addressing her male companion, whose arm she rather touched than leaned on, to steady her own light but firm footing, "this is like a view of the ocean you so much love!"

"So much for ignorance, and a girl's fancy, Magnet"—a term of affection the sailor often used in allusion to his niece's personal attractions; "no one but a child would think of likening this handful of leaves to a look at the real Atlantic. You might seize all these tree-tops to Neptune's jacket, and they would make no more than a nosegay for his bosom."

"More fanciful than true, I think, uncle. Look thither; it must be miles on miles, and yet we see nothing but leaves! what more could one behold, if looking at the ocean?"

"More!" returned the uncle, giving an impatient gesture with the elbow the other touched, for his arms were crossed, and the hands were thrust into the bosom of a vest of red cloth, a fashion of the times—"more, Magnet! say, rather, what less? Where are your combing seas, your blue water, your rollers, your breakers, your whales, or your waterspouts, and your end-less motion, in this bit of a forest, child?"

"And where are your tree-tops, your solemn silence, your fragrant leaves, and your beautiful green, uncle, on the ocean?"

"Tut, Magnet! if you understood the thing, you would know that green water is a sailor's bane. He scarcely relishes a green-horn less."

"But green trees are a different thing. Hist! that sound is the air breathing among the leaves!"

"You should hear a nor-wester breathe, girl, if you fancy wind aloft. Now, where are your gales, and hurricanes, and trades, and levanters, and such like incidents, in this bit of a forest? and what fishes have you swimming beneath yonder tame surface?"

"That there have been tempests here, these signs around us plainly show; and beasts, if not fishes, are beneath those leaves."

"I do not know that," returned the uncle, with a sailor's dogmatism. "They told us many stories at Albany of the wild animals we should fall in with, and yet we have seen nothing to frighten a seal. I doubt if any of your inland animals will com-pare with a low latitude shark."

"See!" exclaimed the niece, who was more occupied with the sublimity and beauty of the "boundless wood" than with her uncle's arguments; "yonder is a smoke curling over the tops of the trees—can it come from a house?"

"Ay, ay; there is a look of humanity in that smoke," returned the old seaman, "which is worth a thousand trees. I must show it to Arrowhead, who may be running past a port without know-ing it. It is probable there is a caboose where there is a smoke."

As he concluded, the uncle drew a hand from his bosom, touched the male Indian, who was standing near him, lightly on the shoulder, and pointed out a thin line of vapor which was stealing slowly out of the wilderness of leaves, at a distance of about a mile, and was diffusing itself in almost imperceptible threads of humidity in the quivering atmosphere. The Tuscarora was one of those noble-looking warriors oftener met with among the aborigines of this continent a century since than to-day; and, while he had mingled sufficiently with the colonists to be familiar with their habits and even with their language, he had lost little, if any, of the wild grandeur and simple dignity of a chief. Between him and the old seaman the intercourse had been friendly, but distant; for the Indian had been too much accustomed to mingle with the officers of the different military posts he had frequented not to understand that his present companion was only a subordinate. So imposing, indeed, had been the quiet superiority of the Tuscarora's reserve, that Charles Cap, for so was the seaman named, in his most dogmatical or facetious moments, had not ventured on familiarity in an intercourse which had now lasted more than a week. The sight of the curling smoke, however, had struck the latter like the sudden appearance of a sail at sea; and, for the first time since they met, he ventured to touch the warrior, as has been related.

The quick eye of the Tuscarora instantly caught a sight of the smoke; and for full a minute he stood, slightly raised on tiptoe, with distended nostrils, like the buck that scents a taint in the air, and a gaze as riveted as that of the trained pointer while he waits his master's aim. Then, falling back on his feet, a low exclamation, in the soft tones that form so singular a contrast to its harsher cries in the Indian warrior's voice, was barely audible; otherwise, he was undisturbed. His countenance was calm, and his quick, dark, eagle eye moved over the leafy panorama, as if to take in at a glance every circumstance that might enlighten his mind. That the long journey they had attempted to make through a broad belt of wilderness was necessarily attended with danger, both uncle and niece well knew; though neither could at once determine whether the sign that others were in their vicinity was the harbinger of good or evil.

"There must be Oneidas or Tuscaroras near us, Arrowhead," said Cap, addressing his Indian companion by his conventional English name; "will it not be well to join company with them, and get a comfortable berth for the night in their wigwam?"

"No wigwam there," Arrowhead answered in his unmoved manner—"too much tree."

"But Indians must be there; perhaps some old messmates of your own, Master Arrowhead."

"No Tuscarora—no Oneida—no Mohawk—pale-face fire."

"The devil it is! Well, Magnet, this surpasses a seaman's philosophy: we old sea-dogs can tell a lubber's nest from a mate's hammock; but I do not think the oldest admiral in his Majesty's fleet can tell a king's smoke from a collier's."

The idea that human beings were in their vicinity, in that ocean of wilderness, had deepened the flush on the blooming cheek and brightened the eye of the fair creature at his side; but she soon turned with a look of surprise to her relative, and said hesitatingly, for both had often admired the Tuscarora's knowledge, or, we might almost say, instinct—

"A pale-face's fire! Surely, uncle, he cannot know *that*?"

"Ten days since, child, I would have sworn to it; but now I hardly know what to believe. May I take the liberty of asking, Arrowhead, why you fancy that smoke, now, a pale-face's smoke, and not a red-skin's?"

"Wet wood," returned the warrior, with the calmness with which the pedagogue might point out an arithmetical demonstration to his puzzled pupil. "Much wet—much smoke; much water—black smoke."

"But, begging your pardon, Master Arrowhead, the smoke is not black, nor is there much of it. To my eye, now, it is as light and fanciful a smoke as ever rose from a captain's tea-kettle, when nothing was left to make the fire but a few chips from the dunnage."

"Too much water," returned Arrowhead, with a slight nod of the head; "Tuscarora too cunning to make fire with water! pale-face too much book, and burn anything; much book, little know."

"Well, that's reasonable, I allow," said Cap, who was no devotee of learning: "he means that as a hit at your reading, Magnet; for the chief has sensible notions of things in his own way. How far, now, Arrowhead, do you make us, by your calculation, from the bit of a pond that you call the Great Lake, and towards which we have been so many days shaping our course?"

The Tuscarora looked at the seaman with quiet superiority as he answered, "Ontario, like heaven; one sun, and the great traveller will know it."

"Well, I have been a great traveller, I cannot deny; but of all my v'y'ges this has been the longest, the least profitable, and the farthest inland. If this body of fresh water is so nigh, Arrowhead, and so large, one might think a pair of good eyes would find it out; for apparently everything within thirty miles is to be seen from this lookout."

"Look," said Arrowhead, stretching an arm before him with quiet grace; "Ontario!"

"Uncle, you are accustomed to cry 'Land ho!' but not 'Water ho!' and you do not see it," cried the niece, laughing, as girls will laugh at their own idle conceits.

"How now, Magnet! dost suppose that I shouldn't know my native element, if it were in sight?"

"But Ontario is not your native element, dear uncle; for you come from the salt water, while this is fresh."

"That might make some difference to your young mariner, but none to the old one. I should know water, child, were I to see it in China."

"Ontario," repeated Arrowhead, with emphasis, again stretching his hand towards the north-west.

Cap looked at the Tuscarora, for the first time since their acquaintance, with something like an air of contempt, though he did not fail to follow the direction of the chief's eye and arm, both of which were directed towards a vacant point in the heavens, a short distance above the plain of leaves.

"Ay, ay; this is much as I expected, when I left the coast in search of a fresh-water pond," resumed Cap, shrugging his shoulders like one whose mind was made up, and who thought no more need be said. "Ontario may be there, or, for that matter, it may be in my pocket. Well, I suppose there will be room enough, when we reach it, to work our canoe. But, Arrowhead, if there be pale-faces in our neighborhood, I confess I should like to get within hail of them."

The Tuscarora now gave a quiet inclination of his head, and the whole party descended from the roots of the uptorn tree in silence. When they reached the ground, Arrowhead intimated his intention to go towards the fire, and ascertain who had lighted it; while he advised his wife and the two others to return to a canoe, which they had left in the adjacent stream, and await his return.

"Why, chief, this might do on soundings, and in an offing where one knew the channel," returned old Cap; "but in an unknown region like this, I think it unsafe to trust the pilot alone too far from the ship: so, with your leave, we will not part company."

"What my brother want?" asked the Indian gravely, though

without taking offence at a distrust that was sufficiently plain.

"Your company, Master Arrowhead, and no more. I will go with you and speak these strangers."

The Tuscarora assented without difficulty, and again he directed his patient and submissive little wife, who seldom turned her full rich black eye on him but to express equally her respect, her dread, and her love, to proceed to the boat. But here Magnet raised a difficulty. Although spirited, and of unusual energy under circumstances of trial, she was but woman; and the idea of being entirely deserted by her two male protectors, in the midst of a wilderness that her senses had just told her was seemingly illimitable, became so keenly painful, that she expressed a wish to accompany her uncle.

"The exercise will be a relief, dear sir, after sitting so long in the canoe," she added, as the rich blood slowly returned to a cheek that had paled in spite of her efforts to be calm; "and there may be females with the strangers."

"Come, then, child; it is but a cable's length, and we shall return an hour before the sun sets."

With this permission, the girl, whole real name was Mabel Dunham, prepared to be of the party; while the Dew-of-June, as the wife of Arrowhead was called, passively went her way towards the canoe, too much accustomed to obedience, solitude, and the gloom of the forest to feel apprehension.

The three who remained in the wind-row now picked their way around its tangled maze, and gained the margin of the woods. A few glances of the eye sufficed for Arrowhead; but old Cap deliberately set the smoke by a pocket-compass, before he trusted himself within the shadows of the trees.

"This steering by the nose, Magnet, may do well enough for an Indian, but your thoroughbred knows the virtue of the needle," said the uncle, as he trudged at the heels of the light-stepping Tuscarora. "America would never have been discovered, take my word for it, if Columbus had been nothing but nostrils. Friend Arrowhead, didst ever see a machine like this?"

The Indian turned, cast a glance at the compass, which Cap held in a way to direct his course, and gravely answered, "A pale-face eye. The Tuscarora see in his head. The Saltwater (for so the Indian styled his companion) all eye now; no tongue."

"He means, uncle, that we had needs be silent; perhaps he distrusts the persons we are about to meet."

"Ay, 'tis an Indian's fashion of going to quarters. You perceive he has examined the priming of his rifle, and it may be as well if I look to that of my own pistols."

Without betraying alarm at these preparations, to which she had become accustomed by her long journey in the wilderness, Mabel followed with a step as elastic as that of the Indian, keeping close in the rear of her companions. For the first half mile no other caution beyond a rigid silence was observed; but as the party drew nearer to the spot where the fire was known to be, much greater care became necessary.

The forest, as usual, had little to intercept the view below the branches but the tall straight trunks of trees. Everything belonging to vegetation had struggled towards the light, and beneath the leafy canopy one walked, as it might be, through a vast natural vault, upheld by myriads of rustic columns. These columns or trees, however, often served to conceal the adventurer, the hunter, or the foe; and, as Arrowhead swiftly approached the spot where his practised and unerring senses told him the strangers ought to be, his footstep gradually became lighter, his eye more vigilant, and his person was more carefully concealed.

"See, Saltwater," said he exultingly, pointing through the vista of trees; "pale-face fire!"

"By the Lord, the fellow is right!" muttered Cap; "there they are, sure enough, and eating their grub as quietly as if they were in the cabin of a three-decker."

"Arrowhead is but half right!" whispered Mabel; "for there are two Indians and only one white man."

"Pale-faces," said the Tuscarora, holding up two fingers; "red man," holding up one.

"Well," rejoined Cap, "it is hard to say which is right and which is wrong. One is entirely white, and a fine comely lad he is, with an air of respectability about him; one is a red-skin as plain as paint and nature can make him; but the third chap is half-rigged, being neither brig nor schooner."

"Pale-faces," repeated Arrowhead, again raising two fingers; "red man," showing but one.

"He must be right, uncle; for his eye seems never to fail. But it is now urgent to know whether we meet as friends or foes. They may be French."

"One hail will soon satisfy us on that head," returned Cap. "Stand you behind the tree, Magnet, lest the knaves take it into their heads to fire a broadside without a parley, and I will soon learn what colors they sail under."

The uncle had placed his two hands to his mouth to form a trumpet, and was about to give the promised hail, when a rapid movement from the hand of Arrowhead defeated the intention by deranging the instrument.

"Red man, Mohican," said the Tuscarora; "good; pale-faces, Yengeese."

"These are heavenly tidings," murmured Mabel, who little relished the prospect of a deadly fray in that remote wilderness. "Let us approach at once, dear uncle, and proclaim ourselves friends."

"Good," said the Tuscarora; "red man cool, and know; pale-face hurried, and fire. Let the squaw go."

"What!" said Cap in astonishment; "send little Magnet ahead as a lookout, while two lubbers, like you and me, lie-to to see what sort of a land-fall she will make! If I do, I——"

"It is wisest, uncle," interrupted the generous girl, "and I have no fear. No Christian, seeing a woman approach alone, would fire upon her; and my presence will be a pledge of peace. Let me go forward, as Arrowhead wishes, and all will be well. We are, as yet, unseen, and the surprise of the strangers will not partake of alarm."

"Good," returned Arrowhead, who did not conceal his approbation of Mabel's spirit.

"It has an unseaman-like look," answered Cap; "but, being in the woods, no one will know it. If you think, Mabel——"

"Uncle, I know. There is no cause to fear for me; and you are always nigh to protect me."

"Well, take one of the pistols, then——"

"Nay, I had better rely on my youth and feebleness," said the girl, smiling, while her color heightened under her feelings. "Among Christian men, a woman's best guard is her claim to their protection. I know nothing of arms, and wish to live in ignorance of them."

The uncle desisted; and, after receiving a few cautious instructions from the Tuscarora, Mabel rallied all her spirit, and advanced alone towards the group seated near the fire. Although the heart of the girl beat quick, her step was firm, and her movements, seemingly, were without reluctance. A death-like silence reigned in the forest, for they towards whom she approached were too much occupied in appeasing their hunger to avert their looks for an instant from the important business in which they were all engaged. When Mabel, however, had got within a hundred feet of the fire, she trod upon a dried stick, and the trifling noise produced by her light footstep caused the Mohican, as Arrowhead had pronounced the Indian to be, and his companion, whose character had been thought so equivocal, to rise to their feet, as quick as thought. Both glanced at the rifles that leaned against a tree; and then each stood without stretching out an arm, as his eyes fell on the form of the girl. The Indian uttered a few words to his companion, and resumed his seat and his meal as calmly as if no interruption had occurred. On the contrary, the white man left the fire, and came forward to meet Mabel.

The latter saw, as the stranger approached, that she was about to be addressed by one of her own color, though his dress was so strange a mixture of the habits of the two races, that it required a near look to be certain of the fact. He was of middle age; but there was an open honesty, a total absence of guile, in his face, which otherwise would not have been thought handsome, that at once assured Magnet she was in no danger. Still she paused.

"Fear nothing, young woman," said the hunter, for such his attire would indicate him to be; "you have met Christian men in the wilderness, and such as know how to treat all kindly who are disposed to peace and justice. I am a man well known in all these parts, and perhaps one of my names may have reached your ears. By the Frenchers and the red-skins on the other side of the Big Lakes, I am called La Longue Carabine; by the Mohicans, a just-minded and upright tribe, what is left of them, Hawk Eye; while the troops and rangers along this side of the water call me Pathfinder, inasmuch as I have never been known to miss one end of the trail, when there was a Mingo, or a friend who stood in need of me, at the other."

This was not uttered boastfully, but with the honest confidence of one who well knew that by whatever name others might have heard of him, he had no reason to blush at the reports. The effect on Mabel was instantaneous. The moment she heard the last *sobriquet* she clasped her hands eagerly and repeated the word "Pathfinder!"

"So they call me, young woman, and many a great lord has got a title that he did not half so well merit; though, if truth be said, I rather pride myself in finding my way where there is no path, than in finding it where there is. But the regular troops are by no means particular, and half the time they don't know the difference between a trail and a path, though one is a matter for the eye, while the other is little more than scent."

"Then you are the friend my father promised to send to meet us?"

"If you are Sergeant Dunham's daughter, the great Prophet of the Delawares never uttered more truth."

"I am Mabel; and yonder, hid by the trees, are my uncle, whose name is Cap, and a Tuscarora called Arrowhead. We did not hope to meet you until we had nearly reached the shores of the lake."

"I wish a juster-minded Indian had been your guide," said Pathfinder; "for I am no lover of the Tuscaroras, who have travelled too far from the graves of their fathers always to remember the Great Spirit; and Arrowhead is an ambitious chief. Is the Dew-of-June with him?"

"His wife accompanies us, and a humble and mild creature she is."

"Ay, and true-hearted; which is more than any who know him will say of Arrowhead. Well, we must take the fare that Providence bestows, while we follow the trail of life. I suppose worse guides might have been found than the Tuscarora; though he has too much Mingo blood for one who consorts altogether with the Delawares."

"It is, then, perhaps, fortunate we have met," said Mabel.

"It is not misfortunate, at any rate; for I promised the Sergeant I would see his child safe to the garrison, though I died for it. We expected to meet you before you reached the Falls, where we have left our own canoe; while we thought it might do no harm to come up a few miles, in order to be of service if wanted. It is lucky we did, for I doubt if Arrowhead be the man to shoot the current."

"Here come my uncle and the Tuscarora, and our parties can now join." As Mabel concluded, Cap and Arrowhead, who saw that the conference was amicable, drew nigh; and a few words sufficed to let them know as much as the girl herself had learned from the strangers. As soon as this was done, the party proceeded towards the two who still remained near the fire.

CHAPTER II

Yea! long as Nature's humblest child
Hath kept her temple undefiled
By simple sacrifice,
Earth's fairest scenes are all his own,
He is a monarch, and his throne
Is built amid the skies!   WILSON

THE Mohican continued to eat, though the second white man rose, and courteously took off his cap to Mabel Dunham. He was young, healthful, and manly in appearance; and he wore a dress which, while it was less rigidly professional than that of the uncle, also denoted one accustomed to the water. In that age, real seamen were a class entirely apart from the rest of mankind, their ideas, ordinary language, and attire being as strongly indicative of their calling as the opinions, speech, and dress of a Turk denote a Mussulman. Although the Pathfinder was scarcely in the prime of life, Mabel had met him with a steadiness that may have been the consequence of having braced her nerves for the interview; but when her eyes encountered those of the young man at the fire, they fell before the gaze of admiration with which she saw, or fancied she saw, he greeted her. Each, in truth, felt that interest in the other which similarity of age, condition, mutual comeliness, and their novel situation would be likely to inspire in the young and ingenuous.

"Here," said Pathfinder, with an honest smile bestowed on Mabel, "are the friends your worthy father has sent to meet you. This is a great Delaware; and one who has had honors as well as troubles in his day. He has an Indian name fit for a chief, but, as the language is not always easy for the inexperienced to pronounce, we naturally turn it into English, and call him the Big Sarpent. You are not to suppose, however, that by this name we wish to say that he is treacherous, beyond what is lawful in a red-skin; but that he is wise, and has the cunning which becomes a warrior. Arrowhead, there, knows what I mean."

While the Pathfinder was delivering this address, the two Indians gazed on each other steadily, and the Tuscarora advanced and spoke to the other in an apparently friendly manner.

"I like to see this," continued Pathfinder; "the salutes of two red-skins in the woods, Master Cap, are like the hailing of friendly vessels on the ocean. But speaking of water, it reminds me of my young friend, Jasper Western here, who can claim to know something of these matters, seeing that he has passed his days on Ontario."

"I am glad to see you, friend," said Cap, giving the young fresh-water sailor a cordial grip; "though you must have something still to learn, considering the school to which you have been sent. This is my niece Mabel; I call her Magnet, for a reason she never dreams of, though you may possibly have education enough to guess at it, having some pretensions to understand the compass, I suppose."

"The reason is easily comprehended," said the young man, involuntarily fastening his keen dark eye, at the same time, on the suffused face of the girl; "and I feel sure that the sailor who steers by your Magnet will never make a bad land-fall."

"Ha! you do make use of some of the terms, I find, and that with propriety; though, on the whole, I fear you have seen more green than blue water."

"It is not surprising that we should get some of the phrases which belong to the land; for we are seldom out of sight of it twenty-four hours at a time."

"More's the pity, boy, more's the pity! A very little land ought to go a great way with a seafaring man. Now, if the truth were known, Master Western, I suppose there is more or less land all round your lake."

"And, uncle, is there not more or less land around the ocean?" said Magnet quickly; for she dreaded a premature display of the old seaman's peculiar dogmatism, not to say pedantry.

"No, child, there is more or less ocean all round the land;

that's what I tell the people ashore, youngster. They are living, as it might be, in the midst of the sea, without knowing it; by sufferance, as it were, the water being so much the more powerful and the largest. But there is no end to conceit in this world: for a fellow who never saw salt water often fancies he knows more than one who has gone round the Horn. No, no, this earth is pretty much an island; and all that can be truly said not to be so is water."

Young Western had a profound deference for a mariner of the ocean, on which he had often pined to sail; but he had also a natural regard for the broad sheet on which he had passed his life, and which was not without its beauties in his eyes.

"What you say, sir," he answered modestly, "may be true as to the Atlantic; but we have a respect for the land up here on Ontario."

"That is because you are always land-locked," returned Cap, laughing heartily; "but yonder is the Pathfinder, as they call him, with some smoking platters, inviting us to share in his mess; and I will confess that one gets no venison at sea. Master Western, civility to girls, at your time of life, comes as easy as taking in the slack of the ensign halyards; and if you will just keep an eye to her kid and can, while I join the mess of the Pathfinder and our Indian friends, I make no doubt she will remember it."

Master Cap uttered more than he was aware of at the time. Jasper Western did attend to the wants of Mabel, and she long remembered the kind, manly attention of the young sailor at this their first interview. He placed the end of a log for a seat, obtained for her a delicious morsel of the venison, gave her a draught of pure water from the spring, and as he sat near her, fast won his way to her esteem by his gentle but frank manner of manifesting his care; homage that woman always wishes to receive, but which is never so flattering or so agreeable as when it comes from the young to those of their own age—from the manly to the gentle. Like most of those who pass their time excluded from the society of the softer sex, young Western was earnest, sincere, and kind in his attentions, which, though they wanted a conventional refinement, which, perhaps, Mabel never missed, had those winning qualities that prove very sufficient as substitutes. Leaving these two unsophisticated young people to become acquainted through their feelings, rather than their expressed thoughts, we will turn to the group in which the uncle had already become a principal actor.

The party had taken their places around a platter of venison steaks, which served for the common use, and the discourse naturally partook of the characters of the different individuals which composed it. The Indians were silent and industrious, the appetite of the aboriginal American for venison being seemingly inappeasable, while the two white men were communicative, each of the latter being garrulous and opinionated in his way. But, as the dialogue will put the reader in possession of certain facts that may render the succeeding narrative more clear, it will be well to record it.

"There must be satisfaction in this life of yours, no doubt, Mr. Pathfinder," continued Cap, when the hunger of the travellers was so far appeased that they began to pick and choose among the savory morsels; "it has some of the chances and luck that we seamen like; and if ours is all water, yours is all land."

"Nay, we have water too, in our journeyings and marches," returned his white companion; "we bordermen handle the paddle and the spear almost as much as the rifle and the hunting-knife."

"Ay; but do you handle the brace and the bow-line, the wheel and the lead-line, the reef-point and the top-rope? The paddle is a good thing, out of doubt, in a canoe; but of what use is it in the ship?"

"Nay, I respect all men in their callings, and I can believe the things you mention have their uses. One who has lived, like myself, in company with many tribes, understands differences in usages. The paint of a Mingo is not the paint of a Delaware; and he who should expect to see a warrior in the dress of a squaw might be disappointed. I am not yet very old, but I have lived in the woods, and have some acquaintance with human natur'. I never believe much in the learning of them that dwell in towns, for I never yet met with one that had an eye for a rifle or a trail."

"That's my manner of reasoning, Master Pathfinder, to a yarn. Walking about streets, going to church of Sundays, and hearing sermons, never yet made a man of a human being. Send the boy out upon the broad ocean, if you wish to open his eyes,

osophy which I hold to be equal to steering in a dark night
the edges of the sand."

"It's no great secret," returned Pathfinder, laughing w
great inward glee, though habitual caution prevented the em
sion of any noise. "Nothing is easier to us who pass our time
the great school of Providence than to larn its lessons. V
should be as useless on a trail, or in carrying tidings through t
wilderness, as so many woodchucks, did we not soon come to
knowledge of these niceties. Eau-douce, as we call him, is
fond of the water, that he gathered a damp stick or two for o
fire; and wet will bring dark smoke, as I suppose even you f
lowers of the sea must know. It's no great secret, though all
mystery to such as doesn't study the Lord and His mighty wa
with humility and thankfulness."

"That must be a keen eye of Arrowhead's to see so slight
difference."

"He would be but a poor Indian if he didn't. No, no; it is wa
time, and no red-skin is outlying without using his sense
Every skin has its own natur', and every natur' has its own law
as well as its own skin. It was many years before I could maste
all these higher branches of a forest education; for red-ski
knowledge doesn't come as easy to white-skin natur', as wha
I suppose is intended to be white-skin knowledge; though
have but little of the latter, having passed most of my time i
the wilderness."

"You have been a ready scholar, Master Pathfinder, as i
seen by your understanding these things so well. I suppose i
would be no great matter for a man regularly brought up to th
sea to catch these trifles, if he could only bring his mind fairl
to bear upon them."

"I don't know that. The white man has his difficulties in get
ting red-skin habits, quite as much as the Indian in getting
white-skin ways. As for the real natur', it is my opinion that
neither can actually get that of the other."

"And yet we sailors, who run about the world so much, say
there is but one nature, whether it be in the Chinaman or a
Dutchman. For my own part, I am much of that way of thinking too; for I have generally found that all nations like gold and
silver, and most men relish tobacco."

"Then you seafaring men know little of the red-skins. Have

and let him look upon foreign nations, or what I call the face of
nature, if you wish him to understand his own character. Now,
there is my brother-in-law, the Sergeant: he is as good a fellow
as ever broke a biscuit, in his way; but what is he, after all?
Why, nothing but a soldier. A sergeant, to be sure, but that is
a sort of a soldier, you know. When he wished to marry poor
Bridget, my sister, I told the girl what he was, as in duty bound,
and what she might expect from such a husband; but you know
how it is with girls when their minds are jammed by an inclination. It is true, the Sergeant has risen in his calling, and they say
he is an important man at the fort; but his poor wife has not
lived to see it all, for she has now been dead these fourteen
years."

"A soldier's calling is honorable, provided he has fi't only on
the side of right," returned the Pathfinder; "and as the Frenchers are always wrong, and his sacred Majesty and these colonies
are always right, I take it the Sergeant has a quiet conscience
as well as a good character. I have never slept more sweetly
than when I have fi't the Mingos, though it is the law with me
to fight always like a white man and never like an Indian. The
Sarpent, here, has his fashions, and I have mine; and yet have
we fi't side by side these many years, without either thinking a
hard thought consarning the other's ways. I tell him there is
but one heaven and one hell, notwithstanding his traditions,
though there are many paths to both."

"That is rational; and he is bound to believe you, though, I
fancy, most of the roads to the last are on dry land. The sea is
what my poor sister Bridget used to call a 'purifying place,' and
one is out of the way of temptation when out of sight of land.
I doubt if as much can be said in favor of your lakes up hereaway."

"That towns and settlements lead to sin, I will allow; but our
lakes are bordered by the forests, and one is every day called
upon to worship God in such a temple. That men are not always
the same, even in the wilderness, I must admit, for the difference between a Mingo and a Delaware is as plain to be seen as
the difference between the sun and the moon. I am glad, friend
Cap, that we have met, however, if it be only that you may tell
the Big Sarpent here that there are lakes in which the water is
salt. We have been pretty much of one mind since our acquaint-

ance began, and if the Mohican has only half the faith in me that I have in him, he believes all that I have told him touching the white men's ways and natur's laws; but it has always seemed to me that none of the red-skins have given as free a belief as an honest man likes to the accounts of the Big Salt Lakes, and to that of their being rivers that flow up stream."

"This comes of getting things wrong end foremost," answered Cap, with a condescending nod. "You have thought of your lakes and rifts as the ship; and of the ocean and the tides as the boat. Neither Arrowhead nor the Serpent need doubt what you have said concerning both, though I confess myself to some difficulty in swallowing the tale about there being inland seas at all, and still more that there is any sea of fresh water. I have come this long journey as much to satisfy my own eyes concerning these facts, as to oblige the Sergeant and Magnet, though the ·first was my sister's husband, and I love the last like a child."

"You are wrong, friend Cap, very wrong, to distrust the power of God in any thing," returned Pathfinder earnestly. "They that live in the settlements and the towns have confined and unjust opinions consarning the might of His hand; but we, who pass our time in His very presence, as it might be, see things differently—I mean, such of us as have white natur's. A red-skin has his notions, and it is right that it should be so; and if they are not exactly the same as a Christian white man's, there is no harm in it. Still, there are matters which belong altogether to the ordering of God's providence; and these salt and fresh-water lakes are some of them. I do not pretend to account for these things, but I think it the duty of all to believe in them."

"Hold on there, Master Pathfinder," interrupted Cap, not without some heat; "in the way of a proper and manly faith, I will turn my back on no one, when afloat. Although more accustomed to make all snug aloft, and to show the proper canvas, than to pray when the hurricane comes, I know that we are but helpless mortals at times, and I hope I pay reverence where reverence is due. All I mean to say is this: that, being accustomed to see water in large bodies salt, I should like to taste it before I can believe it to be fresh."

"God has given the salt lick to the deer; and He has given to man, red-skin and white, the delicious spring at which to slake

his thirst. It is unreasonable to think that He given lakes of pure water to the west, and lakes of to the east."

Cap was awed, in spite of his overweening dogmatis earnest simplicity of the Pathfinder, though he did n the idea of believing a fact which, for many years, he had naciously insisted could not be true. Unwilling to give up point, and, at the same time, unable to maintain it against reasoning to which he was unaccustomed, and which possess equally the force of truth, faith, and probability, he was glad to get rid of the subject by evasion.

"Well, well, friend Pathfinder," said he, "we will leave the argument where it is; and we can try the water when we once reach it. Only mark my words—I do not say that it may not be fresh on the surface; the Atlantic is sometimes fresh on the surface, near the mouths of great rivers; but, rely on it, I shall show you a way of tasting the water many fathoms deep, of which you never dreamed; and then we shall know more about it."

The guide seemed content to let the matter rest, and the conversation changed.

"We are not over-conceited consarning our gifts," observed the Pathfinder, after a short pause, "and well know that such as live in the towns, and near the sea——"

"On the sea," interrupted Cap.

"On the sea, if you wish it, friend—have opportunities which do not befall us of the wilderness. Still, we know our own callings, and they are what I consider natural callings, and are not parvarted by vanity and wantonness. Now, my gifts are with the rifle, and on a trail, and in the way of game and scouting; for, though I can use the spear and the paddle, I pride not myself on either. The youth Jasper, there, who is discoursing with the Sergeant's daughter, is a different cratur'; for he may b said to breathe the water, as it might be, like a fish. The Indi and Frenchers of the north shore call him Eau-douce, or count of his gifts in this particular. He is better at the oa the rope too, than in making fires on a trail."

"There must be something about these gifts of y speak, after all," said Cap. "Now this fire, I will ac has overlaid all my seamanship. Arrowhead, th smoke came from a pale-face's fire, and that is

you ever known any of your Chinamen who could sing their death-songs, with their flesh torn with splinters and cut with knives, the fire raging around their naked bodies, and death staring them in the face? Until you can find me a Chinaman, or a Christian man, that can do all this, you cannot find a man with a red-skin natur', let him look ever so valiant, or know how to read all the books that were ever printed."

"It is the savages only that play each other such hellish tricks," said Master Cap, glancing his eyes about him uneasily at the apparently endless arches of the forest. "No white man is ever condemned to undergo these trials."

"Nay, therein you are again mistaken," returned the Pathfinder, coolly selecting a delicate morsel of the venison as his *bonne bouche*; "for though these torments belong only to the red-skin natur', in the way of bearing them like braves, white-skin natur' may be, and often has been, agonized by them."

"Happily," said Cap, with an effort to clear his throat, "none of his Majesty's allies will be likely to attempt such damnable cruelties on any of his Majesty's loyal subjects. I have not served much in the royal navy, it is true; but I have served, and that is something; and, in the way of privateering and worrying the enemy in his ships and cargoes, I've done my full share. But I trust there are no French savages on this side the lake, and I think you said that Ontario is a broad sheet of water?"

"Nay, it is broad in our eyes," returned Pathfinder, not caring to conceal the smile which lighted a face which had been burnt by exposure to a bright red; "though I mistrust that some may think it narrow; and narrow it is, if you wish it to keep off the foe. Ontario has two ends, and the enemy that is afraid to cross it will be certain to come round it."

"Ah! that comes of your d——d fresh-water ponds!" growled Cap, hemming so loudly as to cause him instantly to repent the indiscretion. "No man, now, ever heard of a pirate or a ship getting round one end of the Atlantic!"

"Mayhap the ocean has no ends?"

"That it hasn't; nor sides, nor bottom. The nation which is snugly moored on one of its coasts need fear nothing from the one anchored abeam, let it be ever so savage, unless it possesses the art of ship-building. No, no! the people who live on the shores of the Atlantic need fear but little for their skins or their scalps. A man may lie down at night, in those regions, in the hope of finding the hair on his head in the morning, unless he wears a wig."

"It isn't so here. I don't wish to flurry the young woman, and therefore I will be in no way particular, though she seems pretty much listening to Eau-douce, as we call him; but without the edication I have received, I should think it, at this very moment, a risky journey to go over the very ground that lies between us and the garrison, in the present state of this frontier. There are about as many Iroquois on this side of Ontario as there are on the other. It is for this very reason, friend Cap, that the Sergeant has engaged us to come out and show you the path."

"What! do the knaves dare to cruise so near the guns of one of his Majesty's works?"

"Do not the ravens resort near the carcass of the deer, though the fowler is at hand? They come this-a-way, as it might be, naturally. There are more or less whites passing between the forts and the settlements, and they are sure to be on their trails. The Sarpent has come up one side of the river, and I have come up the other, in order to scout for the outlying rascals, while Jasper brought up the canoe, like a bold-hearted sailor as he is. The Sergeant told him, with tears in his eyes, all about his child, and how his heart yearned for her, and how gentle and obedient she was, until I think the lad would have dashed into a Mingo camp single-handed, rather than not a-come."

"We thank him, and shall think the better of him for his readiness; though I suppose the boy has run no great risk, after all."

"Only the risk of being shot from a cover, as he forced the canoe up a swift rift, or turned an elbow in the stream, with his eyes fastened on the eddies. Of all the risky journeys, that on an ambushed river is the most risky, in my judgment, and that risk has Jasper run."

"And why the devil has the Sergeant sent for me to travel a hundred and fifty miles in this outlandish manner? Give me an offing, and the enemy in sight, and I'll play with him in his own fashion, as long as he pleases, long bows or close quarters; but to be shot like a turtle asleep is not to my humor. If it were not for little Magnet there, I would tack ship this instant, make the best of my way back to York, and let Ontario take care of itself, salt water or fresh water."

"That wouldn't mend the matter much, friend mariner, as the road to return is much longer, and almost as bad as the road to go on. Trust to us, and we will carry you through safely, or lose our scalps."

Cap wore a tight solid queue, done up in eelskin, while the top of his head was nearly bald; and he mechanically passed his hand over both, as if to make certain that each was in its right place. He was at the bottom, however, a brave man, and had often faced death with coolness, though never in the frightful forms in which it presented itself under the brief but graphic picture of his companion. It was too late to retreat; and he determined to put the best face on the matter, though he could not avoid muttering inwardly a few curses on the indiscretion with which his brother-in-law, the Sergeant, had led him into his present dilemma.

"I make no doubt, Master Pathfinder," he answered, when these thoughts had found time to glance through his mind, "that we shall reach port in safety. What distance may we now be from the fort?"

"Little more than fifteen miles; and swift miles too, as the river runs, if the Mingos let us go clear."

"And I suppose the woods will stretch along starboard and larboard, as heretofore?"

"Anan?"

"I mean that we shall have to pick our way through these damned trees."

"Nay, nay, you will go in the canoe, and the Oswego has been cleared of its flood-wood by the troops. It will be floating down stream, and that, too, with a swift current."

"And what the devil is to prevent these minks of which you speak from shooting us as we double a headland, or are busy in steering clear of the rocks?"

"The Lord!—He who has so often helped others in greater difficulties. Many and many is the time that my head would have been stripped of hair, skin, and all, hadn't the Lord fi't of my side. I never go into a scrimmage, friend mariner, without thinking of this great ally, who can do more in battle than all the battalions of the 60th, were they brought into a single line."

"Ay, ay, this may do well enough for a scouter; but we seamen like our offing, and to go into action with nothing in our minds but the business before us—plain broadside and broadside work, and no trees or rocks to thicken the water."

"And no Lord too, I dare to say, if the truth were known. Take my word for it, Master Cap, that no battle is the worse fi't for having the Lord on your side. Look at the head of the Big Sarpent, there; you can see the mark of a knife all along by his left ear: now nothing but a bullet from this long rifle of mine saved his scalp that day; for it had fairly started, and half a minute more would have left him without the war-lock. When the Mohican squeezes my hand, and intermates that I befriended him in that matter, I tell him no; it was the Lord who led me to the only spot where execution could be done, or his necessity be made known, on account of the smoke. Sartain, when I got the right position, I finished the affair of my own accord. For a friend under the tomahawk is apt to make a man think quick and act at once, as was my case, or the Sarpent's spirit would be hunting in the happy land of his people at this very moment."

"Come, come, Pathfinder, this palaver is worse than being skinned from stem to stem; we have but a few hours of sun, and had better be drifting down this said current of yours while we may. Magnet dear, are you not ready to get under way?"

Magnet started, blushed brightly, and made her preparations for immediate departure. Not a syllable of the discourse just related had she heard; for Eau-douce, as young Jasper was oftener called than anything else, had been filling her ears with a description of the yet distant part towards which she was journeying, with accounts of her father, whom she had not seen since a child, and with the manner of life of those who lived in the frontier garrisons. Unconsciously she had become deeply interested, and her thoughts had been too intently directed to these matters to allow any of the less agreeable subjects discussed by those so near to reach her ears. The bustle of departure put an end to the conversation, and, the baggage of the scouts or guides being trifling, in a few minutes the whole party was ready to proceed. As they were about to quit the spot, however, to the surprise of even his fellow-guides, Pathfinder collected a quantity of branches and threw them upon the embers of the fire, taking care even to see that some of the wood was damp, in order to raise as dark and dense a smoke as possible.

"When you can hide your trail, Jasper," said he, "a smoke at leaving an encampment may do good instead of harm. If there are a dozen Mingos within ten miles of us, some on 'em are on the heights, or in the trees, looking out for smokes; let them see this, and much good may it do them. They are welcome to our leavings."

"But may they not strike and follow on our trail?" asked the youth, whose interest in the hazard of his situation had much increased since the meeting with Magnet. "We shall leave a broad path to the river."

"The broader the better; when there, it will surpass Mingo cunning, even, to say which way the canoe has gone—up stream or down. Water is the only thing in natur' that will thoroughly wash out a trail, and even water will not always do it when the scent is strong. Do you not see, Eau-douce, that if any Mingos have seen our path below the falls, they will strike off towards this smoke, and that they will naturally conclude that they who began by going up stream will end by going up stream. If they know anything, they now know a party is out from the fort, and it will exceed even Mingo wit to fancy that we have come up here just for the pleasure of going back again, and that, too, the same day, and at the risk of our scalps."

"Certainly," added Jasper, who was talking apart with the Pathfinder, as they moved towards the wind-row, "they cannot know anything about the Sergeant's daughter, for the greatest secrecy has been observed on her account."

"And they will learn nothing here," returned Pathfinder, causing his companion to see that he trod with the utmost care on the impression left on the leaves by the little foot of Mabel; "unless this old salt-water fish has been taking his niece about in the wind-row, like a fa'n playing by the side of the old doe."

"Buck, you mean, Pathfinder."

"Isn't he a queerity? Now I can consort with such a sailor as yourself, Eau-douce, and find nothing very contrary in our gifts, though yours belong to the lakes and mine to the woods. Hark'e, Jasper," continued the scout, laughing in his noiseless manner; "suppose we try the temper of his blade, and run him over the falls?"

"And what would be done with the pretty niece in the meanwhile?"

"Nay, nay, no harm shall come to her; she must walk round the portage, at any rate; but you and I can try this Atlantic oceaner, and then all parties will become better acquainted. We shall find out whether his flint will strike fire; and he may come to know something of frontier tricks."

Young Jasper smiled, for he was not averse to fun, and had been a little touched by Cap's superciliousness; but Mabel's fair face, light, agile form, and winning smiles, stood like a shield between her uncle and the intended experiment.

"Perhaps the Sergeant's daughter will be frightened," said he.

"Not she, if she has any of the Sergeant's spirit in her. She doesn't look like a skeary thing, at all. Leave it to me, then, Eau-douce, and I will manage the affair alone."

"Not you, Pathfinder; you would only drown both. If the canoe goes over, I must go in it."

"Well, have it so, then: shall we smoke the pipe of agreement on the bargain?"

Jasper laughed, nodded his head by way of consent, and then the subject was dropped, as the party had reached the canoe so often mentioned, and fewer words had determined much greater things between the parties.

CHAPTER III

> Before these fields were shorn and till'd,
>   Full to the brim our rivers flow'd;
> The melody of waters fill'd
>   The fresh and boundless wood;
> And torrents dash'd, and rivulets play'd,
> And fountains spouted in the shade.   BRYANT

IT IS generally known that the waters which flow into the southern side of Ontario are, in general, narrow, sluggish, and deep. There are some exceptions to this rule, for many of the rivers have rapids, or, as they are termed in the language of the region, "rifts," and some have falls. Among the latter was the particular stream on which our adventurers were now journeying. The Oswego is formed by the junction of the Oneida and the Onondaga, both of which flow from lakes; and it pursues its way, through a gently undulating country, some eight or ten miles, until it reaches the margin of a sort of natural terrace, down which it tumbles some ten or fifteen feet, to another level, across which it glides with the silent, stealthy progress of deep water, until it throws its tribute into the broad receptacle of the Ontario. The canoe in which Cap and his party had travelled from Fort Stanwix, the last military station on the Mohawk, lay by the side of this river, and into it the whole party now entered, with the exception of Pathfinder, who remained on the land, in order to shove the light vessel off.

"Let her starn drift down stream, Jasper," said the man of the woods to the young mariner of the lake, who had dispossessed Arrowhead of his paddle and taken his own station as steersman; "let it go down with the current. Should any of these infarnals, the Mingos, strike our trail, or follow it to this point, they will not fail to look for the signs in the mud; and if they discover that we have left the shore with the nose of the canoe up stream, it is a natural belief to think we went up stream."

This direction was followed; and, giving a vigorous shove, the Pathfinder, who was in the flower of his strength and activity, made a leap, landing lightly, and without disturbing its equilibrium, in the bow of the canoe. As soon as it had reached the centre of the river or the strength of the current, the boat was turned, and it began to glide noiselessly down the stream.

The vessel in which Cap and his niece had embarked for their long and adventurous journey was one of the canoes of bark which the Indians are in the habit of constructing, and which, by their exceeding lightness and the ease with which they are propelled, are admirably adapted to a navigation in which shoals, flood-wood, and other similar obstructions so often occur. The two men who composed its original crew had several times carried it, when emptied of its luggage, many hundred yards; and it would not have exceeded the strength of a single man to lift its weight. Still it was long, and, for a canoe, wide; a want of steadiness being its principal defect in the eyes of the uninitiated. A few hours' practice, however, in a great measure remedied this evil, and both Mabel and her uncle had learned so far to humor its movements, that they now maintained their places with perfect composure; nor did the additional weight of the three guides tax its power in any particular degree, the breath of the rounded bottom allowing the necessary quantity of water to be displaced without bringing the gunwale very sensibly nearer to the surface of the stream. Its workmanship was neat; the timbers were small, and secured by thongs; and the whole fabric, though it was so slight to the eye, was probably capable of conveying double the number of persons which it now contained.

Cap was seated on a low thwart, in the centre of the canoe; the Big Serpent knelt near him. Arrowhead and his wife occupied places forward of both, the former having relinquished his post aft. Mabel was half reclining behind her uncle, while the Pathfinder and Eau-douce stood erect, the one in the bow, and the other in the stern, each using a paddle, with a long, steady, noiseless sweep. The conversation was carried on in low tones, all the party beginning to feel the necessity of prudence, as they drew nearer to the outskirts of the fort, and had no longer the cover of the woods.

The Oswego, just at that place, was a deep dark stream of no great width, its still, gloomy-looking current winding its way among overhanging trees, which, in particular spots, almost shut out the light of the heavens. Here and there some half-fallen giant of the forest lay nearly across its surface, rendering care necessary to avoid the limbs; and most of the distance, the lower branches and leaves of the trees of smaller growth were laved by its waters. The picture so beautifully described by our own admirable poet, and which we have placed at the head of this chapter, was here realized; the earth fattened by the decayed vegetation of centuries, and black with loam, the stream that filled the banks nearly to overflowing, and the "fresh and boundless wood," being all as visible to the eye as the pen of Bryant has elsewhere vividly presented them to the imagination. In short, the entire scene was one of a rich and benevolent nature, before it had been subjected to the uses and desires of man; luxuriant, wild, full of promise, and not without the charm of the picturesque, even in its rudest state. It will be remembered that this was in the year 175-, or long before even speculation had brought any portion of western New York within the bounds of civilization. At that distant day there were two great channels of military communication between the inhabited portion of the colony of New York and the frontiers which lay adjacent to the Canadas—that by Lakes Champlain and George, and that by means of the Mohawk, Wood Creek, the Oneida, and the rivers we have been describing. Along both these lines of communication military posts had been established, though there existed a blank space of a hundred miles between the last fort at the head of the Mohawk and the outlet of the Oswego, which embraced most of the distance that Cap and Mabel had journeyed under the protection of Arrowhead.

"I sometimes wish for peace again," said the Pathfinder, "when one can range the forest without searching for any other enemy than the beasts and fishes. Ah's me! many is the day that the Sarpent, there, and I have passed happily among the streams, living on venison, salmon, and trout, without thought of a Mingo or a scalp! I sometimes wish that them blessed days might come back, for it is not my real gift to slay my own kind. I'm sartain the Sergeant's daughter don't think me a wretch that takes pleasure in preying on human natur'?"

As this remark, a sort of half interrogatory, was made, Pathfinder looked behind him; and, though the most partial friend could scarcely term his sunburnt and hard features handsome, even Mabel thought his smile attractive, by its simple ingenuousness and the uprightness that beamed in every lineament of his honest countenance.

"I do not think my father would have sent one like those you mention to see his daughter through the wilderness," the young woman answered, returning the smile as frankly as it was given, but much more sweetly.

"That he wouldn't; the Sergeant is a man of feeling, and many is the march and the fight that we have had—stood shoulder to shoulder in, as *he* would call it—though I always keep my limbs free when near a Frencher or a Mingo."

"You are, then, the young friend of whom my father has spoken so often in his letters?"

"His *young* friend—the Sergeant has the advantage of me by thirty years; yes, he is thirty years my senior, and as many my better."

"Not in the eyes of the daughter, perhaps, friend Pathfinder," put in Cap, whose spirits began to revive when he found the water once more flowing around him. "The thirty years that you mention are not often thought to be an advantage in the eyes of girls of nineteen."

Mabel colored; and, in turning aside her face to avoid the looks of those in the bow of the canoe, she encountered the admiring gaze of the young man in the stern. As a last resource, her spirited but soft blue eyes sought refuge in the water. Just at this moment a dull, heavy sound swept up the avenue formed by the trees, borne along by a light air that hardly produced a ripple on the water.

"That sounds pleasantly," said Cap, pricking up his ears like a dog that hears a distant baying; "it is the surf on the shores of your lake, I suppose?"

"Not so—not so," answered the Pathfinder; "it is merely this river tumbling over some rocks half a mile below us."

"Is there a fall in the stream?" demanded Mabel, a still brighter flush glowing in her face.

"The devil! Master Pathfinder, or you, Mr. Eau-douce" (for so Cap began to style Jasper), "had you not better give the canoe a sheer, and get nearer to the shore? These waterfalls have generally rapids above them, and one might as well get into the Maelstrom at once as to run into their suction."

"Trust to us, friend Cap," answered Pathfinder; "we are but fresh-water sailors, it is true, and I cannot boast of being much even of that; but we understand rifts and rapids and cataracts; and in going down these we shall do our endeavors not to disgrace our edication."

"In going down!" exclaimed Cap. "The devil, man! you do not dream of going down a waterfall in this eggshell of bark!"

"Sartain; the path lies over the falls, and it is much easier to shoot them than to unload the canoe and to carry that and all it contains around a portage of a mile by hand."

Mabel turned her pallid countenance towards the young man in the stern of the canoe; for, just at that moment, a fresh roar of the fall was borne to her ears by a new current of the air, and it really sounded terrific, now that the cause was understood.

"We thought that, by landing the females and the two Indians," Jasper quietly observed, "we three white men, all of whom are used to the water, might carry the canoe over in safety, for we often shoot these falls."

"And we counted on you, friend mariner, as a mainstay," said Pathfinder, winking to Jasper over his shoulder; "for you are accustomed to see waves tumbling about; and without some one to steady the cargo, all the finery of the Sergeant's daughter might be washed into the river and be lost."

Cap was puzzled. The idea of going over a waterfall was, perhaps, more serious in his eyes than it would have been in those of one totally ignorant of all that pertained to boats; for he understood the power of the element, and the total feebleness of man when exposed to its fury. Still his pride revolted at the thought of deserting the boat, while others not only steadily, but coolly, proposed to continue in it. Notwithstanding the latter feeling, and his innate as well as acquired steadiness in danger, he would probably have deserted his post, had not the images of Indians tearing scalps from the human head taken so strong hold of his fancy as to induce him to imagine the canoe a sort of sanctuary.

"What is to be done with Magnet?" he demanded, affection for his niece raising another qualm in his conscience. "We can not allow Magnet to land if there are enemy Indians near?"

"Nay, no Mingo will be near the portage; for that is a spot too public for their devilries," answered the Pathfinder confidently. "Natur' is natur', and it is an Indian's natur' to be found where he is least expected. No fear of him on a beaten path; for he wishes to come upon you when unprepared to meet him, and the fiery villains make it a point to deceive you, one way or another. Sheer in, Eau-douce, and we will land the Sergeant's daughter on the end of that log, where she can reach the shore with a dry foot."

The injunction was obeyed, and in a few minutes the whole party had left the canoe, with the exception of Pathfinder and the two sailors. Notwithstanding his professional pride, Cap would have gladly followed; but he did not like to exhibit so unequivocal a weakness in the presence of a fresh-water sailor.

"I call all hands to witness," said he, as those who had landed moved away, "that I do not look on this affair as anything more than canoeing in the woods. There is no seamanship in tumbling over a waterfall, which is a feat the greatest lubber can perform as well as the oldest mariner."

"Nay, nay, you needn't despise the Oswego Falls, neither,"

put in Pathfinder; "for, though they may not be Niagara, nor the Genesee, nor the Cahoos, nor Glenn's, nor those on the Canada, they are narvous enough for a new beginner. Let the Sergeant's daughter stand on yonder rock, and she will see the manner in which we ignorant backwoodsmen get over a difficulty that we can't get under. Now, Eau-douce, a steady hand and a true eye, for all rests on you, seeing that we can count Master Cap for no more than a passenger."

The canoe was leaving the shore as he concluded, while Mabel went hurriedly and trembling to the rock that had been pointed out, talking to her companion of the danger her uncle so unnecessarily ran, while her eyes were riveted on the agile and vigorous form of Eau-douce, as he stood erect in the stern of the light boat, governing its movements. As soon, however, as she reached a point where she got a view of the fall, she gave an involuntary but suppressed scream, and covered her eyes. At the next instant, the latter were again free, and the entranced girl stood immovable as a statue, a scarcely breathing observer of all that passed. The two Indians seated themselves passively on a log, hardly looking towards the stream, while the wife of Arrowhead came near Mabel, and appeared to watch the motions of the canoe with some such interest as a child regards the leaps of a tumbler.

As soon as the boat was in the stream, Pathfinder sank on his knees, continuing to use the paddle, though it was slowly, and in a manner not to interfere with the efforts of his companion. The latter still stood erect; and, as he kept his eye on some object beyond the fall, it was evident that he was carefully looking for the spot proper for their passage.

"Farther west, boy; farther west," muttered Pathfinder; "there where you see the water foam. Bring the top of the dead oak in a line with the stem of the blasted hemlock."

Eau-douce made no answer; for the canoe was in the centre of the stream, with its head pointed towards the fall, and it had already begun to quicken its motion by the increased force of the current. At that moment Cap would cheerfully have renounced every claim to glory that could possibly be acquired by the feat, to have been safe again on shore. He heard the roar of the water, thundering, as it might be, behind a screen, but becoming more and more distinct, louder and louder, and before him he saw its line cutting the forest below, along which the green and angry element seemed stretched and shining, as if the particles were about to lose their principle of cohesion.

"Down with your helm, down with your helm, man!" he exclaimed, unable any longer to suppress his anxiety, as the canoe glided towards the edge of the fall.

"Ay, ay, down it is sure enough," answered Pathfinder, looking behind him for a single instant, with his silent, joyous laugh —"down we go, of a sartainty! Heave her starn up, boy; farther up with her starn!"

The rest was like the passage of the viewless wind. Eau-douce gave the required sweep with his paddle, the canoe glanced into the channel, and for a few seconds it seemed to Cap that he was tossing in a caldron. He felt the bow of the canoe tip, saw the raging, foaming water careering madly by his side, was sensible that the light fabric in which he floated was tossed about like an egg-shell, and then, not less to his great joy than to his surprise, he discovered that it was gliding across the basin of still water below the fall, under the steady impulse of Jasper's paddle.

The Pathfinder continued to laugh; but he arose from his knees, and, searching for a tin pot and a horn spoon, he began deliberately to measure the water that had been taken in the passage.

"Fourteen spoonfuls, Eau-douce; fourteen fairly measured spoonfuls. I have, you must acknowledge, known you to go down with only ten."

"Master Cap leaned so hard up stream," returned Jasper seriously, "that I had difficulty in trimming the canoe."

"It may be so; no doubt it *was* so, since you say it; but I have known you go over with only ten."

Cap now gave a tremendous hem, felt for his queue as if to ascertain its safety, and then looked back in order to examine the danger he had gone through. His safety is easily explained. Most of the river fell perpendicularly ten or twelve feet; but near its centre the force of the current had so far worn away the rock as to permit the water to shoot through a narrow passage, at an angle of about forty or forty-five degrees. Down this ticklish descent the canoe had glanced, amid fragments of broken rock, whirlpools, foam, and furious tossings of the element, which an uninstructed eye would believe menaced inevitable destruction to an object so fragile. But the very lightness of the canoe had favored its descent; for, borne on the crest of the waves, and directed by a steady eye and an arm full of muscle, it had passed like a feather from one pile of foam to another, scarcely permitting its glossy side to be wetted. There were a few rocks to be avoided, the proper direction was to be rigidly observed, and the fierce current did the rest.[1]

To say that Cap was astonished would not be expressing half his feelings; he felt awed: for the profound dread of rocks which most seamen entertain came in aid of his admiration of the boldness of the exploit. Still he was indisposed to express all he felt, lest it might be conceding too much in favor of fresh water and inland navigation; and no sooner had he cleared his throat with the aforesaid hem, than he loosened his tongue in the usual strain of superiority.

"I do not gainsay your knowledge of the channel, Master Eau-douce, and, after all, to know the channel in such a place is the main point. I have had cockswains with me who could come down that shoot too, if they only knew the channel."

"It isn't enough to know the channel," said Pathfinder; "it needs narves and skill to keep the canoe straight, and to keep her clear of the rocks too. There isn't another boatman in all this region that can shoot the Oswego, but Eau-douce there, with any sartainty; though, now and then, one has blundered through. I can't do it myself unless by means of Providence, and it needs Jasper's hand and eye to make sure of a dry passage. Fourteen spoonfuls, after all, are no great matter, though I wish it had been but ten, seeing that the Sergeant's daughter was a looker-on."

"And yet you conned the canoe; you told him how to head and how to sheer."

"Human frailty, master mariner; that was a little of white-skin natur'. Now, had the Sarpent, yonder, been in the boat, not a word would he have spoken or thought would he have given to the public. An Indian knows how to hold his tongue; but we white folk fancy we are always wiser than our fellows.

[1] Lest the reader suppose we are dealing purely in fiction, the writer will add that he has known a long thirty-two pounder carried over these same falls in perfect safety.

I'm curing myself fast of the weakness, but it needs time to root up the tree that has been growing more than thirty years."

"I think little of this affair, sir; nothing at all, to speak my mind freely. It's a mere wash of spray to shooting London Bridge, which is done every day by hundreds of persons, and often by the most delicate ladies in the land. The king's Majesty has shot the bridge in his royal person."

"Well, I want no delicate ladies or king's majesties (God bless 'em!) in the canoe, in going over these falls; for a boat's breath, either way, may make a drowning matter of it. Eau-douce, we shall have to carry the Sergeant's brother over Niagara yet, to show him what may be done in a frontier."

"The devil! Master Pathfinder, you must be joking now! Surely it is not possible for a bark canoe to go over that mighty cataract?"

"You never were more mistaken, Master Cap, in your life. Nothing is easier, and many is the canoe I have seen go over it with my own eyes; and if we both live I hope to satisfy you that the feat can be done. For my part, I think the largest ship that ever sailed on the ocean might be carried over, could she once get into the rapids."

Cap did not perceive the wink which Pathfinder exchanged with Eau-douce, and he remained silent for some time; for, sooth to say, he had never suspected the possibility of going down Niagara, feasible as the thing must appear to every one on a second thought, the real difficulty existing in going up it.

By this time the party had reached the place where Jasper had left his own canoe, concealed in the bushes, and they all re-embarked; Cap, Jasper, and his niece in one boat, and Pathfinder, Arrowhead, and the wife of the latter in the other. The Mohican had already passed down the banks of the river by land, looking cautiously and with the skill of his people for the signs of an enemy.

The cheek of Mabel did not recover all its bloom until the canoe was again in the current, down which it floated swiftly, occasionally impelled by the paddle of Jasper. She witnessed the descent of the falls with a degree of terror which had rendered her mute; but her fright had not been so great as to prevent admiration of the steadiness of the youth who directed the movement from blending with the passing terror. In truth, one much less sensitive might have had her feelings awakened by the cool and gallant air with which Eau-douce had accomplished this clever exploit. He had stood firmly erect, notwithstanding the plunge; and to those on the shore it was evident that, by a timely application of his skill and strength, the canoe had received a sheer which alone carried it clear of a rock over which the boiling water was leaping in *jets d'eau*—now leaving the brown stone visible, and now covering it with a limpid sheet, as if machinery controlled the play of the element. The tongue cannot always express what the eyes view; but Mabel saw enough, even in that moment of fear, to blend for ever in her mind the pictures presented by the plunging canoe and the unmoved steersman. She admitted that insidious feeling which binds woman so strongly to man, by feeling additional security in finding herself under his care; and, for the first time since leaving Fort Stanwix, she was entirely at her ease in the frail bark in which she travelled. As the other canoe kept quite near her own, however, and the Pathfinder, by floating at her side, was most in view, the conversation was principally maintained with that person; Jasper seldom speaking unless addressed, and constantly exhibiting a weariness in the management of his own boat, which might have been remarked by one accustomed to his ordinarily confident, careless manner.

"We know too well a woman's gifts to think of carrying the Sergeant's daughter over the falls," said Pathfinder, looking at Mabel, while he addressed her uncle; "though I've been acquainted with some of her sex that would think but little of doing the thing."

"Mabel is faint-hearted, like her mother," returned Cap; "and you did well, friend, to humor her weakness. You will remember the child has never been at sea."

"No, no, it was easy to discover that; by your own fearlessness, any one might have seen how little you cared about the matter. I went over once with a raw hand, and he jumped out of the canoe just as it tipped, and you may judge what a time he had of it."

"What became of the poor fellow?" asked Cap, scarcely knowing how to take the other's manner, which was so dry, while it was so simple, that a less obtuse subject than the old sailor might well have suspected its sincerity. "One who has passed the place knows how to feel for him."

"He was a *poor* fellow, as you say; and a poor frontier man too, though he came out to show his skill among us ignoranters. What became of him? Why, he went down the falls topsy-turvy like, as would have happened to a court-house or a fort."

"If it should jump out of a canoe," interrupted Jasper, smiling, though he was evidently more disposed than his friend to let the passage of the falls be forgotten.

"The boy is right," rejoined Pathfinder, laughing in Mabel's face, the canoes being now so near that they almost touched; "he is sartainly right. But you have not told us what you think of the leap we took?"

"It was perilous and bold," said Mabel; "while looking at it, I could have wished that it had not been attempted, though, now it is over, I can admire its boldness and the steadiness with which it was made."

"Now, do not think that we did this thing to set ourselves off in female eyes. It may be pleasant to the young to win each other's good opinions by doing things which may seem praiseworthy and bold; but neither Eau-douce nor myself is of that race. My natur' has few turns in it, and is a straight natur'; nor would it be likely to lead me into a vanity of this sort while out on duty. As for Jasper, he would sooner go over the Oswego Falls, without a looker-on, than do it before a hundred pair of eyes. I know the lad well from much consorting, and I am sure he is not boastful or vain-glorious."

Mabel rewarded the scout with a smile, which served to keep the canoes together for some time longer; for the sight of youth and beauty was so rare on that remote frontier, that even the rebuked and self-mortified feelings of this wanderer of the forest were sensibly touched by the blooming loveliness of the girl.

"We did it for the best," Pathfinder continued; " 'twas all for the best. Had we waited to carry the canoe across the portage, time would have been lost, and nothing is so precious as time when you are mistrustful of Mingos."

"But we can have little to fear now. The canoes move swiftly, and two hours, you have said, will carry us down to the fort."

"It shall be a cunning Iroquois who hurts a hair of your head, pretty one; for all here are bound to the Sergeant, and most, I think, to yourself, to see you safe from harm. Ha, Eau-douce! what is that in the river, at the lower turn, yonder, beneath the bushes—I mean standing on the rock?"

" 'Tis the Big Serpent, Pathfinder; he is making signs to us in a way I don't understand."

" 'Tis the Sarpent, as sure as I'm a white man, and he wishes us to drop in nearer to his shore. Mischief is brewing, or one of his deliberation and steadiness would never take this trouble. Courage, all! we are men, and must meet devilry as becomes our color and our callings. Ah, I never knew good come of boasting! and here, just as I was vaunting of our safety, comes danger to give me the lie."

CHAPTER IV

Art, stryving to compare
With nature, did an arber greene dispred,
Fram'd of wanton yvie flowing fayre,
Through which the fragrant eglantines did spred.   SPENSER

THE Oswego, below the falls, is a more rapid, unequal stream than it is above them. There are places where the river flows in the quiet stillness of deep water, but many shoals and rapids occur; and at that distant day, when everything was in its natural state, some of the passes were not altogether without hazard. Very little exertion was required on the part of those who managed the canoes, except in those places where the swiftness of the current and the presence of the rocks required care; then, indeed, not only vigilance, but great coolness, readiness, and strength of arm became necessary, in order to avoid the dangers. Of all this the Mohican was aware, and he had judiciously selected a spot where the river flowed tranquilly to intercept the canoes, in order to make his communication without hazard to those he wished to speak.

The Pathfinder had no sooner recognized the form of his red friend, than, with a strong sweep of his paddle, he threw the head of his own canoe towards the shore, motioning for Jasper to follow. In a minute both boats were silently drifting down the stream, within reach of the bushes that overhung the water, all observing a profound silence; some from alarm, and others from habitual caution. As the travellers drew nearer the Indian, he made a sign for them to stop; and then he and Pathfinder had a short but earnest conference.

"The chief is not apt to see enemies in a dead log," observed the white man to his red associate; "why does he tell us to stop?"

"Mingos are in the woods."

"That we have believed these two days: does the chief know it?"

The Mohican quietly held up the head of a pipe formed of stone.

"It lay on a fresh trail that led towards the garrison"—for so it was the usage of that frontier to term a military work, whether it was occupied or not.

"That may be the bowl of a pipe belonging to a soldier. Many use the red-skin pipes."

"See," said the Big Serpent, again holding the thing he had found up to the view of his friend.

The bowl of the pipe was of soap-stone, and was carved with great care and with a very respectable degree of skill; in its centre was a small Latin cross, made with an accuracy which permitted no doubt of its meaning.

"That does foretell devilry and wickedness," said the Pathfinder, who had all the provincial horror of the holy symbol in question which then pervaded the country, and which became so incorporated with its prejudices, by confounding men with things, as to have left its traces strong enough on the moral feeling of the community to be discovered even at the present hour; "no Indian who had not been parvarted by the cunning priests of the Canadas would dream of carving a thing like that on his pipe. I'll warrant ye, the knave prays to the image every time he wishes to sarcumvent the innocent, and work his fearful wickedness. It looks fresh, too, Chingachgook?"

"The tobacco was burning when I found it."

"That is close work, chief. Where was the trail?"

The Mohican pointed to a spot not a hundred yards from that where they stood.

The matter now began to look very serious, and the two principal guides conferred apart for several minutes, when both ascended the bank, approached the indicated spot, and examined the trail with the utmost care. After this investigation had lasted a quarter of an hour, the white man returned alone, his red friend having disappeared in the forest.

The ordinary expression of the countenance of the Pathfinder was that of simplicity, integrity, and sincerity, blended in an air of self-reliance which usually gave great confidence to those who found themselves under his care; but now a look of concern cast a shade over his honest face, that struck the whole party.

"What cheer, Master Pathfinder?" demanded Cap, permitting a voice that was usually deep, loud, and confident to sink into the cautious tones that better suited the dangers of the wilderness. "Has the enemy got between us and our port?"

"Anan?"

"Have any of these painted scaramouches anchored off the harbor towards which we are running, with the hope of cutting us off in entering?"

"It may be all as you say, friend Cap, but I am none the wiser for your words; and in ticklish times the plainer a man makes his English the easier he is understood. I know nothing of ports and anchors; but there is a direful Mingo trail within a hundred yards of this very spot, and as fresh as venison without salt. If one of the fiery devils has passed, so have a dozen; and, what is worse, they have gone down towards the garrison, and not a soul crosses the clearing around it that some of their piercing eyes will not discover, when sartain bullets will follow."

"Cannot this said fort deliver a broadside, and clear everything within the sweep of its hawse?"

"Nay, the forts this-a-way are not like forts in the settlements, and two or three light cannon are all they have down at the mouth of the river; and then, broadsides fired at a dozen outlying Mingos, lying behind logs and in a forest, would be powder spent in vain. We have but one course, and that is a very nice one. We are judgmatically placed here, both canoes being hid by the high bank and the bushes, from all eyes, except those of any lurker directly opposite. Here, then, we may stay without much present fear; but how to get the bloodthirsty devils up the stream again? Ha! I have it, I have it! if it does no good, it can do no harm. Do you see the wide-topped chestnut here, Jasper, at the last turn in the river—on our own side of the stream, I mean?"

"That near the fallen pine?"

"The very same. Take the flint and tinder-box, creep along the bank, and light a fire at that spot; maybe the smoke will draw them above us. In the meanwhile, we will drop the canoes carefully down beyond the point below, and find another shelter. Bushes are plenty, and covers are easily to be had in this region, as witness the many ambushments."

"I will do it, Pathfinder," said Jasper, springing to the shore. "In ten minutes the fire shall be lighted."

"And, Eau-douce, use plenty of damp wood this time," half whispered the other, laughing heartily, in his own peculiar manner; "when smoke is wanted, water helps to thicken it."

The young man was soon off, making his way rapidly towards the desired point. A slight attempt of Mabel to object to the risk was disregarded, and the party immediately prepared to change its position, as it could be seen from the place where Jasper intended to light his fire. The movement did not require haste, and it was made leisurely and with care. The canoes were got clear of the bushes, then suffered to drop down with the stream until they reached the spot where the chestnut, at the foot of which Jasper was to light the fire, was almost shut out from view, when they stopped, and every eye was turned in the direction of the adventurer.

"There goes the smoke!" exclaimed the Pathfinder, as a current of air whirled a little column of the vapor from the land, allowing it to rise spirally above the bed of the river. "A good flint, a small bit of steel, and plenty of dry leaves make a quick fire. I hope Eau-douce will have the wit to bethink him of the damp wood now when it may serve us all a good turn."

"Too much smoke—too much cunning," said Arrowhead sententiously.

"That is gospel truth, Tuscarora, if the Mingos didn't know that they are near soldiers; but soldiers commonly think more of their dinner at a halt than of their wisdom and danger. No, no; let the boy pile on his logs, and smoke them well too; it will all be laid to the stupidity of some Scotch or Irish blunderer, who is thinking more of his oatmeal or his potatoes than of Indian sarcumventions or Indian rifles."

"And yet I should think, from all we have heard in the towns, that the soldiers on this frontier are used to the artifices of their enemies," said Mabel, "and become almost as wily as the red men themselves."

"Not they. Experience makes them but little wiser; and they wheel, and platoon, and battalion it about, here in the forest, just as they did in their parks at home, of which they are all so fond of talking. One red-skin has more cunning in his natur' than a whole regiment from the other side of the water; that is, what I call cunning of the woods. But there is smoke enough, of all conscience, and we had better drop into another cover. The lad has thrown the river on his fire, and there is danger that the Mingos will believe a whole regiment is out."

While speaking, the Pathfinder permitted his canoe to drift away from the bush by which it had been retained, and in a couple of minutes the bend in the river concealed the smoke and the tree. Fortunately a small indentation in the shore presented itself, within a few yards of the point they had just passed; and the two canoes glided into it, under the impulsion of the paddles.

A better spot could not have been found for the purpose. The bushes were thick, and overhung the water, forming a complete canopy of leaves. There was a small gravelly strand at the bottom of the little bay, where most of the party landed to be more at their ease, and the only position from which they could possibly be seen was a point on the river directly opposite. There was little danger, however, of discovery from that quarter, as the thicket there was even denser than common, and the land beyond it was so wet and marshy as to render it difficult to be trodden.

"This is a safe cover," said the Pathfinder, after he had taken a scrutinizing survey of his position; "but it may be necessary to make it safer. Master Cap, I ask nothing of you but silence, and a quieting of such gifts as you may have got at sea, while the Tuscarora and I make provision for the evil hour."

The guide then went a short distance into the bushes, accompanied by the Indian, where the two cut off the larger stems of several alders and other bushes, using the utmost care not to make a noise. The ends of these little trees were forced into the mud, outside of the canoes, the depth of the water being very trifling; and in the course of ten minutes a very effectual screen was interposed between them and the principal point of danger. Much ingenuity and readiness were manifested in making this simple arrangement, in which the two workmen were essentially favored by the natural formation of the bank, the indentation in the shore, the shallowness of the water, and the manner in which the tangled bushes dipped into the stream. The Pathfinder had the address to look for bushes which had curved stems, things easily found in such a place; and by cutting them some distance beneath the bend, and permitting the latter to touch the water, the artificial little thicket had not the appearance of growing in the stream, which might have excited suspicion; but one passing it would have thought that the bushes shot out horizontally from the bank before they inclined upwards towards the light. In short, none but an unusually distrustful eye would have been turned for an instant towards the spot in quest of a hiding-place.

"This is the best cover I ever yet got into," said the Pathfinder, with his quiet laugh, after having been on the outside to reconnoitre; "the leaves of our new trees fairly touch those of the bushes over our heads. Hist!—yonder comes Eau-douce, wading, like a sensible boy, as he is, to leave his trail in the water; and we shall soon see whether our cover is good for anything or not."

Jasper had indeed returned from his duty above; and missing the canoes, he at once inferred that they had dropped round the next bend in the river, in order to get out of sight of the fire. His habits of caution immediately suggested the expediency of stepping into the water, in order that there might exist no visible communication between the marks left on the shore by the party and the place where he believed them to have taken refuge below. Should the Canadian Indians return on their own trail, and discover that made by the Pathfinder and the Serpent in their ascent from and descent to the river, the clue to their movements would cease at the shore, water leaving no prints of footsteps. The young man had therefore waded, knee-deep, as far as the point, and was now seen making his way slowly down the margin of the stream, searching curiously for the spot in which the canoes were hid.

It was in the power of those behind the bushes, by placing their eyes near the leaves, to find many places to look through, while one at a little distance lost this advantage. To those who watched his motions from behind their cover, and they were all in the canoes, it was evident that Jasper was totally at a loss to imagine where the Pathfinder had secreted himself. When fairly round the curvature in the shore, and out of sight of the fire he had lighted above, the young man stopped and began examining the bank deliberately and with great care. Occasionally he advanced eight or ten paces, and then halted again, to renew the search. The water being much shallower than common, he stepped aside, in order to walk with greater ease to himself, and came so near the artificial plantation that he might have touched it with his hand. Still he detected nothing, and was actually passing the spot when Pathfinder made an opening beneath the branches, and called to him in a low voice to enter.

"This is pretty well," said the Pathfinder, laughing; "though pale-face eyes and red-skin eyes are as different as human spy-glasses. I would wager, with the Sergeant's daughter here, a horn of powder against a wampum-belt for her girdle, that her father's rijiment should march by this embankment of ours and never find out the fraud! But if the Mingos actually get down into the bed of the river where Jasper passed, I should tremble for the plantation. It will do for their eyes, even across the stream, however, and will not be without its use."

"Don't you think, Master Pathfinder, that it would be wisest, after all," said Cap, "to get under way at once, and carry sail hard down stream, as soon as we are satisfied that these rascals are fairly astern of us? We seamen call a stern chase a long chase."

"I wouldn't move from this spot until we hear from the Sarpent, with the Sergeant's pretty daughter here in our company, for all the powder in the magazine of the fort below. Sartain captivity or sartain death would follow. If a tender fa'n, such as the maiden we have in charge, could thread the forest like old deer, it might, indeed, do to quit the canoes; for by making a circuit we could reach the garrison before morning."

"Then let it be done," said Mabel, springing to her feet under the sudden impulse of awakened energy. "I am young, active, used to exercise, and could easily out-walk my dear uncle. Let no one think me a hindrance. I cannot bear that all your lives should be exposed on my account."

"No, no, pretty one; we think you anything but a hindrance or anything that is unbecoming, and would willingly run twice this risk to do you and the honest Sergeant a service. Do I not speak your mind, Eau-douce?"

"To do *her* a service!" said Jasper with emphasis. "Nothing shall tempt me to desert Mabel Dunham until she is safe in her father's arms."

"Well said, lad; bravely and honestly said, too; and I join in it, heart and hand. No, no! you are not the first of your sex I have led through the wilderness, and never but once did any harm befall any of them:—that was a sad day, certainly; but its like may never come again."

Mabel looked from one of her protectors to the other, and her fine eyes swam in tears. Frankly placing a hand in that of each, she answered them, though at first her voice was choked, "I have no right to expose you on my account. My dear father will thank you, I thank you, God will reward you; but let there be no unnecessary risk. I can walk far, and have often gone miles on some girlish fancy; why not now exert myself for my life?—nay, for your precious lives?"

"She is a true dove, Jasper," said the Pathfinder, neither relinquishing the hand he held until the girl herself, in native modesty, saw fit to withdraw it, "and wonderfully winning! We get to be rough, and sometimes even hard-hearted, in the woods, Mabel; but the sight of one like you brings us back again to our young feelings, and does us good for the remainder of our days. I daresay Jasper here will tell you the same; for, like me in the forest, the lad sees but few such as yourself on Ontario, to soften his heart and remind him of love for his kind. Speak out now, Jasper, and say if it is not so?"

"I question if many like Mabel Dunham are to be found anywhere," returned the young man gallantly, an honest sincerity glowing in his face that spoke more eloquently than his tongue; "you need not mention woods and lakes to challenge her equals, but I would go into the settlements and towns."

"We had better leave the canoes," Mabel hurriedly rejoined; "for I feel it is no longer safe to be here."

"You can never do it; you can never do it. It would be a

march of more than twenty miles, and that, too, of tramping over brush and roots, and through swamps, in the dark; the trail of such a party would be wide, and we might have to fight our way into the garrison after all. We will wait for the Mohican."

Such appearing to be the decision of him to whom all, in their present strait, looked up for counsel, no more was said on the subject. The whole party now broke up into groups: Arrowhead and his wife sitting apart under the bushes, conversing in a low tone, though the man spoke sternly, and the woman answered with the subdued mildness that marks the degraded condition of a savage's wife. Pathfinder and Cap occupied one canoe, chatting of their different adventures by sea and land; while Jasper and Mabel sat in the other, making greater progress in intimacy in a single hour than might have been effected under other circumstances in a twelvemonth. Notwithstanding their situation as regards the enemy, the time flew by swiftly, and the young people, in particular, were astonished when Cap informed them how long they had been thus occupied.

"If one could smoke, Master Pathfinder," observed the old sailor, "this berth would be snug enough; for, to give the devil his due, you have got the canoes handsomely land-locked, and into moorings that would defy a monsoon. The only hardship is the denial of the pipe."

"The scent of the tobacco would betray us; and where is the use of taking all these precautions against the Mingo's eyes, if we are to tell him where the cover is to be found through the nose? No, no; deny your appetites; and learn one virtue from a red-skin, who will pass a week without eating even, to get a single scalp. Did you hear nothing, Jasper?"

"The Serpent is coming."

"Then let us see if Mohican eyes are better than them of a lad who follows the water."

The Mohican had indeed made his appearance in the same direction as that by which Jasper had rejoined his friends. Instead of coming directly on, however, no sooner did he pass the bend, where he was concealed from any who might be higher up stream, than he moved close under the bank; and, using the utmost caution, got a position where he could look back, with his person sufficiently concealed by the bushes to prevent its being seen by any in that quarter.

"The Sarpent sees the knaves!" whispered Pathfinder. "As I'm a Christian white man, they have bit at the bait, and have ambushed the smoke!"

Here a hearty but silent laugh interrupted his words, and nudging Cap with his elbow, they all continued to watch the movements of Chingachgook in profound stillness. The Mohican remained stationary as the rock on which he stood full ten minutes; and then it was apparent that something of interest had occurred within his view, for he drew back with a hurried manner, looked anxiously and keenly along the margin of the stream, and moved quickly down it, taking care to lose his trail in the shallow water. He was evidently in a hurry and concerned, now looking behind him, and then casting eager glances towards every spot on the shore where he thought a canoe might be concealed.

"Call him in," whispered Jasper, scarcely able to restrain his impatience—"call him in, or it will be too late! See! he is actually passing us."

"Not so, not so, lad; nothing presses, depend on it," returned his companion, "or the Sarpent would begin to creep. The Lord help us and teach us wisdom! I *do* believe even Chingachgook, whose sight is as faithful as the hound's scent, overlooks us, and will not find out the ambushment we have made!"

This exultation was untimely; for the words were no sooner spoken than the Indian, who had actually got several feet lower down the stream than the artificial cover, suddenly stopped; fastened a keen-riveted glance among the transplanted bushes; made a few hasty steps backward; and, bending his body and carefully separating the branches, he appeared among them.

"The accursed Mingos!" said Pathfinder, as soon as his friend was near enough to be addressed with prudence.

"Iroquois," returned the sententious Indian.

"No matter, no matter; Iroquois, devil, Mingo, Mengwes, or furies—all are pretty much the same. I call all rascals Mingos. Come hither, chief, and let us converse rationally."

When their private communication was over, Pathfinder rejoined the rest, and made them acquainted with all he had learned.

The Mohican had followed the trail of their enemies some distance towards the fort, until the latter caught a sight of the smoke of Jasper's fire, when they instantly retraced their steps. It now became necessary for Chingachgook, who ran the greatest risk of detection, to find a cover where he could secrete himself until the party might pass. It was perhaps fortunate for him that the savages were so intent on this recent discovery, that they did not bestow the ordinary attention on the signs of the forest. At all events, they passed him swiftly, fifteen in number, treading lightly in each other's footsteps; and he was enabled again to get into their rear. After proceeding to the place where the footsteps of Pathfinder and the Mohican had joined the principal trail, the Iroquois had struck off to the river, which they reached just as Jasper had disappeared behind the bend below. The smoke being now in plain view, the savages plunged into the woods and endeavored to approach the fire unseen. Chingachgook profited by this occasion to descend to the water, and to gain the bend in the river also, which he thought had been effected undiscovered. Here he paused, as has been stated, until he saw his enemies at the fire, where their stay, however, was very short.

Of the motives of the Iroquois the Mohican could judge only by their acts. He thought they had detected the artifice of the fire, and were aware that it had been kindled with a view to mislead them; for, after a hasty examination of the spot, they had separated, some plunging again into the woods, while six or eight had followed the footsteps of Jasper along the shore, and come down the stream towards the place where the canoes had landed. What course they might take on reaching that spot was only to be conjectured; for the Serpent had felt the emergency to be too pressing to delay looking for his friends any longer. From some indications that were to be gathered from their gestures, however, he thought it probable that their enemies might follow down in the margin of the stream, but could not be certain.

As the Pathfinder related these facts to his companions, the professional feelings of the two other white men came uppermost, and both naturally reverted to their habits, in quest of the means of escape.

"Let us run out the canoes at once," said Jasper eagerly;

"the current is strong, and by using the paddles vigorously we shall soon be beyond the reach of these scoundrels!"

"And this poor flower, that first blossomed in the clearings—shall it wither in the forest?" objected his friend, with a poetry which he had unconsciously imbibed by his long association with the Delawares.

"We must all die first," answered the youth, a generous color mounting to his temples; "Mabel and Arrowhead's wife may lie down in the canoes, while we do our duty, like men, on our feet."

"Ay, you are active at the paddle and the oar, Eau-douce, I will allow, but an accursed Mingo is more active at his mischief; the canoes are swift, but a rifle bullet is swifter."

"It is the business of men, engaged as we have been by a confiding father, to run this risk——"

"But it is not their business to overlook prudence."

"Prudence! a man may carry his prudence so far as to forget his courage."

The group was standing on the narrow strand, the Pathfinder leaning on his rifle, the butt of which rested on the gravelly beach, while both his hands clasped the barrel at the height of his own shoulders. As Jasper threw out this severe and unmerited imputation, the deep red of his comrade's face maintained its hue unchanged, though the young man perceived that the fingers grasped the iron of the gun with the tenacity of a vise. Here all betrayal of emotion ceased.

"You are young and hot-headed," returned Pathfinder, with a dignity that impressed his listeners with a keen sense of his moral superiority; "but my life has been passed among dangers of this sort, and my experience and gifts are not to be mastered by the impatience of a boy. As for courage, Jasper, I will not send back an angry and unmeaning word to meet an angry and an unmeaning word; for I know that you are true in your station and according to your knowledge; but take the advice of one who faced the Mingos when you were a child, and know that their cunning is easier sarcumvented by prudence than outwitted by foolishness."

"I ask your pardon, Pathfinder," said the repentant Jasper, eagerly grasping the hand that the other permitted him to seize; "I ask your pardon, humbly and sincerely. 'Twas a foolish, as well as wicked thing to hint of a man whose heart, in a good cause, is known to be as firm as the rocks on the lake shore."

For the first time the color deepened on the cheek of the Pathfinder, and the solemn dignity which he had assumed, under a purely natural impulse, disappeared in the expression of the earnest simplicity inherent in all his feelings. He met the grasp of his young friend with a squeeze as cordial as if no chord had jarred between them, and a slight sternness that had gathered about his eye disappeared in a look of natural kindness.

" 'Tis well, Jasper," he answered, laughing; "I bear no ill-will, nor shall any one on my behalf. My natur' is that of a white man, and that is to bear no malice. It might have been ticklish work to have said half as much to the Sarpent here, though he is a Delaware, for color will have its way——"

A touch on his shoulder caused the speaker to cease. Mabel was standing erect in the canoe, her light, but swelling form bent forward in an attitude of graceful earnestness, her finger on her lips, her head averted, her spirited eyes riveted on an opening in the bushes, and one arm extended with a fishing-rod, the end of which had touched the Pathfinder. The latter bowed his head to a level with a look-out near which he had intentionally kept himself, and then whispered to Jasper—

"The accursed Mingos! Stand to your arms, my men, but lay quiet as the corpses of dead trees!"

Jasper advanced rapidly, but noiselessly, to the canoe, and with a gentle violence induced Mabel to place herself in such an attitude as concealed her entire body, though it would have probably exceeded his means to induce the girl so far to lower her head that she could not keep her gaze fastened on their enemies. He then took his own post near her, with his rifle cocked and poised, in readiness to fire. Arrowhead and Chingachgook crawled to the cover, and lay in wait like snakes, with their arms prepared for service, while the wife of the former bowed her head between her knees, covered it with her calico robe, and remained passive and immovable. Cap loosened both his pistols in their belt, but seemed quite at a loss what course to pursue. The Pathfinder did not stir. He had originally got a position where he might aim with deadly effect through the leaves, and where he could watch the movements of his enemies;

and he was far too steady to be disconcerted at a moment so critical.

It was truly an alarming instant. Just as Mabel touched the shoulder of her guide, three of the Iroquois had appeared in the water, at the bend of the river, within a hundred yards of the cover, and halted to examine the stream below. They were all naked to the waist, armed for an expedition against their foes, and in their war-paint. It was apparent that they were undecided as to the course they ought to pursue in order to find the fugitives. One pointed down the river, a second up the stream, and the third towards the opposite bank. They evidently doubted.

CHAPTER V

Death is here, and death is there,
Death is busy everywhere.   SHELLEY

IT WAS a breathless moment. The only clue the fugitives possessed to the intentions of their pursuers was in their gestures and the indications which escaped them in the fury of disappointment. That a party had returned already, on their own footsteps, by land, was pretty certain; and all the benefit expected from the artifice of the fire was necessarily lost. But that consideration became of little moment just then; for the party was menaced with an immediate discovery by those who had kept on a level with the river. All the facts presented themselves clearly, and as it might be by intuition, to the mind of Pathfinder, who perceived the necessity of immediate decision and of being in readiness to act in concert. Without making any noise, therefore, he managed to get the two Indians and Jasper near him, when he opened his communications in a whisper.

"We must be ready, we must be ready," he said. "There are but three of the scalping devils, and we are five, four of whom may be set down as manful warriors for such a scrimmage. Eau-douce, do you take the fellow that is painted like death: Chingachgook, I give you the chief; and Arrowhead must keep his eye on the young one. There must be no mistake, for two bullets in the same body would be sinful waste, with one like the Sergeant's daughter in danger. I shall hold myself in resarve against accident, lest a fourth reptile appear, for one of your hands may prove unsteady. By no means fire until I give the word; we must not let the crack of the rifle be heard except in the last resort, since all the rest of the miscreants are still within hearing. Jasper, boy, in case of any movement behind us on the bank, I trust to you to run out the canoe with the Sergeant's daughter, and to pull for the garrison, by God's leave."

The Pathfinder had no sooner given these directions than the near approach of their enemies rendered profound silence necessary. The Iroquois in the river were slowly descending the stream, keeping of necessity near the bushes which overhung the water, while the rustling of leaves and the snapping of twigs soon gave fearful evidence that another party was moving along the bank, at an equally graduated pace, and directly abreast of them. In consequence of the distance between the bushes planted by the fugitives and the true shore, the two parties became visible to each other when opposite that precise point. Both stopped, and a conversation ensued, that may be said to have passed directly over the heads of those who were concealed. Indeed, nothing sheltered the travellers but the branches and leaves of plants, so pliant that they yielded to every current of air, and which a puff of wind a little stronger than common would have blown away. Fortunately the line of sight carried the eyes of the two parties of savages, whether they stood in the water or on the land, above the bushes, and the leaves appeared blended in a way to excite no suspicion. Perhaps the very boldness of the expedient alone prevented an immediate exposure. The conversation which took place was conducted earnestly, but in guarded tones, as if those who spoke wished to defeat the intentions of any listeners. It was in a dialect that both the Indian warriors beneath, as well as the Pathfinder, understood. Even Jasper comprehended a portion of what was said.

"The trail is washed away by the water!" said one from below, who stood so near the artificial cover of the fugitives, that he might have been struck by the salmon-spear that lay in the bottom of Jasper's canoe. "Water has washed it so clear that a Yengeese hound could not follow."

"The pale-faces have left the shore in their canoes," answered the speaker on the bank.

"It cannot be. The rifles of our warriors below are certain."

The Pathfinder gave a significant glance at Jasper, and he clinched his teeth in order to suppress the sound of his own breathing.

"Let my young men look as if their eyes were eagles'," said the eldest warrior among those who were wading in the river. "We have been a whole moon on the war-path, and have found but one scalp. There is a maiden among them, and some of our braves want wives."

Happily these words were lost on Mabel; but Jasper's frown became deeper, and his face fiercely flushed.

The savages now ceased speaking, and the party which was concealed heard the slow and guarded movements of those who were on the bank, as they pushed the bushes aside in their wary progress. It was soon evident that the latter had passed the cover; but the group in the water still remained, scanning the shore with eyes that glared through their war-paint like coals of living fire. After a pause of two or three minutes, these three began also to descend the stream, though it was step by step, as men move who look for an object that has been lost. In this manner they passed the artificial screen, and Pathfinder opened his mouth in that hearty but noiseless laugh that nature and habit had contributed to render a peculiarity of the man. His triumph, however, was premature; for the last of the retiring party, just at this moment casting a look behind him, suddenly stopped; and his fixed attitude and steady gaze at once betrayed the appalling fact that some neglected bush had awakened his suspicions.

It was perhaps fortunate for the concealed that the warrior who manifested these fearful signs of distrust was young, and had still a reputation to acquire. He knew the importance of discretion and modesty in one of his years, and most of all did he dread the ridicule and contempt that would certainly follow a false alarm. Without recalling any of his companions, therefore, he turned on his own footsteps; and, while the others continued to descend the river, he cautiously approached the bushes, on which his looks were still fastened, as by a charm. Some of the leaves which were exposed to the sun had drooped a little, and this slight departure from the usual natural laws had caught the quick eyes of the Indian; for so practised and acute do the senses of the savage become, more especially when he is on the war-path, that trifles apparently of the most insignificant sort often prove to be clues to lead him to his object.

The trifling nature of the change which had aroused the suspicion of this youth was an additional motive for not acquainting his companions with his discovery. Should he really detect anything, his glory would be the greater for being unshared; and should he not, he might hope to escape that derision which the young Indian so much dreads. Then there were the dangers of an ambush and a surprise, to which every warrior of the woods is keenly alive, to render his approach slow and cautious. In consequence of the delay that proceeded from these combined causes, the two parties had descended some fifty or sixty yards before the young savage was again near enough to the bushes of the Pathfinder to touch them with his hand.

Notwithstanding their critical situation, the whole party behind the cover had their eyes fastened on the working countenance of the young Iroquois, who was agitated by conflicting feelings. First came the eager hope of obtaining success where some of the most experienced of his tribe had failed, and with it a degree of glory that had seldom fallen to the share of one of his years or a brave on his first war-path; then followed doubts, as the drooping leaves seemed to rise again and to revive in the currents of air; and distrust of hidden danger lent its exciting feeling to keep the eloquent features in play. So very slight, however, had been the alteration produced by the heat on the bushes of which the stems were in the water, that when the Iroquois actually laid his hand on the leaves, he fancied that he had been deceived. As no man ever distrusts strongly without using all convenient means of satisfying his doubts, however, the young warrior cautiously pushed aside the branches and advanced a step within the hiding-place, when the forms of the concealed party met his gaze, resembling so many breathless statues. The low exclamation, the slight start, and the glaring eye, were hardly seen and heard, before the arm of Chingachgook was raised, and the tomahawk of the Delaware descended on the shaven head of his foe. The Iroquois raised his hands frantically, bounded backward, and fell into the water, at a spot where the current swept the body away, the struggling limbs still tossing and writhing in the agony of death. The Delaware made a vigorous but unsuccessful attempt to seize an arm, with the hope of securing the scalp; but the bloodstained waters whirled down the current, carrying with them their quivering burthen.

All this passed in less than a minute, and the events were so sudden and unexpected, that men less accustomed than the Pathfinder and his associates to forest warfare would have been at a loss how to act.

"There is not a moment to lose," said Jasper, tearing aside the bushes, as he spoke earnestly, but in a suppressed voice. "Do as I do, Master Cap, if you would save your niece; and you, Mabel, lie at your length in the canoe."

The words were scarcely uttered when, seizing the bow of the light boat, he dragged it along the shore, wading himself, while Cap aided behind, keeping so near the bank as to avoid being seen by the savages below, and striving to gain the turn in the river above him which would effectually conceal the party from the enemy. The Pathfinder's canoe lay nearest to the bank, and was necessarily the last to quit the shore. The Delaware leaped on the narrow strand and plunged into the forest, it being his assigned duty to watch the foe in that quarter, while Arrowhead motioned to his white companion to seize the bow of the boat and to follow Jasper. All this was the work of an instant; but when the Pathfinder reached the current that was sweeping round the turn, he felt a sudden change in the weight he was dragging, and, looking back, he found that both the Tuscarora and his wife had deserted him. The thought of treachery flashed upon his mind, but there was no time to pause, for the wailing shout that arose from the party below proclaimed that the body of the young Iroquois had floated as low as the spot reached by his friends. The report of a rifle followed; and then the guide saw that Jasper, having doubled the bend in the river, was crossing the stream, standing erect in the stern of the canoe, while Cap was seated forward, both propelling the light boat with vigorous strokes of the paddles. A glance, a thought, and an expedient followed each other quickly in one so trained in the vicissitudes of the frontier warfare. Springing into the stern of his own canoe, he urged it by a vigorous shove into the current, and commenced crossing the stream himself, at a point so much lower than that of his companions as to offer his own person for a target to the enemy, well knowing that their keen desire to secure a scalp would control all other feelings.

"Keep well up the current, Jasper," shouted the gallant guide, as he swept the water with long, steady, vigorous strokes of the paddle; "keep well up the current, and pull for the alder bushes opposite. Presarve the Sergeant's daughter before all things, and leave these Mingo knaves to the Sarpent and me."

Jasper flourished his paddle as a signal of understanding, while shot succeeded shot in quick succession, all now being aimed at the solitary man in the nearest canoe.

"Ay, empty your rifles like simpletons as you are," said the Pathfinder, who had acquired a habit of speaking when alone, from passing so much of his time in the solitude of the forest; "empty your rifles with an unsteady aim, and give me time to put yard upon yard of river between us. I will not revile you like a Delaware or a Mohican; for my gifts are a white man's gifts, and not an Indian's; and boasting in battle is no part of a Christian warrior; but I may say here, all alone by myself, that you are little better than so many men from the town shooting at robins in the orchards. That was well meant," throwing back his head, as a rifle bullet cut a lock of hair from his temple; "but the lead that misses by an inch is as useless as the lead that never quits the barrel. Bravely done, Jasper! the Sergeant's sweet child must be saved, even if we go in without our own scalps."

By this time the Pathfinder was in the centre of the river, and almost abreast of his enemies, while the other canoe, impelled by the vigorous arms of Cap and Jasper, had nearly gained the opposite shore at the precise spot that had been pointed out to them. The old mariner now played his part manfully; for he was on his proper element, loved his niece sincerely, had a proper regard for his own person, and was not unused to fire, though his experience certainly lay in a very different species of warfare. A few strokes of the paddles were given, and the canoe shot into the bushes, Mabel was hurried to land by Jasper, and for the present all three of the fugitives were safe.

Not so with the Pathfinder: his hardy self-devotion had brought him into a situation of unusual exposure, the hazards of which were much increased by the fact that, just as he drifted nearest to the enemy the party on the shore rushed down the bank and joined their friends who still stood in the water. The Oswego was about a cable's length in width at this point, and, the canoe being in the centre, the object was only a hundred yards from the rifles that were constantly discharged at it; or, at the usual target distance for that weapon.

In this extremity the steadiness and skill of the Pathfinder did him good service. He knew that his safety depended altogether on keeping in motion; for a stationary object, at that distance, would have been hit nearly every shot. Nor was motion of itself sufficient; for, accustomed to kill the bounding deer, his enemies probably knew how to vary the line of aim so as to strike him, should he continue to move in any one direction. He was consequently compelled to change the course of the canoe—at one moment shooting down with the current, with the swiftness of an arrow; and at the next checking its progress in that direction, to glance athwart the stream. Luckily the Iroquois could not reload their pieces in the water, and the bushes that everywhere fringed the shore rendered it difficult to keep the fugitive in view when on the land. Aided by these circumstances, and having received the fire of all his foes, the Pathfinder was gaining fast in distance, both downwards and across the current, when a new danger suddenly, if not unexpectedly, presented itself, by the appearance of the party that had been left in ambush below with a view to watch the river.

These were the savages alluded to in the short dialogue already related. They were no less than ten in number; and, understanding all the advantages of their bloody occupation, they had posted themselves at a spot where the water dashed among rocks and over shallows, in a way to form a rapid which, in the language of the country, is called a rift. The Pathfinder saw that, if he entered this rift, he should be compelled to approach a point where the Iroquois had posted themselves, for the current was irresistible, and the rocks allowed no other safe passage, while death or captivity would be the probable result of the attempt. All his efforts, therefore, were turned toward reaching the western shore, the foe being all on the eastern side of the river; but the exploit surpassed human power, and to attempt to stem the stream would at once have so far diminished the motion of the canoe as to render aim certain. In this exigency the guide came to a decision with his usual cool promptitude, making his preparations accordingly. Instead of endeavoring to gain the channel, he steered towards the shallowest part of the stream, on reaching which he seized his rifle and pack, leaped into the water, and began to wade from rock to rock, taking the direction of the western shore. The canoe whirled about in the furious current, now rolling over some slippery stone, now filling, and then emptying itself, until it lodged on the shore, within a few yards of the spot where the Iroquois had posted themselves.

In the meanwhile the Pathfinder was far from being out of danger; for the first minute, admiration of his promptitude and daring, which are so high virtues in the mind of an Indian, kept his enemies motionless; but the desire of revenge, and the cravings for the much-prized trophy, soon overcame this transient feeling, and aroused them from their stupor. Rifle flashed after rifle, and the bullets whistled around the head of the fugitive, amid the roar of the waters. Still he proceeded like one who bore a charmed life; for, while his rude frontier garments were more than once cut, his skin was not grazed.

As the Pathfinder, in several instances, was compelled to wade in water which rose nearly to his arms, while he kept his rifle and ammunition elevated above the raging current, the toil soon fatigued him, and he was glad to stop at a large stone, or a small rock, which rose so high above the river that its upper surface was dry. On this stone he placed his powder-horn, getting behind it himself, so as to have the advantage of a partial cover for his body. The western shore was only fifty feet distant, but the quiet, swift, dark current that glanced through the interval sufficiently showed that here he would be compelled to swim.

A short cessation in the firing now took place on the part of the Indians, who gathered about the canoe, and, having found the paddles, were preparing to cross the river.

"Pathfinder," called a voice from among the bushes, at the point nearest to the person addressed, on the western shore.

"What would you have, Jasper?"

"Be of good heart—friends are at hand, and not a single Mingo shall cross without suffering for his boldness. Had you not better leave the rifle on the rock, and swim to us before the rascals can get afloat?"

"A true woodsman never quits his piece while he has any powder in his horn or a bullet in his pouch. I have not drawn a trigger this day, Eau-douce, and shouldn't relish the idea of parting with those reptiles without causing them to remember my name. A little water will not harm my legs; and I see that blackguard, Arrowhead, among the scamps, and wish to send him the wages he has so faithfully earned. You have not brought the Sergeant's daughter down here in a range with their bullets, I hope, Jasper?"

"She is safe for the present at least; though all depends on our keeping the river between us and the enemy. They must know our weakness now; and, should they cross, no doubt some of their party will be left on the other side."

"This canoeing touches your gifts rather than mine, boy, though I will handle a paddle with the best Mingo that ever struck a salmon. If they cross below the rift, why can't we cross in the still water above, and keep playing at dodge and turn with the wolves?"

"Because, as I have said, they will leave a party on the other shore; and then, Pathfinder, would you expose Mabel, to the rifles of the Iroquois?"

"The Sergeant's daughter must be saved," returned the guide, with calm energy. "You are right, Jasper; she has no gift to authorize her in offering her sweet face and tender body to a Mingo rifle. What can be done, then? They must be kept from crossing for an hour or two, if possible, when we must do our best in the darkness."

"I agree with you, Pathfinder, if it can be effected; but are we strong enough for such a purpose?"

"The Lord is with us, boy, the Lord is with us; and it is unreasonable to suppose that one like the Sergeant's daughter will be altogether abandoned by Providence in such a strait. There is not a boat between the falls and the garrison, except these two canoes, to my sartain knowledge; and I think it will go beyond red-skin gifts to cross in the face of two rifles like these of yourn and mine. I will not vaunt, Jasper; but it is well known on all this frontier that Killdeer seldom fails."

"Your skill is admitted by all, far and near, Pathfinder; but a rifle takes time to be loaded; nor are you on the land, aided by a good cover, where you can work to the advantage you are used to. If you had our canoe, might you not pass to the shore with a dry rifle?"

"Can an eagle fly, Jasper?" returned the other, laughing in his usual manner, and looking back as he spoke. "But it would be unwise to expose yourself on the water; for them miscreants are beginning to bethink them again of powder and bullets."

"It can be done without any such chances. Master Cap has gone up to the canoe, and will cast the branch of a tree into the river to try the current, which sets from the point above in the direction of your rock. See, there it comes already; if it float fairly, you must raise your arm, when the canoe will follow. At all events, if the boat should pass you, the eddy below will bring it up, and I can recover it."

While Jasper was still speaking, the floating branch came in sight; and, quickening its progress with the increasing velocity of the current, it swept swiftly down towards the Pathfinder, who seized it as it was passing, and held it in the air as a sign of success. Cap understood the signal, and presently the canoe was launched into the stream, with a caution and an intelligence that the habits of the mariner had fitted him to observe. It floated in the same direction as the branch, and in a minute was arrested by the Pathfinder.

"This has been done with a frontier man's judgment, Jasper," said the guide, laughing; "but you have your gifts, which incline most to the water, as mine incline to the woods. Now let them Mingo knaves cock their rifles and get rests, for this is the last chance they are likely to have at a man without a cover."

"Nay, shove the canoe towards the shore, quartering the current, and throw yourself into it as it goes off," said Jasper eagerly. "There is little use in running any risk."

"I love to stand up face to face with my enemies like a man, while they set me the example," returned the Pathfinder proudly. "I am not a red-skin born, and it is more a white man's gifts to fight openly than to lie in ambushment."

"And Mabel?"

"True, boy, true; the Sergeant's daughter must be saved;

and, as you say, foolish risks only become boys. Think you that you can catch the canoe where you stand?"

"There can be no doubt, if you give a vigorous push."

Pathfinder made the necessary effort; the light bark shot across the intervening space, and Jasper seized it as it came to land. To secure the canoe, and to take proper positions in the cover, occupied the friends but a moment, when they shook hands cordially, like those who had met after a long separation.

"Now, Jasper, we shall see if a Mingo of them all dares cross the Oswego in the teeth of Killdeer! You are handier with the oar and the paddle and the sail than with the rifle, perhaps; but you have a stout heart and a steady hand, and them are things that count in a fight."

"Mabel will find me between her and her enemies," said Jasper calmly.

"Yes, yes, the Sergeant's daughter must be protected. I like you, boy, on your own account; but I like you all the better that you think of one so feeble at a moment when there is need of all your manhood. See, Jasper! three of the knaves are actually getting into the canoe! They must believe we have fled, or they would not surely venture so much, directly in the very face of Killdeer."

Sure enough the Iroquois did appear bent on venturing across the stream; for, as the Pathfinder and his friends now kept their persons strictly concealed, their enemies began to think that the latter had taken to flight. Such a course was that which most white men would have followed; but Mabel was under the care of those who were much too well skilled in forest warfare to neglect to defend the only pass that, in truth, now offered even a probable chance for protection.

As the Pathfinder had said, three warriors were in the canoe, two holding their rifles at a poise, as they knelt in readiness to aim the deadly weapons, and the other standing erect in the stern to wield the paddle. In this manner they left the shore, having had the precaution to haul the canoe, previously to entering it, so far up the stream as to have got into the comparatively still water above the rift. It was apparent at a glance that the savage who guided the boat was skilled in the art; for the long steady sweep of his paddle sent the light bark over the glassy surface of the tranquil river as if it were a feather floating in air.

"Shall I fire?" demanded Jasper in a whisper, trembling with eagerness to engage.

"Not yet, boy, not yet. There are but three of them, and if Master Cap yonder knows how to use the popguns he carries in his belt, we may even let them land, and then we shall recover the canoe."

"But Mabel——?"

"No fear for the Sergeant's daughter. She is safe in the hollow stump, you say, with the opening judgmatically hid by the brambles. If what you tell me of the manner in which you concealed the trail be true, the sweet one might lie there a month and laugh at the Mingos."

"We are never certain. I wish we had brought her nearer to our own cover!"

"What for, Eau-douce? To place her pretty little head and leaping heart among flying bullets? No, no: she is better where she is, because she is safer."

"We are never certain. We thought ourselves safe behind the bushes, and yet you saw that we were discovered."

"And the Mingo imp paid for his curiosity, as these knaves are about to do."

The Pathfinder ceased speaking; for at that instant the sharp report of a rifle was heard, when the Indian in the stern of the canoe leaped high into the air, and fell into the water, holding the paddle in his hand. A small wreath of smoke floated out from among the bushes of the eastern shore, and was soon absorbed by the atmosphere.

"That is the Sarpent hissing!" exclaimed the Pathfinder exultingly. "A bolder or a truer heart never beat in the breast of a Delaware. I am sorry that he interfered; but he could not have known our condition."

The canoe had no sooner lost its guide than it floated with the stream, and was soon sucked into the rapids of the rift. Perfectly helpless, the two remaining savages gazed wildly about them, but could offer no resistance to the power of the element. It was perhaps fortunate for Chingachgook that the attention of most of the Iroquois was intently given to the situation of those in the boat, else would his escape have been to the last degree difficult, if not totally impracticable. But not a foe moved, except to conceal his person behind some cover; and every eye was riveted on the two remaining adventurers. In less time than has been necessary to record these occurrences, the canoe was whirling and tossing in the rift, while both the savages had stretched themselves in its bottom, as the only means of preserving the equilibrium. This natural expedient soon failed them; for, striking a rock, the light craft rolled over, and the two warriors were thrown into the river. The water is seldom deep on a rift, except in particular places where it may have worn channels; and there was little to be apprehended from drowning, though their arms were lost; and the two savages were fain to make the best of their way to the friendly shore, swimming and wading as circumstances required. The canoe itself lodged on a rock in the centre of the stream, where for the moment it became useless to both parties.

"Now is our time, Pathfinder," cried Jasper, as the two Iroquois exposed most of their persons while wading in the shallowest part of the rapids: "the fellow up stream is mine, and you can take the lower."

So excited had the young man become by all the incidents of the stirring scene, that the bullet sped from his rifle as he spoke, but uselessly, as it would seem, for both the fugitives tossed their arms in disdain. The Pathfinder did not fire.

"No, no, Eau-douce," he answered; "I do not seek blood without a cause; and my bullet is well leathered and carefully driven down, for the time of need. I love no Mingo, as is just, seeing how much I have consorted with the Delawares, who are their mortal and natural enemies; but I never pull trigger on one of the miscreants unless it be plain that his death will lead to some good end. The deer never leaped that fell by my hand wantonly. By living much alone with God in the wilderness a man gets to feel the justice of such opinions. One life is sufficient for our present wants; and there may yet be occasion to use Killdeer in behalf of the Sarpent, who has done an untimorsome thing to let them rampant devils so plainly know that he is in their neighborhood. As I'm a wicked sinner, there is one of them prowling along the bank this very moment, like one of the boys of the garrison skulking behind a fallen tree to get a shot at a squirrel!"

As the Pathfinder pointed with his finger while speaking, the quick eye of Jasper soon caught the object towards which it was directed. One of the young warriors of the enemy, burning with a desire to distinguish himself, had stolen from his party towards the cover in which Chingachgook had concealed himself; and as the latter was deceived by the apparent apathy of his foes, as well as engaged in some further preparations of his own, he had evidently obtained a position where he got a sight of the Delaware. This circumstance was apparent by the arrangements the Iroquois was making to fire, for Chingachgook himself was not visible from the western side of the river. The rift was at a bend in the Oswego, and the sweep of the eastern shore formed a curve so wide that Chingachgook was quite near to his enemies in a straight direction, though separated by several hundred feet on the land, owing to which fact air lines brought both parties nearly equidistant from the Pathfinder and Jasper. The general width of the river being a little less than two hundred yards, such necessarily was about the distance between his two observers and the skulking Iroquois.

"The Sarpent must be thereabouts," observed Pathfinder, who never turned his eye for an instant from the young warrior; "and yet he must be strangely off his guard to allow a Mingo devil to get his stand so near, with manifest signs of bloodshed in his heart."

"See!" interrupted Jasper—"there is the body of the Indian the Delaware shot! It has drifted on a rock, and the current has forced the head and face above the water."

"Quite likely, boy, quite likely. Human natur' is little better than a log of driftwood when the life that was breathed into its nostrils has departed. That Iroquois will never harm any one more; but yonder skulking savage is bent on taking the scalp of my best and most tried friend."

The Pathfinder suddenly interrupted himself by raising his rifle, a weapon of unusual length, with admirable precision, and firing the instant it had got its level. The Iroquois on the opposite shore was in the act of aiming when the fatal messenger from Killdeer arrived. His rifle was discharged, it is true, but it was with the muzzle in the air, while the man himself plunged into the bushes, quite evidently hurt, if not slain.

"The skulking reptyle brought it on himself," muttered Pathfinder sternly, as, dropping the butt of his rifle, he carefully commenced reloading it. "Chingachgook and I have consorted together since we were boys, and have fi't in company on the Horican, the Mohawk, the Ontario, and all the other bloody passes between the country of the Frenchers and our own; and did the foolish knave believe that I would stand by and see my best friend cut off in an ambushment?"

"We have served the Sarpent as good a turn as he served us. Those rascals are troubled, Pathfinder, and are falling back into their covers, since they find we can reach them across the river."

"The shot is no great matter, Jasper, no great matter. Ask any of the 60th, and they can tell you what Killdeer can do, and has done, and that, too, when the bullets were flying about our heads like hailstones. No, no! this is no great matter, and the unthoughtful vagabond drew it down on himself."

"Is that a dog, or a deer, swimming towards this shore?"

Pathfinder started, for sure enough an object was crossing the stream, above the rift, towards which, however, it was gradually setting by the force of the current. A second look satisfied both the observers that it was a man, and an Indian, though so concealed as at first to render it doubtful. Some stratagem was apprehended, and the closest attention was given to the movements of the stranger.

"He is pushing something before him as he swims, and his head resembles a drifting bush," said Jasper.

" 'Tis Indian devilry, boy; but Christian honesty shall circumvent their arts."

As the man slowly approached, the observers began to doubt the accuracy of their first impressions, and it was only when two-thirds of the stream were passed that the truth was really known.

"The Big Sarpent, as I live!" exclaimed Pathfinder, looking at his companion, and laughing until the tears came into his eyes with pure delight at the success of the artifice. "He has tied bushes to his head, so as to hide it, put the horn on top, lashed the rifle to that bit of log he is pushing before him, and has come over to join his friends. Ah's me! The times and times that he and I have cut such pranks, right in the teeth of Mingos raging for our blood, in the great thoroughfare round and about Ty!"

"It may not be the Serpent after all, Pathfinder; I can see no feature that I remember."

"Feature! Who looks for features in an Indian? No, no, boy; 'tis the paint that speaks, and none but a Delaware would wear that paint: them are his colors, Jasper, just as your craft on the lake wears St. George's Cross, and the Frenchers set their tablecloths to fluttering in the wind, with all the stains of fish-bones and venison steaks upon them. Now, you see the eye, lad, and it is the eye of a chief. But, Eau-douce, fierce as it is in battle, and glassy as it looks from among the leaves"—here the Pathfinder laid his fingers lightly but impressively on his companion's arm—"I have seen it shed tears like rain. There is a soul and a heart under that red skin, rely on it; although they are a soul and a heart with gifts different from our own."

"No one who is acquainted with the chief ever doubted that."

"I _know_ it," returned the other proudly, "for I have consorted with him in sorrow and in joy: in one I have found him a man, however stricken; in the other, a chief who knows that the women of his tribe are the most seemly in light merriment. But hist! It is too much like the people of the settlements to pour soft speeches into another's ear; and the Sarpent has keen senses. He knows I love him, and that I speak well of him behind his back; but a Delaware has modesty in his inmost natur', though he will brag like a sinner when tied to a stake."

The Serpent now reached the shore, directly in the front of his two comrades, with whose precise position he must have been acquainted before leaving the eastern side of the river, and rising from the water he shook himself like a dog, and made the usual exclamation—"Hugh!"

CHAPTER VI

These, as they change, Almighty Father, these,
Are but the varied God.   THOMSON

As THE chief landed he was met by the Pathfinder, who addressed him in the language of the warrior's people: "Was it well done, Chingachgook," said he reproachfully, "to ambush a dozen Mingos alone? Killdeer seldom fails me, it is true; but the Oswego makes a distant mark, and that miscreant showed little more than his head and shoulders above the bushes, and an onpractysed hand and eye might have failed. You should have thought of this, chief—you should have thought of this!"

"The Great Serpent is a Mohican warrior—he sees only his enemies when he is on the war-path, and his fathers have struck the Mingos from behind, since the waters began to run."

"I know your gifts, I know your gifts, and respect them too. No man shall hear me complain that a red-skin obsarved red-skin natur'. But prudence as much becomes a warrior as valor; and had not the Iroquois devils been looking after their friends who were in the water, a hot trail they would have made of yourn."

"What is the Delaware about to do?" exclaimed Jasper, who observed at that moment that the chief had suddenly left the Pathfinder and advanced to the water's edge, apparently with an intention of again entering the river. "He will not be so mad as to return to the other shore for any trifle he may have forgotten?"

"Not he, not he; he is as prudent as he is brave, in the main, though so forgetful of himself in the late ambushment. Hark'e, Jasper," leading the other a little aside, just as they heard the Indian's plunge into the water—"hark'e, lad; Chingachgook is not a Christian white man, like ourselves, but a Mohican chief, who has his gifts and traditions to tell him what he ought to do; and he who consorts with them that are not strictly and altogether of his own kind had better leave natur' and use to govern his comrades. A king's soldier will swear and he will drink, and it is of little use to try to prevent him; a gentleman likes his delicacies, and a lady her feathers, and it does not avail much to struggle against either; whereas an Indian's natur' and gifts are much stronger than these, and no doubt were bestowed by the Lord for wise ends, though neither you nor me can follow them in all their windings."

"What does this mean? See, the Delaware is swimming towards the body that is lodged on the rock? Why does he risk this?"

"For honor and glory and renown, as great gentlemen quit their quiet homes beyond seas—where, as they tell me, heart has nothing left to wish for; that is, such hearts as can be satisfied in a clearing—to come hither to live on game and fight the Frenchers."

"I understand you—your friend has gone to secure the scalp."

" 'Tis his gift, and let him enjoy it. We are white men, and cannot mangle a dead enemy; but it is honor in the eyes of a red-skin to do so. It may seem singular to you, Eau-douce, but I've known white men of great name and character manifest as remarkable idees consarning their honor, I have."

"A savage will be a savage, Pathfinder, let him keep what company he may."

"It is well for us to say so, lad; but, as I tell you, white honor will not always conform to reason or to the will of God. I have passed days thinking of these matters, out in the silent woods, and I have come to the opinion, boy, that, as Providence rules all things, no gift is bestowed without some wise and reasonable end."

"The Serpent greatly exposes himself to the enemy, in order to get his scalp! This may lose us the day."

"Not in his mind, Jasper. That one scalp has more honor in it, according to the Sarpent's notions of warfare, than a field covered with slain, that kept the hair on their heads. Now, there was the fine young captain of the 6oth that threw away his life in trying to bring off a three-pounder from among the Frenchers in the last scrimmage we had; he thought he was sarving honor; and I have known a young ensign wrap himself up in his colors, and go to sleep in his blood, fancying that he was lying on something softer even than buffalo-skins."

"Yes, yes; one can understand the merit of not hauling down an ensign."

"And these are Chingachgook's colors—he will keep them to show his children's children—" Here the Pathfinder interrupted himself, shook his head in melancholy, and slowly added, "Ah's me! no shoot of the old Mohican stem remains! He has no children to delight with his trophies; no tribe to honor by his deeds; he is a lone man in this world, and yet he stands true to his training and his gifts! There is something honest and respectable in these, you must allow, Jasper."

Here a great outcry from the Iroquois was succeeded by the quick reports of their rifles, and so eager did the enemy become, in the desire to drive the Delaware back from his victim, that a dozen rushed into the river, several of whom even advanced near a hundred feet into the foaming current, as if they actually meditated a serious sortie. But Chingachgook continued unmoved, as he remained unhurt by the missiles, accomplishing his task with the dexterity of long habit. Flourishing his reeking trophy, he gave the war-whoop in its most frightful intonations, and for a minute the arches of the silent woods and the deep vista formed by the course of the river echoed with cries so terrific that Mabel bowed her head in irrepressible fear, while her uncle for a single instant actually meditated flight.

"This surpasses all I have heard from the wretches," Jasper exclaimed, stopping his ears, equally in horror and disgust.

" 'Tis their music, boy; their drum and fife; their trumpets and clarions. No doubt they love those sounds; for they stir up in them fierce feelings, and a desire for blood," returned the Pathfinder, totally unmoved. "I thought them rather frightful when a mere youngster; but they have become like the whistle of the whip-poor-will or the song of the cat-bird in my ear now. All the screeching reptyles that could stand between the falls and the garrison would have no effect on my narves at this time of day. I say it not in boasting, Jasper; for the man that lets in cowardice through the ears must have but a weak heart at the best; sounds and outcries being more intended to alarm women and children than such as scout the forest and face the foe. I hope the Sarpent is now satisfied, for here he comes with the scalp at his belt."

Jasper turned away his head as the Delaware rose from the water, in pure disgust at his late errand; but the Pathfinder regarded his friend with the philosophical indifference of one who had made up his mind to be indifferent to things he deemed immaterial. As the Delaware passed deeper into the bushes with a view to wring his trifling calico dress and to prepare his rifle for service, he gave one glance of triumph at his companions, and then all emotion connected with the recent exploit seemed to cease.

"Jasper," resumed the guide, "step down to the station of Master Cap, and ask him to join us: we have little time for a council, and yet our plans must be laid quickly, for it will not be long before them Mingos will be plotting our ruin."

The young man complied; and in a few minutes the four were assembled near the shore, completely concealed from the view of their enemies, while they kept a vigilant watch over the proceedings of the latter, in order to consult on their own future movements.

By this time the day had so far advanced as to leave but a few minutes between the passing light and an obscurity that promised to be even deeper than common. The sun had already set, and the twilight of a low latitude would soon pass into the darkness of deep night. Most of the hopes of the party rested on this favorable circumstance, though it was not without its dangers also, as the very obscurity which would favor their escape would be as likely to conceal the movements of their wily enemies.

"The moment has come, men," Pathfinder commenced, "when our plans must be coolly laid, in order that we may act together, and with a right understanding of our errand and gifts. In an hour's time these woods will be as dark as midnight; and if we are ever to gain the garrison, it must be done under favor of this advantage. What say you, Master Cap? for, though none of the most experienced in combats and retreats in the woods, your years entitle you to speak first in a matter like this and in a council."

"Well, in my judgment, all we have to do is to go on board the canoe when it gets to be so dark the enemy's look-outs can't see us, and run for the haven, as wind and tide will allow."

"That is easily said, but not so easily done," returned the

guide. "We shall be more exposed in the river than by following the woods; and then there is the Oswego rift below us, and I am far from sartain that Jasper himself can carry a boat safely through it in the dark. What say you, lad, as to your own skill and judgment?"

"I am of Master Cap's opinion about using the canoe. Mabel is too tender to walk through swamps and among roots of trees in such a night as this promises to be, and then I always feel myself stouter of heart and truer of eye when afloat than when ashore."

"Stout of heart you always be, lad, and I think tolerably true of eye for one who has lived so much in broad sunshine and so little in the woods. Ah's me! the Ontario has no trees, or it would be a plain to delight a hunter's heart! As to your opinion, friends, there is much for and much against it. For it, it may be said water leaves no trail——"

"What do you call the wake?" interrupted the pertinacious and dogmatical Cap.

"Anan?"

"Go on," said Jasper; "Master Cap thinks he is on the ocean —water leaves no trail——"

"It leaves none, Eau-douce, hereaway, though I do not pretend to say what it may leave on the sea. Then a canoe is both swift and easy when it floats with the current, and the tender limbs of the Sergeant's daughter will be favored by its motion. But, on the other hand, the river will have no cover but the clouds in the heavens; the rift is a ticklish thing for boats to venture into, even by daylight; and it is six fairly measured miles, by water, from this spot to the garrison. Then a trail on land is not easy to be found in the dark. I am troubled, Jasper, to say which way we ought to counsel and advise."

"If the Serpent and myself could swim into the river and bring off the other canoe," the young sailor replied, "it would seem to me that our safest course would be the water."

"If, indeed! and yet it might easily be done, as soon as it is a little darker. Well, well, I am not sartain it will not be the best. Though, were we only a party of men, it would be like a hunt to the lusty and brave to play at hide-and-seek with yonder miscreants on the other shore. Jasper," continued the guide, into whose character there entered no ingredient which belonged to vain display or theatrical effect, "will you undertake to bring in the canoe?"

"I will undertake anything that will serve and protect Mabel, Pathfinder."

"That is an upright feeling, and I suppose it is natur'. The Sarpent, who is nearly naked already, can help you; and this will be cutting off one of the means of them devils to work their harm."

This material point being settled, the different members of the party prepared themselves to put the project in execution. The shades of evening fell fast upon the forest; and by the time all was ready for the attempt, it was found impossible to discern objects on the opposite shore. Time now pressed; for Indian cunning could devise so many expedients for passing so narrow a stream, that the Pathfinder was getting impatient to quit the spot. While Jasper and his companion entered the river, armed with nothing but their knives and the Delaware's tomahawk, observing the greatest caution not to betray their movements, the guide brought Mabel from her place of concealment, and, bidding her and Cap proceed along the shore to the foot of the rapids, he got into the canoe that remained in his possession, in order to carry it to the same place.

This was easily effected. The canoe was laid against the bank, and Mabel and her uncle entered it, taking their seats as usual; while the Pathfinder, erect in the stern, held by a bush, in order to prevent the swift stream from sweeping them down its current. Several minutes of intense and breathless expectation followed, while they awaited the results of the bold attempt of their comrades.

It will be understood that the two adventurers were compelled to swim across a deep and rapid channel before they could reach a part of the rift that admitted of wading. This portion of the enterprise was soon effected; and Jasper and the Serpent struck the bottom side by side at the same instant. Having secured firm footing, they took hold of each other's hands, and waded slowly and with extreme caution in the supposed direction of the canoe. But the darkness was already so deep that they soon ascertained they were to be but little aided by the sense of sight, and that their search must be conducted on that species of instinct which enables the woodsman to find his way when the sun is hid, no stars appear, and all would seem chaos to one less accustomed to the mazes of the forest. Under these circumstances, Jasper submitted to be guided by the Delaware, whose habits best fitted him to take the lead. Still it was no easy matter to wade amid the roaring element at that hour, and retain a clear recollection of the localities. By the time they believed themselves to be in the centre of the stream, the two shores were discernible merely by masses of obscurity denser than common, the outlines against the clouds being barely distinguishable by the ragged tops of the trees. Once or twice the wanderers altered their course, in consequence of unexpectedly stepping into deep water; for they knew that the boat had lodged on the shallowest part of the rift. In short, with this fact for their compass, Jasper and his companion wandered about in the water for nearly a quarter of an hour; and at the end of that period, which began to appear interminable to the young man, they found themselves apparently no nearer the object of their search than they had been at its commencement. Just as the Delaware was about to stop, in order to inform his associate that they would do well to return to the land, in order to take a fresh departure, he saw the form of a man moving about in the water, almost within reach of his arm. Jasper was at his side, and he at once understood that the Iroquois were engaged on the same errand as he was himself.

"Mingo!" he uttered in Jasper's ear. "The Serpent will show his brother how to be cunning."

The young sailor caught a glimpse of the figure at that instant, and the startling truth also flashed on his mind. Understanding the necessity of trusting all to the Delaware chief, he kept back, while his friend moved cautiously in the direction in which the strange form had vanished. In another moment it was seen again, evidently moving towards themselves. The waters made such an uproar that little was to be apprehended from ordinary sounds, and the Indian, turning his head, hastily said, "Leave it to the cunning of the Great Serpent."

"Hugh!" exclaimed the strange savage, adding, in the language of his people, "The canoe is found, but there were none to help me. Come, let us raise it from the rock."

"Willingly," answered Chingachgook, who understood the dialect. "Lead; we will follow."

The stranger, unable to distinguish between voices and accents amid the raging of the rapid, led the way in the necessary direction; and, the two others keeping close at his heels, all three speedily reached the canoe. The Iroquois laid hold of one end, Chingachgook placed himself in the centre, and Jasper went to the opposite extremity, as it was important that the stranger should not detect the presence of a pale-face, a discovery that might be made by the parts of the dress the young man still wore, as well as by the general appearance of his head.

"Lift," said the Iroquois in the sententious manner of his race; and by a trifling effort the canoe was raised from the rock, held a moment in the air to empty it, and then placed carefully on the water in its proper position. All three held it firmly, lest it should escape from their hands under the pressure of the violent current, while the Iroquois, who led, of course, being at the upper end of the boat, took the direction of the eastern shore, or towards the spot where his friends waited his return.

As the Delaware and Jasper well knew there must be several more of the Iroquois on the rift, from the circumstance that their own appearance had occasioned no surprise in the individual they had met, both felt the necessity of extreme caution. Men less bold and determined would have thought that they were incurring too great a risk by thus venturing into the midst of their enemies; but these hardy borderers were unacquainted with fear, were accustomed to hazards, and so well understood the necessity of at least preventing their foes from getting the boat, that they would have cheerfully encountered even greater risks to secure their object. So all-important to the safety of Mabel, indeed, did Jasper deem the possession or the destruction of this canoe, that he had drawn his knife, and stood ready to rip up the bark, in order to render the boat temporarily unserviceable, should anything occur to compel the Delaware and himself to abandon their prize.

In the meantime, the Iroquois, who led the way, proceeded slowly through the water in the direction of his own party, still grasping the canoe, and dragging his reluctant followers in his train. Once Chingachgook raised his tomahawk, and was about to bury it in the brain of his confiding and unsuspicious neighbor; but the probability that the death-cry or the floating body might give the alarm induced that wary chief to change his purpose. At the next moment he regretted this indecision, for the three who clung to the canoe suddenly found themselves in the centre of a party of no less than four others who were in quest of it.

After the usual brief characteristic exclamations of satisfaction, the savages eagerly laid hold of the canoe, for all seemed impressed with the necessity of securing this important boat, the one side in order to assail their foes, and the other to secure their retreat. The addition to the party, however, was so unlooked-for, and so completely gave the enemy the superiority, that for a few moments the ingenuity and address of even the Delaware were at fault. The five Iroquois, who seemed perfectly to understand their errand, pressed forward towards their own shore, without pausing to converse; their object being in truth to obtain the paddles, which they had previously secured, and to embark three or four warriors, with all their rifles and powder-horns, the want of which had alone prevented their crossing the river by swimming as soon as it was dark.

In this manner, the body of friends and foes united reached the margin of the eastern channel, where, as in the case of the western, the river was too deep to be waded. Here a short pause succeeded, it being necessary to determine the manner in which the canoe was to be carried across. One of the four who had just reached the boat was a chief; and the habitual deference which the American Indian pays to merit, experience, and station kept the others silent until this individual had spoken.

The halt greatly added to the danger of discovering the presence of Jasper, in particular, who, however, had the precaution to throw the cap he wore into the bottom of the canoe. Being without his jacket and shirt, the outline of his figure, in the obscurity, would now be less likely to attract observation. His position, too, at the stern of the canoe a little favored his concealment, the Iroquois naturally keeping their looks directed the other way. Not so with Chingachgook. This warrior was literally in the midst of his most deadly foes, and he could scarcely move without touching one of them. Yet he was apparently unmoved, though he kept all his senses on the alert, in readiness to escape, or to strike a blow at the proper moment. By carefully abstaining from looking towards those behind him, he lessened the chances of discovery, and waited with the indomitable patience of an Indian for the instant when he should be required to act.

"Let all my young men but two, one at each end of the canoe, cross and get their arms," said the Iroquois chief. "Let the two push over the boat."

The Indians quietly obeyed, leaving Jasper at the stern, and the Iroquois who had found the canoe at the bow of the light raft, Chingachgook burying himself so deep in the river as to be passed by the others without detection. The splashing in the water, the tossing arms, and the calls of one to another, soon announced that the four who had last joined the party were already swimming. As soon as this fact was certain, the Delaware rose, resumed his former station, and began to think the moment for action was come.

One less habitually under self-restraint than this warrior would probably have now aimed his meditated blow; but Chingachgook knew there were more Iroquois behind him on the rift, and he was a warrior much too trained and experienced to risk anything unnecessarily. He suffered the Indian at the bow of the canoe to push off into the deep water, and then all three were swimming in the direction of the eastern shore. Instead, however, of helping the canoe across the swift current, no sooner did the Delaware and Jasper find themselves within the influence of its greatest force than both began to swim in a way to check their farther progress across the stream. Nor was this done suddenly, or in the incautious manner in which a civilized man would have been apt to attempt the artifice, but warily, and so gradually that the Iroquois at the bow fancied at first he was merely struggling against the strength of the current. Of course, while acted on by these opposing efforts, the canoe drifted down stream, and in about a minute it was floating in still deeper water at the foot of the rift. Here, however, the Iroquois was not slow in finding that something unusual retarded their advance, and, looking back, he first learned that he was resisted by the efforts of his companions.

That second nature which grows up through habit instantly told the young Iroquois that he was alone with enemies. Dashing the water aside, he sprang at the throat of Chingachgook, and the two Indians, relinquishing their hold of the canoe, seized each other like tigers. In the midst of the darkness of that gloomy night, and floating in an element so dangerous to man when engaged in deadly strife, they appeared to forget everything but their fell animosity and their mutual desire to conquer.

Jasper had now complete command of the canoe, which flew off like a feather impelled by the breath under the violent reaction of the struggles of the two combatants. The first impulse of the youth was to swim to the aid of the Delaware, but the importance of securing the boat presented itself with tenfold force, while he listened to the heavy breathings of the warriors as they throttled each other, and he proceeded as fast as possible towards the western shore. This he soon reached; and after a short search he succeeded in discovering the remainder of the party and in procuring his clothes. A few words sufficed to explain the situation in which he had left the Delaware and the manner in which the canoe had been obtained.

When those who had been left behind had heard the explanations of Jasper, a profound stillness reigned among them, each listening intently in the vain hope of catching some clue to the result of the fearful struggle that had just taken place, if it were not still going on in the water. Nothing was audible beyond the steady roar of the rushing river; it being a part of the policy of their enemies on the opposite shore to observe the most deathlike stillness.

"Take this paddle, Jasper," said Pathfinder calmly, though the listeners thought his voice sounded more melancholy than usual, "and follow with your own canoe. It is unsafe for us to remain here longer."

"But the Serpent?"

"The Great Sarpent is in the hands of his own Deity, and will live or die, according to the intentions of Providence. We can do him no good, and may risk too much by remaining here in idleness, like women talking over their distresses. This darkness is very precious."

A loud, long, piercing yell came from the shore, and cut short the words of the guide.

"What is the meaning of that uproar, Master Pathfinder?" demanded Cap. "It sounds more like the outcries of devils than anything that can come from the throats of Christians and men."

"Christians they are not, and do not pretend to be, and do

not wish to be; and in calling them devils you have scarcely misnamed them. That yell is one of rejoicing, and it is as conquerors they have given it. The body of the Sarpent, no doubt, dead or alive, is in their power."

"And we!" exclaimed Jasper, who felt a pang of generous regret, as the idea that he might have averted the calamity presented itself to his mind, had he not deserted his comrade.

"We can do the chief no good, lad, and must quit this spot as fast as possible."

"Without one attempt to rescue him?—without even knowing whether he be dead or living?"

"Jasper is right," said Mabel, who could speak, though her voice sounded huskily and smothered; "I have no fears, uncle, and will stay here until we know what has become of our friend."

"This seems reasonable, Pathfinder," put in Cap. "Your true seaman cannot well desert a messmate; and I am glad to find that motives so correct exist among those fresh-water people."

"Tut! tut!" returned the impatient guide, forcing the canoe into the stream as he spoke; "ye know nothing and ye fear nothing. If ye value your lives, think of reaching the garrison, and leave the Delaware in the hands of Providence. Ah's me! the deer that goes too often to the tick meets the hunter at last!"

CHAPTER VII

And is this—Yarrow?—this the stream
Of which my fancy cherish'd
So faithfully a waking dream?
An image that hath perish'd?
Oh that some minstrel's harp were near,
To utter notes of gladness,
And chase this silence from the air,
That fills my heart with sadness.   WORDSWORTH

THE scene was not without its sublimity, and the ardent, generous-minded Mabel felt her blood thrill in her veins and her cheeks flush, as the canoe shot into the strength of the stream, to quit the spot. The darkness of the night had lessened, by the dispersion of the clouds; but the overhanging woods rendered the shore so obscure, that the boats floated down the current in a belt of gloom that effectually secured them from detection. Still, there was necessarily a strong feeling of insecurity in all on board them; and even Jasper, who by this time began to tremble, in behalf of the girl, at every unusual sound that arose from the forest, kept casting uneasy glances around him as he drifted on in company. The paddle was used lightly, and only with exceeding care; for the slightest sound in the breathing stillness of that hour and place might apprise the watchful ears of the Iroquois of their position.

All these accessories added to the impressive grandeur of her situation, and contributed to render the moment much the most exciting which had ever occurred in the brief existence of Mabel Dunham. Spirited, accustomed to self-reliance, and sustained by the pride of considering herself a soldier's daughter, she could hardly be said to be under the influence of fear, yet her heart often beat quicker than common, her fine blue eye lighted with an exhibition of a resolution that was wasted in the darkness, and her quickened feelings came in aid of the real sublimity that belonged to the scene and to the incidents of the night.

"Mabel!" said the suppressed voice of Jasper, as the two canoes floated so near each other that the hand of the young man held them together; "you have no dread? you trust freely to our care and willingness to protect you?"

"I am a soldier's daughter, as you know, Jasper Western, and ought to be ashamed to confess fear."

"Rely on me—on us all. Your uncle, Pathfinder, the Delaware, were the poor fellow here, I myself, will risk everything rather than harm should reach you."

"I believe you, Jasper," returned the girl, her hand unconsciously playing in the water. "I know that my uncle loves me, and will never think of himself until he has first thought of me; and I believe you are all my father's friends, and would willingly assist his child. But I am not so feeble and weak-minded as you may think; for, though only a girl from the towns, and, like most of that class, a little disposed to see danger where there is none, I promise you, Jasper, no foolish fears of mine shall stand in the way ot your doing your duty."

"The Sergeant's daughter is right, and she is worthy of being honest Thomas Dunham's child," put in the Pathfinder. "Ah's me, pretty one! many is the time that your father and I have scouted and marched together on the flanks and rear of the enemy, in nights darker than this, and that, too, when we did not know but the next moment would lead us into a bloody ambushment. I was at his side when he got the wound in his shoulder; and the honest fellow will tell you, when you meet, the manner in which we contrived to cross the river which lay in our rear, in order to save his scalp."

"He *has* told me," said Mabel, with more energy perhaps than her situation rendered prudent. "I have his letters, in which he has mentioned all that, and I thank you from the bottom of my heart for the service. God will remember it, Pathfinder; and there is no gratitude that you can ask of the daughter which she will not cheerfully repay for her father's life."

"Ay, that is the way with all your gentle and pure-hearted creatures. I have seen some of you before, and have heard of others. The Sergeant himself has talked to me of his own young days, and of your mother, and of the manner in which he courted her, and of all the crossings and disappointments, until he succeeded at last."

"My mother did not live long to repay him for what he did to win her," said Mabel, with a trembling lip.

"So he tells me. The honest Sergeant has kept nothing back; for, being so many years my senior, he has looked on me, in our many scoutings together, as a sort of son."

"Perhaps, Pathfinder," observed Jasper, with a huskiness in his voice that defeated the attempt at pleasantry, "he would be glad to have you for one in reality."

"And if he did, Eau-douce, where would be the sin of it? He knows what I am on a trail or a scout, and he has seen me often face to face with the Frenchers. I have sometimes thought, lad, that we all ought to seek for wives; for the man that lives altogether in the woods, and in company with his enemies or his prey, gets to lose some of the feeling of kind in the end. It is not easy to dwell always in the presence of God and not feel the power of His goodness. I have attended church-sarvice in the garrisons, and tried hard, as becomes a true soldier, to join in the prayers; for, though no enlisted sarvant of the king, I fight his battles and sarve his cause, and so I have endeavored to worship garrison-fashion, but never could raise within me the solemn feelings and true affection that I feel when alone with God in the forest. There I seem to stand face to face with my Master; all around me is fresh and beautiful, as it came from His hand; and there is no nicety of doctrine to chill the feelings. No no; the woods are the true temple after all, for there the thoughts are free to mount higher even than the clouds."

"You speak the truth, Master Pathfinder," said Cap, "and a truth that all who live much in solitude know. What, for instance, is the reason that seafaring men in general are so religious and conscientious in all they do, but the fact that they are so often alone with Providence, and have so little to do with the wickedness of the land. Many and many is the time that I have stood my watch, under the equator perhaps, or in the Southern Ocean, when the nights are lighted up with the fires of heaven; and that is the time, I can tell you, my hearties, to bring a man to his bearings in the way of his sins. I have rattled down mine again and again under such circumstances, until the shrouds and lanyards of conscience have fairly creaked with the strain. I agree with you, Master Pathfinder, therefore, in saying, if you want a truly religious man, go to sea, or go into the woods."

"Uncle, I thought seamen had little credit generally for their respect for religion?"

"All d——d slander, girl; for all the essentials of Christianity the seaman beats the landsman hand-over-hand."

"I will not answer for all this, Master Cap," returned Pathfinder; "but I daresay some of it may be true. I want no thunder and lightning to remind me of my God, nor am I as apt to bethink on most of all His goodness in trouble and tribulations as on a calm, solemn, quiet day in a forest, when His voice is heard in the creaking of a dead branch or in the song of a bird, as much in my ears at least as it is ever heard in uproar and gales. How is it with you, Eau-douce? you face the tempests as well as Master Cap, and ought to know something of the feelings of storms."

"I fear that I am too young and too inexperienced to be able to say much on such a subject," modestly answered Jasper.

"But you have your feelings!" said Mabel quickly. "You cannot —no one can live among such scenes without feeling how much they ought to trust in God!"

"I shall not belie my training so much as to say I do not sometimes think of these things, but I fear it is not so often or so much as I ought."

"Fresh water," resumed Cap pithily; "you are not to expect too much of the young man, Mabel. I think they call you sometimes by a name which would insinuate all this: Eau-de-vie, is it not?"

"Eau-douce," quietly replied Jasper, who from sailing on the lake had acquired a knowledge of French, as well as of several of the Indian dialects. "It is a name the Iroquois have given me to distinguish me from some of my companions who once sailed upon the sea, and are fond of filling the ears of the natives with stories of their great salt-water lakes."

"And why shouldn't they? I daresay they do the savages no harm. Ay, ay, Eau-deuce; that must mean the white brandy, which may well enough be called the deuce, for deuced stuff it is!"

"The signification of Eau-douce is sweet-water, and it is the manner in which the French express fresh-water," rejoined Jasper, a little nettled.

"And how the devil do they make water out of Eau-in-deuce, when it means brandy in Eau-de-vie? Besides, among seamen, Eau always means brandy; and Eau-de-vie, brandy of a high proof. I think nothing of your ignorance, young man; for it is natural to your situation, and cannot be helped. If you will return with me, and make a v'y'ge or two on the Atlantic, it will serve you a good turn the remainder of your days; and Mabel there, and all the other young women near the coast, will think all the better of you should you live to be as old as one of the trees in this forest."

"Nay, nay," interrupted the single-hearted and generous guide; "Jasper wants not for friends in this region, I can assure you; and though seeing the world, according to his habits, may do him good as well as another, we shall think none the worse of him if he never quits us. Eau-douce or Eau-de-vie, he is a brave, true-hearted youth, and I always sleep as soundly when he is on the watch as if I was up and stirring myself; ay, and for that matter, sounder too. The Sergeant's daughter here doesn't believe it necessary for the lad to go to sea in order to make a man of him, or one who is worthy to be respected and esteemed."

Mabel made no reply to this appeal, and she even looked towards the western shore, although the darkness rendered the natural movements unnecessary to conceal her face. But Jasper felt that there was a necessity for his saying something, the pride of youth and manhood revolting at the idea of his being in a condition not to command the respect of his fellows or the smiles of his equals of the other sex. Still he was unwilling to utter aught that might be considered harsh to the uncle of Mabel; and his self-command was perhaps more creditable than his modesty and spirit.

"I pretend not to things I don't possess," he said, "and lay no claim to any knowledge of the ocean or of navigation. We steer by the stars and the compass on these lakes, running from headland to headland; and having little need of figures and calculations, make no use of them. But we have our claims notwithstanding, as I have often heard from those who have passed years on the ocean. In the first place, we have always the land aboard, and much of the time on a lee-shore, and that I have frequently heard makes hardy sailors. Our gales are sudden and severe, and we are compelled to run for our ports at all hours."

"You have your leads," interrupted Cap.

"They are of little use, and are seldom cast."

"The deep-seas."

"I have heard of such things, but confess I never saw one."

"Oh! deuce, with a vengeance. A trader, and no deep-sea! Why, boy, you cannot pretend to be anything of a mariner. Who the devil ever heard of a seaman without his deep-sea?"

"I do not pretend to any particular skill, Master Cap."

"Except in shooting falls, Jasper, except in shooting falls and rifts," said Pathfinder, coming to the rescue; "in which business even you, Master Cap, must allow he has some handiness. In my judgment, every man is to be esteemed or condemned according to his gifts; and if Master Cap is useless in running the Oswego Falls, I try to remember that he is useful when out of sight of land; and if Jasper be useless when out of sight of land, I do not forget that he has a true eye and steady hand when running the falls."

"But Jasper is not useless—would not be useless when out of sight of land," said Mabel, with a spirit and energy that caused her clear sweet voice to be startling amid the solemn stillness of that extraordinary scene. "No one can be useless there, who can do so much here, is what I mean; though, I daresay, he is not as well acquainted with ships as my uncle."

"Ay, bolster each other up in your ignorance," returned Cap, with a sneer. "We seamen are so much outnumbered when ashore, that it is seldom we get our dues; but when you want to be defended, or trade is to be carried on, there is outcry enough for us."

"But, uncle, landsmen do not come to attack our coasts; so that seamen only meet seamen."

"So much for ignorance! Where are all the enemies that have landed in this country, French and English, let me inquire, niece?"

"Sure enough, where are they?" ejaculated Pathfinder. "None can tell better than we who dwell in the woods, Master Cap. I have often followed their line of march by bones bleaching in the rain, and have found their trail by graves, years after they and their pride had vanished together. Generals and privates, they lay scattered throughout the land, so many proofs of what men are when led on by their love of great names and the wish to be more than their fellows."

"I must say, Master Pathfinder, that you sometimes utter opinions that are a little remarkable for a man who lives by the rifle; seldom snuffing the air but he smells gunpowder, or turning out of his berth but to bear down on an enemy."

"If you think I pass my days in warfare against my kind, you know neither me nor my history. The man that lives in the woods and on the frontiers must take the chances of the things among which he dwells. For this I am not accountable, being but an humble and powerless hunter and scout and guide. My real calling is to hunt for the army, on its marches and in times of peace; although I am more especially engaged in the service of one officer, who is now absent in the settlements, where I never follow him. No, no; bloodshed and warfare are not my real gifts, but peace and mercy. Still, I must face the enemy as well as another; and as for a Mingo, I look upon him as man looks on a snake, a creatur' to be put beneath the heel whenever a fitting occasion offers."

"Well, well; I have mistaken your calling, which I had thought as regularly warlike as that of a ship's gunner. There is my brother-in-law, now; he has been a soldier since he was sixteen, and he looks upon his trade as every way as respectable as that of a seafaring man, a point I hardly think it worth while to dispute with him."

"My father has been taught to believe that it is honorable to carry arms," said Mabel, "for his father was a soldier before him."

"Yes, yes," resumed the guide; "most of the Sergeant's gifts are martial, and he looks at most things in this world over the barrel of his musket. One of his notions, now, is to prefer a king's piece to a regular, double-sighted, long-barrelled rifle. Such conceits will come over men from long habit; and prejudice is, perhaps, the commonest failing of human natur'."

While the desultory conversation just related had been carried on in subdued voices, the canoes were dropping slowly down with the current within the deep shadows of the western shore, the paddles being used merely to preserve the desired direction and proper positions. The strength of the stream varied materially, the water being seemingly still in places, while in other reaches it flowed at a rate exceeding two or even three miles in the hour. On the rifts it even dashed forward with a velocity that was appalling to the unpractised eye. Jasper was of opinion that they might drift down with the current to the mouth of the river in two hours from the time they left the shore, and he and the Pathfinder had agreed on the expediency of suffering the canoes to float of themselves for a time, or at least until they had passed the first dangers of their new movement. The dialogue had been carried on in voices, too, guardedly low; for though the quiet of deep solitude reigned in that vast and nearly boundless forest, nature was speaking with her thousand tongues in the eloquent language of night in a wilderness. The air sighed through ten thousand trees, the water rippled, and at places even roared along the shores; and now and then was heard the creaking of a branch or a trunk, as it rubbed against some object similar to itself, under the vibrations of a nicely balanced body. All living sounds had ceased. Once, it is true, the Pathfinder fancied he heard the howl of a distant wolf, of which a few prowled through these woods; but it was a transient and doubtful cry, that might possibly have been attributed to the imagination. When he desired his companions, however, to cease talking, his vigilant ear had caught the peculiar sound which is made by the parting of a dried branch of a tree, and which, if his senses did not deceive him, came from the western shore. All who are accustomed to that particular sound will understand how readily the ear receives it, and how easy it is to distinguish the tread which breaks the branch from every other noise of the forest.

"There is the footstep of a man on the bank," said Pathfinder to Jasper, speaking in neither a whisper nor yet in a voice loud enough to be heard at any distance. "Can the accursed Iroquois have crossed the river already, with their arms, and without a boat?"

"It may be the Delaware. He would follow us, of course, down this bank, and would know where to look for us. Let me draw closer into the shore, and reconnoitre."

"Go, boy, but be light with the paddle, and on no account venture ashore on an onsartainty."

"Is this prudent?" demanded Mabel, with an impetuosity that rendered her incautious in modulating her sweet voice.

"Very imprudent, if you speak so loud, fair one. I like your voice, which is soft and pleasing, after listening so long to the tones of men; but it must not be heard too much, or too freely, just now. Your father, the honest Sergeant, will tell you, when you meet him, that silence is a double virtue on a trail. Go, Jasper, and do justice to your own character for prudence."

Ten anxious minutes succeeded the disappearance of the canoe of Jasper, which glided away from that of the Pathfinder so noiselessly, that it had been swallowed up in the gloom before Mabel allowed herself to believe the young man would really venture alone on a service which struck her imagination as singularly dangerous. During this time, the party continued to float with the current, no one speaking, and, it might almost be said, no one breathing, so strong was the general desire to catch the minutest sound that should come from the shore. But the same solemn, we might, indeed, say sublime, quiet reigned as before; the washing of the water, as it piled up against some slight obstruction, and the sighing of the trees, alone interrupting the slumbers of the forest. At the end of the period mentioned, the snapping of dried branches was again faintly heard, and the Pathfinder fancied that the sound of smothered voices reached him.

"I may be mistaken," he said, "for the thoughts often fancy what the heart wishes; but these were notes like the low tones of the Delaware."

"Do the dead of the savages ever walk?" demanded Cap.

"Ay, and run too, in their happy hunting-grounds, but no-where else. A red-skin finishes with the 'arth, after the breath quits the body. It is not one of his gifts to linger around his wigwam when his hour has passed."

"I see some object on the water," whispered Mabel, whose eye had not ceased to dwell on the body of gloom, with close inten-sity, since the disappearance of Jasper.

"It is the canoe," returned the guide, greatly relieved. "All must be safe, or we should have heard from the lad."

In another minute the two canoes, which became visible to those they carried only as they drew near each other, again floated side by side, and the form of Jasper was recognized at the stern of his own boat. The figure of a second man was seated in the bow; and, as the young sailor so wielded his paddle as to bring the face of his companion near the eyes of the Pathfinder and Mabel, they both recognized the person of the Delaware.

"Chingachgook—my brother!" said the guide in the dialect of the other's people, a tremor shaking his voice that betrayed the strength of his feelings. "Chief of the Mohicans! my heart is very glad. Often have we passed through blood and strife together, but I was afraid it was never to be so again."

"Hugh! The Mingos are squaws! Three of their scalps hang at my girdle. They do not know how to strike the Great Serpent of the Delawares. Their hearts have no blood; and their thoughts are on their return path, across the waters of the Great Lake."

"Have you been among them, chief? and what has become of the warrior who was in the river?"

"He has turned into a fish, and lies at the bottom with the eels! Let his brothers bait their hooks for him. Pathfinder, I have counted the enemy, and have touched their rifles."

"Ah, I thought he would be venturesome!" exclaimed the

guide in English. "The risky fellow has been in the midst of them, and has brought us back their whole history. Speak, Chingachgook, and I will make our friends as knowing as ourselves."

The Delaware now related in a low earnest manner the substance of all his discoveries, since he was last seen struggling with his foe in the river. Of the fate of his antagonist he said no more, it not being usual for a warrior to boast in his more direct and useful narratives. As soon as he had conquered in that fearful strife, however, he swam to the eastern shore, landed with caution, and wound his way in amongst the Iroquois, concealed by the darkness, undetected, and, in the main, even unsuspected. Once, indeed, he had been questioned; but answering that he was Arrowhead, no further inquiries were made. By the passing remarks, he soon ascertained that the party was out expressly to intercept Mabel and her uncle, concerning whose rank, however, they had evidently been deceived. He also ascertained enough to justify the suspicion that Arrowhead had betrayed them to their enemies, for some motive that it was not now easy to reach, as he had not yet received the reward of his services.

Pathfinder communicated no more of this intelligence to his companions than he thought might relieve their apprehensions, intimating, at the same time, that now was the moment for exertion, the Iroquois not having yet entirely recovered from the confusion created by their losses.

"We shall find them at the rift, I make no manner of doubt," continued he; "and there it will be our fate to pass them, or to fall into their hands. The distance to the garrison will then be so short, that I have been thinking of a plan of landing with Mabel myself, that I may take her in, by some of the by-ways, and leave the canoes to their chances in the rapids."

"It will never succeed, Pathfinder," eagerly interrupted Jasper. "Mabel is not strong enough to tramp the woods in a night like this. Put her in my skiff, and I will lose my life, or carry her through the rift safely, dark as it is."

"No doubt you will, lad; no one doubts your willingness to do anything to serve the Sergeant's daughter; but it must be the eye of Providence, and not your own, that will take you safely through the Oswego rift in a night like this."

"And who will lead her safely to the garrison if she land? Is not the night as dark on shore as on the water? or do you think I know less of my calling than you know of yours?"

"Spiritedly said, lad; but if I should lose my way in the dark— and I believe no man can say truly that such a thing ever yet happened to me—but, if I *should* lose my way, no other harm would come of it than to pass a night in the forest; whereas a false turn of the paddle, or a broad sheer of the canoe, would put you and the young woman into the river, out of which it is more than probable the Sergeant's daughter would never come alive."

"I will leave it to Mabel herself; I am certain that she will feel more secure in the canoe."

"I have great confidence in you both," answered the girl; "and have no doubts that either will do all he can to prove to my father how much he values him; but I confess I should not like to quit the canoe, with the certainty we have of there being enemies like those we have seen in the forest. But my uncle can decide for me in this matter."

"I have no liking for the woods," said Cap, "while one has a clear drift like this on the river. Besides, Master Pathfinder, to say nothing of the savages, you overlook the sharks."

"Sharks! who ever heard of sharks in the wilderness?"

"Ay! sharks, or bears, or wolves—no matter what you call a thing, so it has the mind and power to bite."

"Lord, lord, man! do you dread any creatur' that is to be found in the American forest? A catamount is a skeary animal, I will allow, but then it is nothing in the hands of a practysed hunter. Talk of the Mingos and their devilries if you will; but do not raise a false alarm about bears and wolves."

"Ay, ay, Master Pathfinder, this is all well enough for you, who probably know the name of every creature you would meet. Use is everything, and it makes a man bold when he might otherwise be bashful. I have known seamen in the low latitudes swim for hours at a time among sharks fifteen or twenty feet long."

"This is extraordinary!" exclaimed Jasper, who had not yet acquired that material part of his trade, the ability to spin a yarn. "I have always heard that it was certain death to venture in the water among sharks."

"I forgot to say, that the lads always took capstan-bars, or gunners' handspikes, or crows with them, to rap the beasts over the noses if they got to be troublesome. No, no, I have no liking for bears and wolves, though a whale, in my eye, is very much the same sort of fish as a red herring after it is dried and salted. Mabel and I had better stick to the canoe."

"Mabel would do well to change canoes," added Jasper. "This of mine is empty, and even Pathfinder will allow that my eye is surer than his own on the water."

"That I will, cheerfully, boy. The water belongs to your gifts, and no one will deny that you have improved them to the utmost. You are right enough in believing that the Sergeant's daughter will be safer in your canoe than in this; and though I would gladly keep her near myself, I have her welfare too much at heart not to give her honest advice. Bring your canoe close alongside, Jasper, and I will give you what you must consider as a precious treasure."

"I do so consider it," returned the youth, not losing a moment in complying with the request; when Mabel passed from one canoe to the other taking her seat on the effects which had hitherto composed its sole cargo.

As soon as this arrangement was made, the canoes separated a short distance, and the paddles were used, though with great care to avoid making any noise. The conversation gradually ceased; and as the dreaded rift was approached, all became impressed with the gravity of the moment. That their enemies would endeavor to reach this point before them was almost certain; and it seemed so little probable any one should attempt to pass it, in the profound obscurity which reigned, that Pathfinder was confident parties were on both sides of the river, in the hope of intercepting them when they might land. He would not have made the proposal he did had he not felt sure of his own ability to convert this very anticipation of success into a means of defeating the plans of the Iroquois. As the arrangement now stood, however, everything depended on the skill of those who guided the canoes; for should either hit a rock, if not split asunder, it would almost certainly be upset, and then would come not only all the hazards of the river itself, but, for Mabel, the certainty of falling into the hands of her pursuers. The utmost circumspection consequently became necessary, and each one was too much engrossed with his own thoughts to feel a disposition to utter more than was called for by the exigencies of the case.

As the canoes stole silently along, the roar of the rift became audible, and it required all the fortitude of Cap to keep his seat, while these boding sounds were approached, amid a darkness which scarcely permitted a view of the outlines of the wooded shore and of the gloomy vault above his head. He retained a vivid impression of the falls, and his imagination was not now idle in swelling the dangers of the rift to a level with those of the headlong descent he had that day made, and even to increase them, under the influence of doubt and uncertainty. In this, however, the old mariner was mistaken, for the Oswego Rift and the Oswego Falls are very different in their characters and violence; the former being no more than a rapid, that glances among shallows and rocks, while the latter really deserved the name it bore, as has been already shown.

Mabel certainly felt distrust and apprehension; but her entire situation was so novel, and her reliance on her guide so great, that she retained a self-command which might not have existed had she clearer perceptions of the truth, or been better acquainted with the helplessness of men when placed in opposition to the power and majesty of Nature.

"Is that the spot you have mentioned?" she said to Jasper, when the roar of the rift first came distinctly on her ears.

"It is; and I beg you to have confidence in me. We are not old acquaintances, Mabel; but we live many days in one, in this wilderness. I think, already, that I have known you years!"

"And I do not feel as if you were a stranger to me, Jasper. I have every reliance on your skill, as well as on your disposition to serve me."

"We shall see, we shall see. Pathfinder is striking the rapids too near the centre of the river; the bed of the water is closer to the eastern shore; but I cannot make him hear me now. Hold firmly to the canoe, Mabel, and fear nothing."

At the next moment the swift current had sucked them into the rift, and for three or four minutes the awe-struck, rather than the alarmed, girl saw nothing around her but sheets of glancing foam, heard nothing but the roar of waters. Twenty times did the canoe appear about to dash against some curling and bright wave that showed itself even amid that obscurity; and as often did it glide away again unharmed, impelled by the vigorous arm of him who governed its movements. Once, and once only, did Jasper seem to lose command of his frail bark, during which brief space it fairly whirled entirely round; but by a desperate effort he brought it again under control, recovered the lost channel, and was soon rewarded for all his anxiety by finding himself floating quietly in the deep water below the rapids, secure from every danger, and without having taken in enough of the element to serve for a draught.

"All is over, Mabel," the young man cried cheerfully. "The danger is past, and you may now indeed hope to meet your father this very night."

"God be praised! Jasper, we shall owe this great happiness to you."

"The Pathfinder may claim a full share in the merit; but what has become of the other canoe?"

"I see something near us on the water; is it not the boat of our friends?"

A few strokes of the paddle brought Jasper to the side of the object in question: it was the other canoe, empty and bottom upwards. No sooner did the young man ascertain this fact, than he began to search for the swimmers, and, to his great joy, Cap was soon discovered drifting down with the current; the old seaman preferring the chances of drowning to those of landing among savages. He was hauled into the canoe, though not without difficulty, and then the search ended; for Jasper was persuaded that the Pathfinder would wade to the shore, the water being shallow, in preference to abandoning his beloved rifle.

The remainder of the passage was short, though made amid darkness and doubt. After a short pause, a dull roaring sound was heard, which at times resembled the mutterings of distant thunder, and then again brought with it the washing of waters. Jasper announced to his companions that they now heard the surf of the lake. Low curved spits of land lay before them, into the bay formed by one of which the canoe glided, and then it shot up noiselessly upon a gravelly beach. The transition that followed was so hurried and great, that Mabel scarcely knew what passed. In the course of a few minutes, however, sentinels had been passed, a gate was opened, and the agitated girl found herself in the arms of a parent who was almost a stranger to her.

CHAPTER VIII

A land of love, and a land of light,
Withouten sun, or moon, or night:
Where the river swa'd a living stream,
And the light a pure celestial beam:
The land of vision, it would seem
A still, an everlasting dream.   *Queen's Wake*

THE rest that succeeds fatigue, and which attends a newly awakened sense of security, is generally sweet and deep. Such was the fact with Mabel, who did not rise from her humble pallet —such a bed as a sergeant's daughter might claim in a remote frontier post—until long after the garrison had obeyed the usual summons of the drums, and had assembled at the morning parade. Sergeant Dunham, on whose shoulders fell the task of attending to these ordinary and daily duties, had got through all his morning avocations, and was beginning to think of his breakfast, before his child left her room, and came into the fresh air, equally bewildered, delighted, and grateful, at the novelty and security of her new situation.

At the time of which we are writing, Oswego was one of the extreme frontier posts of the British possessions on this continent. It had not been long occupied, and was garrisoned by a battalion of a regiment which had been originally Scotch, but into which many Americans had been received since its arrival in this country; an innovation that had led the way to Mabel's father filling the humble but responsible situation of the oldest sergeant. A few young officers also, who were natives of the colonies, were to be found in the corps. The fort itself, like most works of that character, was better adapted to resist an attack of savages than to withstand a regular siege; but the great difficulty of transporting heavy artillery and other necessaries rendered the occurrence of the latter a probability so remote as scarcely to enter into the estimate of the engineers who had planned the defences. There were bastions of earth and logs, a dry ditch, a stockade, a parade of considerable extent, and barracks of logs, that answered the double purpose of dwellings and

fortifications. A few light field-pieces stood in the area of the
fort, ready to be conveyed to any point where they might be
wanted, and one or two heavy iron guns looked out from the
summits of the advanced angles, as so many admonitions to the
audacious to respect their power.

When Mabel, quitting the convenient, but comparatively retired hut where her father had been permitted to place her,
issued into the pure air of the morning, she found herself at the
foot of a bastion, which lay invitingly before her, with a promise
of giving a *coup d'œil* of all that had been concealed in the darkness of the preceding night. Tripping up the grassy ascent, the
light-hearted as well as light-footed girl found herself at once on
a point where the sight, at a few varying glances, could take in
all the external novelties of her new situation.

To the southward lay the forest, through which she had been
journeying so many weary days, and which had proved so full of
dangers. It was separated from the stockade by a belt of open
land, that had been principally cleared of its woods to form the
martial constructions around her. This glacis, for such in fact
was its military use, might have covered a hundred acres; but
with it every sign of civilization ceased. All beyond was forest;
that dense, interminable forest which Mabel could now picture
to herself, through her recollections, with its hidden glassy lakes,
its dark rolling stream, and its world of nature.

Turning from this view, our heroine felt her cheek fanned by
a fresh and grateful breeze, such as she had not experienced since
quitting the far distant coast. Here a new scene presented itself:
although expected, it was not without a start, and a low exclamation indicative of pleasure, that the eager eyes of the girl drank
in its beauties. To the north, and east, and west, in every direction, in short, over one entire half of the novel panorama, lay a
field of rolling waters. The element was neither of that glassy
green which distinguishes the American waters in general, nor
yet of the deep blue of the ocean, the color being of a slightly
amber hue, which scarcely affected its limpidity. No land was to
be seen, with the exception of the adjacent coast, which stretched
to the right and left in an unbroken outline of forest with wide
bays and low headlands or points; still, much of the shore was
rocky, and into its caverns the sluggish waters occasionally
rolled, producing a hollow sound, which resembled the concus-

sions of a distant gun. No sail whitened the surface, no whale or other fish gambolled on its bosom, no sign of use or service rewarded the longest and most minute gaze at its boundless expanse. It was a scene, on one side, of apparently endless forests, while a waste of seemingly interminable water spread itself on the other. Nature appeared to have delighted in producing grand effects, by setting two of her principal agents in bold relief to each other, neglecting details; the eye turning from the broad carpet of leaves to the still broader field of fluid, from the endless but gentle heavings of the lake to the holy calm and poetical solitude of the forest, with wonder and delight.

Mabel Dunham, though unsophisticated, like most of her countrywomen of that period, and ingenuous and frank as any warm-hearted and sincere-minded girl well could be, was not altogether without a feeling for the poetry of this beautiful earth of ours. Although she could scarcely be said to be educated at all, for few of her sex at that day and in this country received much more than the rudiments of plain English instruction, still she had been taught much more than was usual for young women in her own station in life; and, in one sense certainly, she did credit to her teaching. The widow of a field-officer, who formerly belonged to the same regiment as her father, had taken the child in charge at the death of its mother; and under the care of this lady Mabel had acquired some tastes and many ideas which otherwise might always have remained strangers to her. Her situation in the family had been less that of a domestic than of a humble companion, and the results were quite apparent in her attire, her language, her sentiments, and even in her feelings, though neither, perhaps, rose to the level of those which would properly characterize a lady. She had lost the less refined habits and manners of one in her original position, without having quite reached a point that disqualified her for the situation in life that the accidents of birth and fortune would probably compel her to fill. All else that was distinctive and peculiar in her belonged to natural character.

With such antecedents it will occasion the reader no wonder if he learns that Mabel viewed the novel scene before her with a pleasure far superior to that produced by vulgar surprise. She felt its ordinary beauties as most would have felt them, but she had also a feeling for its sublimity—for that softened solitude,

that calm grandeur, and eloquent repose, which ever pervades
broad views of natural objects yet undisturbed by the labors and
struggles of man.

"How beautiful!" she exclaimed, unconscious of speaking, as
she stood on the solitary bastion, facing the air from the lake,
and experiencing the genial influence of its freshness pervading
both her body and her mind. "How very beautiful! and yet how
singular!"

The words, and the train of her ideas, were interrupted by a
touch of a finger on her shoulder, and turning, in the expectation
of seeing her father, Mabel found Pathfinder at her side. He was
leaning quietly on his long rifle, and laughing in his quiet manner, while, with an outstretched arm, he swept over the whole
panorama of land and water.

"Here you have both our domains," said he—"Jasper's and
mine. The lake is for him, and the woods are for me. The lad
sometimes boasts of the breadth of his dominions; but I tell him
my trees make as broad a plain on the face of this 'arth as all his
water. Well, Mabel, you are fit for either; for I do not see that
fear of the Mingos, or night-marches, can destroy your pretty
looks."

"It is a new character for the Pathfinder to appear in, to compliment a silly girl."

"Not silly, Mabel; no, not in the least silly. The Sergeant's
daughter would do discredit to her worthy father, were she to do
or say anything that could be called silly."

"Then she must take care and not put too much faith in
treacherous, flattering words. But, Pathfinder, I rejoice to see
you among us again; for, though Jasper did not seem to feel
much uneasiness, I was afraid some accident might have happened to you and your friend on that frightful rift."

"The lad knows us both, and was sartain that we should not
drown, which is scarcely one of my gifts. It would have been
hard swimming of a sartainty, with a long-barrelled rifle in the
hand; and what between the game, and the savages and the
French, Killdeer and I have gone through too much in company
to part very easily. No, no; we waded ashore, the rift being
shallow enough for that with small exceptions, and we landed
with our arms in our hands. We had to take our time for it, on
account of the Iroquois, I will own; but, as soon as the skulking

vagabonds saw the lights that the Sergeant sent down to your canoe, we well understood they would decamp, since a visit might have been expected from some of the garrison. So it was only sitting patiently on the stones for an hour, and all the danger was over. Patience is the greatest of virtues in a woodsman."

"I rejoice to hear this, for fatigue itself could scarcely make me sleep, for thinking of what might befall you."

"Lord bless your tender little heart, Mabel! but this is the way with all you gentle ones. I must say, on my part, however, that I was right glad to see the lanterns come down to the waterside, which I knew to be a sure sign of *your* safety. We hunters and guides are rude beings; but we have our feelings and our idees, as well as any general in the army. Both Jasper and I would have died before you should have come to harm—we would."

"I thank you for all you did for me, Pathfinder; from the bottom of my heart, I thank you; and, depend on it, my father shall know it. I have already told him much, but have still a duty to perform on this subject."

"Tush, Mabel! The Sergeant knows what the woods be, and what men—true red men—be, too. There is little need to tell him anything about it. Well, now you have met your father, do you find the honest old soldier the sort of person you expected to find?"

"He is my own dear father, and received me as a soldier and a father should receive a child. Have you known him long, Pathfinder?"

"That is as people count time. I was just twelve when the Sergeant took me on my first scouting, and that is now more than twenty years ago. We had a tramping time of it; and, as it was before your day, you would have had no father, had not the rifle been one of my natural gifts."

"Explain yourself."

"It is too simple for many words. We were ambushed, and the Sergeant got a bad hurt, and would have lost his scalp, but for a sort of inbred turn I took to the weapon. We brought him off, however, and a handsomer head of hair, for his time of life, is not to be found in the rijiment than the Sergeant carries about with him this blessed day."

"You saved my father's life, Pathfinder!" exclaimed Mabel,

unconsciously, though warmly, taking one of his hard, sinewy hands into both her own. "God bless you for this, too, among your other good acts!"

"Nay, I did not say that much, though I believe I did save his scalp. A man might live without a scalp, and so I cannot say I saved his life. Jasper may say that much consarning you; for without his eye and arm the canoe would never have passed the rift in safety on a night like the last. The gifts of the lad are for the water, while mine are for the hunt and the trail. He is yonder, in the cove there, looking after the canoes, and keeping his eye on his beloved little craft. To my eye, there is no likelier youth in these parts than Jasper Western."

For the first time since she had left her room, Mabel now turned her eyes beneath her, and got a view of what might be called the foreground of the remarkable picture she had been studying with so much pleasure. The Oswego threw its dark waters into the lake, between banks of some height; that on its eastern side being bolder and projecting farther north than that on its western. The fort was on the latter, and immediately beneath it were a few huts of logs, which, as they could not interfere with the defence of the place, had been erected along the strand for the purpose of receiving and containing such stores as were landed, or were intended to be embarked, in the communications between the different ports on the shores of Ontario. Two low, curved, gravelly points had been formed with surprising regularity by the counteracting forces of the northerly winds and the swift current, and, inclining from the storms of the lake, formed two coves within the river: that on the western side was the most deeply indented; and, as it also had the most water, it formed a sort of picturesque little port for the post. It was along the narrow strand that lay between the low height of the fort and the water of this cove, that the rude buildings just mentioned had been erected.

Several skiffs, bateaux, and canoes were hauled up on the shore, and in the cove itself lay the little craft from which Jasper obtained his claim to be considered a sailor. She was cutter-rigged, might have been of forty tons burthen, was so neatly constructed and painted as to have something of the air of a vessel of war, though entirely without quarters, and rigged and sparred with so scrupulous a regard to proportions and beauty, as well as fitness and judgment, as to give her an appearance that even Mabel at once distinguished to be gallant and trim. Her mould was admirable, for a wright of great skill had sent her drafts from England, at the express request of the officer who had caused her to be constructed; her paint dark, warlike, and neat; and the long coach-whip pennant that she wore at once proclaimed her to be the property of the king. Her name was the *Scud*.

"That, then, is the vessel of Jasper!" said Mabel, who associated the master of the little craft very naturally with the cutter itself. "Are there many others on this lake?"

"The Frenchers have three: one of which, they tell me, is a real ship, such as are used on the ocean; another a brig; and a third is a cutter, like the *Scud* here, which they call the *Squirrel*, in their own tongue, however; and which seems to have a natural hatred of our own pretty boat, for Jasper seldom goes out that the *Squirrel* is not at his heels."

"And is Jasper one to run from a Frenchman, though he appears in the shape of a squirrel, and that, too, on the water?"

"Of what use would valor be without the means of turning it to account? Jasper is a brave boy, as all on this frontier know; but he has no gun except a little howitzer, and then his crew consists only of two men besides himself, and a boy. I was with him in one of his trampooses, and the youngster was risky enough, for he brought us so near the enemy that rifles began to talk; but the Frenchers carry cannon and ports, and never show their faces outside of Frontenac, without having some twenty men, besides their *Squirrel*, in their cutter. No, no; this *Scud* was built for flying, and the major says he will not put her in a fighting humor by giving her men and arms, lest she should take him at his word, and get her wings clipped. I know little of these things, for my gifts are not at all in that way; but I see the reason of the thing—I see its reason, though Jasper does not."

"Ah! here is my uncle, none the worse for his swim, coming to look at this inland sea."

Sure enough, Cap, who had announced his approach by a couple of lusty hems, now made his appearance on the bastion, where, after nodding to his niece and her companion, he made a deliberate survey of the expanse of water before him. In order to effect this at his ease, the mariner mounted on one of the old iron guns, folded his arms across his breast, and balanced his body, as if he felt the motion of a vessel. To complete the picture, he had a short pipe in his mouth.

"Well, Master Cap," asked the Pathfinder innocently, for he did not detect the expression of contempt that was gradually settling on the features of the other; "is it not a beautiful sheet, and fit to be named a sea?"

"This, then, is what you call your lake?" demanded Cap, sweeping the northern horizon with his pipe. "I say, is this really your lake?"

"Sartain; and, if the judgment of one who has lived on the shores of many others can be taken, a very good lake it is."

"Just as I expected. A pond in dimensions, and a scuttle-butt in taste. It is all in vain to travel inland, in the hope of seeing anything either full-grown or useful. I knew it would turn out just in this way."

"What is the matter with Ontario, Master Cap? It is large, and fair to look at, and pleasant enough to drink, for those who can't get at the water of the springs."

"Do you call this large?" asked Cap, again sweeping the air with the pipe. "I will just ask you what there is large about it? Didn't Jasper himself confess that it was only some twenty leagues from shore to shore?"

"But, uncle," interposed Mabel, "no land is to be seen, except here on our own coast. To me it looks exactly like the ocean."

"This bit of a pond look like the ocean! Well, Magnet, that from a girl who has had real seamen in her family is downright nonsense. What is there about it, pray, that has even the outline of a sea on it?"

"Why, there is water—water—water—nothing but water, for miles on miles—far as the eye can see."

"And isn't there water—water—water—nothing but water for miles on miles in your rivers, that you have been canoeing through, too?—ay, and 'as far as the eye can see,' in the bargain?"

"Yes, uncle, but the rivers have their banks, and there are trees along them, and they are narrow."

"And isn't this a bank where we stand? don't these soldiers call this the bank of the lake? and aren't there trees in thousands? and aren't twenty leagues narrow enough of all conscience? Who the devil ever heard of the banks of the ocean, unless it might be the banks that are under water?"

"But, uncle, we cannot see across this lake, as we can see across a river."

"There you are out, Magnet. Aren't the Amazon and Orinoco and La Plata rivers, and can you see across them? Hark'e, Pathfinder, I very much doubt if this stripe of water here be even a lake; for to me it appears to be only a river. You are by no means particular about your geography, I find, up here in the woods."

"There *you* are out, Master Cap. There is a river, and a noble one too, at each end of it; but this is old Ontario before you; and, though it is not my gift to live on a lake, to my judgment there are few better than this."

"And, uncle, if we stood on the beach at Rockaway, what more should we see than we now behold? There is a shore on one side, or banks there, and trees too, as well as those which are here."

"This is perverseness, Magnet, and young girls should steer clear of anything like obstinacy. In the first place, the ocean has coasts, but no banks, except the Grand Banks, as I tell you, which are out of sight of land; and you will not pretend that this bank is out of sight of land, or even under water?"

As Mabel could not very plausibly set up this extravagant opinion, Cap pursued the subject, his countenance beginning to discover the triumph of a successful disputant.

"And then them trees bear no comparison to these trees. The coasts of the ocean have farms and cities and country-seats, and in some parts of the world, castles and monasteries and lighthouses—ay, ay—lighthouses, in particular, on them; not one of all which things is to be seen here. No, no, Master Pathfinder; I never heard of an ocean that hadn't more or less lighthouses on it; whereas, hereaway there is not even a beacon."

"There is what is better, there is what is better; a forest and noble trees, a fit temple of God."

"Ay, your forest may do for a lake; but of what use would an ocean be if the earth all around it were forest? Ships would be unnecessary, as timber might be floated in rafts, and there would be an end of trade, and what would a world be without trade? I am of that philosopher's opinion who says human nature was invented for the purposes of trade. Magnet, I am astonished that you should think this water even looks like sea-water! Now, I daresay that there isn't such a thing as a whale in all your lake, Master Pathfinder?"

"I never heard of one, I will confess; but I am no judge of animals that live in the water, unless it be the fishes of the rivers and the brooks."

"Nor a grampus, nor a porpoise even? not so much as a poor devil of a shark?"

"I will not take it on myself to say there is either. My gifts are not in that way, I tell you, Master Cap."

"Nor herring, nor albatross, nor flying-fish?" continued Cap, who kept his eye fastened on the guide, in order to see how far he might venture. "No such thing as a fish that can fly, I daresay?"

"A fish that can fly! Master Cap, Master Cap, do not think, because we are mere borderers, that we have no idees of natur', and what she has been pleased to do. I know there are squirrels that can fly——"

"A squirrel fly!—the devil, Master Pathfinder! Do you suppose that you have got a boy on his first v'y'ge up here among you?"

"I know nothing of your v'y'ges, Master Cap, though I suppose them to have been many; for as for what belongs to natur' in the woods, what I have seen I may tell, and not fear the face of man."

"And do you wish me to understand that you have seen a squirrel fly?"

"If you wish to understand the power of God, Master Cap, you will do well to believe that, and many other things of a like natur', for you may be quite sartain it is true."

"And yet, Pathfinder," said Mabel, looking so prettily and sweetly even while she played with the guide's infirmity, that he forgave her in his heart, "you, who speak so reverently of the power of the Deity, appear to doubt that a fish can fly."

"I have not said it, I have not said it; and if Master Cap is ready to testify to the fact, unlikely as it seems, I am willing to try to think it true. I think it every man's duty to believe in the power of God, however difficult it may be."

"And why isn't my fish as likely to have wings as your squirrel?" demanded Cap, with more logic than was his wont. "That fishes do and can fly is as true as it is reasonable."

"Nay, that is the only difficulty in believing the story," rejoined the guide. "It seems unreasonable to give an animal that lives in the water wings, which seemingly can be of no use to it."

"And do you suppose that the fishes are such asses as to fly about under water, when they are once fairly fitted out with wings?"

"Nay, I know nothing of the matter; but that fish should fly in the air seems more contrary to natur' still, than that they should fly in their own element—that in which they were born and brought up, as one might say."

"So much for contracted ideas, Magnet. The fish fly out of water to run away from their enemies in the water; and there you see not only the fact, but the reason for it."

"Then I suppose it must be true," said the guide quietly. "How long are their flights?"

"Not quite as far as those of pigeons, perhaps; but far enough to make an offing. As for those squirrels of yours, we'll say no more about them, friend Pathfinder, as I suppose they were mentioned just as a make-weight to the fish, in favor of the woods. But what is this thing anchored here under the hill?"

"That is the cutter of Jasper, uncle," said Mabel hurriedly; "and a very pretty vessel I think it is. Its name, too, is the *Scud*."

"Ay, it will do well enough for a lake, perhaps, but it's no great affair. The lad has got a standing bowsprit, and who ever saw a cutter with a standing bowsprit before?"

"But may there not be some good reason for it, on a lake like this, uncle?"

"Sure enough—I must remember this is not the ocean, though it does look so much like it."

"Ah, uncle! then Ontario does look like the ocean, after all?"

"In your eyes, I mean, and those of Pathfinder; not in the least in mine, Magnet. Now you might set me down out yonder, in the middle of this bit of a pond, and that, too, in the darkest night that ever fell from the heavens, and in the smallest canoe, and I could tell you it was only a lake. For that matter, the *Dorothy*" (the name of his vessel) "would find it out as quick a

I could myself. I do not believe that brig would make more than a couple of short stretches, at the most, before she would perceive the difference between Ontario and the old Atlantic. I once took her down into one of the large South American bays, and she behaved herself as awkwardly as a booby would in a church with the congregation in a hurry. And Jasper sails that boat? I must have a cruise with the lad, Magnet, before I quit you, just for the name of the thing. It would never do to say I got in sight of this pond, and went away without taking a trip on it."

"Well, well, you needn't wait long for that," returned Pathfinder; "for the Sergeant is about to embark with a party, to relieve a post among the Thousand Islands; and as I heard him say he intended that Mabel should go along, you can join company too."

"Is this true, Magnet?"

"I believe it is," returned the girl, a flush so imperceptible as to escape the observation of her companions glowing on her cheeks; "though I have had so little opportunity to talk with my dear father that I am not quite certain. Here he comes, however, and you can inquire of himself."

Notwithstanding his humble rank, there was something in the mien and character of Sergeant Dunham that commanded respect: of a tall, imposing figure, grave and saturnine disposition, and accurate and precise in his acts and manner of thinking, even Cap, dogmatical and supercilious as he usually was with landsmen, did not presume to take the same liberties with the old soldier as he did with his other friends. It was often remarked that Sergeant Dunham received more true respect from Duncan of Lundie, the Scotch laird who commanded the post, than most of the subalterns; for experience and tried services were of quite as much value in the eyes of the veteran major as birth and money. While the Sergeant never even hoped to rise any higher, he so far respected himself and his present station as always to act in a way to command attention; and the habit of mixing so much with inferiors, whose passions and dispositions he felt it necessary to restrain by distance and dignity, had so far colored his whole deportment, that few were altogether free from its influence. While the captains treated him kindly and as an old comrade, the lieutenants seldom ventured to dissent from his military opinions; and the ensigns, it was remarked, actually manifested a species of respect that amounted to something very like deference. It is no wonder, then, that the announcement of Mabel put a sudden termination to the singular dialogue we have just related, though it had been often observed that the Pathfinder was the only man on that frontier, beneath the condition of a gentleman, who presumed to treat the Sergeant at all as an equal, or even with the cordial familiarity of a friend.

"Good morrow, brother Cap," said the Sergeant giving the military salute, as he walked, in a grave, stately manner, on the bastion. "My morning duty has made me seem forgetful of you and Mabel; but we have now an hour or two to spare, and to get acquainted. Do you not perceive, brother, a strong likeness in the girl to her we have so long lost?"

"Mabel is the image of her mother, Sergeant, as I have always said, with a little of your firmer figure; though, for that matter, the Caps were never wanting in spring and activity."

Mabel cast a timid glance at the stern, rigid countenance of her father, of whom she had ever thought, as the warm-hearted dwell on the affection of their absent parents; and, as she saw that the muscles of his face were working, notwithstanding the stiffness and method of his manner, her very heart yearned to throw herself on his bosom and to weep at will. But he was so much colder in externals, so much more formal and distant than she had expected to find him, that she would not have dared to hazard the freedom, even had they been alone.

"You have taken a long and troublesome journey, brother, on my account; and we will try to make you comfortable while you stay among us."

"I hear you are likely to receive orders to lift your anchor, Sergeant, and to shift your berth into a part of the world where they say there are a thousand islands."

"Pathfinder, this is some of your forgetfulness?"

"Nay, nay, Sergeant, I forgot nothing; but it did not seem to me necessary to hide your intentions so very closely from your own flesh and blood."

"All military movements ought to be made with as little conversation as possible," returned the Sergeant, tapping the guide's shoulder in a friendly but reproachful manner. "You have passed too much of your life in front of the French not to know the value of silence. But no matter; the thing must soon be known, and there is no great use in trying now to conceal it. We shall embark a relief party shortly for a post on the lake, though I do not say it is for the Thousand Islands, and I may have to go with it; in which case I intend to take Mabel to make my broth for me; and I hope, brother, you will not despise a soldier's fare for a month or so."

"That will depend on the manner of marching. I have no love for woods and swamps."

"We shall sail in the *Scud;* and, indeed, the whole service, which is no stranger to us, is likely enough to please one accustomed to the water."

"Ay, to salt-water if you will, but not to lake-water. If you have no person to handle that bit of a cutter for you, I have no objection to ship for the v'y'ge, notwithstanding; though I shall look on the whole affair as so much time thrown away, for I consider it an imposition to call sailing about this pond going to sea."

"Jasper is every way able to manage the *Scud*, brother Cap; and in that light I cannot say that we have need of your services, though we shall be glad of your company. You cannot return to the settlement until a party is sent in, and that is not likely to happen until after my return. Well, Pathfinder, this is the first time I ever knew men on the trail of the Mingos and you not at their head."

"To be honest with you, Sergeant," returned the guide, not without a little awkwardness of manner, and a perceptible difference in the hue of a face that had become so uniformly red by exposure, "I have not felt that it was my gift this morning. In the first place, I very well know that the soldiers of the 55th are not the lads to overtake Iroquois in the woods; and the knaves did not wait to be surrounded when they knew that Jasper had reached the garrison. Then a man may take a little rest after a summer of hard work, and no impeachment of his good-will. Besides, the Sarpent is out with them; and if the miscreants are to be found at all, you may trust to his inmity and sight: the first being stronger, and the last nearly, if not quite, as good as my own. He loves the skulking vagabonds as little as myself; and, for that matter, I may say that my own feelings towards a Mingo are not much more than the gifts of a Delaware grafted on a Christian stock. No, no; I thought I would leave the honor this time, if honor there is to be, to the young ensign that commands, who, if he don't lose his scalp, may boast of his campaign in his letters to his mother, when he gets in. I thought I would play idler once in my life."

"And no one has a better right, if long and faithful service entitles a man to a furlough," returned the Sergeant kindly. "Mabel will think none the worse of you for preferring her company to the trail of the savages; and, I daresay, will be happy to give you a part of her breakfast if you are inclined to eat. You must not think, girl, however, that the Pathfinder is in the habit of letting prowlers around the fort beat a retreat without hearing the crack of his rifle."

"If I thought she did, Sergeant, though not much given to showy and parade evolutions, I would shoulder Killdeer and quit the garrison before her pretty eyes had time to frown. No, no; Mabel knows me better, though we are but new acquaintances, for there has been no want of Mingos to enliven the short march we have already made in company."

"It would need a great deal of testimony, Pathfinder, to make me think ill of you in any way, and more than all in the way you mention," returned Mabel, coloring with the sincere earnestness with which she endeavored to remove any suspicion to the contrary from his mind. "Both father and daughter, I believe, owe you their lives, and believe me, that neither will ever forget it."

"Thank you, Mabel, thank you with all my heart. But I will not take advantage of your ignorance neither, girl, and therefore shall say, I do not think the Mingos would have hurt a hair of your head, had they succeeded by their devilries and contrivances in getting you into their hands. My scalp, and Jasper's, and Master Cap's there, and the Sarpent's too, would sartainly have been smoked; but as for the Sergeant's daughter, I do not think they would have hurt a hair of her head."

"And why should I suppose that enemies, known to spare neither women nor children, would have shown more mercy to me than to another? I feel, Pathfinder, that I owe you my life."

"I say nay, Mabel; they wouldn't have had the heart to hurt you. No, not even a fiery Mingo devil would have had the heart to hurt a hair of your head. Bad as I suspect the vampires to be, I do not suspect them of anything so wicked as that. They might have wished you, nay, forced you to become the wife of one of their chiefs, and that would be torment enough to a Christian young woman; but beyond that I do not think even the Mingos themselves would have gone."

"Well, then, I shall owe my escape from this great misfortune to you," said Mabel, taking his hard hand into her own frankly and cordially, and certainly in a way to delight the honest guide. "To me it would be a lighter evil to be killed than to become the wife of an Indian."

"That is her gift, Sergeant," exclaimed Pathfinder, turning to his old comrade with gratification written on every lineament of his honest countenance, "and it will have its way. I tell the Sarpent that no Christianizing will ever make even a Delaware a white man; nor any whooping and yelling convert a pale-face into a red-skin. That is the gift of a young woman born of Christian parents, and it ought to be maintained."

"You are right, Pathfinder; and so far as Mabel Dunham is concerned, it *shall* be maintained. But it is time to break your fasts; and if you will follow me, brother Cap, I will show you how we poor soldiers live here on a distant frontier."

CHAPTER IX

> Now, my co-mates and partners in exile,
> Hath not old custom made this life more sweet
> Than that of painted pomp? Are not these woods
> More free from peril than the envious court?
> Here feel we but the penalty of Adam.   *As You Like It*

SERGEANT DUNHAM made no empty vaunt when he gave the promise conveyed in the closing words of the last chapter. Notwithstanding the remote frontier position of the post, they who lived at it enjoyed a table that, in many respects, kings and princes might have envied. At the period of our tale, and, indeed, for half a century later, the whole of that vast region which has been called the West, or the new countries since the war of the revolution, lay a comparatively unpeopled desert, teeming with all the living productions of nature that properly belonged to the climate, man and the domestic animals excepted. The few Indians that roamed its forests then could produce no visible effects on the abundance of the game; and the scattered garrisons, or occasional hunters, that here and there were to be met with on that vast surface, had no other influence than the bee on the buckwheat field, or the humming-bird on the flower.

The marvels that have descended to our own times, in the way of tradition, concerning the quantities of beasts, birds, and fishes that were then to be met with, on the shores of the great lakes in particular, are known to be sustained by the experience of living men, else might we hesitate about relating them; but having been eyewitnesses of some of these prodigies, our office shall be discharged with the confidence that certainty can impart. Oswego was particularly well placed to keep the larder of an epicure amply supplied. Fish of various sorts abounded in its river, and the sportsman had only to cast his line to haul in a bass or some other member of the finny tribe, which then peopled the waters, as the air above the swamps of this fruitful latitude is known to be filled with insects. Among others was the salmon of the lakes, a variety of that well-known species, that is scarcely inferior to the delicious salmon of northern Europe. Of the different migratory birds that frequent forests and waters, there was the same affluence, hundreds of acres of geese and ducks being often seen at a time in the great bays that indent the shores of the lake. Deer, bears, rabbits, and squirrels, with divers other quadrupeds, among which was sometimes included the elk, or moose, helped to complete the sum of the natural supplies on which all the posts depended, more or less, to relieve the unavoidable privations of their remote frontier positions.

In a place where viands that would elsewhere be deemed great luxuries were so abundant, no one was excluded from their enjoyment. The meanest individual at Oswego habitually feasted on game that would have formed the boast of a Parisian table; and it was no more than a healthful commentary on the caprices of taste, and of the waywardness of human desires, that the very diet which in other scenes would have been deemed the subject of envy and repinings got to pall on the appetite. The coarse and regular food of the army, which it became necessary to husband on account of the difficulty of transportation, rose in the estimation of the common soldier; and at any time he would cheerfully desert his venison, and ducks, and pigeons, and salmon, to banquet on the sweets of pickled pork, stringy turnips, and half-cooked cabbage.

The table of Sergeant Dunham, as a matter of course, partook of the abundance and luxuries of the frontier, as well as of its privations. A delicious broiled salmon smoked on a homely platter, hot venison steaks sent up their appetizing odors, and several dishes of cold meats, all of which were composed of game, had been set before the guests, in honor of the newly arrived visitors, and in vindication of the old soldier's hospitality.

"You do not seem to be on short allowance in this quarter of the world, Sergeant," said Cap, after he had got fairly initiated into the mysteries of the different dishes; "your salmon might satisfy a Scotsman."

"It fails to do it, notwithstanding, brother Cap; for among two or three hundred of the fellows that we have in this garrison, there are not half a dozen who will not swear that the fish is unfit to be eaten. Even some of the lads, who never tasted venison except as poachers at home, turn up their noses at the fattest haunches that we get here."

"Ay, that is Christian natur'," put in Pathfinder; "and I must say it is none to its credit. Now, a red-skin never repines, but is always thankful for the food he gets, whether it be fat or lean, venison or bear, wild turkey's breast or wild goose's wing. To the shame of us white men be it said, that we look upon blessings without satisfaction, and consider trifling evils as matters of great account."

"It is so with the 55th, as I can answer, though I cannot say as much for their Christianity," returned the Sergeant. "Even the major himself, old Duncan of Lundie, will sometimes swear that an oatmeal cake is better fare than the Oswego bass, and sigh for a swallow of Highland water, when, if so minded, he has the whole of Ontario to quench his thirst in."

"Has Major Duncan a wife and children?" asked Mabel, whose thoughts naturally turned towards her own sex in her new situation.

"Not he, girl; though they do say that he has a betrothed at home. The lady, it seems, is willing to wait, rather than suffer the hardships of service in this wild region; all of which, brother

Cap, is not according to my notions of a woman's duties. Your sister thought differently."

"I hope, Sergeant, you do not think of Mabel for a soldier's wife," returned Cap gravely. "Our family has done its share in that way already, and it's high time that the sea was again remembered."

"I do not think of finding a husband for the girl in the 55th, or any other regiment, I can promise you, brother; though I do think it getting to be time that the child were respectably married."

"Father!"

" 'Tis not their gifts, Sergeant, to talk of these matters in so open a manner," said the guide; "for I've seen it verified by experience, that he who would follow the trail of a virgin's good-will must not go shouting out his thoughts behind her. So, if you please, we will talk of something else."

"Well, then, brother Cap, I hope that bit of a cold roasted pig is to your mind; you seem to fancy the food."

"Ay, ay; give me civilized grub if I must eat," returned the pertinacious seaman. "Venison is well enough for your inland sailors, but we of the ocean like a little of that which we understand."

Here Pathfinder laid down his knife and fork, and indulged in a hearty laugh, though in his always silent manner; then he asked, with a little curiosity in his manner—

"Don't you miss the skin, Master Cap? don't you miss the skin?"

"It would have been better for its jacket, I think myself, Pathfinder; but I suppose it is a fashion of the woods to serve up shoats in this style."

"Well, well, a man may go round the 'arth and not know everything. If you had had the skinning of that pig, Master Cap, it would have left you sore hands. The cratur' is a hedgehog!"

"Blast me, if I thought it wholesome natural pork either!" returned Cap. "But then I believed even a pig might lose some of its good qualities up hereaway in the woods."

"If the skinning of it, brother, does not fall to my duty. Pathfinder, I hope you didn't find Mabel disobedient on the march?"

"Not she, not she. If Mabel is only half as well satisfied with

Jasper and Pathfinder as the Pathfinder and Jasper are satisfied with her, Sergeant, we shall be friends for the remainder of our days."

As the guide spoke, he turned his eyes towards the blushing girl, with a sort of innocent desire to know her opinion; and then, with an inborn delicacy, which proved he was far superior to the vulgar desire to invade the sanctity of feminine feeling, he looked at his plate, and seemed to regret his own boldness.

"Well, well, we must remember that women are not men, my friend," resumed the Sergeant, "and make proper allowances for nature and education. A recruit is not a veteran. Any man knows that it takes longer to make a good soldier than it takes to make anything else."

"This is new doctrine, Sergeant," said Cap with some spirit. "We old seamen are apt to think that six soldiers, ay, and capital soldiers too, might be made while one sailor is getting his education."

"Ay, brother Cap, I've seen something of the opinions which seafaring men have of themselves," returned the brother-in-law, with a smile as bland as comported with his saturnine features; "for I was many years one of the garrison in a seaport. You and I have conversed on the subject before, and I'm afraid we shall never agree. But if you wish to know what the difference is between a real soldier and man in what I should call a state of nature, you have only to look at a battalion of the 55th on parade this afternoon, and then, when you get back to York, examine one of the militia regiments making its greatest efforts."

"Well, to my eye, Sergeant, there is very little difference, not more than you'll find between a brig and a snow. To me they seem alike: all scarlet, and feathers, and powder, and pipeclay."

"So much, sir, for the judgment of a sailor," returned the Sergeant with dignity; "but perhaps you are not aware that it requires a year to teach a true soldier how to eat?"

"So much the worse for him. The militia know how to eat at starting; for I have often heard that, on their marches, they commonly eat all before them, even if they do nothing else."

"They have their gifts, I suppose, like other men," observed Pathfinder, with a view to preserve the peace, which was evidently in some danger of being broken by the obstinate predilection of each of the disputants in favor of his own calling; "and when a man has his gift from Providence, it is commonly idle to endeavor to bear up against it. The 55th, Sergeant, is a judicious regiment in the way of eating, as I know from having been so long in its company, though I daresay militia corps could be found that would outdo them in feats of that natur' too."

"Uncle," said Mabel, "if you have breakfasted, I will thank you to go out upon the bastion with me again. We have neither of us half seen the lake, and it would be hardly seemly for a young woman to be walking about the fort, the first day of her arrival, quite alone."

Cap understood the motive of Mabel; and having, at the bottom, a hearty friendship for his brother-in-law, he was willing enough to defer the argument until they had been longer together, for the idea of abandoning it altogether never crossed the mind of one so dogmatical and obstinate. He accordingly accompanied his niece, leaving Sergeant Dunham and his friend, the Pathfinder, alone together. As soon as his adversary had beat a retreat, the Sergeant, who did not quite so well understand the manœuvre of his daughter, turned to his companion, and, with a smile which was not without triumph, he remarked—

"The army, Pathfinder, has never yet done itself justice in the way of asserting its rights; and though modesty becomes a man, whether he is in a red coat or a black one, or, for that matter, in his shirt-sleeves, I don't like to let a good opportunity slip of saying a word in its behalf. Well, my friend," laying his own hand on one of the Pathfinder's, and giving it a hearty squeeze, "how do you like the girl?"

"You have reason to be proud of her, Sergeant. I have seen many of her sex, and some that were great and beautiful; but never before did I meet with one in whom I thought Providence had so well balanced the different gifts."

"And the good opinion, I can tell you, Pathfinder, is mutual. She told me last night all about your coolness, and spirit, and kindness—particularly the last, for kindness counts for more than half with females, my friend—and the first inspection seems to give satisfaction on both sides. Brush up the uniform, and pay a little more attention to the outside, Pathfinder, and you will have the girl heart and hand."

"Nay, nay, Sergeant, I've forgotten nothing that you have told me, and grudge no reasonable pains to make myself as pleasant in the eyes of Mabel as she is getting to be in mine. I cleaned and brightened up Killdeer this morning as soon as the sun rose; and, in my judgment, the piece never looked better than it does at this very moment."

"That is according to your hunting notions, Pathfinder; but firearms should sparkle and glitter in the sun, and I never yet could see any beauty in a clouded barrel."

"Lord Howe thought otherwise, Sergeant; and he was accounted a good soldier."

"Very true; his lordship had all the barrels of his regiment darkened, and what good came of it? You can see his 'scutcheon hanging in the English church at Albany. No, no, my worthy friend, a soldier should be a soldier, and at no time ought he to be ashamed or afraid to carry about him the signs and symbols of his honorable trade. Had you much discourse with Mabel, Pathfinder, as you came along in the canoe?"

"There was not much opportunity, Sergeant, and then I found myself so much beneath her in idees, that I was afraid to speak of much beyond what belonged to my own gifts."

"Therein you are partly right and partly wrong, my friend. Women love trifling discourse, though they like to have most of it to themselves. Now you know I'm a man that do not loosen my tongue at every giddy thought; and yet there were days when I could see that Mabel's mother thought none the worse of me because I descended a little from my manhood. It is true, I was twenty-two years younger then than I am to-day; and, moreover, instead of being the oldest sergeant in the regiment, I was the youngest. Dignity is commanding and useful, and there is no getting on without it, as respects the men; but if you would be thoroughly esteemed by a woman, it is necessary to condescend a little on occasions."

"Ah's me, Sergeant, I sometimes fear it will never do."

"Why do you think so discouragingly of a matter on which I thought both our minds were made up?"

"We did agree, if Mabel should prove what you told me she was, and if the girl could fancy a rude hunter and guide, that I should quit some of my wandering ways, and try to humanize my mind down to a wife and children. But since I have seen the girl, I will own that many misgivings have come over me."

"How's this?" interrupted the Sergeant sternly; "did I not

understand you to say that you were pleased?—and is Mabel a young woman to disappoint expectation?"

"Ah, Sergeant, it is not Mabel that I distrust, but myself. I am but a poor ignorant woodsman, after all; and perhaps I'm not, in truth, as good as even you and I may think me."

"If you doubt your own judgment of yourself, Pathfinder, I beg you will not doubt mine. Am I not accustomed to judge men's character? and am I often deceived? Ask Major Duncan, sir, if you desire any assurances in this particular."

"But, Sergeant, we have long been friends; have fi't side by side a dozen times, and have done each other many services. When this is the case, men are apt to think over kindly of each other; and I fear me that the daughter may not be so likely to view a plain ignorant hunter as favorably as the father does."

"Tut, tut, Pathfinder! you don't know yourself, man, and may put all faith in my judgment. In the first place you have experience; and, as all girls must want that, no prudent young woman would overlook such a qualification. Then you are not one of the coxcombs that strut about when they first join a regiment; but a man who has seen service, and who carries the marks of it on his person and countenance. I daresay you have been under fire some thirty or forty times, counting all the skirmishes and ambushes that you've seen."

"All of that, Sergeant, all of that; but what will it avail in gaining the good-will of a tender-hearted young female?"

"It will gain the day. Experience in the field is as good in love as in war. But you are as honest-hearted and as loyal a subject as the king can boast of—God bless him!"

"That may be too; but I'm afeared I'm too rude and too old and too wild like to suit the fancy of such a young and delicate girl as Mabel, who has been unused to our wilderness ways, and may think the settlements better suited to her gifts and inclinations."

"These are new misgivings for you, my friend; and I wonder they were never paraded before."

"Because I never knew my own worthlessness, perhaps, until I saw Mabel. I have travelled with some as fair, and have guided them through the forest, and seen them in their perils and in their gladness; but they were always too much above me to make me think of them as more than so many feeble ones I was bound to protect and defend. The case is now different. Mabel and I are so nearly alike, that I feel weighed down with a load that is hard to bear, at finding us so unlike. I do wish, Sergeant, that I was ten years younger, more comely to look at, and better suited to please a handsome young woman's fancy."

"Cheer up, my brave friend, and trust to a father's knowledge of womankind. Mabel half loves you already, and a fortnight's intercourse and kindness, down among the islands yonder, will close ranks with the other half. The girl as much as told me this herself last night."

"Can this be so, Sergeant?" said the guide, whose meek and modest nature shrank from viewing himself in colors so favorable. "Can this be truly so? I am but a poor hunter, and Mabel, I see, is fit to be an officer's lady. Do you think the girl will consent to quit all her beloved settlement usages, and her visitings and church-goings, to dwell with a plain guide and hunter up hereaway in the woods? Will she not in the end, crave her old ways, and a better man?"

"A better man, Pathfinder, would be hard to find," returned the father. "As for town usages, they are soon forgotten in the freedom of the forest, and Mabel has just spirit enough to dwell on a frontier. I've not planned this marriage, my friend, without thinking it over, as a general does his campaign. At first, I thought of bringing you into the regiment, that you might succeed me when I retire, which must be sooner or later; but on reflection, Pathfinder, I think you are scarcely fitted for the office. Still, if not a soldier in all the meanings of the word, you are a soldier in its best meaning, and I know that you have the good-will of every officer in the corps. As long as I live, Mabel can dwell with me, and you will always have a home when you return from your scoutings and marches."

"This is very pleasant to think of, Sergeant, if the girl can only come into our wishes with good-will. But, ah's me! it does not seem that one like myself can ever be agreeable in her handsome eyes. If I were younger, and more comely, now, as Jasper Western is, for instance, there might be a chance—yes, then, indeed, there might be some chance."

"That for Jasper Eau-douce, and every younker of them in or about the fort!" returned the Sergeant, snapping his fingers. "If not actually a younger, you are a younger-looking, ay, and a better-looking man than the *Scud's* master——"

"Anan?" said Pathfinder, looking up at his companion with an expression of doubt, as if he did not understand his meaning.

"I say if not actually younger in days and years, you look more hardy and like whipcord than Jasper, or any of them; and there will be more of you, thirty years hence, than of all of them put together. A good conscience will keep one like you a mere boy all his life."

"Jasper has as clear a conscience as any youth I know, Sergeant, and is as likely to wear on that account as any young man in the colony."

"Then you are my friend," squeezing the other's hand—"my tried, sworn, and constant friend."

"Yes, we have been friends, Sergeant, near twenty years before Mabel was born."

"True enough; before Mabel was born, we were well-tried friends; and the hussy would never dream of refusing to marry a man who was her father's friend before she was born."

"We don't know, Sergeant, we don't know. Like loves like. The young prefer the young for companions, and the old the old."

"Not for wives, Pathfinder; I never knew an old man, now, who had an objection to a young wife. Then you are respected and esteemed by every officer in the fort, as I have said already, and it will please her fancy to like a man that every one else likes."

"I hope I have no enemies but the Mingos," returned the guide, stroking down his hair meekly, and speaking thoughtfully. "I've *tried* to do right, and that ought to make friends, though it sometimes fails."

"And you may be said to keep the best company; for even old Duncan of Lundie is glad to see you, and you pass hours in his society. Of all the guides, he confides most in you."

"Ay, even greater than he is have marched by my side for days, and have conversed with me as if I were their brother; but, Sergeant, I have never been puffed up by their company, for I know that the woods often bring men to a level who would not be so in the settlements."

"And you are known to be the greatest rifle shot that ever pulled trigger in all this region."

"If Mabel could fancy a man for that, I might have no great reason to despair; and yet, Sergeant, I sometimes think that it is all as much owing to Killdeer as to any skill of my own. It is sartainly a wonderful piece, and might do as much in the hands of another."

"That is your own humble opinion of yourself, Pathfinder; but we have seen too many fail with the same weapon, and you succeed too often with the rifles of other men, to allow me to agree with you. We will get up a shooting match in a day or two, when you can show your skill, and when Mabel will form some judgment concerning your true character."

"Will that be fair, Sergeant? Everybody knows that Killdeer seldom misses; and ought we to make a trial of this sort when we all know what must be the result?"

"Tut, tut, man! I foresee I must do half this courting for you. For one who is always inside of the smoke in a skirmish, you are the faintest-hearted suitor I ever met with. Remember, Mabel comes of a bold stock; and the girl will be as likely to admire a man as her mother was before her."

Here the Sergeant arose, and proceeded to attend to his never-ceasing duties, without apology; the terms on which the guide stood with all in the garrison rendering this freedom quite a matter of course.

The reader will have gathered from the conversation just related, one of the plans that Sergeant Dunham had in view in causing his daughter to be brought to the frontier. Although necessarily much weaned from the caresses and blandishments that had rendered his child so dear to him during the first year or two of his widowerhood, he had still a strong but somewhat latent love for her. Accustomed to command and to obey, without being questioned himself or questioning others, concerning the reasonableness of the mandates, he was perhaps too much disposed to believe that his daughter would marry the man he might select, while he was far from being disposed to do violence to her wishes. The fact was, few knew the Pathfinder intimately without secretly believing him to be one of extraordinary qualities. Ever the same, simple-minded, faithful, utterly without fear, and yet prudent, foremost in all warrantable enterprises, or what the opinion of the day considered as such, and never engaged in anything to call a blush to his cheek or censure on his acts, it was not possible to live much with this being and not feel a respect and admiration for him which had no reference to his position in life. The most surprising peculiarity about the man himself was the entire indifference with which he regarded all distinctions which did not depend on personal merit. He was respectful to his superiors from habit; but had often been known to correct their mistakes and to reprove their vices with a fearlessness that proved how essentially he regarded the more material points, and with a natural discrimination that appeared to set education at defiance. In short, a disbeliever in the ability of man to distinguish between good and evil without the aid of instruction, would have been staggered by the character of this extraordinary inhabitant of the frontier. His feelings appeared to possess the freshness and nature of the forest in which he passed so much of his time; and no casuist could have made clearer decisions in matters relating to right and wrong; and yet he was not without his prejudices, which, though few, and colored by the character and usages of the individual, were deep-rooted, and almost formed a part of his nature. But the most striking feature about the moral organization of Pathfinder was his beautiful and unerring sense of justice. This noble trait—and without it no man can be truly great, with it no man other than respectable—probably had its unseen influence on all who associated with him; for the common and unprincipled brawler of the camp had been known to return from an expedition made in his company rebuked by his sentiments, softened by his language, and improved by his example. As might have been expected, with so elevated a quality his fidelity was like the immovable rock; treachery in him was classed among the things which are impossible; and as he seldom retired before his enemies, so was he never known, under any circumstances that admitted of an alternative, to abandon a friend. The affinities of such a character were, as a matter of course, those of like for like. His associates and intimates, though more or less determined by chance, were generally of the highest order as to moral propensities; for he appeared to possess a species of instinctive discrimination, which led him, insensibly to himself, most probably, to cling closest to those whose characters would best reward his friendship. In short, it was said of the Pathfinder, by one accustomed to study his fellows, that he was a fair example of what a just-minded and pure man might be, while untempted by unruly or ambitious desires, and left to follow the bias of his feelings, amid the solitary grandeur and ennobling influences of a sublime nature; neither led aside by the inducements which influence all to do evil amid the incentives of civilization, nor forgetful of the Almighty Being whose spirit pervades the wilderness as well as the towns.

Such was the man whom Sergeant Dunham had selected as the husband of Mabel. In making this choice, he had not been as much governed by a clear and judicious view of the merits of the individual, perhaps, as by his own likings; still no one knew the Pathfinder so intimately as himself without always conceding to the honest guide a high place in his esteem on account of these very virtues. That his daughter could find any serious objections to the match the old soldier did not apprehend; while, on the other hand, he saw many advantages to himself in dim perspective, connected with the decline of his days, and an evening of life passed among descendants who were equally dear to him through both parents. He had first made the proposition to his friend, who had listened to it kindly, but who, the Sergeant was now pleased to find, already betrayed a willingness to come into his own views that was proportioned to the doubts and misgivings proceeding from his humble distrust of himself.

CHAPTER X

Think not I love him, though I ask for him;
'Tis but a peevish boy:—yet he talks well—
But what care I for words?

A WEEK passed in the usual routine of a garrison. Mabel was becoming used to a situation that, at first, she had found not only novel, but a little irksome; and the officers and men in their turn, gradually familiarized to the presence of a young and blooming girl, whose attire and carriage had that air of modest gentility about them which she had obtained in the family of her patroness, annoyed her less by their ill-concealed admiration, while they gratified her by the respect which, she was fain to think, they paid her on account of her father; but which, in truth, was more to be attributed to her own modest but spirited deportment, then to any deference for the worthy Sergeant.

Acquaintances made in a forest, or in any circumstances of unusual excitement, soon attain their limits. Mabel found one week's residence at Oswego sufficient to determine her as to those with whom she might be intimate and those whom she ought to avoid. The sort of neutral position occupied by her father, who was not an officer, while he was so much more than a common soldier, by keeping her aloof from the two great classes of military life, lessened the number of those whom she was compelled to know, and made the duty of decision comparatively easy. Still she soon discovered that there were a few, even among those that could aspire to a seat at the Commandant's table, who were disposed to overlook the halbert for the novelty of a well-turned figure and of a pretty, winning face; and by the end of the first two or three days she had admirers even among the gentlemen. The Quartermaster, in particular, a middle-aged soldier, who had more than once tried the blessings of matrimony already, but was now a widower, was evidently disposed to increase his intimacy with the Sergeant, though their duties often brought them together; and the youngsters among his messmates did not fail to note that this man of method, who was a Scotsman of the name of Muir, was much more frequent in his visits to the quarters of his subordinate than had formerly been his wont. A laugh, or a joke, in honor of the "Sergeant's daughter," however, limited their strictures; though "Mabel Dunham" was soon a toast that even the ensign, or the lieutenant, did not disdain to give.

At the end of the week, Duncan of Lundie sent for Sergeant Dunham, after evening roll-call, on business of a nature that, it was understood, required a personal conference. The old veteran dwelt in a movable hut, which, being placed on trucks, he could order to be wheeled about at pleasure, sometimes living in one part of the area within the fort, and sometimes in another. On the present occasion, he had made a halt near the centre; and there he was found by his subordinate, who was admitted to his presence without any delay or dancing attendance in an antechamber. In point of fact, there was very little difference in the quality of the accommodations allowed to the officers and those allowed to the men, the former being merely granted the most room.

"Walk in, Sergeant, walk in, my good friend," said old Lundie heartily, as his inferior stood in a respectful attitude at the door of a sort of library and bedroom into which he had been ushered; —"walk in, and take a seat on that stool. I have sent for you, man, to discuss anything but rosters and pay-rolls this evening. It is now many years since we have been comrades, and 'auld lang syne' should count for something, even between a major and his orderly, a Scot and a Yankee. Sit ye down, man, and just put yourself at your ease. It has been a fine day, Sergeant."

"It has indeed, Major Duncan," returned the other, who, though he complied so far as to take the seat, was much too practised not to understand the degree of respect it was necessary to maintain in his manner; "a very fine day, sir, it has been, and we may look for more of them at this season."

"I hope so with all my heart. The crops look well as it is, man, and you'll be finding that the 55th make almost as good farmers as soldiers. I never saw better potatoes in Scotland than we are likely to have in that new patch of ours."

"They promise a good yield, Major Duncan; and, in that light, a more comfortable winter than the last."

"Life is progressive, Sergeant, in its comforts as well as in its need of them. We grow old, and I begin to think it time to retire and settle in life. I feel that my working days are nearly over."

"The king, God bless him! sir, has much good service in your honor yet."

"It may be so, Sergeant Dunham, especially if he should happen to have a spare lieutenant-colonelcy left."

"The 55th will be honored the day that commission is given to Duncan of Lundie, sir."

"And Duncan of Lundie will be honored the day he receives it. But, Sergeant, if you have never had a lieutenant-colonelcy, you have had a good wife, and that is the next thing to rank in making a man happy."

"I have been married, Major Duncan; but it is now a long time since I have had no drawback on the love I bear his majesty and my duty."

"What, man! not even the love you bear that active little

round-limbed, rosy-cheeked daughter that I have seen in the fort these last few days! Out upon you, Sergeant! old fellow as I am, I could almost love that little lassie myself, and send the lieutenant-colonelcy to the devil."

"We all know where Major Duncan's heart is, and that is in Scotland, where a beautiful lady is ready and willing to make him happy, as soon as his own sense of duty shall permit."

"Ay, hope is ever a far-off thing, Sergeant," returned the superior, a shade of melancholy passing over his hard Scottish features as he spoke; "and bonnie Scotland is a far-off country. Well, if we have no heather and oatmeal in this region, we have venison for the killing of it and salmon as plenty as at Berwick-upon-Tweed. Is it true, Sergeant, that the men complain of having been over-venisoned and over-pigeoned of late?"

"Not for some weeks, Major Duncan, for neither deer nor birds are so plenty at this season as they have been. They begin to throw their remarks about concerning the salmon, but I trust we shall get through the summer without any serious disturbance on the score of food. The Scotch in the battalion do, indeed, talk more than is prudent of their want of oatmeal, grumbling occasionally of our wheaten bread."

"Ah, that is human nature, Sergeant! pure, unadulterated Scotch human nature. A cake, man, to say the truth, is an agreeable morsel, and I often see the time when I pine for a bite myself."

"If the feeling gets to be troublesome, Major Duncan—in the men, I mean, sir, for I would not think of saying so disrespectful a thing to your honor—but if the men ever pine seriously for their natural food, I would humbly recommend that some oatmeal be imported, or prepared in this country for them, and I think we shall hear no more of it. A very little would answer for a cure, sir."

"You are a wag, Sergeant; but hang me if I am sure you are not right. There may be sweeter things in this world, after all, than oatmeal. You have a sweet daughter, Dunham, for one."

"The girl is like her mother, Major Duncan, and will pass inspection," said the Sergeant proudly. "Neither was brought up on anything better than good American flour. The girl will pass inspection, sir."

"That would she, I'll answer for it. Well, I may as well come to the point at once, man, and bring up my reserve into the front of the battle. Here is Davy Muir, the quartermaster, disposed to make your daughter his wife, and he has just got me to open the matter to you, being fearful of compromising his own dignity; and I may as well add that half the youngsters in the fort toast her, and talk of her from morning till night."

"She is much honored, sir," returned the father stiffly; "but I trust the gentlemen will find something more worthy of them to talk about ere long. I hope to see her the wife of an honest man before many weeks, sir."

"Yes, Davy is an honest man, and that is more than can be said for all in the quartermaster's department, I'm thinking, Sergeant," returned Lundie, with a slight smile. "Well, then may I tell the Cupid-stricken youth that the matter is as good as settled?"

"I thank your honor; but Mabel is betrothed to another."

"The devil she is! That will produce a stir in the fort; though I'm not sorry to hear it either, for, to be frank with you, Sergeant, I'm no great admirer of unequal matches."

"I think with your honor, and have no desire to see my daughter an officer's lady. If she can get as high as her mother was before her, it ought to satisfy any reasonable woman."

"And may I ask, Sergeant, who is the lucky man that you intend to call son-in-law?"

"The Pathfinder, your honor."

"Pathfinder!"

"The same, Major Duncan; and in naming him to you, I give you his whole history. No one is better known on this frontier than my honest, brave, true-hearted friend."

"All that is true enough; but is he, after all, the sort of person to make a girl of twenty happy?"

"Why not, your honor? The man is at the head of his calling. There is no other guide or scout connected with the army who has half the reputation of Pathfinder, or who deserves to have it half as well."

"Very true, Sergeant; but is the reputation of a scout exactly the sort of renown to captivate a girl's fancy?"

"Talking of girls' fancies, sir, is in my humble opinion much like talking of a recruit's judgment. If we were to take the movements of the awkward squad, sir, as a guide, we should never form a decent line in battalion, Major Duncan."

"But your daughter has nothing awkward about her; for a genteeler girl of her class could not be found in old Albion itself. Is she of your way of thinking in this matter?—though I suppose she must be, as you say she is betrothed."

"We have not yet conversed on the subject, your honor; but I consider her mind as good as made up, from several little circumstances which might be named."

"And what are these circumstances, Sergeant?" asked the Major, who began to take more interest than he had at first felt on the subject. "I confess a little curiosity to know something about a woman's mind, being, as you know, a bachelor myself."

"Why, your honor, when I speak of the Pathfinder to the girl, she always looks me full in the face; chimes in with everything I say in his favor, and has a frank open way with her, which says as much as if she half considered him already as a husband."

"Hum! and these signs, you think, Dunham, are faithful tokens of your daughter's feelings?"

"I do, your honor, for they strike me as natural. When I find a man, sir, who looks me full in the face, while he praises an officer—for, begging your honor's pardon, the men will sometimes pass their strictures on their betters—and when I find a man looking me in the eyes as he praises his captain, I always set it down that the fellow is honest, and means what he says."

"Is there not some material difference in the age of the intended bridegroom and that of his pretty bride, Sergeant?"

"You are quite right, sir; Pathfinder is well advanced towards forty, and Mabel has every prospect of happiness that a young woman can derive from the certainty of possessing an experienced husband. I was quite forty myself, your honor, when I married her mother."

"But will your daughter be as likely to admire a green hunting-shirt, such as that our worthy guide wears, with a fox-skin cap, as the smart uniform of the 55th?"

"Perhaps not, sir; and therefore she will have the merit of self-denial, which always makes a young woman wiser and better."

"And are you not afraid that she may be left a widow while still a young woman? what between wild beasts, and wilder savages, Pathfinder may be said to carry his life in his hand."

" 'Every bullet has its billet,' Lundie," for so the Major was fond of being called in his moments of condescension, and when not engaged in military affairs; "and no man in the 55th can call himself beyond or above the chances of sudden death. In that particular, Mabel would gain nothing by a change. Besides, sir, if I may speak freely on such a subject, I much doubt if ever Pathfinder dies in battle, or by any of the sudden chances of the wilderness."

"And why so, Sergeant?" asked the Major. "He is a soldier, so far as danger is concerned, and one that is much more than usually exposed; and, being free of his person, why should he expect to escape when others do not?"

"I do not believe, your honor, that the Pathfinder considers his own chances better than any one's else, but the man will never die by a bullet. I have seen him so often handling his rifle with as much composure as if it were a shepherd's crook, in the midst of the heaviest showers of bullets, and under so many extraordinary circumstances, that I do not think Providence means he should ever fall in that manner. And yet, if there be a man in his Majesty's dominions who really deserves such a death, it is Pathfinder."

"We never know, Sergeant," returned Lundie, with a countenance grave with thought; "and the less we say about it, perhaps, the better. But will your daughter—Mabel, I think, you call her—will Mabel be as willing to accept one who, after all, is a mere hanger-on of the army, as to take one from the service itself? There is no hope of promotion for the guide, Sergeant."

"He is at the head of his corps already, your honor. In short, Mabel has made up her mind on this subject; and, as your honor has had the condescension to speak to me about Mr. Muir, I trust you will be kind enough to say that the girl is as good as billeted for life."

"Well, well, this is your own matter, and, now—Sergeant Dunham!"

"Your honor," said the other, rising, and giving the customary salute.

"You have been told it is my intention to send you down among the Thousand Islands for the next month. All the old subalterns have had their tours of duty in that quarter—all that I like to trust at least; and it has at length come to your turn. Lieutenant Muir, it is true, claims his right; but, being quartermaster, I do not like to break up well-established arrangements. Are the men drafted?"

"Everything is ready, your honor. The draft is made, and I understood that the canoe which got in last night brought a message to say that the party already below is looking out for the relief."

"It did; and you must sail the day after to-morrow, if not to-morrow night. It will be wise, perhaps, to sail in the dark."

"So Jasper thinks, Major Duncan; and I know no one more to be depended on in such an affair than young Jasper Western."

"Young Jasper Eau-douce!" said Lundie, a slight smile gathering around his usually stern mouth. "Will that lad be of your party, Sergeant?"

"Your honor will remember that the *Scud* never quits port without him."

"True; but all general rules have their exceptions. Have I not seen a seafaring person about the fort within the last few days?"

"No doubt, your honor; it is Master Cap, a brother-in-law of mine, who brought my daughter from below."

"Why not put him in the *Scud* for this cruise, Sergeant, and leave Jasper behind? Your brother-in-law would like the variety of a fresh-water cruise, and you would enjoy more of his company."

"I intended to ask your honor's permission to take him along; but he must go as a volunteer. Jasper is too brave a lad to be turned out of his command without a reason, Major Duncan; and I'm afraid brother Cap despises fresh water too much to do duty on it."

"Quite right, Sergeant, and I leave all this to your own discretion. Eau-douce must retain his command, on second thoughts. You intend that Pathfinder shall also be of the party?"

"If your honor approves of it. There will be service for both the guides, the Indian as well as the white man."

"I think you are right. Well, Sergeant, I wish you good luck in the enterprise; and remember the post is to be destroyed and abandoned when your command is withdrawn. It will have done its work by that time, or we shall have failed entirely, and it is too ticklish a position to be maintained unnecessarily. You can retire."

Sergeant Dunham gave the customary salute, turned on his heels as if they had been pivots, and had got the door nearly drawn to after him, when he was suddenly recalled.

"I had forgotten, Sergeant, the younger officers have begged for a shooting match, and to-morrow has been named for the day. All competitors will be admitted, and the prizes will be a silver-mounted powder horn, a leathern flask ditto," reading from a piece of paper, "as I see by the professional jargon of this bill, and a silk calash for a lady. The latter is to enable the victor to show his gallantry by making an offering of it to her he best loves."

"All very agreeable, your honor, at least to him that succeeds. Is the Pathfinder to be permitted to enter?"

"I do not well see how he can be excluded, if he choose to come forward. Latterly, I have observed that he takes no share in these sports, probably from a conviction of his own unequalled skill."

"That's it, Major Duncan; the honest fellow knows there is not a man on the frontier who can equal him, and he does not wish to spoil the pleasure of others. I think we may trust to his delicacy in anything, sir. Perhaps it may be as well to let him have his own way?"

"In this instance we must, Sergeant. Whether he will be as successful in all others remains to be seen. I wish you good evening, Dunham."

The Sergeant now withdrew, leaving Duncan of Lundie to his own thoughts: that they were not altogether disagreeable was to be inferred from the smiles which occasionally covered a countenance hard and martial in its usual expression, though there were moments in which all its severe sobriety prevailed. Half an hour might have passed, when a tap at the door was answered by a direction to enter. A middle-aged man, in the dress of an officer, but whose uniform wanted the usual smartness of the profession, made his appearance, and was saluted as "Mr. Muir."

"I have come sir, at your bidding, to know my fortune," said the Quartermaster, in a strong Scotch accent, as soon as he had taken the seat which was proffered to him. "To say the truth to you, Major Duncan, this girl is making as much havoc in the garrison as the French did before Ty: I never witnessed so general a rout in so short a time!"

"Surely, Davy, you don't mean to persuade me that your young and unsophisticated heart is in such a flame, after one week's ignition? Why, man, this is worse than the affair in Scotland, where it was said the heat within was so intense that it just burnt a hole through your own precious body, and left a place for all the lassies to peer in at, to see what the combustible material was worth."

"Ye'll have your own way, Major Duncan; and your father and mother would have theirs before ye, even if the enemy were in the camp. I see nothing so extraordinar' in young people following the bent of their inclinations and wishes."

"But you've followed yours so often, Davy, that I should think by this time it had lost the edge of novelty. Including that informal affair in Scotland, when you were a lad, you've been married four times already."

"Only three, Major, as I hope to get another wife. I've not yet had my number: no, no; only three."

"I'm thinking, Davy, you don't include the first affair I mentioned; that in which there was no parson."

"And why should I, Major? The courts decided that it was no marriage; and what more could a man want? The woman took advantage of a slight amorous propensity that may be a weakness in my disposition, perhaps, and inveigled me into a contract which was found to be illegal."

"If I remember right, Muir, there were thought to be two sides to that question, in the time of it?"

"It would be but an indifferent question, my dear Major, that hadn't two sides to it; and I've known many that had three. But the poor woman's dead, and there was no issue; so nothing came of it after all. Then, I was particularly unfortunate with my second wife; I say second, Major, out of deference to you, and on the mere supposition that the first was a marriage at all; but first or second, I was particularly unfortunate with Jeannie Graham, who died in the first lustrum, leaving neither chick nor chiel behind her. I do think, if Jeannie had survived, I never should have turned my thoughts towards another wife."

"But as she did not, you married twice after her death; and are desirous of doing so a third time."

"The truth can never justly be gainsaid, Major Duncan, and I am always ready to avow it. I'm thinking, Lundie, you are melancholar this fine evening?"

"No, Muir, not melancholy absolutely; but a little thoughtful, I confess. I was looking back to my boyish days, when I, the laird's son, and you, the parson's, roamed about our native hills, happy and careless boys, taking little heed to the future; and then have followed some thoughts, that may be a little painful, concerning that future as it has turned out to be."

"Surely, Lundie, ye do not complain of yer portion of it. You've risen to be a major, and will soon be a lieutenant-colonel, if letters tell the truth; while I am just one step higher than when your honored father gave me my first commission, and a poor deevil of a quartermaster."

"And the four wives?"

"Three, Lundie; three only that were legal, even under our own liberal and sanctified laws."

"Well, then, let it be three. Ye know, Davy," said Major Duncan, insensibly dropping into the pronunciation and dialect of his youth, as is much the practice with educated Scotchmen as they warm with a subject that comes near the heart—"ye know, Davy, that my own choice has long been made, and in how anxious and hope-wearied a manner I've waited for that happy hour when I can call the woman I've so long loved a wife; and here have you, without fortune, name, birth, or merit— I mean particular merit——"

"Na, na; dinna say that, Lundie. The Muirs are of gude bluid."

"Well, then, without aught but bluid, ye've wived four times——"

"I tall ye but thrice, Lundie. Ye'll weaken auld friendship if ye call it four."

"Put it at yer own number, Davy; and it's far more than yer share. Our lives have been very different, on the score of matrimony, at least; you must allow that, my old friend."

"And which do you think has been the gainer, Major, speaking as frankly thegither as we did when lads?"

"Nay, I've nothing to conceal. My days have passed in hope deferred, while yours have passed in——"

"Not in hope realized, I give you mine honor, Major Duncan," interrupted the Quartermaster. "Each new experiment I have thought might prove an advantage; but disappointment seems the lot of man. Ah! this is a vain world of ours, Lundie, it must be owned; and in nothing vainer than in matrimony."

"And yet you are ready to put your neck into the noose for the fifth time?"

"I desire to say, it will be but the fourth, Major Duncan," said the Quartermaster positively; then, instantly changing the expression of his face to one of boyish rapture, he added, "But this Mabel Dunham is a *rara avis!* Our Scotch lassies are fair and pleasant; but it must be owned these colonials are of surpassing comeliness."

"You will do well to recollect your commission and blood. Davy. I believe all four of your wives——"

"I wish, my dear Lundie, ye'd be more accurate in yer arithmetic. Three times one make three."

"All three, then, were what might be termed gentlewomen?"

"That's just it, Major. Three were gentlewomen, as you say, and the connections were suitable."

"And the fourth being the daughter of my father's gardener, the connection was unsuitable. But have you no fear that marrying the child of a non-commissioned officer, who is in the same corps with yourself, will have the effect to lessen your consequence in the regiment?"

"That's just been my weakness through life, Major Duncan; for I've always married without regard to consequences. Every man has his besetting sin, and matrimony, I fear, is mine. And now that we have discussed what may be called the principles of the connection, I will just ask if you did me the favor to speak to the Sergeant on the trifling affair?"

"I did, David; and am sorry to say, for your hopes, that I see no great chance of your succeeding."

"Not succeeding! An officer, and a quartermaster in the bargain, and not succeed with a sergeant's daughter!"

"It's just that, Davy."

"And why not, Lundie? Will ye have the goodness to answer just that?"

"The girl is betrothed. Hand plighted, word passed, love pledged—no, hang me if I believe that either; but she is betrothed."

"Well, that's an obstacle, it must be avowed, Major, though it counts for little if the heart is free."

"Quite true; and I think it probable the heart is free in this case; for the intended husband appears to be the choice of the father rather than of the daughter."

"And who may it be, Major?" asked the Quartermaster, who viewed the whole matter with the philosophy and coolness acquired by use. "I do not recollect any plausible suitor that is likely to stand in my way."

"No, *you* are the only *plausible* suitor on the frontier, Davy. The happy man is Pathfinder."

"Pathfinder, Major Duncan!"

"No more, nor any less, David Muir. Pathfinder is the man; but it may relieve your jealousy a little to know that, in my judgment at least, it is a match of the father's rather than of the daughter's seeking."

"I thought as much!" exclaimed the Quartermaster, drawing a long breath, like one who felt relieved; "it's quite impossible that with my experience in human nature——"

"Particularly hu-woman's nature, David."

"Ye will have yer joke, Lundie, let who will suffer. But I did not think it possible I could be deceived as to the young woman's inclinations, which I think I may boldly pronounce to be altogether above the condition of Pathfinder. As for the individual himself—why, time will show."

"Now, tell me frankly, Davy Muir," said Lundie, stopping short in his walk, and looking the other earnestly in the face with a comical expression of surprise, that rendered the veteran's countenance ridiculously earnest—"do you really suppose a girl like the daughter of Sergeant Dunham can take a serious fancy to a man of your years and appearance, and experience, I might add?"

"Hout, awa', Lundie! ye dinna know the sax, and that's the reason yer unmarried in yer forty-fifth year. It's a fearfu' time ye've been a bachelor, Major!"

"And what may be *your* age, Lieutenant Muir, if I may presume to ask so delicate a question?"

"Forty-seven; I'll no' deny it, Lundie; and if I get Mabel, there'll be just a wife for every twa lustrums. But I didna think Sergeant Dunham would be so humble minded as to dream of giving that sweet lass of his to one like the Pathfinder."

"There's no dream about it, Davy; the man is as serious as a soldier about to be flogged."

"Well, well, Major, we are auld friends"—both ran into the Scotch or avoided it, as they approached or drew away from their younger days, in the dialogue—"and ought to know how to take and give a joke, off duty. It is possible the worthy man has not understood my hints, or he never would have thought of such a thing. The difference between an officer's consort and a guide's woman is as vast as that between the antiquity of Scotland and the antiquity of America. I'm auld blood, too, Lundie."

"Take my word for it, Davy, your antiquity will do you no good in this affair; and as for your blood, it is not older than your bones. Well, well, man, ye know the Sergeant's answer; and so ye perceive that my influence, on which ye counted so much, can do nought for ye. Let us take a glass thegither, Davy, for auld acquaintance sake; and then ye'll be doing well to remember the party that marches the morrow, and to forget Mabel Dunham as fast as ever you can."

"Ah, Major! I have always found it easier to forget a wife than to forget a sweetheart. When a couple are fairly married, all is settled but the death, as one may say, which must finally part us all; and it seems to me awfu' irreverent to disturb the departed; whereas there is so much anxiety and hope and felicity in expectation like, with the lassie, that it keeps thought alive."

"That is just my idea of your situation, Davy; for I never supposed you expected any more felicity with either of your wives. Now, I've heard of fellows who were so stupid as to look forward to happiness with their wives even beyond the grave. I drink to your success, or to your speedy recovery from this attack, Lieutenant; and I admonish you to be more cautious in future, as some of these violent cases may yet carry you off."

"Many thanks, dear Major; and a speedy termination to an old courtship, of which I know something. This is real mountain dew, Lundie, and it warms the heart like a gleam of bonnie Scotland. As for the men you've just mentioned, they could have had but one wife a piece; for where there are several, the deeds of the women themselves may carry them different ways. I think a reasonable husband ought to be satisfied with passing his allotted time with any particular wife in this world, and not to go about moping for things unattainable. I'm infinitely obliged to you, Major Duncan, for this and all your other acts of friendship; and if you could but add another, I should think you had not altogether forgotten the playfellow of your boyhood."

"Well, Davy, if the request be reasonable, and such as a superior ought to grant, out with it, man."

"If ye could only contrive a little service for me, down among the Thousand Isles, for a fortnight or so, I think this matter might be settled to the satisfaction of all parties. Just remember, Lundie, the lassie is the only marriageable white female on this frontier."

"There is always duty for one in your line at a post, however small; but this below can be done by the Sergeant as well as by the Quartermaster-general, and better too."

"But not better than by a regimental officer. There is great waste, in common, among the orderlies."

"I'll think of it, Muir," said the Major, laughing, "and you shall have my answer in the morning. Here will be a fine occasion, man, the morrow, to show yourself off before the lady; you are expert with the rifle, and prizes are to be won. Make up your mind to display your skill, and who knows what may yet happen before the *Scud* sails."

"I'm thinking most of the young men will try their hands in this sport, Major!"

"That will they, and some of the old ones too, if you appear. To keep you in countenance, I'll try a shot or two myself, Davy; and you know I have some name that way."

"It might, indeed, do good. The female heart, Major Duncan, is susceptible in many different modes, and sometimes in a way that the rules of philosophy might reject. Some require a suitor to sit down before them, as it might be, in a regular siege, and only capitulate when the place can hold out no longer; others, again, like to be carried by storm; while there are hussies who can only be caught by leading them into an ambush. The first is the most creditable and officer-like process, perhaps; but I must say I think the last the most pleasing."

"An opinion formed from experience, out of all question. And what of the storming parties?"

"They may do for younger men, Lundie," returned the Quartermaster, rising and winking, a liberty that he often took with his commanding officer on the score of a long intimacy; "every period of life has its necessities, and at forty-seven it's just as well to trust a little to the head. I wish you a very good even, Major Duncan, and freedom from gout, with a sweet and refreshing sleep."

"The same to yourself, Mr. Muir, with many thanks. Remember the passage of arms for the morrow."

The Quartermaster withdrew, leaving Lundie in his library to reflect on what had just passed. Use had so accustomed Major Duncan to Lieutenant Muir and all his traits and humors, that the conduct of the latter did not strike the former with the same force as it will probably the reader. In truth, while all men act under one common law that is termed nature, the varieties in their dispositions, modes of judging, feelings, and selfishness are infinite.

CHAPTER XI

Compel the hawke to sit that is unmann'd,
Or make the hound, untaught, to draw the deere,
Or bring the free against his will in band,
Or move the sad a pleasant tale to heere,
Your time is lost, and you no whit the neere!
So love ne learnes, of force the heart to knit:
She serves but those that feel sweet fancies' fit.
Mirror for Magistrates

It is not often that hope is rewarded by fruition so completely as the wishes of the young men of the garrison were met by the state of the weather on the succeeding day. The heats of summer were little felt at Oswego at the period of which we are writing; for the shade of the forest, added to the refreshing breezes from the lake, so far reduced the influence of the sun as to render the nights always cool and the days seldom oppressive.

It was now September, a month in which the strong gales of

the coast often appear to force themselves across the country as far as the great lakes, where the inland sailor sometimes feels that genial influence which characterizes the winds of the ocean invigorating his frame, cheering his spirits, and arousing his moral force. Such a day was that on which the garrison of Oswego assembled to witness what its commander had jocularly called a "passage of arms." Lundie was a scholar in military matters at least, and it was one of his sources of honest pride to direct the reading and thoughts of the young men under his orders to the more intellectual parts of their profession. For one in his situation, his library was both good and extensive, and its books were freely lent to all who desired to use them. Among other whims that had found their way into the garrison through these means, was a relish for the sort of amusement in which it was now about to indulge; and around which some chronicles of the days of chivalry had induced them to throw a parade and romance not unsuited to the characters and habits of soldiers, or to the insulated and wild post occupied by this particular garrison. While so earnestly bent on pleasure, however, they on whom that duty devolved did not neglect the safety of the garrison. One standing on the ramparts of the fort, and gazing on the waste of glittering water that bounded the view all along the northern horizon, and on the slumbering and seemingly boundless forest which filled the other half of the panorama, would have fancied the spot the very abode of peacefulness and security; but Duncan of Lundie too well knew that the woods might, at any moment, give up their hundreds, bent on the destruction of the fort and all it contained; and that even the treacherous lake offered a highway of easy approach by which his more civilized and scarcely less wily foes, the French, could come upon him at an unguarded moment. Parties were sent out under old and vigilant officers, men who cared little for the sports of the day, to scour the forest; and one entire company held the fort, under arms, with orders to maintain a vigilance as strict as if an enemy of superior force was known to be near. With these precautions, the remainder of the officers and men abandoned themselves, without apprehension, to the business of the morning.

The spot selected for the sports was a sort of esplanade, a little west of the fort, and on the immediate bank of the lake. It had been cleared of its trees and stumps, that it might answer the purpose of a parade-ground, as it possessed the advantages of having its rear protected by the water, and one of its flanks by the works. Men drilling on it could be attacked, consequently, on two sides only; and as the cleared space beyond it, in the direction of the west and south, was large, any assailants would be compelled to quit the cover of the woods before they could make an approach sufficiently near to render them dangerous.

Although the regular arms of the regiment were muskets, some fifty rifles were produced on the present occasion. Every officer had one as a part of his private provision for amusement; many belonged to the scouts and friendly Indians, of whom more or less were always hanging about the fort; and there was a public provision of them for the use of those who followed the game with the express object of obtaining supplies. Among those who carried the weapon were some five or six, who had reputation for knowing how to use it particularly well—so well, indeed, as to have given them a celebrity on the frontier; twice that number who were believed to be much better than common; and many who would have been thought expert in almost any situation but the precise one in which they now happened to be placed.

The distance was a hundred yards, and the weapon was to be used without a rest; the target, a board, with the customary circular lines in white paint, having the bull's-eye in the centre. The first trials in skill commenced with challenges among the more ignoble of the competitors to display their steadiness and dexterity in idle competition. None but the common men engaged in this strife, which had little to interest the spectators, among whom no officer had yet appeared.

Most of the soldiers were Scotch, the regiment having been raised at Stirling and its vicinity not many years before, though, as in the case of Sergeant Dunham, many Americans had joined it since its arrival in the colonies. As a matter of course, the provincials were generally the most expert marksmen; and after a desultory trial of half an hour it was necessarily conceded that a youth who had been born in the colony of New York, and who coming of Dutch extraction, was the most expert of all who had yet tried their skill. It was just as this opinion prevailed that the oldest captain, accompanied by most of the gentlemen and ladies of the fort, appeared on the parade. A train of some twenty females of humbler condition followed, among whom was seen the well-turned form, intelligent, blooming, animated countenance, and neat, becoming attire of Mabel Dunham.

Of females who were officially recognized as belonging to the class of ladies, there were but three in the fort, all of whom were officers' wives; Mabel being strictly, as had been stated by the Quartermaster, the only real candidate for matrimony among her sex.

Some little preparation had been made for the proper reception of the females, who were placed on a low staging of planks near the immediate bank of the lake. In this vicinity the prizes were suspended from a post. Great care was taken to reserve the front seat of the stage for the three ladies and their children; while Mabel and those who belonged to the non-commissioned officers of the regiment, occupied the second. The wives and daughters of the privates were huddled together in the rear, some standing and some sitting, as they could find room. Mabel, who had already been admitted to the society of the officers' wives, on the footing of a humble companion, was a good deal noticed by the ladies in front, who had a proper appreciation of modest self-respect and gentle refinement, though they were all fully aware of the value of rank, more particularly in a garrison.

As soon as this important portion of the spectators had got into their places, Lundie gave orders for the trial of skill to proceed in the manner that had been prescribed in his previous orders. Some eight or ten of the best marksmen of the garrison now took possession of the stand, and began to fire in succession. Among them were officers and men indiscriminately placed, nor were the casual visitors in the fort excluded from the competition.

As might have been expected of men whose amusements and comfortable subsistence equally depended on skill in the use of their weapons, it was soon found that they were all sufficiently expert to hit the bull's-eye, or the white spot in the centre of the target. Others who succeeded them, it is true, were less sure, their bullets striking in the different circles that surrounded the centre of the target without touching it.

According to the rules of the day, none could proceed to the second trial who had failed in the first, and the adjutant of the place, who acted as master of the ceremonies, or marshal of the day, called upon the successful adventurers by name to get ready for the next effort, while he gave notice that those who failed to present themselves for the shot at the bull's-eye would necessarily be excluded from all the higher trials. Just at this moment Lundie, the Quartermaster, and Jasper Eau-douce appeared in the group at the stand, while the Pathfinder walked leisurely on the ground without his beloved rifle, for him a measure so unusual, as to be understood by all present as a proof that he did not consider himself a competitor for the honors of the day. All made way for Major Duncan, who, as he approached the stand in a good-humored way, took his station, levelled his rifle carelessly, and fired. The bullet missed the required mark by several inches.

"Major Duncan is excluded from the other trials!" proclaimed the Adjutant, in a voice so strong and confident that all the elder officers and the sergeants well understood that this failure was preconcerted, while all the younger gentlemen and the privates felt new encouragement to proceed on account of the evident impartiality with which the laws of the sports were administered.

"Now, Master Eau-douce, comes your turn," said Muir; "and if you do not beat the Major, I shall say that your hand is better skilled with the oar than with the rifle."

Jasper's handsome face flushed, he stepped upon the stand, cast a hasty glance at Mabel, whose pretty form he ascertained was bending eagerly forward as if to note the result, dropped the barrel of his rifle with but little apparent care into the palm of his left hand, raised the muzzle for a single instant with exceeding steadiness, and fired. The bullet passed directly through the centre of the bull's-eye, much the best shot of the morning, since the others had merely touched the paint.

"Well performed, Master Jasper," said Muir, as soon as the result was declared; "and a shot that might have done credit to an older head and a more experienced eye. I'm thinking, notwithstanding, there was some of a youngster's luck in it; for ye were no' partic'lar in the aim ye took. Ye may be quick, Eaudouce, in the movement, but yer not philosophic nor scientific in yer management of the weepon. Now, Sergeant Dunham, I'll thank you to request the ladies to give a closer attention than common; for I'm about to make that use of the rifle which may be called the intellectual. Jasper would have killed, I allow; but then there would not have been half the satisfaction in receiving such a shot as in receiving one that is discharged scientifically."

All this time the Quartermaster was preparing himself for the scientific trial; but he delayed his aim until he saw that the eye of Mabel, in common with those of her companions, was fastened on him in curiosity. As the others left him room, out of respect to his rank, no one stood near the competitor but his commanding officer, to whom he now said in his familiar manner—

"Ye see, Lundie, that something is to be gained by exciting a female's curiosity. It's an active sentiment is curiosity, and properly improved may lead to gentler innovations in the end."

"Very true, Davy; but ye keep us all waiting while ye make your preparations; and here is Pathfinder drawing near to catch a lesson from your greater experience."

"Well, Pathfinder, and so *you* have come to get an idea too, concerning the philosophy of shooting? I do not wish to hide my light under a bushel, and yer welcome to all ye'll learn. Do ye no' mean to try a shot yersel', man?"

"Why should I, Quartermaster, why should I? I want none of the prizes; and as for honor, I have had enough of that, if it's any honor to shoot better than yourself. I'm not a woman to wear a calash."

"Very true; but ye might find a woman that is precious in your eyes to wear it for ye, as——"

"Come, Davy," interrupted the Major, "your shot or a retreat. The Adjutant is getting impatient."

"The Quartermaster's department and the Adjutant's department are seldom compliable, Lundie; but I'm ready. Stand a little aside, Pathfinder, and give the ladies an opportunity."

Lieutenant Muir now took his attitude with a good deal of studied elegance, raised his rifle slowly, lowered it, raised it again, repeated the manœuvres, and fired.

"Missed the target altogether!" shouted the man whose duty it was to mark the bullets, and who had little relish for the Quartermaster's tedious science. "Missed the target!"

"It cannot be!" cried Muir, his face flushing equally with indignation and shame; "it cannot be, Adjutant; for I never did so awkward a thing in my life. I appeal to the ladies for a juster judgment."

"The ladies shut their eyes when you fired!" exclaimed the regimental wags. "Your preparations alarmed them."

"I will na believe such calumny of the leddies, nor sic' a reproach on my own skill," returned the Quartermaster, growing more and more Scotch as he warmed with his feelings; "it's a conspiracy to rob a meritorious man of his dues."

"It's a dead miss, Muir," said the laughing Lundie, "and ye'll jist sit down quietly with the disgrace."

"No, no, Major," Pathfinder at length observed; "the Quartermaster *is* a good shot for a slow one and a measured distance, though nothing extr'ornary for real service. He has covered Jasper's bullet, as will be seen, if any one will take the trouble to examine the target."

The respect for Pathfinder's skill and for his quickness and accuracy of sight was so profound and general, that, the instant he made this declaration, the spectators began to distrust their own opinions, and a dozen rushed to the target in order to ascertain the fact. There, sure enough, it was found that the Quartermaster's bullet had gone through the hole made by Jasper's, and that, too, so accurately as to require a minute examination to be certain of the circumstance; which, however, was soon clearly established, by discovering one bullet over the other in the stump against which the target was placed.

"I told ye, ladies, ye were about to witness the influence of science on gunnery," said the Quartermaster, advancing towards the staging occupied by the females. "Major Duncan derides the idea of mathematics entering into target-shooting; but I tell him philosophy colors, and enlarges, and improves, and dilates, and explains everything that belongs to human life, whether it be a shooting-match or a sermon. In a word, philosophy is philosophy, and that is saying all that the subject requires."

"I trust you exclude love from the catalogue," observed the wife of a captain who knew the history of the Quartermaster's marriages, and who had a woman's malice against the monopolizer of her sex; "it seems that philosophy has little in common with love."

"You wouldn't say that, madam, if your heart had experienced many trials. It's the man or the woman that has had many occasions to improve the affections that can best speak of such matters; and, believe me, of all love, philosophical is the most lasting, as it is the most rational."

"You would then recommend experience as an improvement on the passion?"

"Your quick mind has conceived the idea at a glance. The happiest marriages are those in which youth and beauty and confidence on one side, rely on the sagacity, moderation, and prudence of years—middle age, I mean, madam, for I'll no' deny that there is such a thing as a husband's being too old for a wife. Here is Sergeant Dunham's charming daughter, now, to approve of such sentiments, I'm certain; her character for discretion being already well established in the garrison, short as has been her residence among us."

"Sergeant Dunham's daughter is scarcely a fitting interlocutor in a discourse between you and me, Lieutenant Muir," rejoined the captain's lady, with careful respect for her own dignity; "and yonder is the Pathfinder about to take his chance, by way of changing the subject."

"I protest, Major Duncan, I protest," cried Muir, hurrying back towards the stand, with both arms elevated by way of enforcing his words—"I protest in the strongest terms, gentlemen, against Pathfinder's being admitted into these sports with Killdeer, which is a piece, to say nothing of long habit, that is altogether out of proportion for a trial of skill against Government rifles."

"Killdeer is taking its rest, Quartermaster," returned Pathfinder calmly, "and no one here thinks of disturbing it. I did not think, myself, of pulling a trigger to-day; but Sergeant Dunham has been persuading me that I shall not do proper honor to his handsome daughter, who came in under my care, if I am backward on such an occasion. I'm using Jasper's rifle, Quartermaster, as you may see, and that is no better than your own."

Lieutenant Muir was now obliged to acquiesce, and every eye turned towards the Pathfinder, as he took the required station. The air and attitude of this celebrated guide and hunter were extremely fine, as he raised his tall form and levelled the piece, showing perfect self-command, and a thorough knowledge of the power of the human frame as well as of the weapon. Pathfinder was not what is usually termed a handsome man, though his appearance excited so much confidence and commanded respect.

Tall, and even muscular, his frame might have been esteemed nearly perfect, were it not for the total absence of everything like flesh. Whipcord was scarcely more rigid than his arms and legs, or, at need, more pliable; but the outlines of his person were rather too angular for the proportion that the eye most approves. Still, his motions, being natural, were graceful, and, being calm and regulated, they gave him an air and dignity that associated well with the idea, which was so prevalent, of his services and peculiar merits. His honest, open features were burnt to a bright red, that comported well with the notion of exposure and hardships, while his sinewy hands denoted force, and a species of use removed from the stiffening and deforming effects of labor. Although no one perceived any of those gentler or more insinuating qualities which are apt to win upon a woman's affections, as he raised his rifle not a female eye was fastened on him without a silent approbation of the freedom of his movements and the manliness of his air. Thought was scarcely quicker than his aim; and, as the smoke floated above his head, the butt-end of the rifle was seen on the ground, the hand of the Pathfinder was leaning on the barrel, and his honest countenance was illuminated by his usual silent, hearty laugh.

"If one dared to hint at such a thing," cried Major Duncan, "I should say that the Pathfinder had also missed the target."

"No, no, Major," returned the guide confidently; "that would be a risky declaration. I didn't load the piece, and can't say what was in it; but if it was lead, you will find the bullet driving down those of the Quartermaster and Jasper, else is not my name Pathfinder."

A shout from the target announced the truth of this assertion.

"That's not all, that's not all, boys," called out the guide, who was now slowly advancing towards the stage occupied by the females; "if you find the target touched at all, I'll own to a miss. The Quartermaster cut the wood, but you'll find no wood cut by that last messenger."

"Very true, Pathfinder, very true," answered Muir, who was lingering near Mabel, though ashamed to address her particularly in the presence of the officers' wives. "The Quartermaster did cut the wood, and by that means he opened a passage for your bullet, which went through the hole he had made."

"Well, Quartermaster, there goes the nail and we'll see who

can drive it closer, you or I; for, though I did not think of showing what a rifle can do to-day, now my hand is in, I'll turn my back to no man that carries King George's commission. Chingachgook is outlying, or he might force me into some of the niceties of the art; but, as for you, Quartermaster, if the nail don't stop you, the potato will."

"You're over boastful this morning, Pathfinder; but you'll find you've no green boy fresh from the settlements and the towns to deal with, I will assure ye!"

"I know that well, Quartermaster; I know that well, and shall not deny your experience. You've lived many years on the frontiers, and I've heard of you in the colonies, and among the Indians, too, quite a human life ago."

"Na, na," interrupted Muir in his broadest Scotch, "this is injustice, man. I've no' lived so very long, neither."

"I'll do you justice, Lieutenant, even if you get the best in the potato trial. I say you've passed a good human life, for a soldier, in places where the rifle is daily used, and I know you are a creditable and ingenious marksman; but then you are not a true rifle-shooter. As for boasting, I hope I'm not a vain talker about my own exploits; but a man's gifts are his gifts, and it's flying in the face of Providence to deny them. The Sergeant's daughter, here, shall judge between us, if you have the stomach to submit to so pretty a judge."

The Pathfinder had named Mabel as the arbiter because he admired her, and because, in his eyes, rank had little or no value; but Lieutenant Muir shrank at such a reference in the presence of the wives of the officers. He would gladly keep himself constantly before the eyes and the imagination of the object of his wishes; but he was still too much under the influence of old prejudices, and perhaps too wary, to appear openly as her suitor, unless he saw something very like a certainty of success. On the discretion of Major Duncan he had a full reliance, and he apprehended no betrayal from that quarter; but he was quite aware, should it ever get abroad that he had been refused by the child of a non-commissioned officer, he would find great difficulty in making his approaches to any other woman of a condition to which he might reasonably aspire. Notwithstanding these doubts and misgivings, Mabel looked so prettily, blushed so charmingly, smiled so sweetly, and altogether presented so winning a picture of youth, spirit, modesty, and beauty, that he found it exceedingly tempting to be kept so prominently before her imagination, and to be able to address her freely.

"You shall have it your own way, Pathfinder," he answered, as soon as his doubts had settled down into determination; "let the Sergeant's daughter—his charming daughter, I should have termed her—be the umpire then; and to her we will both dedicate the prize, that one or the other must certainly win. Pathfinder must be humored, ladies, as you perceive, else, no doubt, we should have had the honor to submit ourselves to one of your charming society."

A call for the competitors now drew the Quartermaster and his adversary away, and in a few moments the second trial of skill commenced. A common wrought nail was driven lightly into the target, its head having been first touched with paint, and the marksman was required to hit it, or he lost his chances in the succeeding trials. No one was permitted to enter, on this occasion, who had already failed in the essay against the bull's-eye.

There might have been half a dozen aspirants for the honors of this trial; one or two, who had barely succeeded in touching the spot of paint in the previous strife, preferring to rest their reputations there, feeling certain that they could not succeed in the greater effort that was now exacted of them. The first three adventurers failed, all coming very near the mark, but neither touching it. The fourth person who presented himself was the Quartermaster, who, after going through his usual attitudes, so far succeeded as to carry away a small portion of the head of the nail, planting his bullet by the side of its point. This was not considered an extraordinary shot, though it brought the adventurer within the category.

"You've saved your bacon, Quartermaster, as they say in the settlements of their creaturs," cried Pathfinder, laughing; "but it would take a long time to build a house with a hammer no better than yours. Jasper, here, will show you how a nail is to be started, or the lad has lost some of his steadiness of hand and sartainty of eye. You would have done better yourself, Lieutenant, had you not been so much bent on soldierizing your figure. Shooting is a natural gift, and is to be exercised in a natural way."

"We shall see, Pathfinder; I call that a pretty attempt at a nail; and I doubt if the 55th has another hammer, as you call it, that can do just the same thing over again."

"Jasper is not in the 55th, but there goes his rap."

As the Pathfinder spoke, the bullet of Eau-douce hit the nail square, and drove it into the target, within an inch of the head.

"Be all ready to clench it, boys!" cried out Pathfinder, stepping into his friend's tracks the instant they were vacant. "Never mind a new nail; I can see that, though the paint is gone, and what I can see I can hit, at a hundred yards, though it were only a mosquito's eye. Be ready to clench!"

The rifle cracked, the bullet sped its way, and the head of the nail was buried in the wood, covered by the piece of flattened lead.

"Well, Jasper, lad," continued Pathfinder, dropping the butt-end of his rifle to the ground, and resuming the discourse, as if ne thought nothing of his own exploit, "you improve daily. A few more tramps on land in my company, and the best marksman on the frontiers will have occasion to look keenly when he takes his stand ag'in you. The Quartermaster is respectable, but he will never get any farther; whereas you, Jasper, have the gift, and may one day defy any who pull trigger."

"Hoot, hoot!" exclaimed Muir; "do you call hitting the head of the nail respectable only, when it's the perfection of the art? Any one the least refined and elevated in sentiment knows that the delicate touches denote the master; whereas your sledge-hammer blows come from the rude and uninstructed. If 'a miss is as good as a mile,' a hit ought to be better, Pathfinder, whether it wound or kill."

"The surest way of settling this rivalry will be to make another trial," observed Lundie, "and that will be of the potato. You're Scotch, Mr. Muir, and might fare better were it a cake or a thistle; but frontier law has declared for the American fruit, and the potato it shall be."

As Major Duncan manifested some impatience of manner, Muir had too much tact to delay the sports any longer with his discursive remarks, but judiciously prepared himself for the next appeal. To say the truth, the Quartermaster had little or no faith in his own success in the trial of skill that was to follow, nor would he have been so free in presenting himself as a competitor at all had he anticipated it would have been made; but Major Duncan, who was somewhat of a humorist in his own quiet Scotch way, had secretly ordered it to be introduced expressly to mortify him; for, a laird himself, Lundie did not relish the notion that one who might claim to be a gentleman should bring discredit on his caste by forming an unequal alliance. As soon as everything was prepared, Muir was summoned to the stand, and the potato was held in readiness to be thrown. As the sort of feat we are about to offer to the reader, however, may be new to him, a word in explanation will render the matter more clear. A potato of large size was selected, and given to one who stood at the distance of twenty yards from the stand. At the word "heave!" which was given by the marksman, the vegetable was thrown with a gentle toss into the air, and it was the business of the adventurer to cause a ball to pass through it before it reached the ground.

The Quartermaster, in a hundred experiments, had once succeeded in accomplishing this difficult feat; but he now essayed to perform it again, with a sort of blind hope that was fated to be disappointed. The potato was thrown in the usual manner, the rifle was discharged, but the flying target was untouched.

"To the right-about, and fall out, Quartermaster," said Lundie, smiling at the success of the artifice. "The honor of the silken calash will lie between Jasper Eau-douce and Pathfinder."

"And how is the trial to end, Major?" inquired the latter. "Are we to have the two-potato trial, or is it to be settled by centre and skin?"

"By centre and skin, if there is any perceptible difference; otherwise the double shot must follow."

"This is an awful moment to me, Pathfinder," observed Jasper, as he moved towards the stand, his face actually losing its color in intensity of feeling.

Pathfinder gazed earnestly at the young man; and then, begging Major Duncan to have patience for a moment, he led his friend out of the hearing of all near him before he spoke.

"You seem to take this matter to heart, Jasper?" the hunter remarked, keeping his eyes fastened on those of the youth.

"I must own, Pathfinder, that my feelings were never before so much bound up in success."

"And do you so much crave to outdo me, an old and tried

friend?—and that, as it might be, in my own way? Shooting is my gift, boy, and no common hand can equal mine."

"I know it—I know it, Pathfinder; but yet——"

"But what, Jasper, boy?—speak freely; you talk to a friend."

The young man compressed his lips, dashed a hand across his eye, and flushed and paled alternately, like a girl confessing her love. Then, squeezing the other's hand, he said calmly, like one whose manhood has overcome all other sensations, "I would lose an arm, Pathfinder, to be able to make an offering of that calash to Mabel Dunham."

The hunter dropped his eyes to the ground, and as he walked slowly back towards the stand, he seemed to ponder deeply on what he had just heard.

"You never could succeed in the double trial, Jasper!" he suddenly remarked.

"Of that I am certain, and it troubles me."

"What a creature is mortal man! he pines for things which are not of his gift, and treats the bounties of Providence lightly. No matter, no matter. Take your station, Jasper, for the Major is waiting; and harkee, lad—I must touch the skin, for I could not show my face in the garrison with less than that."

"I suppose I must submit to my fate," returned Jasper, flushing and losing his color as before; "but I will make the effort, if I die."

"What a thing is mortal man!" repeated Pathfinder, falling back to allow his friend room to take his aim; "he overlooks his own gifts, and craves those of another!"

The potato was thrown, Jasper fired, and the shout that followed preceded the announcement of the fact that he had driven his bullet through its centre, or so nearly so as to merit that award.

"Here is a competitor worthy of you, Pathfinder," cried Major Duncan with delight, as the former took his station; "and we may look to some fine shooting in the double trial."

"What a thing is mortal man!" repeated the hunter, scarcely seeming to notice what was passing around him, so much were his thoughts absorbed in his own reflections. "Toss!"

The potato was tossed, the rifle cracked—it was remarked just as the little black ball seemed stationary in the air, for the marksman evidently took unusual heed to his aim—and then a look of disappointment and wonder succeeded among those who caught the falling target.

"Two holes in one?" called out the Major.

"The skin, the skin!" was the answer; "only the skin!"

"How's this, Pathfinder? Is Jasper Eau-douce to carry off the honors of the day?"

"The calash is his," returned the other, shaking his head and walking quietly away from the stand. "What a creature is mortal man! never satisfied with his own gifts, but for ever craving that which Providence denies!"

As Pathfinder had not buried his bullet in the potato, but had cut through the skin, the prize was immediately adjudged to Jasper. The calash was in the hands of the latter when the Quartermaster approached, and with a polite air of cordiality he wished his successful rival joy of his victory.

"But now you've got the calash, lad, it's of no use to you," he added; "it will never make a sail, nor even an ensign. I'm thinking, Eau-douce, you'd no' be sorry to see its value in good siller of the king?"

"Money cannot buy it, Lieutenant," returned Jasper, whose eye lighted with all the fire of success and joy. "I would rather have won this calash than have obtained fifty new suits of sails for the *Scud!*"

"Hoot, hoot, lad! you are going mad like all the rest of them. I'd even venture to offer half a guinea for the trifle rather than it should lie kicking about in the cabin of your cutter, and in the end become an ornament for the head of a squaw."

Although Jasper did not know that the wary Quartermaster had not offered half the actual cost of the prize, he heard the proposition with indifference. Shaking his head in the negative, he advanced towards the stage, where his approach excited a little commotion, the officers' ladies, one and all, having determined to accept the present, should the gallantry of the young sailor induce him to offer it. But Jasper's diffidence, no less than admiration for another, would have prevented him from aspiring to the honor of complimenting any whom he thought so much his superiors.

"Mabel," said he, "this prize is for you, unless——"

"Unless what, Jasper?" answered the girl, losing her own bashfulness in the natural and generous wish to relieve his embarrassment, though both reddened in a way to betray strong feeling.

"Unless you may think too indifferently of it, because it is offered by one who may have no right to believe his gift will be accepted."

"I do accept it, Jasper; and it shall be a sign of the danger I have passed in your company, and of the gratitude I feel for your care of me—your care, and that of the Pathfinder."

"Never mind me, never mind me!" exclaimed the latter; "this is Jasper's luck, and Jasper's gift: give him full credit for both. My turn may come another day; mine and the Quartermaster's, who seems to grudge the boy the calash; though what *he* can want of it I cannot understand, for he has no wife."

"And has Jasper Eau-douce a wife? or have you a wife yoursel', Pathfinder? I may want it to help to get a wife, or as a memorial that I have had a wife, or as proof how much I admire the sex, or because it is a female garment, or for some other equally respectable motive. It's not the unreflecting that are the most prized by the thoughtful, and there is no surer sign that a man made a good husband to his first consort, let me tell you all, than to see him speedily looking round for a competent successor. The affections are good gifts from Providence, and they that have loved one faithfully prove how much of this bounty has been lavished upon them by loving another as soon as possible."

"It may be so, it may be so. I am no practitioner in such things, and cannot gainsay it. But Mabel here, the Sergeant's daughter, will give you full credit for the words. Come, Jasper, although our hands are out, let us see what the other lads can do with the rifle."

Pathfinder and his companions retired, for the sports were about to proceed. The ladies, however, were not so much engrossed with rifle-shooting as to neglect the calash. It passed from hand to hand; the silk was felt, the fashion criticized, and the work examined, and divers opinions were privately ventured concerning the fitness of so handsome a thing passing into the possession of a non-commissioned officer's child.

"Perhaps you will be disposed to sell that calash, Mabel, when it has been a short time in your possession?" inquired the captain's lady. "Wear it, I should think, you never can."

"I may not wear it, madam," returned our heroine modestly; "but I should not like to part with it either."

"I daresay Sergeant Dunham keeps you above the necessity of selling your clothes, child; but, at the same time, it is money thrown away to keep an article of dress you can never wear."

"I should be unwilling to part with the gift of a friend."

"But the young man himself will think all the better of you for your prudence after the triumph of the day is forgotten. It is a pretty and a becoming calash, and ought not to be thrown away."

"I've no intention to throw it away, ma'am; and, if you please, would rather keep it."

"As you will, child; girls of your age often overlook their real advantages. Remember, however, if you do determine to dispose of the thing, that it is bespoke, and that I will not take it if you ever even put it on your own head."

"Yes, ma'am," said Mabel, in the meekest voice imaginable, though her eyes looked like diamonds, and her cheeks reddened to the tints of two roses, as she placed the forbidden garment over her well-turned shoulders, where she kept it a minute, as if to try its fitness, and then quietly removed it again.

The remainder of the sports offered nothing of interest. The shooting was reasonably good; but the trials were all of a scale lower than those related, and the competitors were soon left to themselves. The ladies and most of the officers withdrew, and the remainder of the females soon followed their example. Mabel was returning along the low flat rocks that line the shore of the lake, dangling her pretty calash from a prettier finger, when Pathfinder met her. He carried the rifle which he had used that day; but his manner had less of the frank ease of the hunter about it than usual, while his eye seemed roving and uneasy. After a few unmeaning words concerning the noble sheet of water before them, he turned towards his companion with strong interest in his countenance, and said—

"Jasper earned that calash for you, Mabel, without much trial of his gifts."

"It was fairly done, Pathfinder."

"No doubt, no doubt. The bullet passed neatly through the potato, and no man could have done more; though others might have done as much."

"But no one did as much!" exclaimed Mabel, with an animation that she instantly regretted; for she saw by the pained look of the guide that he was mortified equally by the remark and by the feeling with which it was uttered.

"It is true, it is true, Mabel, no one did as much then; but— yet there is no reason I should deny my gifts which come from Providence—yes, yes; no one did as much there, but you shall know what *can* be done here. Do you observe the gulls that are flying over our heads?"

"Certainly, Pathfinder; there are too many to escape notice."

"Here, where they cross each other in sailing about." he added, cocking and raising his rifle; "the two—the two. Now look!"

The piece was presented quick as thought, as two of the birds came in a line, though distant from each other many yards; the report followed, and the bullet passed through the bodies of both the victims. No sooner had the gulls fallen into the lake, than Pathfinder dropped the butt-end of the rifle, and laughed in his own peculiar manner, every shade of dissatisfaction and morti- fied pride having left his honest face.

"That is something, Mabel, that is something; although I have no calash to give you! But ask Jasper himself; I'll leave it all to Jasper, for a truer tongue and heart are not in America."

"Then it was not Jasper's fault that he gained the prize?"

"Not it. He did his best, and he did well. For one that has water gifts, rather than land gifts, Jasper is uncommonly expert, and a better backer no one need wish, ashore or afloat. But it was my fault, Mabel, that he got the calash; though it makes no dif- ference—it makes no difference, for the thing has gone to the right person."

"I believe I understand you, Pathfinder," said Mabel, blush- ing in spite of herself, "and I look upon the calash as the joint gift of yourself and Jasper."

"That would not be doing justice to the lad, neither. He won the garment, and had a right to give it away. The most you may think, Mabel, is to believe that, had I won it, it would have gone to the same person."

"I will remember that, Pathfinder, and take care that others know your skill, as it has been proved upon the poor gulls in my presence."

"Lord bless you, Mabel! there is no more need of your talking in favor of my shooting on this frontier, than of your talking about the water in the lake or the sun in the heavens. Everybody knows what I can do in that way, and your words would be thrown away, as much as French would be thrown away on an American bear."

"Then you think that Jasper knew you were giving him this advantage, of which he had so unhandsomely availed himself?" said Mabel, the color which had imparted so much lustre to her eyes gradually leaving her face, which became grave and thoughtful.

"I do not say that, but very far from it. We all forget things that we have known, when eager after our wishes. Jasper is satisfied that I can pass one bullet through two potatoes, as I sent my bullet through the gulls; and he knows no other man on the frontier can do the same thing. But with the calash before his eyes, and the hope of giving it to you, the lad was inclined to think better of himself, just at that moment, perhaps, than he ought. No, no, there's nothing mean or distrustful about Jasper Eau-douce, though it is a gift natural to all young men to wish to appear well in the eyes of handsome young women."

"I'll try to forget all, but the kindness you've both shown to a poor motherless girl," said Mabel, struggling to keep down emotions she scarcely knew how to account for herself. "Believe me, Pathfinder, I can never forget all you have already done for me—you and Jasper; and this new proof of your regard is not thrown away. Here, here is a brooch that is of silver, and I offer it as a token that I owe you life or liberty."

"What shall I do with this, Mabel?" asked the bewildered hunter, holding the simple trinket in his hand. "I have neither buckle nor button about me, for I wear nothing but leathern strings, and them of good deer-skins. It's pretty to the eye, but it is prettier far on the spot it came from than it can be about me."

"Nay, put it in your hunting-shirt; it will become it well. Remember, Pathfinder, that it is a token of friendship between us, and a sign that I can never forget you or your services."

Mabel then smiled an adieu; and, bounding up the bank, she was soon lost to view behind the mound of the fort.

CHAPTER XII

Lo! dusky masses steal in dubious sight,
Along the leaguer'd wall, and bristling bank,
Of the arm'd river; while with straggling light,
The stars peep through the vapor, dim and dank.

BYRON

A FEW hours later Mabel Dunham was on the bastion that overlooked the river and the lake, seemingly in deep thought. The evening was calm and soft, and the question had arisen whether the party for the Thousand Islands would be able to get out that night or not, on account of the total absence of wind. The stores, arms, and ammunition were already shipped, and even Mabel's effects were on board; but the small draft of men that was to go was still ashore, there being no apparent prospect of the cutter's getting under way. Jasper had warped the *Scud* out of the cove, and so far up the stream as to enable him to pass through the outlet of the river whenever he chose; but there he still lay, riding at single anchor. The drafted men were lounging about the shore of the cove, undecided whether or not to pull off.

The sports of the morning had left a quiet in the garrison which was in harmony with the whole of the beautiful scene, and Mabel felt its influence on her feelings, though probably too little accustomed to speculate on such sensations to be aware of the cause. Everything near appeared lovely and soothing, while the solemn grandeur of the silent forest and placid expanse of the lake lent a sublimity that other scenes might have wanted. For the first time, Mabel felt the hold that the towns and civilization had gained on her habits sensibly weakened; and the warm-hearted girl began to think that a life passed amid objects such as those around her might be happy. How far the experience of the last days came in aid of the calm and holy eventide, and contributed towards producing that young conviction, may be suspected, rather than affirmed, in this early portion of our legend.

"A charming sunset, Mabel!" said the hearty voice of her uncle, so close to the ear of our heroine as to cause her to start—

"a charming sunset, girl, for a fresh-water concern, though we should think but little of it at sea."

"And is not nature the same on shore or at sea—on a lake like this or on the ocean? Does not the sun shine on all alike, dear uncle; and can we not feel gratitude for the blessings of Providence as strongly on this remote frontier as in our own Manhattan?"

"The girl has fallen in with some of her mother's books. Is not nature the same, indeed! Now, Mabel, do you imagine that the nature of a soldier is the same as that of a seafaring man? You've relations in both callings, and ought to be able to answer."

"But, uncle, I mean human nature."

"So do I, girl; the human nature of a seaman, and the human nature of one of these fellows of the 55th, not even excepting your own father. Here have they had a shooting-match—target-firing I should call it—this day, and what a different thing has it been from a target-firing afloat! There we should have sprung our broadside, sported with round shot, at an object half a mile off, at the very nearest; and the potatoes, if there happened to be any on board, as very likely would not have been the case, would have been left in the cook's coppers. It may be an honorable calling, that of a soldier, Mabel; but an experienced hand sees many follies and weaknesses in one of these forts. As for that bit of a lake, you know my opinion of it already, and I wish to disparage nothing. No real seafarer disparages anything; but, d— me, if I regard this here Ontario, as they call it, as more than so much water in a ship's scuttle-butt. Now, look you here, Mabel, if you wish to understand the difference between the ocean and a lake, I can make you comprehend it with a single look: this is what one may call a calm, seeing that there is no wind; though, to own the truth, I do not think the calms are as calm as them we get outside——"

"Uncle, there is not a breath of air. I do not think it possible for the leaves to be more immovably still than those of the entire forest are at this very moment."

"Leaves! what are leaves, child? there are no leaves at sea. If you wish to know whether it is a dead calm or not, try a mould candle—your dips flaring too much—and then you may be certain whether there is or is not any wind. If you were in a latitude where the air was so still that you found a difficulty in stirring it to draw it in in breathing, you might fancy it a calm. People are often on a short allowance of air in the calm latitudes. Here, again, look at that water! It is like milk in a pan, with no more motion now than there is in a full hogshead before the bung is started. On the ocean the water is never still, let the air be as quiet as it may."

"The water of the ocean never still, Uncle Cap? not even in a calm?"

"Bless your heart, no, child! The ocean breathes like a living being, and its bosom is always heaving, as the poetizers call it, though there be no more air than is to be found in a siphon. No man ever saw the ocean still like this lake; but it heaves and sets as if it had lungs."

"And this lake is not absolutely still, for you perceive there is a little ripple on the shore, and you may even hear the surf plunging at moments against the rocks."

"All d—d poetry! Lake Ontario is no more the Atlantic than a Powles Hook periagua is a first-rate. That Jasper, notwithstanding, is a fine lad, and wants instruction only to make a man of him."

"Do you think him ignorant, uncle?" answered Mabel, prettily adjusting her hair, in order to do which she was obliged, or fancied she was obliged, to turn away her face. "To me Jasper Eau-douce appears to know more than most of the young men of his class. He has read but little, for books are not plenty in this part of the world; but he has thought much, at least so it seems to me, for one so young."

"He is ignorant, as all must be who navigate an inland water like this. No, no, Mabel; we both owe something to Jasper and the Pathfinder, and I have been thinking how I can best serve them, for I hold ingratitude to be the vice of a hog; for treat the animal to your own dinner, and he would eat you for the dessert."

"Very true, dear uncle; we ought indeed to do all we can to express our proper sense of the services of both these brave men."

"Spoken like your mother's daughter, girl, and in a way to do credit to the Cap family. Now, I've hit upon a traverse that will just suit all parties; and, as soon as we get back from this little expedition down the lake among them there Thousand Islands, and I am ready to return, it is my intention to propose it."

"Dearest uncle! this is so considerate in you, and will be so just! May I ask what your intentions are?"

"I see no reason for keeping them a secret from you, Mabel, though nothing need be said to your father about them; for the Sergeant has his prejudices, and might throw difficulties in the way. Neither Jasper nor his friend Pathfinder can ever make anything hereabouts, and I propose to take both with me down to the coast, and get them fairly afloat. Jasper would find his sea-legs in a fortnight, and a twelvemonth's v'y'ge would make him a man. Although Pathfinder might take more time, or never get to be rated able, yet one could make something of him too, particularly as a look-out, for he has unusually good eyes."

"Uncle, do you think either would consent to this?" said Mabel, smiling.

"Do I suppose them simpletons? what rational being would neglect his own advancement? Let Jasper alone to push his way, and the lad may yet die the master of some square-rigged craft."

"And would he be any the happier for it, dear uncle? How much better is it to be the master of a square-rigged craft than to be master of a round-rigged craft?"

"Pooh, pooh, Magnet! you are just fit to read lectures about ships before some hysterical society; you don't know what you are talking about; leave these things to me, and they'll be properly managed. Ah! here is the Pathfinder himself, and I may just as well drop him a hint of my benevolent intentions as regards himself. Hope is a great encourager of our exertions."

Cap nodded his head, and then ceased to speak, while the hunter approached, not with his usual frank and easy manner, but in a way to show that he was slightly embarrassed, if not distrustful of his reception.

"Uncle and niece make a family party," said Pathfinder, when near the two, "and a stranger may not prove a welcome companion?"

"You are no stranger, Master Pathfinder," returned Cap, "and no one can be more welcome than yourself. We were talking of you but a moment ago, and when friends speak of an absent man, he can guess what they have said."

"I ask no secrets. Every man has his enemies, and I have mine, though I count neither you, Master Cap, nor pretty Mabel here among the number. As for the Mingos, I will say nothing, though they have no just cause to hate me."

"That I'll answer for, Pathfinder! for you strike my fancy as being well-disposed and upright. There is a method, however, of getting away from the enmity of even these Mingos; and if you choose to take it, no one will more willingly point it out than myself, without a charge for my advice either."

"I wish no enemies, Saltwater," for so the Pathfinder had begun to call Cap, having, insensibly to himself, adopted the term, by translating the name given him by the Indians in and about the fort—"I wish no enemies. I'm as ready to bury the hatchet with the Mingos as with the French, though you know that it depends on One greater than either of us so to turn the heart as to leave a man without enemies."

"By lifting your anchor, and accompanying me down to the coast, friend Pathfinder, when we get back from this short cruise on which we are bound, you will find yourself beyond the sound of the war-whoop, and safe enough from any Indian bullet."

"And what should I do on the salt water? Hunt in your towns? Follow the trails of people going and coming from market, and ambush dogs and poultry? You are no friend to my happiness, Master Cap, if you would lead me out of the shades of the woods to put me in the sun of the clearings."

"I did not propose to leave you in the settlements, Pathfinder, but to carry you out to sea, where a man can only be said to breathe freely. Mabel will tell you that such was my intention, before a word was said on the subject."

"And what does Mabel think would come of such a change? She knows that a man has his gifts, and that it is as useless to pretend to others as to withstand them that come from Providence. I am a hunter, and a scout, or a guide, Saltwater, and it is not in me to fly so much in the face of Heaven as to try to become anything else. Am I right, Mabel, or are you so much a woman as to wish to see a natur' altered?"

"I would wish to see no change in you, Pathfinder," Mabel answered, with a cordial sincerity and frankness that went directly to the hunter's heart; "and much as my uncle admires the sea, and great as is all the good that he thinks may come of it, I could not wish to see the best and noblest hunter of the woods transformed into an admiral. Remain what you are, my brave friend, and you need fear nothing short of the anger of God."

"Do you hear this, Saltwater? do you hear what the Sergeant's daughter is saying, and she is much too upright, and fair-minded, and pretty, not to think what she says. So long as she is satisfied with me as I am, I shall not fly in the face of the gifts of Providence, by striving to become anything else. I may seem useless here in a garrison; but when we get down among the Thousand Islands, there may be an opportunity to prove that a sure rifle is sometimes a Godsend."

"You are then to be of our party?" said Mabel, smiling so frankly and so sweetly on the guide that he would have followed her to the end of the earth. "I shall be the only female, with the exception of one soldier's wife, and shall feel none the less secure, Pathfinder, because you will be among our protectors."

"The Sergeant would do that, Mabel, though you were not of his kin. No one will overlook you. I should think your uncle here would like an expedition of this sort, where we shall go with sails, and have a look at an inland sea?"

"Your inland sea is no great matter, Master Pathfinder, and I expect nothing from it. I confess, however, I should like to know the object of the cruise; for one does not wish to be idle, and my brother-in-law, the Sergeant, is as close-mouthed as a freemason. Do you know, Mabel, what all this means?"

"Not in the least, uncle. I dare not ask my father any questions about his duty, for he thinks it is not a woman's business; and all I can say is, that we are to sail as soon as the wind will permit, and that we are to be absent a month."

"Perhaps Master Pathfinder can give me a useful hint; for a v'y'ge without an object is never pleasant to an old sailor."

"There is no great secret, Saltwater, concerning our port and object, though it is forbidden to talk much about either in the garrison. I am no soldier, however, and can use my tongue as I please, though as little given as another to idle conversation, I hope; still, as we sail so soon, and you are both to be of the party, you may as well be told where you are to be carried. You know that there are such things as the Thousand Islands, I suppose, Master Cap?"

"Ay, what are so called hereaway, though I take it for granted that they are not real islands, such as we fall in with on the ocean; and that the thousand means some such matter as two or three."

"My eyes are good, and yet have I often been foiled in trying to count them very islands."

"Ay, ay, I've known people who couldn't count beyond a certain number. Your real land-birds never know their own roosts, even in a land-fall at sea. How many times have I seen the beach, and houses, and churches, when the passengers have not been able to see anything but water! I have no idea that a man can get fairly out of sight of land on fresh water. The thing appears to me to be irrational and impossible."

"You don't know the lakes, Master Cap, or you would not say that. Before we get to the Thousand Islands, you will have other notions of what natur' has done in this wilderness."

"I have my doubts whether you have such a thing as a real island in all this region."

"We'll show you hundreds of them; not exactly a thousand, perhaps, but so many that eye cannot see them all, nor tongue count them."

"I'll engage, when the truth comes to be known, they'll turn out to be nothing but peninsulas, or promontories, or continents, though these are matters, I daresay, of which you know little or nothing. But, islands or no islands, what is the object of the cruise, Master Pathfinder?"

"There can be no harm in giving you some idea of what we are going to do. Being so old a sailor, Master Cap, you've heard, no doubt, of such a port as Frontenac?"

"Who hasn't? I will not say I've ever been inside the harbor, but I've frequently been off the place."

"Then you are about to go upon ground with which you are acquainted. These great lakes, you must know, make a chain, the water passing out of one into the other, until it reaches Erie, which is a sheet off here to the westward, as large as Ontario itself. Well, out of Erie the water comes, until it reaches a low mountain like, over the edge of which it passes."

"I should like to know how the devil it can do that?"

"Why, easy enough, Master Cap," returned Pathfinder, laughing, "seeing that it has only to fall down hill. Had I said the

water went *up* the mountain, there would have been natur' ag'in
it; but we hold it no great matter for water to run down hill—
that is, *fresh* water."

"Ay, ay, but you speak of the water of a lake's coming down
the side of a mountain; it's in the teeth of reason, it reason has
any teeth."

"Well, well, we will not dispute the point; but what I've seen
I've seen. After getting into Ontario, all the water of *all* the lakes
passes down into the sea by a river; and in the narrow part of
the sheet, where it is neither river nor lake, lie the islands spoken
of. Now Frontenac is a post of the Frenchers above these same
islands; and, as they hold the garrison below, their stores and
ammunition are sent up the river to Frontenac, to be forwarded
along the shores of this and the other lakes, in order to enable
the enemy to play his devilries among the savages, and to take
Christian scalps."

"And will our presence prevent these horrible acts?" demanded
Mabel, with interest.

"It may or it may not, as Providence wills. Lundie, as they
call him, he who commands this garrison, sent a party down to
take a station among the islands, to cut off some of the French
boats; and this expedition of ours will be the second relief. As
yet they've not done much, though two bateaux loaded with
Indian goods have been taken; but a runner came in last week,
and brought such tidings that the Major is about to make a last
effort to circumvent the knaves. Jasper knows the way, and we
shall be in good hands, for the Sergeant is prudent, and of the
first quality at an ambushment; yes, he is both prudent and
alert."

"Is this all?" said Cap contemptuously; "by the preparations
and equipments, I had thought there was a forced trade in the
wind, and that an honest penny might be turned by taking an
adventure. I suppose there are no shares in your fresh-water
prize-money?"

"Anan?"

"I take it for granted the king gets all in these soldiering
parties, and ambushments, as you call them."

"I know nothing about that, Master Cap. I take my share of
the lead and powder if any falls into our hands, and say nothing

to the king about it. If any one fares better, it is not I; though it is time I did begin to think of a house and furniture and a home."

Although the Pathfinder did not dare to look at Mabel while he made this direct allusion to his change of life, he would have given the world to know whether she was listening, and what was the expression of her countenance. Mabel little suspected the nature of the allusion, however; and her countenance was perfectly unembarrassed as she turned her eyes towards the river, where the appearance of some movement on board the *Scud* began to be visible.

"Jasper is bringing the cutter out," observed the guide, whose look was drawn in the same direction by the fall of some heavy article on the deck. "The lad sees the signs of wind, no doubt, and wishes to be ready for it."

"Ay, now we shall have an opportunity of learning seamanship," returned Cap, with a sneer. "There is a nicety in getting a craft under her canvas that shows the thoroughbred mariner as much as anything else. It's like a soldier buttoning his coat, and one can see whether he begins at the top or the bottom."

"I will not say that Jasper is equal to your seafarers below," observed Pathfinder, across whose upright mind an unworthy feeling of envy or of jealousy never passed; "but he is a bold boy, and manages his cutter as skillfully as any man can desire, on this lake at least. You didn't find him backwards at the Oswego Falls, Master Cap, where fresh water contrives to tumble down hill with little difficulty."

Cap made no other answer than a dissatisfied ejaculation, and then a general silence followed, all on the bastion studying the movements of the cutter with the interest that was natural to their own future connection with the vessel. It was still a dead calm, the surface of the lake literally glittering with the last rays of the sun. The *Scud* had been warped up to a kedge that lay a hundred yards above the points of the outlet, where she had room to manœuvre in the river which then formed the harbor of Oswego. But the total want of air prevented any such attempt, and it was soon evident that the light vessel was to be taken through the passage under her sweeps. Not a sail was loosened; but as soon as the kedge was tripped, the heavy fall of the sweeps was heard, when the cutter, with her head up stream, began to sheer towards the centre of the current; on reaching which, the efforts of the men ceased, and she drifted towards the outlet. In the narrow pass itself her movement was rapid, and in less than five minutes the *Scud* was floating outside of the two low gravelly points which intercepted the waves of the lake. No anchor was let go, but the vessel continued to set off from the land, until her dark hull was seen resting on the glossy surface of the lake, full a quarter of a mile beyond the low bluff which formed the eastern extremity of what might be called the outer harbor or roadstead. Here the influence of the river current ceased, and she became, virtually, stationary.

"She seems very beautiful to me, uncle," said Mabel, whose gaze had not been averted from the cutter for a single moment while it had thus been changing its position; "I daresay you can find faults in her appearance, and in the way she is managed; but to my ignorance both are perfect."

"Ay, ay; she drops down with a current well enough, girl, and so would a chip. But when you come to niceties, an old tar like myself has no need of spectacles to find fault."

"Well, Master Cap," put in the guide, who seldom heard anything to Jasper's prejudice without manifesting a disposition to interfere, "I've heard old and experienced salt-water mariners confess that the *Scud* is as pretty a craft as floats. I know nothing of such matters myself; but one may have his own notions about a ship, even though they be wrong notions; and it would take more than one witness to persuade me Jasper does not keep his boat in good order."

"I do not say that the cutter is downright lubberly, Master Pathfinder; but she has faults, and great faults."

"And what are they, uncle? If he knew them, Jasper would be glad to mend them."

"What are they? Why, fifty; ay, for that matter a hundred. Very material and manifest faults."

"Do name them, sir, and Pathfinder will mention them to his friend."

"Name them! it is no easy matter to call off the stars, for the simple reason that they are so numerous. Name them, indeed! Why, my pretty niece, Miss Magnet, what do you think of that main-boom now? To my ignorant eyes, it is topped at least a foot too high; and then the pennant is foul; and—and—ay, d—

me, if there isn't a topsail gasket adrift; and it wouldn't surprise me at all if there should be a round turn in that hawser, if the kedge were to be let go this instant. Faults indeed! No seaman could look at her a moment without seeing that she is as full of faults as a servant who has asked for his discharge."

"This may be very true, uncle, though I much question if Jasper knows of them. I do not think he would suffer these things, Pathfinder, if they were once pointed out to him."

"Let Jasper manage his own cutter, Mabel. His gift lies that-a-way, and I'll answer for it, no one can teach him how to keep the Scud out of the hands of the Frontenackers or their devilish Mingo friends. Who cares for round turns in kedges, and for hawsers that are topped too high, Master Cap, so long as the craft sails well, and keeps clear of the Frenchers? I will trust Jasper against all the seafarers of the coast, up here on the lakes; but I do not say he has any gift for the ocean, for there he has never been tried."

Cap smiled condescendingly, but he did not think it necessary to push his criticisms any further just at that moment. By this time the cutter had begun to drift at the mercy of the currents of the lake, her head turning in all directions, though slowly, and not in a way to attract particular attention. Just at this moment the jib was loosened and hoisted, and presently the canvas swelled towards the land, though no evidences of air were yet to be seen on the surface of the water. Slight, however, as was the impulsion, the light hull yielded; and in another minute the Scud was seen standing across the current of the river with a movement so easy and moderate as to be scarcely perceptible. When out of the stream, she struck an eddy, and shot up towards the land, under the eminence where the fort stood, when Jasper dropped his kedge.

"Not lubberly done," muttered Cap in a sort of soliloquy—"not over lubberly, though he should have put his helm a-starboard instead of a-port; for a vessel ought always to come-to with her head off shore, whether she is a league from the land or only a cable's length, since it has a careful look, and looks are something in this world."

"Jasper is a handy lad," suddenly observed Sergeant Dunham at his brother-in-law's elbow; "and we place great reliance on his skill in our expeditions. But come, one and all, we have but half an hour more of daylight to embark in, and the boats will be ready for us by the time we are ready for them."

On this intimation the whole party separated, each to find those trifles which had not been shipped already. A few taps of the drum gave the necessary signal to the soldiers, and in a minute all were in motion.

CHAPTER XIII

The goblin now the fool alarms,
Hags meet to mumble o'er their charms,
The night-mare rides the dreaming ass,
And fairies trip it on the grass.   COTTON

THE embarkation of so small a party was a matter of no great delay or embarrassment. The whole force confided to the care of Sergeant Dunham consisted of but ten privates and two non-commissioned officers, though it was soon positively known that Mr. Muir was to accompany the expedition. The Quartermaster, however, went as a volunteer, while some duty connected with his own department, as had been arranged between him and his commander, was the avowed object. To these must be added the Pathfinder and Cap, with Jasper and his subordinates, one of whom was a boy. The party, consequently, consisted of less than twenty men, and a lad of fourteen. Mabel and the wife of a common soldier were the only females.

Sergeant Dunham carried off his command in a large bateau, and then returned for his final orders, and to see that his brother-in-law and daughter were properly attended to. Having pointed out to Cap the boat that he and Mabel were to use, he ascended the hill to seek his last interview with Lundie.

It was nearly dark when Mabel found herself in the boat that was to carry her off to the cutter. So very smooth was the surface of the lake, that it was not found necessary to bring the bateaux into the river to receive their freights; but the beach outside being totally without surf, and the water as tranquil as that of a pond, everybody embarked there. When the boat left the land, Mabel would not have known that she was afloat on so broad a sheet of water by any movement which is usual to such circumstances. The oars had barely time to give a dozen strokes, when the boat lay at the cutter's side.

Jasper was in readiness to receive his passengers; and, as the deck of the *Scud* was but two or three feet above the water, no difficulty was experienced in getting on board of her. As soon as this was effected, the young man pointed out to Mabel and her companion the accommodations prepared for their reception. The little vessel contained four apartments below, all between decks having been expressly constructed with a view to the transportation of officers and men, with their wives and families. First in rank was what was called the after-cabin, a small apartment that contained four berths, and which enjoyed the advantage of possessing small windows, for the admission of air and light. This was uniformly devoted to females whenever any were on board; and as Mabel and her companion were alone, they had ample accommodation. The main cabin was larger, and lighted from above. It was now appropriated to the Quartermaster, the Sergeant, Cap, and Jasper; the Pathfinder roaming through any part of the cutter he pleased, the female apartment excepted. The corporals and common soldiers occupied the space beneath the main hatch, which had a deck for such a purpose, while the crew were berthed, as usual, in the forecastle. Although the cutter did not measure quite fifty tons, the draft of officers and men was so light, that there was ample room for all on board, there being space enough to accommodate treble the number, if necessary.

As soon as Mabel had taken possession of her own really comfortable cabin, in doing which she could not abstain from indulging in the pleasant reflection that some of Jasper's favor had been especially manifested in her behalf, she went on deck again. Here all was momentarily in motion; the men were roving to and fro, in quest of their knapsacks and other effects; but method and habit soon reduced things to order, when the stillness on board became even imposing, for it was connected with the idea of future adventure and ominous preparation.

Darkness was now beginning to render objects on shore indistinct, the whole of the land forming one shapeless black outline of even forest summits, to be distinguished from the impending heavens only by the greater light of the sky. The stars, however, soon began to appear in the latter, one after another, in their usual mild, placid lustre, bringing with them that sense of quiet which ordinarily accompanies night. There was something soothing, as well as exciting, in such a scene; and Mabel, who was seated on the quarter-deck, sensibly felt both influences. The Pathfinder was standing near her, leaning, as usual, on his long rifle, and she fancied that, through the growing darkness of the hour, she could trace even stronger lines of thought than usual in his rugged countenance.

"To you, Pathfinder, expeditions like this can be no great novelty," said she; "though I am surprised to find how silent and thoughtful the men appear to be."

"We learn this by making war ag'in Indians. Your militia are great talkers and little doers in general; but the soldier who has often met the Mingos learns to know the value of a prudent tongue. A silent army, in the woods, is doubly strong; and a noisy one, doubly weak. If tongues made soldiers, the women of a camp would generally carry the day."

"But we are neither an army, nor in the woods. There can be no danger of Mingos in the *Scud*."

"No one is safe from a Mingo, who does not understand his very natur'; and even then he must act up to his own knowledge, and that closely. Ask Jasper how he got command of this very cutter."

"And how *did* he get command?" inquired Mabel, with an earnestness and interest that quite delighted her simple-minded and true-hearted companion, who was never better pleased than when he had an opportunity of saying aught in favor of a friend. "It is honorable to him that he has reached this station while yet so young."

"That is it; but he deserved it all, and more. A frigate wouldn't have been too much to pay for so much spirit and coolness, had there been such a thing on Ontario, as there is not, hows'ever, or likely to be."

"But Jasper—you have not yet told me how he got the command of the schooner."

"It is a long story, Mabel, and one your father, the Sergeant, can tell much better than I; for he was present, while I was off on a distant scouting. Jasper is not good at a story, I will own that; I have heard him questioned about this affair, and he never made a good tale of it, although everybody knows it was a good thing. The *Scud* had near fallen into the hands of the French and the Mingos, when Jasper saved her, in a way which none but a quick-witted mind and a bold heart would have attempted. The Sergeant will tell the tale better than I can, and I wish you to question him some day, when nothing better offers."

Mabel determined to ask her father to repeat the incidents of the affair that very night; for it struck her young fancy that nothing better could well offer than to listen to the praises of one who was a bad historian of his own exploits.

"Will the *Scud* remain with us when we reach the island?" she asked, after a little hesitation about the propriety of the question; "or shall we be left to ourselves?"

"That's as may be: Jasper does not often keep the cutter idle when anything is to be done; and we may expect activity on his part. My gifts, however, run so little towards the water and vessels generally, unless it be among rapids and falls and in canoes, that I pretend to know nothing about it. We shall have all right under Jasper, I make no doubt, who can find a trail on Ontario as well as a Delaware can find one on the land."

"And our own Delaware, Pathfinder—the Big Serpent—why is he not with us to-night?"

"Your question would have been more natural had you said, Why are *you* here, Pathfinder? The Sarpent is in his place, while I am not in mine. He is out, with two or three more, scouting the lake shores, and will join us down among the islands, with the tidings he may gather. The Sergeant is too good a soldier to forget his rear while he is facing the enemy in front. It's a thousand pities, Mabel, your father wasn't born a general, as some of the English are who come among us; for I feel sartain he wouldn't leave a Frencher in the Canadas a week, could he have his own way with them."

"Shall we have enemies to face in front?" asked Mabel, smiling, and for the first time feeling a slight apprehension about the dangers of the expedition. "Are we likely to have an engagement?"

"If we have, Mabel, there will be men enough ready and willing to stand between you and harm. But you are a soldier's daughter, and, we all know, have the spirit of one. Don't let the fear of a battle keep your pretty eyes from sleeping."

"I do feel braver out here in the woods, Pathfinder, than I ever felt before amid the weaknesses of the towns, although I have always tried to remember what I owe to my dear father."

"Ay, your mother was so before you. 'You will find Mabel, like her mother, no screamer, or a faint-hearted girl, to trouble a man in his need; but one who would encourage her mate, and help to keep his heart up when sorest prest by danger,' said the Sergeant to me, before I ever laid eyes on that sweet countenance of yours—he did!"

"And why should my father have told you this, Pathfinder?" the girl demanded a little earnestly. "Perhaps he fancied you would think the better of me if you did not believe me a silly coward, as so many of my sex love to make themselves appear."

Deception, unless it were at the expense of his enemies in the field—nay, concealment of even a thought—was so little in accordance with the Pathfinder's very nature, that he was not a little embarrassed by this simple question. In such a strait he involuntarily took refuge in a middle course, not revealing that which he fancied ought not to be told, nor yet absolutely concealing it.

"You must know, Mabel," said he, "that the Sergeant and I are old friends, and have stood side by side—or, if not actually side by side, I a little in advance, as became a scout, and your father with his own men, as better suited a soldier of the king—on many a hard fi't and bloody day. It's the way of us skirmishers to think little of the fight when the rifle has done cracking; and at night, around our fires, or on our marches, we talk of the things we love, just as you young women convarse about your fancies and opinions when you get together to laugh over your idees. Now it was natural that the Sergeant, having such a daughter as you, should love her better than anything else, and that he should talk of her oftener than of anything else—while I, having neither daughter, nor sister, nor mother, nor kith, nor kin, nor anything but the Delawares to love, I naturally chimed in, as it were, and got to love you, Mabel, before I ever saw you —yes, I did—just by talking about you so much."

"And now you *have* seen me," returned the smiling girl, whose unmoved and natural manner proved how little she was thinking of anything more than parental or fraternal regard, "you are beginning to see the folly of forming friendships for people before you know anything about them, except by hearsay."

"It wasn't friendship—it isn't friendship, Mabel, that I feel for you. I am the friend of the Delawares, and have been so from boyhood; but my feelings for them, or for the best of them, are not the same as those I got from the Sergeant for you; and, especially, now that I begin to know you better. I'm sometimes afeared it isn't wholesome for one who is much occupied in a very manly calling, like that of a guide or scout, or a soldier even, to form friendships for women—young women in particular—as they seem to me to lessen the love of enterprise, and to turn the feelings away from their gifts and natural occupations."

"You surely do not mean, Pathfinder, that a friendship for a girl like me would make you less bold, and more unwilling to meet the French than you were before?"

"Not so, not so. With you in danger, for instance, I fear I might become foolhardy; but before we became so intimate, as I may say, I loved to think of my scoutings, and of my marches, and outlyings, and fights, and other adventures: but now my mind cares less about them; I think more of the barracks, and of evenings passed in discourse, of feelings in which there are no wranglings and bloodshed, and of young women, and of their laughs and their cheerful, soft voices, their pleasant looks and their winnings ways. I sometimes tell the Sergeant that he and his daughter will be the spoiling of one of the best and most experienced scouts on the lines."

"Not they, Pathfinder; they will try to make that which is already so excellent, perfect. You do not know us, if you think that either wishes to see you in the least changed. Remain as at present, the same honest, upright, conscientious, fearless, intelligent, trustworthy guide that you are, and neither my dear father nor myself can ever think of you differently from what we now do."

It was too dark for Mabel to note the workings of the countenance of her listener; but her own sweet face was turned towards him, as she spoke with an energy equal to her frankness, in a way to show how little embarrassed were her thoughts, and how sincere were her words. Her countenance was a little flushed, it is true; but it was with earnestness and truth of feel-ing, though no nerve thrilled, no limb trembled, no pulsation quickened. In short, her manner and appearance were those of a sincere-minded and frank girl, making such a declaration of good-will and regard for one of the other sex as she felt that his services and good qualities merited, without any of the emotion that invariably accompanies the consciousness of an inclination which might lead to softer disclosures.

The Pathfinder was too unpractised, however, to enter into distinctions of this kind, and his humble nature was encouraged by the directness and strength of the words he had just heard. Unwilling, if not unable, to say any more, he walked away, and stood leaning on his rifle and looking up at the stars for full ten minutes in profound silence.

In the meanwhile the interview on the bastion, to which we have already alluded, took place between Lundie and the Ser-geant.

"Have the men's knapsacks been examined?" demanded Major Duncan, after he had cast his eye at a written report, handed to him by the Sergeant, but which it was too dark to read.

"All, your honor; and all are right."

"The ammunition—arms?"

"All in order, Major Duncan, and fit for any service."

"You have the men named in my own draft, Dunham?"

"Without an exception, sir. Better men could not be found in the regiment."

"You have need of the best of our men, Sergeant. This ex-periment has now been tried three times; always under one of the ensigns, who have flattered me with success, but have as often failed. After so much preparation and expense, I do not like to abandon the project entirely; but this will be the last effort; and the result will mainly depend on you and on the Pathfinder."

"You may count on us both, Major Duncan. The duty you have given us is not above our habits and experience, and I think it will be well done. I know that the Pathfinder will not be wanting."

"On that, indeed, it will be safe to rely. He is a most extraordinary man, Dunham—one who long puzzled me; but who, now that I understand him, commands as much of my respect as any general in his majesty's service."

"I was in hopes, sir, that you would come to look at the proposed marriage with Mabel as a thing I ought to wish and forward."

"As for that, Sergeant, time will show," returned Lundie, smiling; though here, too, the obscurity concealed the nicer shades of expression; "one woman is sometimes more difficult to manage than a whole regiment of men. By the way, you know that your would-be son-in-law, the Quartermaster, will be of the party; and I trust you will at least give him an equal chance in the trial for your daughter's smiles."

"If respect for his rank, sir, did not cause me to do this, your honor's wish would be sufficient."

"I thank you, Sergeant. We have served much together, and ought to value each other in our several stations. Understand me, however, I ask no more for Davy Muir than a clear field and no favor. In love, as in war, each man must gain his own victories. Are you certain that the rations have been properly calculated?"

"I'll answer for it, Major Duncan; but if they were not, we cannot suffer with two such hunters as Pathfinder and the Serpent in company."

"That will never do, Dunham," interrupted Lundie sharply; "and it comes of your American birth and American training. No thorough soldier ever relies on anything but his commissary for supplies; and I beg that no part of my regiment may be the first to set an example to the contrary."

"You have only to command, Major Duncan, to be obeyed; and yet, if I might presume, sir——"

"Speak freely, Sergeant; you are talking with a friend."

"I was merely about to say that I find even the Scotch soldiers like venison and birds quite as well as pork, when they are difficult to be had."

"That may be very true; but likes and dislikes have nothing to do with system. An army can rely on nothing but its commissaries. The irregularity of the provincials has played the devil with the king's service too often to be winked at any longer."

"General Braddock, your honor, might have been advised by Colonel Washington."

"Out upon your Washington! You're all provincials together, man, and uphold each other as if you were of a sworn confederacy."

"I believe his majesty has no more loyal subjects than the Americans, your honor."

"In that, Dunham, I'm thinking you're right; and I have been a little too warm, perhaps. I do not consider *you* a provincial, however, Sergeant; for, though born in America, a better soldier never shouldered a musket."

"And Colonel Washington, your honor?"

"Well!—and Colonel Washington may be a useful subject too. He is the American prodigy; and I suppose I may as well give him all the credit you ask. You have no doubt of the skill of this Jasper Eau-douce?"

"The boy has been tried, sir, and found equal to all that can be required of him."

"He has a French name, and has passed much of his boyhood in the French colonies; has he French blood in his veins, Sergeant?"

"Not a drop, your honor. Jasper's father was an old comrade of my own, and his mother came of an honest and loyal family in this very province."

"How came he then so much among the French, and whence his name? He speaks the language of the Canadas, too, I find."

"That is easily explained, Major Duncan. The boy was left under the care of one of our mariners in the old war, and he took to the water like a duck. Your honor knows that we have no ports on Ontario that can be named as such, and he naturally passed most of his time on the other side of the lake, where the French have had a few vessels these fifty years. He learned to speak their language, as a matter of course, and got his name from the Indians and Canadians, who are fond of calling men by their qualities, as it might be."

"A French master is but a poor instructor for a British sailor, notwithstanding."

"I beg your pardon, sir: Jasper Eau-douce was brought up under a real English seaman, one that had sailed under the king's pennant, and may be called a thorough-bred; that is to say, a subject born in the colonies, but none the worse at his trade, I hope, Major Duncan, for that."

"Perhaps not, Sergeant, perhaps not; nor any better. This Jasper behaved well, too, when I gave him the command of the *Scud;* no lad could have conducted himself more loyally or better."

"Or more bravely, Major Duncan. I am sorry to see, sir, that you have doubts as to the fidelity of Jasper."

"It is the duty of the soldier who is entrusted with the care of a distant and important post like this, Dunham, never to relax in his vigilance. We have two of the most artful enemies that the world has ever produced, in their several ways, to contend with—the Indians and the French—and nothing should be overlooked that can lead to injury."

"I hope your honor considers me fit to be entrusted with any particular reason that may exist for doubting Jasper, since you have seen fit to entrust me with this command."

"It is not that I doubt you, Dunham, that I hesitate to reveal all I may happen to know; but from a strong reluctance to circulate an evil report concerning one of whom I have hitherto thought well. You must think well of the Pathfinder, or you would not wish to give him your daughter?"

"For the Pathfinder's honesty I will answer with my life, sir," returned the Sergeant firmly, and not without a dignity of manner that struck his superior. "Such a man doesn't know how to be false."

"I believe you are right, Dunham; and yet this last information has unsettled all my old opinions. I have received an anonymous communication, Sergeant, advising me to be on my guard against Jasper Western, or Jasper Eau-douce, as he is called, who, it alleges, has been bought by the enemy, and giving me reason to expect that further and more precise information will soon be sent."

"Letters without signatures to them, sir, are scarcely to be regarded in war."

"Or in peace, Dunham. No one can entertain a lower opinion of the writer of an anonymous letter, in ordinary matters, than myself; the very act denotes cowardice, meanness, and baseness; and it usually is a token of falsehood, as well as of other vices. But in matters of war it is not exactly the same thing. Besides, several suspicious circumstances have been pointed out to me."

"Such as is fit for an orderly to hear, your honor?"

"Certainly, one in whom I confide as much as in yourself, Dunham. It is said, for instance, that your daughter and her party were permitted to escape the Iroquois, when they came in, merely to give Jasper credit with me. I am told that the gentry at Frontenac will care more for the capture of the *Scud*, with Sergeant Dunham and a party of men, together with the defeat of our favorite plan, than for the capture of a girl and the scalp of her uncle."

"I understand the hint, sir, but I do not give it credit. Jasper can hardly be true, and Pathfinder false; and, as for the last, I would as soon distrust your honor as distrust him."

"It would seem so, Sergeant; it would indeed seem so. But Jasper is not the Pathfinder, after all; and I will own, Dunham, I should put more faith in the lad if he didn't speak French."

"It's no recommendation in my eyes, I assure your honor; but the boy learned it by compulsion, as it were, and ought not to be condemned too hastily for the circumstance, by your honor's leave."

"It's a d——d lingo, and never did any one good—at least no British subject; for I suppose the French themselves must talk together in some language or other. I should have much more faith in this Jasper, did he know nothing of their language. This letter has made me uneasy; and, were there another to whom I could trust the cutter, I would devise some means to detain him here. I have spoken to you already of a brother-in-law, who goes with you, Sergeant, and who is a sailor?"

"A real seafaring man, your honor, and somewhat prejudiced against fresh water. I doubt if he could be induced to risk his character on a lake, and I'm certain he never could find the station."

"The last is probably true, and then, the man cannot know enough of this treacherous lake to be fit for the employment. You will have to be doubly vigilant, Dunham. I give you full powers; and should you detect this Jasper in any treachery, make him a sacrifice at once to offended justice."

"Being in the service of the crown, your honor, he is amenable to martial law."

"Very true; then iron him, from his head to his heels, and

send him up here in his own cutter. That brother-in-law of yours must be able to find the way back, after he has once travelled the road."

"I make no doubt, Major Duncan, we shall be able to do all that will be necessary should Jasper turn out as you seem to anticipate; though I think I would risk my life on his truth."

"I like your confidence—it speaks well for the fellow; but that infernal letter! there is such an air of truth about it; nay, there is so much truth in it, touching other matters."

"I think your honor said it wanted the name at the bottom; a great omission for an honest man to make."

"Quite right, Dunham, and no one but a rascal, and a cowardly rascal in the bargain, would write an anonymous letter on private affairs. It *is* different, however, in war; despatches are feigned, and artifice is generally allowed to be justifiable."

"Military manly artifices, sir, if you will; such as ambushes, surprises, feints, false attacks, and even spies; but I never heard of a true soldier who could wish to undermine the character of an honest young man by such means as these."

"I have met with many strange events, and some stranger people, in the course of my experience. But fare you well, Sergeant; I must detain you no longer. You are now on your guard, and I recommend to you untiring vigilance. I think Muir means shortly to retire; and, should you fully succeed in this enterprise, my influence will not be wanting in endeavoring to put you in the vacancy, to which you have many claims."

"I humbly thank your honor," coolly returned the Sergeant, who had been encouraged in this manner any time for the twenty preceding years, "and hope I shall never disgrace my station, whatever it may be. I am what nature and Providence have made me, and hope I'm satisfied."

"You have not forgotten the howitzer?"

"Jasper took it on board this morning, sir."

"Be wary, and do not trust that man unnecessarily. Make a confidant of Pathfinder at once; he may be of service in detecting any villainy that may be stirring. His simple honesty will favor his observation by concealing it. He *must* be true."

"For him, sir, my own head shall answer, or even my rank in the regiment. I have seen him too often tried to doubt him."

"Of all wretched sensations, Dunham, distrust, where one is

compelled to confide, is the most painful. You have bethought you of the spare flints?"

"A sergeant is a safe commander for all such details, your honor."

"Well, then, give me your hand, Dunham. God bless you! and may you be successful! Muir means to retire—by the way, let the man have an equal chance with your daughter, for it may facilitate future operations about the promotion. One would retire more cheerfully with such a companion as Mabel, than in cheerless widowhood, and with nothing but oneself to love—and such a self, too, as Davy's!"

"I hope, sir, my child will make a prudent choice, and I think her mind is already pretty much made up in favor of Pathfinder. Still she shall have fair play, though disobedience is the next crime to mutiny."

"Have all the ammunition carefully examined and dried as soon as you arrive; the damp of the lake may affect it. And now, once more, farewell, Sergeant. Beware of that Jasper, and consult with Muir in any difficulty. I shall expect you to return, triumphant, this day month."

"God bless your honor! If anything should happen to me, I trust to you, Major Duncan, to care for an old soldier's character."

"Rely on me, Dunham—you will rely on a friend. Be vigilant: remember you will be in the very jaws of the lion;—phsaw! of no lion neither; but of treacherous tigers: in their very jaws, and beyond support. Have the flints counted and examined in the morning—and—farewell, Dunham, farewell!"

The Sergeant took the extended hand of his superior with proper respect, and they finally parted; Lundie hastening into his own movable abode, while the other left the fort, descended to the beach, and got into a boat.

It is not to be supposed that Sergeant Dunham, after he had parted from his commanding officer, was likely to forget the injunctions he had received. He thought highly of Jasper in general; but distrust had been insinuated between his former confidence and the obligations of duty; and, as he now felt that everything depended on his own vigilance, by the time the boat reached the side of the *Scud* he was in a proper humor to let no suspicious circumstance go unheeded, or any unusual movement in the young sailor pass without its comment. As a matter of course, he viewed things in the light suited to his peculiar mood; and his precautions, as well as his distrust, partook of the habits, opinions, and education of the man.

The *Scud's* kedge was lifted as soon as the boat with the Sergeant, who was the last person expected, was seen to quit the shore, and the head of the cutter was cast to the eastward by means of the sweeps. A few vigorous strokes of the latter, in which the soldiers aided, now sent the light craft into the line of the current that flowed from the river, when she was suffered to drift into the offing again. As yet there was no wind, the light and almost imperceptible air from the lake, that had existed previously to the setting of the sun, having entirely failed.

All this time an unusual quiet prevailed in the cutter. It appeared as if those on board of her felt that they were entering upon an uncertain enterprise, in the obscurity of night; and that their duty, the hour, and the manner of their departure lent a solemnity to their movements. Discipline also came in aid of these feelings. Most were silent; and those who did speak spoke seldom and in low voices. In this manner the cutter set slowly out into the lake, until she had got as far as the river current would carry her, when she became stationary, waiting for the usual land-breeze. An interval of half an hour followed, during the whole of which time the *Scud* lay as motionless as a log, floating on the water. While the little changes just mentioned were occurring in the situation of the vessel, notwithstanding the general quiet that prevailed, all conversation had not been repressed; for Sergeant Dunham, having first ascertained that both his daughter and her female companion were on the quarter-deck, led the Pathfinder to the after-cabin, where, closing the door with great caution, and otherwise making certain that he was beyond the reach of eavesdroppers, he commenced as follows:—

"It is now many years, my friend, since you began to experience the hardships and dangers of the woods in my company."

"It is, Sergeant; yes, it is. I sometimes fear I am too old for Mabel. who was not born until you and I had fought the Frenchers as comrades."

"No fear on that account, Pathfinder. I was near your age before I prevailed on the mind of her mother; and Mabel is a steady, thoughtful girl, one that will regard character more than anything else. A lad like Jasper Eau-douce, for instance, will have no chance with her, though he is both young and comely."

"Does Jasper think of marrying?" inquired the guide, simply but earnestly.

"I should hope not—at least, not until he has satisfied every one of his fitness to possess a wife."

"Jasper is a gallant boy, and one of great gifts in his way; he may claim a wife as well as another."

"To be frank with you, Pathfinder, I brought you here to talk about this very youngster. Major Duncan has received some information which has led him to suspect that Eau-douce is false, and in the pay of the enemy; I wish to hear your opinion on the subject."

"Anan?"

"I say, the Major suspects Jasper of being a traitor—a French spy—or, what is worse, of being bought to betray us. He has received a letter to this effect, and has been charging me to keep an eye on the boy's movements; for he fears we shall meet with enemies when we least suspect it, and by his means."

"Duncan of Lundie has told you this, Sergeant Dunham?"

"He has indeed, Pathfinder; and, though I have been loath to believe anything to the injury of Jasper, I have a feeling which tells me I ought to distrust him. Do you believe in presentiments, my friend?"

"In what, Sergeant?"

"Presentiments—a sort of secret foreknowledge of events that are about to happen. The Scotch of our regiment are great sticklers for such things; and my opinion of Jasper is changing so fast, that I begin to fear there must be some truth in their doctrines."

"But you've been talking with Duncan of Lundie concerning Jasper, and his words have raised misgivings."

"Not it, not so in the least; for, while conversing with the Major, my feelings were altogether the other way; and I endeavored to convince him all I could that he did the boy injustice. But there is no use in holding out against a presentiment, I find; and I fear there is something in the suspicion after all."

"I know nothing of presentiments, Sergeant; but I have

known Jasper Eau-douce since he was a boy, and I have as much faith in his honesty as I have in my own, or that of the Sarpent himself."

"But the Serpent, Pathfinder, has his tricks and ambushes in war as well as another."

"Ay, them are his nat'ral gifts, and are such as belong to his people. Neither red-skin nor pale-face can deny natur'; but Chingachgook is not a man to feel a presentiment against."

"That I believe; nor should I have thought ill of Jasper this very morning. It seems to me, Pathfinder, since I've taken up this presentiment, that the lad does not bustle about his deck naturally, as he used to do; but that he is silent and moody and thoughtful, like a man who has a load on his conscience."

"Jasper is never noisy; and he tells me noisy ships are generally ill-worked ships. Master Cap agrees in this too. No, no; I will believe naught against Jasper until I see it. Send for your brother, Sergeant, and let us question him in this matter; for to sleep with distrust of one's friend in the heart is like sleeping with lead there. I have no faith in your presentiments."

The Sergeant, although he scarcely knew himself with what object, complied, and Cap was summoned to join in the consultation. As Pathfinder was more collected than his companion, and felt so strong a conviction of the good faith of the party accused, he assumed the office of spokesman.

"We have asked you to come down, Master Cap," he commenced, "in order to inquire if you have remarked anything out of the common way in the movements of Eau-douce this evening."

"His movements are common enough, I daresay, for fresh water, Master Pathfinder, though we should think most of his proceedings irregular down on the coast."

"Yes, yes; we know you will never agree with the lad about the manner the cutter ought to be managed; but it is on another point we wish your opinion."

The Pathfinder then explained to Cap the nature of the suspicions which the Sergeant entertained, and the reasons why they had been excited, so far as the latter had been communicated by Major Duncan.

"The youngster talks French, does he?" said Cap.

"They say he speaks it better than common," returned the Sergeant gravely. "Pathfinder knows this to be true."

"I'll not gainsay it," answered the guide; "at least, they tell me such is the fact. But this would prove nothing ag'in a Mississagua, and, least of all, ag'in one like Jasper. I speak the Mingo dialect myself, having learnt it while a prisoner among the reptiles; but who will say I am their friend? Not that I am an enemy, either, according to Indian notions; though I am their enemy, I will admit, agreeable to Christianity."

"Ay, Pathfinder; but Jasper did not get his French as a prisoner: he took it in boyhood, when the mind is easily impressed, and gets its permanent notions; when nature has a presentiment, as it were, which way the character is likely to incline."

"A very just remark," added Cap, "for that is the time of life when we all learn the catechism, and other moral improvements. The Sergeant's observation shows that he understands human nature, and I agree with him perfectly; it *is* a damnable thing for a youngster, up here, on this bit of fresh water, to talk French. If it were down on the Atlantic, now, where a seafaring man has occasion sometimes to converse with a pilot, or a linguister, in that language, I should not think so much of it—though we always look with suspicion, even there, at a shipmate who knows too much of the tongue; but up here, on Ontario, I hold it to be a most suspicious circumstance."

"But Jasper must talk in French to the people on the other shore," said Pathfinder, "or hold his tongue, as there are none but French to speak to."

"You don't mean to tell me, Pathfinder, that France lies hereaway, on the opposite coast?" cried Cap, jerking a thumb over his shoulder in the direction of the Canadas; "that one side of this bit of fresh water is York, and the other France?"

"I mean to tell you this is York, and that is Upper Canada; and that English and Dutch and Indian are spoken in the first, and French and Indian in the last. Even the Mingos have got many of the French words in their dialect, and it is no improvement, neither."

"Very true: and what sort of people are the Mingos, my friend?" inquired the Sergeant, touching the other on his shoulder, by way of enforcing a remark, the inherent truth of which sensibly increased its value in the eyes of the speaker: "no one knows them better than yourself, and I ask you what sort of a tribe are they?"

"Jasper is no Mingo, Sergeant."

"He speaks French, and he might as well be, in that particular. Brother Cap, can you recollect no movement of this unfortunate young man, in the way of his calling, that would seem to denote treachery?"

"Not distinctly, Sergeant, though he has gone to work wrong-end foremost half his time. It is true that one of his hands coiled a rope against the sun, and he called it *querling* a rope, too, when I asked him what he was about; but I am not certain that anything was meant by it; though, I daresay, the French coil half their running rigging the wrong way, and may call it 'querling it down,' too, for that matter. Then Jasper himself belayed the end of the jib-halyards to a stretcher in the rigging, instead of bringing in to the mast, where they belong, at least among British sailors."

"I daresay Jasper may have got some Canada notions about working his craft, from being so much on the other side," Pathfinder interposed; "but catching an idee, or a word, isn't treachery and bad faith. I sometimes get an idee from the Mingos themselves; but my heart has always been with the Delawares. No, no, Jasper is true; and the king might trust him with his crown, just as he would trust his eldest son, who, as he is to wear it one day, ought to be the last man to wish to steal it."

"Fine talking, fine talking!" said Cap; "all fine talking, Master Pathfinder, but d—d little logic. In the first place, the king's majesty cannot lend his crown, it being contrary to the laws of the realm, which require him to wear it at all times, in order that his sacred person may be known, just as the silver oar is necessary to a sheriff's officer afloat. In the next place, it's high treason, by law, for the eldest son of his majesty ever to covet the crown, or to have a child, except in lawful wedlock, as either would derange the succession. Thus you see, friend Pathfinder, that in order to reason truly, one must get under way, as it might be, on the right tack. Law is reason, and reason is philosophy, and philosophy is a steady drag; whence it follows that crowns are regulated by law, reason, and philosophy."

"I know little of all this, Master Cap; but nothing short of seeing and feeling will make me think Jasper Western a traitor."

"There you are wrong again, Pathfinder; for there is a way of proving a thing much more conclusively than by either seeing or feeling, or by both together; and that is by a circumstance."

"It may be so in the settlements; but it is not so here on the lines."

"It is so in nature, which is monarch over all. There was a circumstance, just after we came on board this evening, that is extremely suspicious, and which may be set down at once as a makeweight against this lad. Jasper bent on the king's ensign with his own hands; and, while he pretended to be looking at Mabel and the soldier's wife, giving directions about showing them below here, and all that, he got the flag union down!"

"That might have been accident," returned the Sergeant, "for such a thing has happened to myself; besides, the halyards lead to a pulley, and the flag would have come right, or not, according to the manner in which the lad hoisted it."

"A pulley!" exclaimed Cap, with strong disgust; "I wish, Sergeant Dunham, I could prevail on you to use proper terms. An ensign-halyard-block is no more a pulley than your halbert is a boarding-pike. It is true that by hoisting on one part, another part would go uppermost; but I look upon that affair of the ensign, now you have mentioned your suspicions, as a circumstance, and shall bear it in mind. I trust supper is not to be overlooked, however, even if we have a hold full of traitors."

"It will be duly attended to, brother Cap; but I shall count on you for aid in managing the *Scud*, should anything occur to induce me to arrest Jasper."

"I'll not fail you, Sergeant; and in such an event you'll probably learn what this cutter can really perform; for, as yet, I fancy it is pretty much matter of guesswork."

"Well, for my part," said Pathfinder, drawing a heavy sigh, "I shall cling to the hope of Jasper's innocence, and recommend plain dealing, by asking the lad himself, without further delay, whether he is or is not a traitor. I'll put Jasper Western against all the presentiments and circumstances in the colony."

"That will never do," rejoined the Sergeant. "The responsibility of this affair rests with me, and I request and enjoin that nothing be said to any one without my knowledge. We will all keep watchful eyes about us, and take proper note of circumstances."

"Ay, ay! circumstances are the things after all," returned Cap. "One circumstance is worth fifty facts. That I know to be the law of the realm. Many a man has been hanged on circumstances."

The conversation now ceased, and, after a short delay, the whole party returned to the deck, each individual disposed to view the conduct of the suspected Jasper in the manner most suited to his own habits and character.

CHAPTER XIV

Even such a man, so faint, so spiritless,
So dull, so dead in look, so woe-begone,
Drew Priam's curtain in the dead of night,
And would have told him, half his Troy was burned.

SHAKESPEARE

ALL this time matters were elsewhere passing in their usual train. Jasper, like the weather and his vessel, seemed to be waiting for the land-breeze; while the soldiers, accustomed to early rising, had, to a man, sought their pallets in the main hold. None remained on deck but the people of the cutter, Mr. Muir, and the two females. The Quartermaster was endeavoring to render himself agreeable to Mabel, while our heroine herself, little affected by his assiduities, which she ascribed partly to the habitual gallantry of a soldier, and partly, perhaps, to her own pretty face, was enjoying the peculiarities of a scene and situation which, to her, were full of the charms of novelty.

The sails had been hoisted, but as yet not a breath of air was in motion; and so still and placid was the lake, that not the smallest motion was perceptible in the cutter. She had drifted in the river-current to a distance a little exceeding a quarter of a mile from the land, and there she lay, beautiful in her symmetry and form, but like a fixture. Young Jasper was on the quarter-deck, near enough to hear occasionally the conversation which passed; but too diffident of his own claim, and too intent on his duties, to attempt to mingle in it. The fine blue eyes of Mabel followed his motions in curious expectation, and more than once the Quartermaster had to repeat his compliments before she heard them, so intent was she on the little occurrences of the vessel, and, we might add, so indifferent to the eloquence of her companion. At length, even Mr. Muir became silent, and there was a deep stillness on the water. Presently an oar-blade fell in a boat beneath the fort, and the sound reached the cutter as distinctly as if it had been produced on her deck. Then came a murmur, like a sigh of the night, a fluttering of the canvas, the creaking of the boom, and the flap of the jib. These well-known sounds were followed by a slight heel in the cutter, and by the bellying of all the sails.

"Here's the wind, Anderson," called out Jasper to the oldest of his sailors; "take the helm."

This brief order was obeyed; the helm was put up, and the cutter's bows fell off, and in a few minutes the water was heard murmuring under her head, as the *Scud* glanced through the lake at the rate of five miles in the hour. All this passed in profound silence, when Jasper again gave the order to "ease off the sheets a little and keep her along the land."

It was at this instant that the party from the after-cabin reappeared on the quarter-deck.

"You've no inclination, Jasper lad, to trust yourself too near our neighbors the French," observed Muir, who took that occasion to recommence the discourse. "Well, well, your prudence will never be questioned by me, for I like the Canadas as little as you can possibly like them yourself."

"I hug this shore, Mr. Muir, on account of the wind. The land-breeze is always freshest close in, provided you are not so near as to make a lee of the trees. We have Mexico Bay to cross; and that, on the present course, will give us quite offing enough."

"I'm right glad it's not the Bay of Mexico," put in Cap, "which is a part of the world I would rather not visit in one of your inland craft. Does your cutter bear a weather helm, master Eau-douce?"

"She is easy on her rudder, Master Cap; but likes looking up at the breeze as well as another, when in lively motion."

"I suppose you have such things as reefs, though you can hardly have occasion to use them?"

Mabel's bright eye detected the smile that gleamed for an instant on Jasper's handsome face; but no one else saw that momentary exhibition of surprise and contempt.

"We have reefs, and often have occasion to use them," quietly returned the young man. "Before we get in, Master Cap, an opportunity may offer to show you the manner in which we do so; for there is easterly weather brewing, and the wind cannot chop, even on the ocean itself, more readily than it flies round on Lake Ontario."

"So much for knowing no better! I have seen the wind in the Atlantic fly round like a coach-wheel, in a way to keep your sails shaking for an hour, and the ship would become perfectly motionless from not knowing which way to turn."

"We have no such sudden changes here, certainly," Jasper mildly answered; "though we think ourselves liable to unexpected shifts of wind. I hope, however, to carry this land-breeze as far as the first islands; after which there will be less danger of our being seen and followed by any of the look-out boats from Frontenac."

"Do you think the French keep spies out on the broad lake, Jasper?" inquired the Pathfinder.

"We know they do; one was off Oswego during the night of Monday last. A bark canoe came close in with the eastern point, and landed an Indian and an officer. Had you been outlying that night, as usual, we should have secured one, if not both of them."

It was too dark to betray the color that deepened on the weather-burnt features of the guide; for he felt the consciousness of having lingered in the fort that night, listening to the sweet tones of Mabel's voice as she sang ballads to her father, and gazing at the countenance which, to him, was radiant with charms. Probity in thought and deed being the distinguishing quality of this extraordinary man's mind, while he felt that a sort of disgrace ought to attach to his idleness on the occasion mentioned, the last thought that could occur would be to attempt to palliate or deny his negligence.

"I confess it, Jasper, I confess it," said he humbly. "Had I been out that night—and I now recollect no sufficient reason why I was not—it might, indeed, have turned out as you say."

"It was the evening you passed with us, Pathfinder," Mabel innocently remarked; "surely one who lives so much of his time in the forest, in front of the enemy, may be excused for giving a few hours of his time to an old friend and his daughter."

"Nay, nay, I've done little else but idle since we reached the garrison," returned the other, sighing; "and it is well that the lad should tell me of it: the idler needs a rebuke—yes, he needs a rebuke."

"Rebuke, Pathfinder! I never dreamt of saying anything disagreeable, and least of all would I think of rebuking you, because a solitary spy and an Indian or two have escaped us. Now I know where you were, I think your absence the most natural thing in the world."

"I think nothing of what you said, Jasper, since it was deserved. We are all human, and all do wrong."

"This is unkind, Pathfinder."

"Give me your hand, lad, give me your hand. It wasn't you that gave the lesson; it was conscience."

"Well, well," interrupted Cap; "now this latter matter is settled to the satisfaction of all parties, perhaps you will tell us how it happened to be known that there were spies near us so lately. This looks amazingly like a circumstance."

As the mariner uttered the last sentence, he pressed a foot slily on that of the Sergeant, and nudged the guide with his elbow, winking at the same time, though this sign was lost in the obscurity.

"It is known, because their trail was found next day by the Serpent, and it was that of a military boot and a moccasin. One of our hunters, moreover, saw the canoe crossing towards Frontenac next morning."

"Did the trail lead near the garrison, Jasper?" Pathfinder asked in a manner so meek and subdued that it resembled the tone of a rebuked schoolboy. "Did the trail lead near the garrison, lad?"

"We thought not; though, of course, it did not cross the river. It was followed down to the eastern point, at the river's mouth, where what was doing in port might be seen; but it did not cross, as we could discover."

"And why didn't you get under way, Master Jasper," Cap

demanded, "and give chase? On Tuesday morning it blew a good breeze; one in which this cutter might have run nine knots."

"That may do on the ocean, Master Cap," put in Pathfinder, "but it would not do here. Water leaves no trail, and a Mingo and a Frenchman are a match for the devil in a pursuit."

"Who wants a trail when the chase can be seen from the deck, as Jasper here said was the case with this canoe? and it mattered nothing if there were twenty of your Mingos and Frenchmen, with a good British-built bottom in their wake. I'll engage, Master Eau-douce, had you given me a call that said Tuesday morning, that we should have overhauled the blackguards."

"I daresay, Master Cap, that the advice of as old a seaman as you might have done no harm to as young a sailor as myself, but it is a long and a hopeless chase that has a bark canoe in it."

"You would have had only to press it hard, to drive it ashore."

"Ashore, Master Cap! You do not understand our lake navigation at all, if you suppose it an easy matter to force a bark canoe ashore. As soon as they find themselves pressed, these bubbles paddle right into the wind's eye, and before you know it, you find yourself a mile or two dead under their lee."

"You don't wish me to believe, Master Jasper, that any one is so heedless of drowning as to put off into this lake in one of them eggshells when there is any wind?"

"I have often crossed Ontario in a bark canoe, even when there has been a good deal of sea on. Well managed, they are the driest boats of which we have any knowledge."

Cap now led his brother-in-law and Pathfinder aside, when he assured him that the admission of Jasper concerning the spies was "a circumstance," and "a strong circumstance," and as such it deserved his deliberate investigation; while his account of the canoes was so improbable as to wear the appearance of brow-beating the listeners. Jasper spoke confidently of the character of the two individuals who had landed, and this Cap deemed pretty strong proof that he knew more about them than was to be gathered from a mere trail. As for moccasins, he said that they were worn in that part of the world by white men as well as by Indians; he had purchased a pair himself; and boots, it was notorious, did not particularly make a soldier.

Although much of this logic was thrown away on the Sergeant, still it produced some effect. He thought it a little singular himself, that there should have been spies detected so near the fort and he know nothing of it; nor did he believe that this was a branch of knowledge that fell particularly within the sphere of Jasper. It was true that the *Scud* had, once or twice, been sent across the lake to land men of this character, or to bring them off; but then the part played by Jasper, to his own certain knowledge, was very secondary, the master of the cutter remaining as ignorant as any one else of the purport of the visits of those whom he had carried to and fro; nor did he see why he alone, of all present, should know anything of the late visit. Pathfinder viewed the matter differently. With his habitual diffidence, he reproached himself with a neglect of duty, and that knowledge, of which the want struck him as a fault in one whose business it was to possess it, appeared a merit in the young man. He saw nothing extraordinary in Jasper's knowing the facts he had related; while he did feel it was unusual, not to say disgraceful, that he himself now heard of them for the first time.

"As for moccasins, Master Cap," said he, when a short pause invited him to speak, "they may be worn by pale-faces as well as by red-skins, it is true, though they never leave the same trail on the foot of one as on the foot of the other. Any one who is used to the woods can tell the footstep of an Indian from the footstep of a white man, whether it be made by a boot or a moccasin. It will need better evidence than this to persuade me into the belief that Jasper is false."

"You will allow, Pathfinder, that there are such things in the world as traitors?" put in Cap logically.

"I never knew an honest-minded Mingo—one that you could put faith in, if he had a temptation to deceive you. Cheating seems to be their gift, and I sometimes think they ought to be pitied for it, rather than persecuted."

"Then why not believe that this Jasper may have the same weakness? A man is a man, and human nature is sometimes but a poor concern, as I know by experience."

This was the opening of another long and desultory conversation, in which the probability of Jasper's guilt or innocence was argued *pro* and *con.*, until both the Sergeant and his brother-in-law had nearly reasoned themselves into settled convictions in favor of the first, while their companion grew sturdier and sturdier in his defence of the accused, and still more fixed in his opinion of his being unjustly charged with treachery. In this there was nothing out of the common course of things; for there is no more certain way of arriving at any particular notion, than by undertaking to defend it; and among the most obstinate of our opinions may be classed those which are derived from discussions in which we affect to search for truth, while in reality we are only fortifying prejudice.

By this time the Sergeant had reached a state of mind that disposed him to view every act of the young sailor with distrust, and he soon got to coincide with his relative in deeming the peculiar knowledge of Jasper, in reference to the spies, a branch of information that certainly did not come within the circle of his regular duties, as "a circumstance."

While this matter was thus discussed near the taffrail, Mabel sat silently by the companion-way, Mr. Muir having gone below to look after his personal comforts, and Jasper standing a little aloof, with his arms crossed, and his eyes wandering from the sails to the clouds, from the clouds to the dusky outline of the shore, from the shore to the lake, and from the lake back again to the sails. Our heroine, too, began to commune with her own thoughts. The excitement of the late journey, the incidents which marked the day of her arrival at the fort, the meeting with a father who was virtually a stranger to her, the novelty of her late situation in the garrison, and her present voyage, formed a vista for the mind's eye to look back through, which seemed lengthened into months. She could with difficulty believe that she had so recently left the town, with all the usages of civilized life; and she wondered in particular that the incidents which had occurred during the descent of the Oswego had made so little impression on her mind. Too inexperienced to know that events, when crowded, have the effect of time, or that the quick succession of novelties that pass before us in travelling elevates objects, in a measure, to the dignity of events, she drew upon her memory for days and dates, in order to make certain that she had known Jasper, and the Pathfinder, and her own father, but little more than a fortnight. Mabel was a girl of heart rather than of imagination, though by no means deficient in the last, and she could not easily account for the strength of her feelings in connection with those who were so lately strangers to her; for she was not sufficiently accustomed to analyze her sensations to understand the nature of the influences that have just been mentioned. As yet, however, her pure mind was free from the blight of distrust, and she had no suspicion of the views of either of her suitors; and one of the last thoughts that could have voluntarily disturbed her confidence would have been to suppose it possible either of her companions was a traitor to his king and country.

America, at the time of which we are writing, was remarkable for its attachment to the German family that then sat on the British throne; for, as is the fact with all provinces, the virtues and qualities that are proclaimed near the centre of power, as incense and policy, get to be a part of political faith with the credulous and ignorant at a distance. This truth is just as apparent to-day, in connection with the prodigies of the republic, as it then was in connection with those distant rulers, whose merits it was always safe to applaud, and whose demerits it was treason to reveal. It is a consequence of this mental dependence, that public opinion is so much placed at the mercy of the designing; and the world, in the midst of its idle boasts of knowledge and improvement, is left to receive its truths, on all such points as touch the interests of the powerful and managing, through such a medium, and such a medium only, as may serve the particular views of those who pull the wires. Pressed upon by the subjects of France, who were then encircling the British colonies with a belt of forts and settlements that completely secured the savages for allies, it would have been difficult to say whether the Americans loved the English more than they hated the French; and those who then lived probably would have considered the alliance which took place between the cis-Atlantic subjects and the ancient rivals of the British crown, some twenty years later, as an event entirely without the circle of probabilities. Disaffection was a rare offence; and, most of all, would treason, that should favor France or Frenchmen, have been odious in the eyes of the provincials. The last thing that Mabel would suspect of Jasper was the very crime with which he now stood secretly charged; and if others near her endured the pains of distrust, she, at least, was filled with the generous confidence of a woman. As yet no whisper had reached her ear to disturb the feeling of reliance with which she had early regarded the young sailor, and her own mind would have been the last to suggest such a thought of itself. The pictures of the past and of the present, therefore, that exhibited themselves so rapidly to her active imagination, were unclouded with a shade that might affect any in whom she felt an interest; and ere she had mused, in the manner related, a quarter of an hour, the whole scene around her was filled with unalloyed satisfaction.

The season and the night, to represent them truly, were of a nature to stimulate the sensations which youth, health, and happiness are wont to associate with novelty. The weather was warm, as is not always the case in that region even in summer, while the air that came off the land, in breathing currents, brought with it the coolness and fragrance of the forest. The wind was far from being fresh, though there was enough of it to drive the *Scud* merrily ahead, and, perhaps, to keep attention alive, in the uncertainty that more or less accompanies darkness. Jasper, however, appeared to regard it with complacency, as was apparent by what he said in a short dialogue that now occurred between him and Mabel.

"At this rate, Eau-douce"—for so Mabel had already learned to style the young sailor—said our heroine, "we cannot be long in reaching our place of destination."

"Has your father then told you what that is, Mabel?"

"He has told me nothing; my father is too much of a soldier, and too little used to have a family around him, to talk of such matters. Is it forbidden to say whither we are bound?"

"It cannot be far, while we steer in this direction, for sixty or seventy miles will take us into the St. Lawrence, which the French might make too hot for us; and no voyage on this lake can be very long."

"So says my uncle Cap; but to me, Jasper, Ontario and the ocean appear very much the same."

"You have then been on the ocean; while I, who pretend to be a sailor, have never yet seen salt water. You must have a great contempt for such a mariner as myself, in your heart, Mabel Dunham?"

"Then I have no such thing in my heart, Jasper Eau-douce.

What right have I, a girl without experience or knowledge, to despise any, much less one like you, who are trusted by the Major, and who command a vessel like this? I have never been on the ocean, though I have seen it; and, I repeat, I see no difference between this lake and the Atlantic."

"Nor in them that sail on both? I was afraid, Mabel, your uncle had said so much against us fresh-water sailors, that you had begun to look upon us as little better than pretenders?"

"Give yourself no uneasiness on that account, Jasper; for I know my uncle, and he says as many things against those who live ashore, when at York, as he now says against those who sail on fresh water. No, no, neither my father nor myself think anything of such opinions. My uncle Cap, if he spoke openly, would be found to have even a worse notion of a soldier than of a sailor who never saw the sea."

"But your father, Mabel, has a better opinion of soldiers than of any one else? he wishes you to be the wife of a soldier?"

"Jasper Eau-douce!—I the wife of a soldier! My father wishes it! Why should he wish any such thing? What soldier is there in the garrison that I could marry—that he could *wish me* to marry?"

"One may love a calling so well as to fancy it will cover a thousand imperfections."

"But one is not likely to love his own calling so well as to cause him to overlook everything else. You say my father wishes me to marry a soldier; and yet there is no soldier at Oswego that he would be likely to give me to. I am in an awkward position; for while I am not good enough to be the wife of one of the gentlemen of the garrison, I think even you will admit, Jasper, I am too good to be the wife of one of the common soldiers."

As Mabel spoke thus frankly she blushed, she knew not why, though the obscurity concealed the fact from her companion; and she laughed faintly, like one who felt that the subject, however embarrassing it might be, deserved to be treated fairly. Jasper, it would seem, viewed her position differently from herself.

"It is true Mabel," said he, "you are not what is called a lady, in the common meaning of the word."

"Not in any meaning, Jasper," the generous girl eagerly interrupted: "on that head, I have no vanities, I hope. Providence has made me the daughter of a sergeant, and I am content to remain in the station in which I was born."

"But all do not remain in the stations in which they were born, Mabel; for some rise above them, and some fall below them. Many sergeants have become officers—even generals; and why may not sergeants' daughters become officers' ladies?"

"In the case of Sergeant Dunham's daughter, I know no better reason than the fact that no officer is likely to wish to make her his wife," returned Mabel, laughing.

"*You* may think so; but there are some in the 55th that know better. There is certainly one officer in that regiment, Mabel, who *does* wish to make you his wife."

Quick as the flashing lightning, the rapid thoughts of Mabel Dunham glanced over the five or six subalterns of the corps, who, by age and inclinations, would be the most likely to form such a wish; and we should do injustice to her habits, perhaps, were we not to say that a lively sensation of pleasure rose momentarily in her bosom, at the thought of being raised above a station which, whatever might be her professions of contentment, she felt that she had been too well educated to fill with perfect satisfaction. But this emotion was as transient as it was sudden; for Mabel Dunham was a girl of too much pure and womanly feeling to view the marriage tie through anything so worldly as the mere advantages of station. The passing emotion was a thrill produced by factitious habits, while the more settled opinion which remained was the offspring of nature and principles.

"I know no officer in the 55th, or any other regiment, who would be likely to do so foolish a thing; nor do I think I myself would do so foolish a thing as to marry an officer."

"Foolish, Mabel!"

"Yes, foolish, Jasper. You know, as well as I can know, what the world would think of such matters; and I should be sorry, very sorry, to find that my husband ever regretted that he had so far yielded to a fancy for a face or a figure as to have married the daughter of one so much his inferior as a sergeant."

"*Your* husband, Mabel, will not be so likely to think of the father as to think of the daughter."

The girl was talking with spirit, though feeling evidently

entered into her part of the discourse; but she paused for nearly a minute after Jasper had made the last observation before she uttered another word. Then she continued, in a manner less playful, and one critically attentive might have fancied in a manner slightly melancholy—

"Parent and child ought so to live as not to have two hearts, or two modes of feeling and thinking. A common interest in all things I should think as necessary to happiness in man and wife, as between the other members of the same family. Most of all, ought neither the man nor the woman to have any unusual cause for unhappiness, the world furnishing so many of itself."

"Am I to understand, then, Mabel, you would refuse to marry an officer, merely because he was an officer?"

"Have you a right to ask such a question, Jasper?" said Mabel, smiling.

"No other right than what a strong desire to see you happy can give, which, after all, may be very little. My anxiety has been increased, from happening to know that it is your father's intention to persuade you to marry Lieutenant Muir."

"My dear, dear father can entertain no notion so ridiculous— no notion so cruel!"

"Would it, then, be cruel to wish you the wife of a quarter-master?"

"I have told you what I think on that subject, and cannot make my words stronger. Having answered you so frankly, Jasper, I have a right to ask how you know that my father thinks of any such thing?"

"That he has chosen a husband for you, I know from his own mouth; for he has told me this much during our frequent conversations while he has been superintending the shipment of the stores; and that Mr. Muir is to offer for you, I know from the officer himself, who has told me as much. By putting the two things together, I have come to the opinion mentioned."

"May not my dear father, Jasper"—Mabel's face glowed like fire while she spoke, though her words escaped her slowly, and by a sort of involuntary impulse—"may not my dear father have been thinking of another? It does not follow, from what you say, that Mr. Muir was in his mind."

"Is it not probable, Mabel, from all that has passed? What

brings the Quartermaster here? He has never found it necessary before to accompany the parties that have gone below. He thinks of you for his wife; and your father has made up his own mind that you shall be so. You must see, Mabel, that Mr. Muir follows *you?*"

Mabel made no answer. Her feminine instinct had, indeed, told her that she was an object of admiration with the Quartermaster; though she had hardly supposed to the extent that Jasper believed; and she, too, had even gathered from the discourse of her father that he thought seriously of having her disposed of in marriage; but by no process of reasoning could she ever have arrived at the inference that Mr. Muir was to be the man. She did not believe it now, though she was far from suspecting the truth. Indeed, it was her own opinion that these casual remarks of her father, which had struck her, had proceeded from a general wish to have her settled, rather than from any desire to see her united to any particular individual. These thoughts, however, she kept secret; for self-respect and feminine reserve showed her the impropriety of making them the subject of discussion with her present companion. By way of changing the conversation, therefore, after the pause had lasted long enough to be embarrassing to both parties, she said, "Of one thing you may be certain, Jasper—and that is all I wish to say on the subject—Lieutenant Muir, though he were a colonel, will never be the husband of Mabel Dunham. And now, tell me of your voyage;—when will it end?"

"That is uncertain. Once afloat, we are at the mercy of the winds and waves. Pathfinder will tell you that he who begins to chase the deer in the morning cannot tell where he will sleep at night."

"But we are not chasing a deer, nor is it morning: so Pathfinder's moral is thrown away."

"Although we are not chasing a deer, we are after that which may be as hard to catch. I can tell you no more than I have said already; for it is our duty to be close-mouthed, whether anything depends on it or not. I am afraid, however, I shall not keep you long enough in the *Scud* to show you what she can do at need."

"I think a woman unwise who ever marries a sailor," said Mabel abruptly, and almost involuntarily.

"This is a strange opinion; why do you hold it?"

"Because a sailor's wife is certain to have a rival in his vessel. My uncle Cap, too, says that a sailor should never marry."

"He means salt-water sailors," returned Jasper, laughing. "If he thinks wives not good enough for those who sail on the ocean, he will fancy them just suited to those who sail on the lakes. I hope, Mabel, you do not take your opinions of us fresh-water mariners from all that Master Cap says."

"Sail, ho!" exclaimed the very individual of whom they were conversing; "or boat, ho! would be nearer the truth."

Jasper ran forward; and, sure enough, a small object was discernible about a hundred yards ahead of the cutter, and nearly on her lee bow. At the first glance, he saw it was a bark canoe; for, though the darkness prevented hues from being distinguished, the eye that had become accustomed to the night might discern forms at some little distance; and the eye which, like Jasper's, had long been familiar with things aquatic, could not be at a loss in discovering the outlines necessary to come to the conclusion he did.

"This may be an enemy," the young man remarked; "and it may be well to overhaul him."

"He is paddling with all his might, lad," observed the Pathfinder, "and means to cross your bows and get to windward, when you might as well chase a full-grown buck on snow-shoes!"

"Let her luff," cried Jasper to the man at the helm. "Luff up, till she shakes. There, steady, and hold all that."

The helmsman complied; and, as the *Scud* was now dashing the water aside merrily, a minute or two put the canoe so far to leeward as to render escape impracticable. Jasper now sprang to the helm himself; and, by judicious and careful handling, he got so near his chase that it was secured by a boat-hook. On receiving an order, the two persons who were in the canoe left it, and no sooner had they reached the deck of the cutter than they were found to be Arrowhead and his wife.

CHAPTER XV

What pearl is it that rich men cannot buy,
That learning is too proud to gather up;
But which the poor and the despised of all
Seek and obtain, and often find unsought?
Tell me—and I will tell thee what is truth.   COWPER

THE meeting with the Indian and his wife excited no surprise in the majority of those who witnessed the occurrence; but Mabel, and all who knew of the manner in which this chief had been separated from the party of Cap, simultaneously entertained suspicions, which it was far easier to feel than to follow out by any plausible clue to certainty. Pathfinder, who alone could converse freely with the prisoners, for such they might now be considered, took Arrowhead aside, and held a long conversation with him, concerning the reasons of the latter for having deserted his charge and the manner in which he had been since employed.

The Tuscarora met these inquiries, and he gave his answers with the stoicism of an Indian. As respects the separation, his excuses were very simply made, and they seemed to be sufficiently plausible. When he found that the party was discovered in its place of concealment, he naturally sought his own safety, which he secured by plunging into the woods. In a word, he had run away in order to save his life.

"This is well," returned Pathfinder, affecting to believe the other's apologies; "my brother did very wisely; but his woman followed?"

"Do not the pale-faces' women follow their husbands? Would not Pathfinder have looked back to see if one he loved was coming?"

This appeal was made to the guide while he was in a most fortunate frame of mind to admit its force; for Mabel and her blandishments and constancy were becoming images familiar to his thoughts. The Tuscarora, though he could not trace the reason, saw that his excuse was admitted, and he stood with quiet dignity awaiting the next inquiry.

"This is reasonable and natural," returned Pathfinder; "this is natural, and may be so. A woman would be likely to follow the man to whom she had plighted faith, and husband and wife are one flesh. Your words are honest, Tuscarora," changing the language to the dialect of the other. "Your words are honest, and very pleasant and just. But why has my brother been so long from the fort? His friends have thought of him often, but have never seen him."

"If the doe follows the buck, ought not the buck to follow the doe?" answered the Tuscarora, smiling, as he laid a finger significantly on the shoulder of his interrogator. "Arrowhead's wife followed Arrowhead; it was right in Arrowhead to follow his wife. She lost her way, and they made her cook in a strange wigwam."

"I understand you, Tuscarora. The woman fell into the hands of the Mingos, and you kept upon their trail."

"Pathfinder can see a reason as easily as he can see the moss on the trees. It is so."

"And how long have you got the woman back, and in what manner has it been done?"

"Two suns. The Dew-of-June was not long in coming when her husband whispered to her the path."

"Well, well, all this seems natural, and according to matrimony. But, Tuscarora, how did you get that canoe, and why are you paddling towards the St. Lawrence instead of the garrison?"

"Arrowhead can tell his own from that of another. This canoe is mine; I found it on the shore near the fort."

"That sounds reasonable, too, for the canoe does belong to the man, and an Indian would make few words about taking it. Still, it is extraordinary that we saw nothing of the fellow and his wife, for the canoe must have left the river before we did ourselves."

This idea, which passed rapidly through the mind of the guide, was now put to the Indian in the shape of a question.

"Pathfinder knows that a warrior can have shame. The father would have asked me for his daughter, and I could not give her to him. I sent the Dew-of-June for the canoe, and no one spoke to the woman. A Tuscarora woman would not be free in speaking to strange men."

All this, too, was plausible, and in conformity with Indian character and customs. As was usual, Arrowhead had received one half of his compensation previously to quitting the Mohawk; and his refraining to demand the residue was a proof of that conscientious consideration of mutual rights that quite as often distinguishes the morality of a savage as that of a Christian. To one as upright as Pathfinder, Arrowhead had conducted himself with delicacy and propriety, though it would have been more in accordance with his own frank nature to have met the father, and abided by the simple truth. Still, accustomed to the ways of Indians, he saw nothing out of the ordinary track of things in the course the other had taken.

"This runs like water flowing down hill, Arrowhead," he answered, after a little reflection, "and truth obliges me to own it. It was the gift of a red-skin to act in this way, though I do not think it was the gift of a pale-face. You would not look upon the grief of the girl's father?"

Arrowhead made a quiet inclination of the body as if to assent.

"One thing more my brother will tell me," continued Pathfinder, "and there will be no cloud between his wigwam and the strong-house of the Yengeese. If he can blow away this bit of fog with his breath, his friends will look at him as he sits by his own fire, and he can look at them as they lay aside their arms, and forget that they are warriors. Why was the head of Arrowhead's canoe looking towards the St. Lawrence, where there are none but enemies to be found?"

"Why were the Pathfinder and his friends looking the same way?" asked the Tuscarora calmly. "A Tuscarora may look in the same direction as a Yengeese."

"Why, to own the truth, Arrowhead, we are out scouting like; that is, sailing—in other words, we are on the king's business, and we have a right to be here, though we may not have a right to say *why* we are here."

"Arrowhead saw the big canoe, and he loves to look on the face of Eau-douce. He was going towards the sun at evening in order to seek his wigwam; but, finding that the young sailor was going the other way, he turned that he might look in the same direction. Eau-douce and Arrowhead were together on the last trail."

"This may all be true, Tuscarora, and you are welcome. You

shall eat of our venison, and then we must separate. The setting sun is behind us, and both of us move quick: my brother will get too far from that which he seeks, unless he turns round."

Pathfinder now returned to the others, and repeated the result of his examination. He appeared himself to believe that the account of Arrowhead might be true, though he admitted that caution would be prudent with one he disliked; but his auditors, Jasper excepted, seemed less disposed to put faith in the explanations.

"This chap must be ironed at once, brother Dunham," said Cap, as soon as Pathfinder finished his narration; "he must be turned over to the master-at-arms, if there is any such officer on fresh water, and a court-martial ought to be ordered as soon as we reach port."

"I think it wisest to detain the fellow," the Sergeant answered; "but irons are unnecessary so long as he remains in the cutter. In the morning the matter shall be inquired into."

Arrowhead was now summoned and told the decision. The Indian listened gravely, and made no objections. On the contrary, he submitted with the calm and reserved dignity with which the American aborigines are known to yield to fate; and he stood apart, an attentive but calm observer of what was passing. Jasper caused the cutter's sails to be filled, and the *Scud* resumed her course.

It was now getting near the hour to set the watch, and when it was usual to retire for the night. Most of the party went below, leaving no one on deck but Cap, the Sergeant, Jasper, and two of the crew. Arrowhead and his wife also remained, the former standing aloof in proud reserve, and the latter exhibiting, by her attitude and passiveness, the meek humility that characterizes an Indian woman.

"You will find a place for your wife below, Arrowhead, where my daughter will attend to her wants," said the Sergeant kindly, who was himself on the point of quitting the deck; "yonder is a sail where you may sleep yourself."

"I thank my father. The Tuscaroras are not poor. The woman will look for my blankets in the canoe."

"As you wish, my friend. We think it necessary to detain you; but not necessary to confine or to maltreat you. Send your squaw into the canoe for the blankets and you may follow her yourself, and hand us up the paddles. As there may be some sleepy heads in the *Scud*, Eau-douce," added the Sergeant in a lower tone, "it may be well to secure the paddles."

Jasper assented, and Arrowhead and his wife, with whom resistance appeared to be out of the question, silently complied with the directions. A few expressions of sharp rebuke passed from the Indian to his wife, while both were employed in the canoe, which the latter received with submissive quiet, immediately repairing an error she had made by laying aside the blanket she had taken and searching for another that was more to her tyrant's mind.

"Come, bear a hand, Arrowhead," said the Sergeant, who stood on the gunwale overlooking the movements of the two, which were proceeding too slowly for the impatience of a drowsy man; "it is getting late; and we soldiers have such a thing as réveille—early to bed and early to rise."

"Arrowhead is coming," was the answer, as the Tuscarora stepped towards the head of his canoe.

One blow of his keen knife severed the rope which held the boat, and then the cutter glanced ahead, leaving the light bubble of bark, which instantly lost its way, almost stationary. So suddenly and dexterously was this manœuvre performed, that the canoe was on the lee quarter of the *Scud* before the Sergeant was aware of the artifice, and quite in her wake ere he had time to announce it to his companions.

"Hard-a-lee!" shouted Jasper, letting fly the jib-sheet with his own hands, when the cutter came swiftly up to the breeze, with all her canvas flapping, or was running into the wind's eye, as seamen term it, until the light craft was a hundred feet to windward of her former position. Quick and dexterous as was this movement, and ready as had been the expedient, it was not quicker or more ready than that of the Tuscarora. With an intelligence that denoted some familiarity with vessels, he had seized his paddle and was already skimming the water, aided by the efforts of his wife. The direction he took was southwesterly, or on a line that led him equally towards the wind and the shore, while it also kept him so far aloof from the cutter as to avoid the danger of the latter falling on board of him when she filled on the other tack. Swiftly as the *Scud* had shot into the wind, and far as she had forced ahead, Jasper knew it was necessary to cast her ere she had lost all her way; and it was not two minutes from the time the helm had been put down before the lively little craft was aback forward, and rapidly falling off, in order to allow her sails to fill on the opposite tack.

"He will escape!" said Jasper the instant he caught a glimpse of the relative bearings of the cutter and the canoe. "The cunning knave is paddling dead to windward, and the *Scud* can never overtake him!"

"You have a canoe!" exclaimed the Sergeant, manifesting the eagerness of a boy to join in the pursuit; "let us launch it, and give chase!"

"It will be useless. If Pathfinder had been on deck, there might have been a chance; but there is none now. To launch the canoe would have taken three or four minutes, and the time lost would be sufficient for the purposes of Arrowhead."

Both Cap and the Sergeant saw the truth of this, which would have been nearly self-evident even to one unaccustomed to vessels. The shore was distant less than half a mile, and the canoe was already glancing into its shadows, at a rate to show that it would reach the land before its pursuers could probably get half the distance. The helm of the *Scud* was reluctantly put up again, and the cutter wore short round on her heel, coming up to her course on the other tack, as if acting on an instinct. All this was done by Jasper in profound silence, his assistants understanding what was necessary, and lending their aid in a sort of mechanical imitation. While these manœuvres were in the course of execution, Cap took the Sergeant by a button, and led him towards the cabin-door, where he was out of ear-shot, and began to unlock his stores of thought.

"Hark'e, brother Dunham," said he, with an ominous face, "this is a matter that requires mature thought and much circumspection."

"The life of a soldier, brother Cap, is one of constant thought and circumspection. On this frontier, were we to overlook either, our scalps might be taken from our heads in the first nap."

"But I consider this capture of Arrowhead as a circumstance; and I might add his escape as another. This Jasper Freshwater must look to it."

"They are both circumstances truly, brother; but they tell different ways. If it is a circumstance against the lad that the

Indian has escaped, it is a circumstance in his favor that he was first taken."

"Ay, ay, but two circumstances do not contradict each other like two negatives. If you will follow the advice of an old seaman, Sergeant, not a moment is to be lost in taking the steps necessary for the security of the vessel and all on board of her. The cutter is now slipping through the water at the rate of six knots, and as the distances are so short on this bit of a pond, we may all find ourselves in a French port before morning, and in a French prison before night."

"This may be true enough. What would you advise me to do, brother?"

"In my opinion you should put this Master Freshwater under arrest on the spot; send him below under the charge of a sentinel, and transfer the command of the cutter to me. All this you have power to perform, the craft belonging to the army, and you being the commanding officer of the troops present."

Sergeant Dunham deliberated more than an hour on the propriety of this proposal; for, though sufficiently prompt when his mind was really made up, he was habitually thoughtful and wary. The habit of superintending the personal police of the garrison had made him acquainted with character, and he had long been disposed to think well of Jasper. Still that subtle poison, suspicion, had entered his soul; and so much were the artifices and intrigues of the French dreaded, that, especially warned as he had been by his commander, it is not to be wondered that the recollection of years of good conduct should vanish under the influence of a distrust so keen, and seemingly so plausible. In this embarrassment the Sergeant consulted the Quartermaster, whose opinion, as his superior, he felt bound to respect, though at the moment independent of his control. It is an unfortunate occurrence for one who is in a dilemma to ask advice of another who is desirous of standing well in his favor, the party consulted being almost certain to try to think in the manner which will be the most agreeable to the party consulting. In the present instance it was equally unfortunate, as respects a candid consideration of the subject, that Cap, instead of the Sergeant himself, made the statement of the case; for the earnest old sailor was not backward in letting his listener perceive to which side he was desirous that the Quartermaster should lean. Lieutenant Muir was much too politic to offend the uncle and father of the woman he hoped and expected to win, had he really thought the case admitted of doubt; but, in the manner in which the facts were submitted to him, he was seriously inclined to think that it would be well to put the control of the *Scud* temporarily into the management of Cap, as a precaution against treachery. This opinion then decided the Sergeant, who forthwith set about the execution of the necessary measures.

Without entering into any explanations, Sergeant Dunham simply informed Jasper that he felt it to be his duty to deprive him temporarily of the command of the cutter, and to confer it on his own brother-in-law. A natural and involuntary burst of surprise, which escaped the young man, was met by a quiet remark, reminding him that military service was often of a nature that required concealment, and a declaration that the present duty was of such a character that this particular arrangement had become indispensable. Although Jasper's astonishment remained undiminished—the Sergeant cautiously abstaining from making any allusion to his suspicions—the young man was accustomed to obey with military submission; and he quietly acquiesced, with his own mouth directing the little crew to receive their further orders from Cap until another change should be effected. When, however, he was told the case required that not only he himself, but his principal assistant, who, on account of his long acquaintance with the lake, was usually termed the pilot, were to remain below, there was an alteration in his countenance and manner that denoted strong feeling, though it was so well mastered as to leave even the distrustful Cap in doubt as to its meaning. As a matter of course, however, when distrust exists, it was not long before the worst construction was put upon it.

As soon as Jasper and the pilot were below, the sentinel at the hatch received private orders to pay particular attention to both; to allow neither to come on deck again without giving instant notice to the person who might then be in charge of the cutter, and to insist on his return below as soon as possible. This precaution, however, was uncalled for; Jasper and his assistant both throwing themselves silently on their pallets, which neither quitted again that night.

"And now, Sergeant," said Cap, as soon as he found himself

master of the deck, "you will just have the goodness to give me the courses and distance, that I may see the boat keeps her head the right way."

"I know nothing of either, brother Cap," returned Dunham, not a little embarrassed at the question. "We must make the best of our way to the station among the Thousand Islands, where 'we shall land, relieve the party that is already out, and get information for our future government.' That's it, nearly word for word, as it stands in the written orders."

"But you can muster a chart—something in the way of bearings and distances, that I may see the road?"

"I do not think Jasper ever had anything of the sort to go by."

"No chart, Sergeant Dunham!"

"Not a scrap of a pen even. Our sailors navigate this lake without any aid from maps."

"The devil they do! They must be regular Yahoos. And do you suppose, Sergeant Dunham, that I can find one island out of a thousand without knowing its name or its position, without even a course or a distance?"

"As for the *name*, brother Cap, you need not be particular, for not one of the whole thousand *has* a name, and so a mistake can never be made on that score. As for the position, never having been there myself, I can tell you nothing about it, nor do I think its position of any particular consequence, provided we find the spot. Perhaps one of the hands on deck can tell us the way."

"Hold on, Sergeant—hold on a moment, if you please, Sergeant Dunham. If I am to command this craft, it must be done, if you please, without holding any councils of war with the cook and cabin-boy. A ship-master is a ship-master, and he must have an opinion of his own, even if it be a wrong one. I suppose you know service well enough to understand that it is better in a commander to go wrong than to go nowhere. At all events, the Lord High Admiral couldn't command a yawl with dignity, if he consulted the cockswain every time he wished to go ashore. No sir, if I sink, I sink! but, d— me, I'll go down ship-shape and with dignity."

"But, brother Cap, I have no wish to go down anywhere, unless it be to the station among the Thousand Islands whither we are bound."

"Well, well, Sergeant, rather than ask advice—that is, direct, barefaced advice—of a foremast hand, or any other than a quarter-deck officer, I would go round to the whole thousand, and examine them one by one until we got the right haven. But there is such a thing as coming at an opinion without manifesting ignorance, and I will manage to rouse all there is out of these hands, and make them think all the while that I am cramming them with my own experience! We are sometimes obliged to use the glass at sea when there is nothing in sight, or to heave the lead long before we strike soundings. When a youngster, I sailed two v'y'ges with a man who navigated his ship pretty much by the latter sort of information, which sometimes answers."

"I know we are steering in the right direction at present," returned the Sergeant; "but in the course of a few hours we shall be up with a headland, where we must feel our way with more caution."

"Leave me to pump the man at the wheel, brother, and you shall see that I will make him suck in a very few minutes."

Cap and the Sergeant now walked aft, until they stood by the sailor who was at the helm, Cap maintaining an air of security and tranquillity, like one who was entirely confident of his own powers.

"This is a wholesome air, my lad," Cap observed, in the manner that a superior on board a vessel sometimes condescends to use to a favored inferior. "Of course you have it in this fashion off the land every night?"

"At this season of the year, sir," the man returned, touching his hat, out of respect to his new commander and Sergeant Dunham's connection.

"The same thing, I take it, among the Thousand Islands? The wind will stand, of course, though we shall then have land on every side of us."

"When we get farther east, sir, the wind will probably shift, for there can then be no particular land-breeze."

"Ay, ay; so much for your fresh water! It has always some trick that is opposed to nature. Now, down among the West India Islands, one is just as certain of having a land-breeze as he is of having a sea-breeze. In that respect there is no difference, though it's quite in rule it should be different up here on this bit of fresh water. Of course, my lad, you know all about these said Thousand Islands?"

"Lord bless you, Master Cap, nobody knows all about them, or anything about them. They are a puzzle to the oldest sailor on the lake, and we don't pretend to know even their names. For that matter, most of them have no more names than a child that dies before it is christened."

"Are you a Roman Catholic?" demanded the Sergeant sharply.

"No, sir, nor anything else. I'm a generalizer about religion, never troubling that which don't trouble me."

"Hum! a generalizer; that is, no doubt, one of the new sects that afflict the country," muttered Mr. Dunham, whose grandfather had been a New Jersey Quaker, his father a Presbyterian, and who had joined the Church of England himself after he entered the army.

"I take it, John—" resumed Cap. "Your name is Jack, I believe?"

"No, sir; I am called Robert."

"Ay, Robert, it's very much the same thing, Jack or Bob; we use the two indifferently. I say, Bob, it's good holding ground, is it, down at this same station for which we are bound?"

"Bless you, sir! I know no more about it than one of the Mohawks, or a soldier of the 55th."

"Did you never anchor there?"

"Never, sir. Master Eau-douce always makes fast to the shore."

"But in running in for the town, you kept the lead going, out of question, and must have tallowed as usual."

"'Tallow!—and town, too! Bless your heart, Master Cap! there is no more town than there is on your chin, and not half as much tallow!"

The Sergeant smiled grimly, but his brother-in-law did not detect this proof of humor.

"No church tower, nor light, nor fort, ha? There is a garrison, as you call it hereaway, at least?"

"Ask Sergeant Dunham, sir, if you wish to know that. All the garrison is on board the *Scud*."

"But in running in, Bob, which of the channels do you think the best? the one you went last, or—or—or—ay, or the other?"

"I can't say, sir; I know nothing of either."

"You didn't go to sleep, fellow, at the wheel, did you?"

"Not at the wheel, sir, but down in the fore-peak in my berth. Eau-douce sent us below, soldiers and all, with the exception of the pilot, and we know no more of the road than if we had never been over it. This he has always done in going in and coming out; and, for the life of me, I could tell you nothing of the channel, or the course, after we are once fairly up with the islands. No one knows anything of either but Jasper and the pilot."

"Here is a circumstance for you, Sergeant," said Cap, leading his brother-in-law a little aside; "there is no one on board to pump, for they all suck from ignorance at the first stroke of the brake. How the devil am I to find the way to this station for which we are bound?"

"Sure enough, brother Cap, your question is more easily put than answered. Is there no such thing as figuring it out by navigation? I thought you salt-water mariners were able to do as small a thing as that. I have often read of their discovering islands, surely."

"That you have, brother, that you have; and this discovery would be the greatest of them all; for it would not only be discovering one island, but one island out of a thousand."

"Still, the sailors of the lake have a method of finding the places they wish to go to."

"If I have understood you, Sergeant, this station or block-house is particularly private."

"It is, indeed, the utmost care having been taken to prevent a knowledge of its position from reaching the enemy."

"And you expect me, a stranger on your lake, to find this place without chart, course, distance, latitude, longitude, or soundings—ay, d— me, or tallow! Allow me to ask if you think a mariner runs by his nose, like one of Pathfinder's hounds?"

"Well, brother, you may yet learn something by questioning the young man at the helm; I can hardly think that he is as ignorant as he pretends to be."

"Hum!—this looks like another circumstance. For that matter, the case is getting to be so full of circumstances that one hardly knows how to foot up the evidence. But we will soon see how much the lad knows."

Cap and the Sergeant now returned to their station near the helm, and the former renewed his inquiries.

"Do you happen to know what may be the latitude and longitude of this said island, my lad?" he asked.

"The what, sir?"

"Why, the latitude or longitude—one or both; I'm not particular which, as I merely inquire in order to see how they bring up young men on this bit of fresh water."

"I'm not particular about either myself, sir, and so I do not happen to know what you mean."

"Not what I mean! You know what latitude is?"

"Not I, sir!" returned the man, hesitating. "Though I believe it is French for the upper lakes."

"Whe—e—e—w—!" whistled Cap, drawing out his breath like the broken stop of an organ; "latitude, French for upper lakes! Hark'e, young man, do you know what longitude means?"

"I believe I do, sir; that is, five feet six, the regulation height for soldiers in the king's service."

"There's the longitude found out for you, Sergeant, in the rattling of a brace-block! You have some notion about a degree, and minutes and seconds, I hope?"

"Yes, sir; degree means my betters; and minutes and seconds are for the short or long log-lines. We all know these things as well as the salt-water people."

"D— me, brother Dunham, if I think even Faith can get along on this lake, much as they say it can do with mountains. Well, my lad, you understand the azimuth, and measuring distances, and how to box the compass."

"As for the first, sir, I can't say I do. The distances we all know, as we measure them from point to point; and as for boxing the compass, I will turn my back to no admiral in his Majesty's fleet. Nothe, nothe and by east, nothe, nothe-east, nothe-east and by nothe, nothe-east; nothe-east and by east, east-nothe-east, east and by nothe-east——"

"That will do, that will do. You'll bring about a shift of wind if you go on in this manner. I see very plainly, Sergeant," walking away again, and dropping his voice, "we've nothing to hope for from that chap. I'll stand on two hours longer on this tack, when we'll heave-to and get the soundings, after which we will be governed by circumstances."

To this the Sergeant made no objections; and as the wind grew lighter, as usual with the advance of night, and there were no immediate obstacles to the navigation, he made a bed of a sail on deck, and was soon lost in the sound sleep of a soldier. Cap continued to walk the deck, for he was one whose iron frame set fatigue at defiance, and not once that night did he close his eyes.

It was broad daylight when Sergeant Dunham awoke, and the exclamation of surprise that escaped him, as he rose to his feet and began to look about him, was stronger than it was usual for one so drilled to suffer to be heard. He found the weather entirely changed, the view bounded by driving mist that limited the visible horizon to a circle of about a mile in diameter, the lake raging and covered with foam, and the *Scud* lying-to. A brief conversation with his brother-in-law let him into the secrets of all these sudden changes.

According to the account of Master Cap, the wind had died away to a calm about midnight, or just as he was thinking of heaving-to, to sound, for islands ahead were beginning to be seen. At one A.M. it began to blow from the north-east, accompanied by a drizzle, and he stood off to the northward and westward, knowing that the coast of New York lay in the opposite direction. At half-past one he stowed the flying-jib, reefed the mainsail, and took the bonnet off the jib. At two he was compelled to get a second reef aft; and by half-past two he had put a balance-reef in the sail, and was lying-to.

"I can't say but the boat behaves well, Sergeant," the old sailor added, "but it blows forty-two pounders. I had no idea there were any such currents of air up here on this bit of fresh water, though I care not the knotting of a yarn for it, as your lake has now somewhat of a natural look; and if this d—d water had a savor of salt about it, one might be comfortable."

"How long have you been heading in this direction, brother Cap?" inquired the prudent soldier; "and at what rate may we be going through the water?"

"Why, two or three hours, mayhap, and she went like a horse for the first pair of them. Oh, we've a fine offing now! for, to own the truth, little relishing the neighborhood of them said islands, although they are to windward, I took the helm myself, and run her off free for some league or two. We are well to leeward of them, I'll engage—I say to leeward; for though one might wish to be well to windward of one island, or even half a dozen, when it comes to a thousand, the better way is to give it up at once, and to slide down under their lee as fast as possible. No, no; there they are up yonder in the dingle; and there they may stay, for anything Charles Cap cares."

"As the north shore lies only some five or six leagues from us, brother, and I know there is a large bay in that quarter, might it not be well to consult some of the crew concerning our position, if, indeed, we do not call up Jasper Eau-douce, and tell him to carry us back to Oswego? For it is quite impossible we should ever reach the station with this wind directly in our teeth."

"There are several serious professional reasons, Sergeant, against all your propositions. In the first place, an admission of ignorance on the part of a commander would destroy discipline. No matter, brother; I understand your shake of the head, but nothing capsizes discipline so much as to confess ignorance. I once knew a master of a vessel who went a week on a wrong course rather than allow he had made a mistake; and it was surprising how much he rose in the opinions of his people, just because they could not understand him."

"That may do on salt water, brother Cap, but it will hardly do on fresh. Rather than wreck my command on the Canada shore, I shall feel it a duty to take Jasper out of arrest."

"And make a haven in Frontenac. No, Sergeant; the *Scud* is in good hands, and will now learn something of seamanship. We have a fine offing, and no one but a madman would think of going upon a coast in a gale like this. I shall ware every watch, and then we shall be safe against all dangers but those of the drift, which, in a light low craft like this, without top-hamper, will be next to nothing. Leave it all to me, Sergeant, and I pledge you the character of Charles Cap that all will go well."

Sergeant Dunham was fain to yield. He had great confidence in his connection's professional skill, and hoped that he would take such care of the cutter as would amply justify his opinion of him. On the other hand, as distrust, like care, grows by what it feeds on, he entertained so much apprehension of treachery, that he was quite willing any one but Jasper should just then have the control of the fate of the whole party. Truth, more-over, compels us to admit another motive. The particular duty on which he was now sent of right should have been confided to a commissioned officer; and Major Duncan had excited a good deal of discontent among the subalterns of the garrison, by having confided it to one of the Sergeant's humble station. To return without having even reached the point of destination, therefore, the latter felt would be a failure from which he was not likely soon to recover, and the measure would at once be the means of placing a superior in his shoes.

CHAPTER XVI

Thou glorious mirror, where the Almighty's form
Glasses itself in tempests; in all time,
Calm or convulsed—in breeze. or gale, or storm,
Icing the pole, or in the torrid clime
Dark heaving;—boundless, endless, and sublime—
The image of eternity; the throne
Of the Invisible; even from out thy slime
The monsters of the deep are made; each zone
Obeys thee; thou goest forth, dread, fathomless, alone. BYRON

As THE day advanced, that portion of the inmates of the vessel which had the liberty of doing so appeared on deck. As yet the sea was not very high, from which it was inferred that the cutter was still under the lee of the islands; but it was apparent to all who understood the lake that they were about to experience one of the heavy autumnal gales of that region. Land was nowhere visible; and the horizon on every side exhibited that gloomy void, which lends to all views on vast bodies of water the sublimity of mystery. The swells, or, as landsmen term them, the waves, were short and curling, breaking of necessity sooner than the longer seas of the ocean; while the element itself, instead of presenting that beautiful hue which rivals the deep tint of the southern sky, looked green and angry, though wanting in the lustre that is derived from the rays of the sun.

The soldiers were soon satisfied with the prospect, and one by one they disappeared, until none were left on deck but the crew, the Sergeant, Cap, Pathfinder, the Quartermaster, and Mabel. There was a shade on the brow of the last, who had been made acquainted with the real state of things, and who had fruitlessly ventured an appeal in favor of Jasper's restoration to the command. A night's rest and a night's reflection appeared also to have confirmed the Pathfinder in his opinion of the young man's innocence; and he, too, had made a warm appeal on behalf of his friend, though with the same want of success.

Several hours passed away, the wind gradually getting heavier and the sea rising, until the motion of the cutter compelled Mabel and the Quartermaster to retreat also. Cap wore several times; and it was now evident that the *Scud* was drifting into the broader and deeper parts of the lake, the seas raging down upon her in a way that none but a vessel of superior mould and build could have long ridden and withstood. All this, however, gave Cap no uneasiness; but, like the hunter that pricks his ears at the sound of the horn, or the war-horse that paws and snorts with pleasure at the roll of the drum, the whole scene awakened all that was man within him; and instead of the captious, supercilious, and dogmatic critic, quarrelling with trifles and exaggerating immaterial things, he began to exhibit the qualities of the hardy and experienced seaman which he truly was. The hands soon imbibed a respect for his skill; and, though they wondered at the disappearance of their old commander and the pilot, for which no reason had been publicly given, they soon yielded an implicit and cheerful obedience to the new one.

"This bit of fresh water, after all, brother Dunham, has some spirit, I find," cried Cap about noon, rubbing his hands in pure satisfaction at finding himself once more wrestling with the elements. "The wind seems to be an honest old-fashioned gale, and the seas have a fanciful resemblance to those of the Gulf Stream. I like this, Sergeant, I like this, and shall get to respect your lake, if it hold out twenty-four hours longer in the fashion in which it has begun."

"Land, ho!" shouted the man who was stationed on the forecastle.

Cap hurried forward; and there, sure enough, the land was visible through the drizzle, at the distance of about half a mile, the cutter heading directly towards it. The first impulse of the old seaman was to give an order to "stand by, to ware off shore"; but the cool-headed soldier restrained him.

"By going a little nearer," said the Sergeant, "some of us may recognize the place. Most of us know the American shore in this part of the lake; and it will be something gained to learn our position."

"Very true, very true; if, indeed, there is any chance of that we will hold on. What is this off here, a little on our weather-bow? It looks like a low headland."

"The garrison, by Jove!" exclaimed the other, whose trained eye sooner recognized the military outlines than the less instructed senses of his connection.

The Sergeant was not mistaken. There was the fort, sure enough, though it looked dim and indistinct through the fine rain, as if it were seen in the dusk of evening or the haze of morning. The low, sodded, and verdant ramparts, the sombre palisades, now darker than ever with water, the roof of a house or two, the tall, solitary flagstaff, with its halyards blown steadily out into a curve that appeared traced in immovable lines in the air, were all soon to be seen, though no sign of animated life could be discovered. Even the sentinel was housed; and at first it was believed that no eye would detect the presence of their own vessel. But the unceasing vigilance of a border garrison did not slumber: one of the look-outs probably made the interesting discovery; a man or two were seen on some elevated stands, and then the entire ramparts next the lake were dotted with human beings.

The whole scene was one in which sublimity was singularly relieved by the picturesque. The raging of the tempest had a character of duration that rendered it easy to imagine it might be a permanent feature of the spot. The roar of the wind was without intermission, and the raging water answered to its dull but grand strains with hissing spray, a menacing wash, and sullen surges. The drizzle made a medium for the eye which closely resembled that of a thin mist, softening and rendering mysterious the images it revealed, while the genial feeling that is apt to accompany a gale of wind on water contributed to aid the milder influences of the moment. The dark interminable forest hove up out of the obscurity, grand, sombre, and impressive, while the solitary, peculiar, and picturesque glimpses of life that were caught in and about the fort, formed a refuge for the eye to retreat to when oppressed with the more imposing objects of nature.

"They see us," said the Sergeant, "and think we have returned on account of the gale, and have fallen to leeward of the port. Yes, there is Major Duncan himself on the north-eastern bastion; I know him by his height, and by the officers around him."

"Sergeant, it would be worth standing a little jeering, if we could fetch into the river, and come safely to an anchor. In that case, too, we might land this Master Eau-douce, and purify the boat."

"It would indeed; but, as poor a sailor as I am, I well know it cannot be done. Nothing that sails the lake can turn to windward against this gale; and there is no anchorage outside in weather like this."

"I know it, I see it, Sergeant; and pleasant as is that sight to you landsmen, we must leave it. For myself, I am never so happy in heavy weather as when I am certain that the land is behind me."

The *Scud* had now forged so near in, that it became indispensable to lay her head off shore again, and the necessary orders were given. The storm-staysail was set forward, the gaff lowered, the helm put up, and the light craft, that seemed to sport with the elements like a duck, fell off a little, drew ahead swiftly, obeyed her rudder, and was soon flying away on the top of the surges, dead before the gale. While making this rapid flight, though the land still remained in view on her larboard beam, the fort and the groups of anxious spectators on its rampart were swallowed up in the mist. Then followed the evolutions necessary to bring the head of the cutter up to the wind, when she again began to wallow her weary way towards the north shore.

Hours now passed before any further change was made, the wind increasing in force, until even the dogmatical Cap fairly admitted it was blowing a thorough gale of wind. About sunset the *Scud* wore again to keep her off the north shore during the hours of darkness; and at midnight her temporary master, who, by questioning the crew in an indirect manner, had obtained some general knowledge of the size and shape of the lake, believed himself to be about midway between the two shores. The height and length of the seas aided this impression; and it must be added that Cap by this time began to feel a respect for fresh water which twenty-four hours earlier he would have derided as impossible. Just as the night turned, the fury of the wind became so great that he found it impossible to bear up against it, the water falling on the deck of the little craft in such masses as to cause it to shake to the centre, and, though a vessel of singularly lively qualities, to threaten to bury it beneath its weight. The people of the *Scud* averred that never before had they been out in such a tempest, which was true; for, possessing a perfect knowledge of all the rivers and headlands and havens, Jasper would have carried the cutter in shore long ere this, and placed her in safety in some secure anchorage. But Cap still disdained to consult the young master, who continued below, determining to act like a mariner of the broad ocean.

It was one in the morning when the storm-staysail was again got on the *Scud*, the head of the mainsail lowered, and the cutter put before the wind. Although the canvas now exposed was merely a rag in surface, the little craft nobly justified the use of the name she bore. For eight hours did she scud in truth; and it was almost with the velocity of the gulls that wheeled wildly over her in the tempest, apparently afraid to alight in the boiling caldron of the lake. The dawn of day brought little change; for no other horizon became visible than the little circle of drizzling sky and water already described, in which it seemed as if the elements were rioting in a sort of chaotic confusion. During this time the crew and passengers of the cutter were of necessity passive. Jasper and the pilot remained below; but, the motion of the vessel having become easier, nearly all the rest were on deck. The morning meal had been taken in silence, and eye met eye, as if their owners asked each other, in dumb show, what was to be the end of this strife in the elements. Cap, however, was perfectly composed, and his face brightened, his step grew firmer, and his whole air more assured, as the storm increased, making larger demands on his professional skill and personal spirit. He stood on the forecastle, his arms crossed, balancing his body with a seaman's instinct, while his eyes watched the caps of the seas, as they broke and glanced past the reeling cutter, itself in such swift motion, as if they were the scud flying athwart the sky. At this sublime instant one of the hands gave the unexpected cry of "A sail!"

There was so much of the wild and solitary character of the wilderness about Ontario, that one scarcely expected to meet with a vessel on its waters. The *Scud* herself, to those who were in her, resembled a man threading the forest alone, and the meeting was like that of two solitary hunters beneath the broad canopy of leaves that then covered so many millions of acres on the continent of America. The peculiar state of the weather served to increase the romantic, almost supernatural appearance of the passage. Cap alone regarded it with practised eyes, and even he felt his iron nerves thrill under the sensations that were awakened by the wild features of the scene.

The strange vessel was about two cables' length ahead of the *Scud*, standing by the wind athwart her bows, and steering a course to render it probable that the latter would pass within a few yards of her. She was a full-rigged ship; and, seen through the misty medium of the tempest, the most experienced eye could detect no imperfection in her gear or construction. The only canvas she had set was a close-reefed main-topsail, and two small storm-staysails, one forward and the other aft. Still the power of the wind pressed so hard upon her as to bear her down nearly to her beam-ends, whenever the hull was not righted by the buoyancy of some wave under her lee. Her spars were all in their places, and by her motion through the water, which might have equalled four knots in the hour, it was apparent that she steered a little free.

"The fellow must know his position well," said Cap, as the cutter flew down towards the ship with a velocity almost equalling that of the gale, "for he is standing boldly to the south-ward, where he expects to find anchorage or a haven. No man in his senses would run off free in that fashion, that was not driven to scudding, like ourselves, who did not perfectly understand where he was going."

"We have made an awful run, captain," returned the man to whom this remark had been addressed. "That is the French king's ship, Lee-my-calm (*Le Montcalm*), and she is standing in for the Niagara, where her owner has a garrison and a port. We've made an awful run of it!"

"Ay, bad luck to him! Frenchman-like, he skulks into port the moment he sees an English bottom."

"It might be well for us if we could follow him," returned the man, shaking his head despondingly, "for we are getting into the end of a bay up here at the head of the lake, and it is uncertain whether we ever get out of it again!"

"Pooh, man, pooh! We have plenty of sea-room, and a good English hull beneath us. We are no Johnny Crapauds to hide ourselves behind a point or a fort on account of a puff of wind. Mind your helm, sir!"

The order was given on account of the menacing appearance of the approaching passage. The *Scud* was now heading directly for the fore-foot of the Frenchman; and, the distance between the two vessels having diminished to a hundred yards, it was momentarily questionable if there was room to pass.

"Port, sir, port," shouted Cap. "Port your helm and pass astern!"

The crew of the Frenchman were seen assembling to wind-ward, and a few muskets were pointed, as if to order the people of the *Scud* to keep off. Gesticulations were observed, but the sea was too wild and menacing to admit of the ordinary expedients of war. The water was dripping from the muzzles of two or three light guns on board the ship, but no one thought of loosening them for service in such a tempest. Her black sides, as they emerged from a wave, glistened and seemed to frown; but the wind howled through her rigging, whistling the thousand notes of a ship; and the hails and cries that escape a Frenchman with so much readiness were inaudible.

"Let him halloo himself hoarse!" growled Cap. "This is no weather to whisper secrets in. Port, sir, port!"

The man at the helm obeyed, and the next send of the sea drove the *Scud* down upon the quarter of the ship, so near her that the old mariner himself recoiled a step, in a vague expectation that, at the next surge ahead, she would drive bows foremost directly into the planks of the other vessel. But this was not to be: rising from the crouching posture she had taken, like a panther about to leap, the cutter dashed onward, and at the next instant she was glancing past the stern of her enemy, just clearing the end of her spanker-boom with her own lower yard.

The young Frenchman who commanded the *Montcalm* leaped

on the taffrail; and, with that high-toned courtesy which relieves
even the worst acts of his countryman, he raised his cap and
smiled a salutation as the *Scud* shot past. There were *bonhomie*
and good taste in this act of courtesy, when circumstances
allowed of no other communications; but they were lost on
Cap, who, with an instinct quite as true to his race, shook his
fist menacingly, and muttered to himself—

"Ay, ay, it's d—d lucky for you I've no armament on board
here, or I'd send you in to get new cabin-windows fitted. Sergeant, he's a humbug."

" 'Twas civil, brother Cap," returned the other, lowering his
hand from the military salute which his pride as a soldier had
induced him to return—" 'twas civil, and that's as much as
you can expect from a Frenchman. What he really meant by
it no one can say."

"He is not heading up to this sea without an object, neither.
Well, let him run in, if he can get there; we will keep the lake,
like hearty English mariners."

This sounded gloriously, but Cap eyed with envy the glittering black mass of the *Montcalm's* hull, her waving topsail, and
the misty tracery of her spars, as she grew less and less distinct,
and finally disappeared in the drizzle, in a form as shadowy as
that of some unreal image. Gladly would he have followed in
her wake had he dared; for, to own the truth, the prospect of
another stormy night in the midst of the wild waters that were
raging around him brought little consolation. Still he had too
much professional pride to betray his uneasiness, and those
under his care relied on his knowledge and resources, with the
implicit and blind confidence that the ignorant are apt to feel.

A few hours succeeded, and darkness came again to increase
the perils of the *Scud*. A lull in the gale, however, had induced
Cap to come by the wind once more, and throughout the night
the cutter was lying-to as before, head-reaching as a matter of
course, and occasionally waring to keep off the land. It is unnecessary to dwell on the incidents of this night, which resembled
those of any other gale of wind. There were the pitching of the
vessel, the hissing of the waters, the dashing of spray, the
shocks that menaced annihilation to the little craft as she
plunged into the seas, the undying howl of the wind, and the
fearful drift. The last was the most serious danger; for, though

exceedingly weatherly under her canvas, and totally without top-hamper, the *Scud* was so light, that the combing of the swells would seem at times to wash her down to leeward with a velocity as great as that of the surges themselves.

During this night Cap slept soundly, and for several hours. The day was just dawning when he felt himself shaken by the shoulder; and arousing himself, he found the Pathfinder standing at his side. During the gale the guide had appeared little on deck, for his natural modesty told him that seamen alone should interfere with the management of the vessel; and he was willing to show the same reliance on those who had charge of the *Scud*, as he expected those who followed through the forest to manifest in his own skill; but he now thought himself justified in interfering, which he did in his own unsophisticated and peculiar manner.

"Sleep is sweet, Master Cap," said he, as soon as the eyes of the latter were fairly open, and his consciousness had sufficiently returned—"sleep is sweet, as I know from experience, but life is sweeter still. Look about you, and say if this is exactly the moment for a commander to be off his feet."

"How now? how now, Master Pathfinder?" growled Cap, in the first moments of his awakened faculties. "Are you, too, getting on the side of the grumblers? When ashore I admired your sagacity in running through the worst shoals without a compass; and since we have been afloat, your meekness and submission have been as pleasant as your confidence on your own ground. I little expected such a summons from you."

"As for myself, Master Cap, I feel I have my gifts, and I believe they'll interfere with those of no other man; but the case may be different with Mabel Dunham. She has her gifts, too, it is true; but they are not rude like ours, but gentle and womanish, as they ought to be. It's on her account that I speak, and not on my own."

"Ay, ay, I begin to understand. The girl is a good girl, my worthy friend; but she is a soldier's daughter and a sailor's niece, and ought not to be too tame or too tender in a gale. Does she show any fear?"

"Not she! not she! Mabel is a woman, but she is reasonable and silent. Not a word have I heard from her concerning our doings; though I do think, Master Cap, she would like it better if Jasper Eau-douce were put into his proper place, and things were restored to their old situation, like. This is human natur'."

"I'll warrant it—girl-like, and Dunham-like, too. Anything is better than an old uncle, and everybody knows more than an old seaman. *This* is human natur', Master Pathfinder, and d— me if I'm the man to sheer a fathom, starboard or port, for all the human natur' that can be found in a minx of twenty—ay, or" (lowering his voice a little) "for all that can be paraded in his Majesty's 55th regiment of foot. I've not been at sea forty years, to come up on this bit of fresh water to be taught human natur'. How this gale holds out! It blows as hard at this moment as if Boreas had just clapped his hand upon the bellows. And what is all this to leeward?" (rubbing his eyes)—"land! as sure as my name is Cap—and high land, too."

The Pathfinder made no immediate answer; but, shaking his head, he watched the expression of his companion's face, with a look of strong anxiety in his own.

"Land, as certain as this is the *Scud!*" repeated Cap; "a lee shore, and that, too, within a league of us, with as pretty a line of breakers as one could find on the beach of all Long Island!"

"And is that encouraging? or is it disheartening?" inquired the Pathfinder.

"Ha! encouraging—disheartening!—why, neither. No, no, there is nothing encouraging about it; and as for disheartening, nothing ought to dishearten a seaman. You never get disheartened or afraid in the woods, my friend?"

"I'll not say that, I'll not say that. When the danger is great, it is my gift to see it, and know it, and to try to avoid it; else would my scalp long since have been drying in a Mingo wigwam. On this lake, however, I can see no trail, and I feel it my duty to submit; though I think we ought to remember there is such a person as Mabel Dunham on board. But here comes her father, and he will naturally feel for his own child."

"We are seriously situated, I believe, brother Cap," said the Sergeant, when he had reached the spot, "by what I can gather from the two hands on the forecastle? They tell me the cutter cannot carry any more sail, and her drift is so great we shall go ashore in an hour or two. I hope their fears have deceived them?"

Cap made no reply; but he gazed at the land with a rueful

face, and then looked to windward with an expression of ferocity, as if he would gladly have quarrelled with the weather.

"It may be well, brother," the Sergeant continued, "to send for Jasper and consult him as to what is to be done. There are no French here to dread; and, under all circumstances, the boy will save us from drowning if possible."

"Ay, ay, 'tis these cursed circumstances that have done all the mischief. But let the fellow come; let him come; a few well-managed questions will bring the truth out of him, I'll warrant you."

This acquiescence on the part of the dogmatical Cap was no sooner obtained, than Jasper was sent for. The young man instantly made his appearance, his whole air, countenance, and mien expressive of mortification, humility, and, as his observers fancied, rebuked deception. When he first stepped on deck, Jasper cast one hurried, anxious glance around, as if curious to know the situation of the cutter; and that glance sufficed, it would seem, to let him into the secret of all her perils. At first he looked to windward, as is usual with every seaman; then he turned round the horizon, until his eye caught a view of the high lands to leeward, when the whole truth burst upon him at once.

"I've sent for you, Master Jasper," said Cap, folding his arms, and balancing his body with the dignity of the forecastle, "in order to learn something about the haven to leeward. We take it for granted you do not bear malice so hard as to wish to drown us all, especially the women; and I suppose you will be man enough to help us run the cutter into some safe berth until this bit of a gale has done blowing!"

"I would die myself rather than harm should come to Mabel Dunham," the young man earnestly answered.

"I knew it! I knew it!" cried the Pathfinder, clapping his hand kindly on Jasper's shoulder. "The lad is as true as the best compass that ever ran a boundary, or brought a man off from a blind trail. It is a mortal sin to believe otherwise."

"Humph!" ejaculated Cap; "especially the women! As if *they* were in any particular danger. Never mind, young man; we shall understand each other by talking like two plain seamen. Do you know of any port under our lee?"

"None. There is a large bay at this end of the lake; but it is unknown to us all, and not easy of entrance."

"And this coast to leeward—it has nothing particular to recommend it, I suppose?"

"It is a wilderness until you reach the mouth of the Niagara in one direction, and Frontenac in the other. North and west, they tell me, there is nothing but forest and prairies for a thousand miles."

"Thank God! then, there can be no French. Are there many savages, hereaway, on the land?"

"The Indians are to be found in all directions; though they are nowhere very numerous. By accident, we might find a party at any point on the shore; or we might pass months there without seeing one."

"We must take our chance, then, as to the blackguards; but, to be frank with you, Master Western, if this little unpleasant matter about the French had not come to pass, what would you now do with the cutter?"

"I am a much younger sailor than yourself, Master Cap," said Jasper modestly, "and am hardly fitted to advise you."

"Ay, ay, we all know that. In a common case, perhaps not. But this is an uncommon case, and a circumstance; and on this bit of fresh water it has what may be called its peculiarities; and so, everything considered, you may be fitted to advise even your own father. At all events, you can speak, and I can judge of your opinions, agreeably to my own experience."

"I think, sir, before two hours are over, the cutter will have to anchor."

"Anchor!—not out here in the lake?"

"No, sir; but in yonder, near the land."

"You do not mean to say, Master Eau-douce, you would anchor on a lee shore in a gale of wind?"

"If I would save my vessel, that is exactly what I would do, Master Cap."

"Whe—e—e—w!—this is fresh water, with a vengeance! Hark'e, young man, I've been a seafaring animal, boy and man, forty-one years, and I never yet heard of such a thing. I'd throw my ground-tackle overboard before I would be guilty of so lubberly an act!"

"That is what we do on this lake," modestly replied Jasper, "when we are hard pressed. I daresay we might do better, had we been better taught."

"That you might, indeed! No; no man induces me to commit such a sin against my own bringing up. I should never dare show my face inside of Sandy Hook again, had I committed so know-nothing an exploit. Why, Pathfinder, here, has more seamanship in him than that comes to. You can go below again, Master Eau-douce."

Jasper quietly bowed and withdrew; still, as he passed down the ladder, the spectators observed that he cast a lingering anxious look at the horizon to windward and the land to lee-ward, and then disappeared with concern strongly expressed in every lineament of his face.

CHAPTER XVII

His still refuted quirks he still repeats;
New-raised objections with new quibbles meets,
Till sinking in the quicksand he defends,
He dies disputing, and the contest ends.   COWPER

As THE soldier's wife was sick in her berth, Mabel Dunham was the only person in the outer cabin when Jasper returned to it; for, by an act of grace in the Sergeant, he had been permitted to resume his proper place in this part of the vessel. We should be ascribing too much simplicity of character to our heroine, if we said that she had felt no distrust of the young man in conse-quence of his arrest; but we should also be doing injustice to her warmth of feeling and generosity of disposition, if we did not add, that this distrust was insignificant and transient. As he now took his seat near her, his whole countenance clouded with the uneasiness he felt concerning the situation of the cut-ter, everything like suspicion was banished from her mind, and she saw in him only an injured man.

"You let this affair weigh too heavily on your mind, Jasper," said she eagerly, or with that forgetfulness of self with which the youthful of her sex are wont to betray their feelings when a strong and generous interest has attained the ascendency; "no one who knows you can, or does, believe you guilty. Pathfinder says he will pledge his life for you."

"Then you, Mabel," returned the youth, his eyes flashing fire, "do not look upon me as the traitor your father seems to believe me to be?"

"My dear father is a soldier, and is obliged to act as one. My father's daughter is not, and will think of you as she ought to think of a man who has done so much to serve her already."

"Mabel, I'm not used to talking with one like you, or saying all I think and feel with any. I never had a sister, and my mother died when I was a child, so that I know little what your sex most likes to hear——"

Mabel would have given the world to know what lay behind the teeming word at which Jasper hesitated; but the indefinable and controlling sense of womanly diffidence made her suppress her curiosity. She waited in silence for him to explain his own meaning.

"I wish to say, Mabel," the young man continued, after a pause which he found sufficiently embarrassing, "that I am unused to the ways and opinions of one like you, and that you must imagine all I would add."

Mabel had imagination enough to fancy anything, but there are ideas and feelings that her sex prefer to have expressed before they yield them all their own sympathies, and she had a vague consciousness that these of Jasper might properly be enumerated in the class. With a readiness that belonged to her sex, therefore, she preferred changing the discourse to permitting it to proceed any further in a manner so awkward and so unsatisfactory.

"Tell me one thing, Jasper, and I shall be content," said she, speaking now with a firmness which denoted confidence, not only in herself, but in her companion: "you do not deserve this cruel suspicion which rests upon you?"

"I do not, Mabel!" answered Jasper, looking into her full blue eyes with an openness and simplicity that might have shaken stronger distrust. "As I hope for mercy hereafter, I do not!"

"I knew it—I could have sworn it!" returned the girl warmly.

"And yet my father means well;—but do not let this matter disturb you, Jasper."

"There is so much more to apprehend from another quarter just now, that I scarcely think of it."

"Jasper!"

"I do not wish to alarm you, Mabel; but if your uncle could be persuaded to change his notions about handling the *Scud*: and yet he is so much more experienced than I am, that he ought, perhaps, to place more reliance on his own judgment than on mine."

"Do you think the cutter in any danger?" demanded Mabel, quick as thought.

"I fear so; at least she would have been thought in great danger by us of the lake; perhaps an old seaman of the ocean may have means of his own to take care of her."

"Jasper, all agree in giving you credit for skill in managing the *Scud*. You know the lake, you know the cutter; you *must* be the best judge of our real situation."

"My concern for you, Mabel, may make me more cowardly than common; but, to be frank, I see but one method of keeping the cutter from being wrecked in the course of the next two or three hours, and that your uncle refuses to take. After all, this may be my ignorance; for, as he says, Ontario is merely fresh water."

"You cannot believe this will make any difference. Think of my dear father, Jasper! Think of yourself; of all the lives that depend on a timely word from you to save them."

"I think of you, Mabel, and that is more, much more, than all the rest put together!" returned the young man, with a strength of expression and an earnestness of look that uttered infinitely more than the words themselves.

Mabel's heart beat quickly, and a gleam of grateful satisfaction shot across her blushing features; but the alarm was too vivid and too serious to admit of much relief from happier thoughts. She did not attempt to repress a look of gratitude, and then she returned to the feeling which was naturally uppermost.

"My uncle's obstinacy must not be permitted to occasion this disaster. Go once more on deck, Jasper; and ask my father to come into the cabin."

While the young man was complying with this request, Mabel sat listening to the howling of the storm and the dashing of the water against the cutter, in a dread to which she had hitherto been a stranger. Constitutionally an excellent sailor, as the term is used among passengers, she had not hitherto bethought her of any danger, and had passed her time since the commencement of the gale in such womanly employments as her situation allowed; but now that alarm was seriously awakened, she did not fail to perceive that never before had she been on the water in such a tempest. The minute or two which elapsed before the Sergeant came appeared an hour, and she scarcely breathed when she saw him and Jasper descending the ladder in company. Quick as language could express her meaning, she acquainted her father with Jasper's opinion of their situation; and entreated him, if he loved her, or had any regard for his own life, or for those of his men, to interfere with her uncle, and to induce him to yield the control of the cutter again to its proper commander.

"Jasper is true, father," added she earnestly; "and if false, he could have no motive in wrecking us in this distant part of the lake at the risk of all our lives, his own included. I will pledge my own life for his truth."

"Ay, this is well enough for a young woman who is frightened," answered the more phlegmatic parent; "but it might not be so excusable in one in command of an expedition. Jasper may think the chance of drowning in getting ashore fully repaid by the chance of escaping as soon as he reaches the land."

"Sergeant Dunham!"

"Father!"

These exclamations were made simultaneously, but they were uttered in tones expressive of different feelings. In Jasper, surprise was the emotion uppermost; in Mabel, reproach. The old soldier, however, was too much accustomed to deal frankly with subordinates to heed either; and after a moment's thought, he continued as if neither had spoken. "Nor is brother Cap a man likely to submit to be taught his duty on board a vessel."

"But, father, when all our lives are in the utmost jeopardy!"

"So much the worse. The fair-weather commander is no great matter; it is when things go wrong that the best officer shows himself in his true colors. Charles Cap will not be likely to quit the helm because the ship is in danger. Besides, Jasper Eau-douce, he says your proposal in itself has a suspicious air about it, and sounds more like treachery than reason."

"He may think so; but let him send for the pilot and hear his opinion. It is well known that I have not seen the man since yesterday evening."

"This does sound reasonably, and the experiment shall be tried. Follow me on deck then, that all may be honest and above-aboard."

Jasper obeyed, and so keen was the interest of Mabel, that she too ventured as far as the companion-way, where her garments were sufficiently protected against the violence of the wind and her person from the spray. Here maiden modesty induced her to remain, though an absorbed witness of what was passing.

The pilot soon appeared, and there was no mistaking the look of concern that he cast around at the scene as soon as he was in the open air. Some rumors of the situation of the *Scud* had found their way below, it is true; but in this instance rumor had lessened instead of magnifying the danger. He was allowed a few minutes to look about him, and then the question was put as to the course which he thought it prudent to follow.

"I see no means of saving the cutter but to anchor," he answered simply, and without hesitation.

"What! out here in the lake?" inquired Cap, as he had previously done of Jasper.

"No: but closer in; just at the outer line of the breakers."

The effect of this communication was to leave no doubt in the mind of Cap that there was a secret arrangement between her commander and the pilot to cast away the *Scud;* most probably with the hope of effecting their escape. He consequently treated the opinion of the latter with the indifference he had manifested towards that of the former.

"I tell you, brother Dunham," said he, in answer to the remonstrances of the Sergeant against his turning a deaf ear to this double representation, "that no seaman would give such an opinion honestly. To anchor on a lee shore in a gale of wind would be an act of madness that I could never excuse to the underwriters, under any circumstances, so long as a rag can be set; but to anchor close to breakers would be insanity."

"His Majesty underwrites the *Scud*, brother, and I am responsible for the lives of my command. These men are better acquainted with Lake Ontario than we can possibly be, and I do think their telling the same tale entitles them to some credit."

"Uncle!" said Mabel earnestly; but a gesture from Jasper induced the girl to restrain her feelings.

"We are drifting down upon the breakers so rapidly," said the young man, "that little need be said on the subject. Hali an hour must settle the matter, one way or the other; but I warn Master Cap that the surest-footed man among us will not be able to keep his feet an instant on the deck of this low craft, should she fairly get within them. Indeed, I make little doubt that we shall fill and founder before the second line of rollers is passed."

"And how would anchoring help the matter?" demanded Cap furiously, as if he felt that Jasper was responsible for the effects of the gale, as well as for the opinion he had just given.

"It would at least do no harm," Eau-douce mildly replied. "By bringing the cutter head to sea we should lessen her drift; and even if we dragged through the breakers, it would be with the least possible danger. I hope, Master Cap, you will allow the pilot and myself to *prepare* for anchoring, since the precaution may do good, and can do no harm."

"Overhaul your ranges, if you will, and get your anchors clear, with all my heart. We are now in a situation that cannot be much affected by anything of that sort. Sergeant, a word with you aft here, if you please."

Cap led his brother-in-law out of ear-shot; and then, with more of human feeling in his voice and manner than he was apt to exhibit, he opened his heart on the subject of their real situation.

"This is a melancholy affair for poor Mabel," said he, blowing his nose, and speaking with a slight tremor. "You and I, Sergeant, are old fellows, and used to being near death, if not to actually dying; our trades fit us for such scenes; but poor Mabel!—she is an affectionate and kind-hearted girl, and I had hoped to see her comfortably settled, and a mother, before my time came. Well, well! we must take the bad with the good in every v'y'ge; and the only serious objection that an old seafaring man can with propriety make to such an event is, that it should happen on this bit of d—d fresh water."

Sergeant Dunham was a brave man, and had shown his spirit in scenes that looked much more appalling than this; but on all such occasions he had been able to act his part against his foes, while here he was pressed upon by an enemy whom he had no means of resisting. For himself he cared far less than for his daughter, feeling some of that self-reliance which seldom deserts a man of firmness who is in vigorous health, and who has been accustomed to personal exertions in moments of jeopardy; but as respects Mabel he saw no means of escape, and, with a father's fondness, he at once determined that, if either was doomed to perish, he and his daughter must perish together.

"Do you think this must come to pass?" he asked of Cap firmly, but with strong feeling.

"Twenty minutes will carry us into the breakers; and look for yourself, Sergeant: what chance will even the stoutest man among us have in that caldron to leeward?"

The prospect was, indeed, little calculated to encourage hope. By this time the *Scud* was within a mile of the shore, on which the gale was blowing at right angles, with a violence that forbade the idea of showing any additional canvas with a view to claw off. The small portion of the mainsail actually set, and which merely served to keep the head of the *Scud* so near the wind as to prevent the waves from breaking over her, quivered under the gusts, as if at each moment the stout threads which held the complicated fabric together were about to be torn asunder. The drizzle had ceased; but the air, for a hundred feet above the surface of the lake, was filled with dazzling spray, which had an appearance not unlike that of a brilliant mist, while above all the sun was shining gloriously in a cloudless sky. Jasper had noted the omen, and had foretold that it announced a speedy termination to the gale, though the next hour or two must decide their fate. Between the cutter and the shore the view was still more wild and appalling. The breakers extended nearly half a mile; while the water within their line was white with foam, the air above them was so far filled with vapor and spray as to render the land beyond hazy and indistinct. Still it could be seen that the latter was high—not a usual thing for the shores of Ontario—and that it was covered with the verdant mantle of the interminable forest.

While the Sergeant and Cap were gazing at this scene in silence, Jasper and his people were actively engaged on the forecastle. No sooner had the young man received permission to resume his old employment, than, appealing to some of the soldiers for aid, he mustered five or six assistants, and set about in earnest the performance of a duty which had been too long delayed. On these narrow waters anchors are never stowed inboard, or cables that are intended for service unbent, and Jasper was saved much of the labor that would have been necessary in a vessel at sea. The two bowers were soon ready to be let go, ranges of the cables were overhauled, and then the party paused to look about them. No changes for the better had occurred, but the cutter was falling slowly in, and each instant rendered it more certain that she could not gain an inch to windward.

One long, earnest survey of the lake ended, Jasper gave new orders in a similar manner to prove how much he thought that the time pressed. Two kedges were got on deck, and hawsers were bent to them; the inner ends of the hawsers were bent, in their turns, to the crowns of the anchors, and everything was got ready to throw them overboard at the proper moment. These preparations completed, Jasper's manner changed from the excitement of exertion to a look of calm but settled concern. He quitted the forecastle, where the seas were dashing in-board at every plunge of the vessel, the duty just mentioned having been executed with the bodies of the crew frequently buried in the water, and walked to a drier part of the deck, aft. Here he was met by the Pathfinder, who was standing near Mabel and the Quartermaster. Most of those on board, with the exception of the individuals who have already been particularly mentioned, were below, some seeking relief from physical suffering on their pallets, and others tardily bethinking them of their sins. For the first time, most probably, since her keel had dipped into the limpid waters of Ontario, the voice of prayer was heard on board the *Scud*.

"Jasper," commenced his friend, the guide, "I have been of no use this morning, for my gifts are of little account, as you know, in a vessel like this; but, should it please God to let the

Sergeant's daughter reach the shore alive, my acquaintance with the forest may still carry her through in safety to the garrison."

" 'Tis a fearful distance thither, Pathfinder!" Mabel rejoined, the party being so near together that all which was said by one was overheard by the others. "I am afraid none of us could live to reach the fort."

"It would be a risky path, Mabel, and a crooked one; though some of your sex have undergone even more than that in this wilderness. But, Jasper, either you or I, or both of us, must man this bark canoe; Mabel's only chance will lie in getting through the breakers in that."

"I would willingly man anything to save Mabel," answered Jasper, with a melancholy smile; "but no human hand, Pathfinder, could carry that canoe through yonder breakers in a gale like this. I have hopes from anchoring, after all; for once before have we saved the *Scud* in an extremity nearly as great as this."

"If we are to anchor, Jasper," the Sergeant inquired, "why not do it at once? Every foot we lose in drifting now would come into the distance we shall probably drag when the anchors are let go."

Jasper drew nearer to the Sergeant, and took his hand, pressing it earnestly, and in a way to denote strong, almost uncontrollable feelings.

"Sergeant Dunham," said he solemnly, "you are a good man, though you have treated me harshly in this business. You love your daughter?"

"That you cannot doubt, Eau-douce," returned the Sergeant huskily.

"Will you give her—give us all—the only chance for life that is left?"

"What would you have me do, boy, what would you have me do? I have acted according to my judgment hitherto—what would you have me do?"

"Support me against Master Cap for five minutes, and all that man can do towards saving the *Scud* shall be done."

The Sergeant hesitated, for he was too much of a disciplinarian to fly in the face of regular orders. He disliked the appearance of vacillation, too; and then he had a profound respect for his kinsman's seamanship. While he was deliberating, Cap came from the post he had some time occupied, which was at the side of the man at the helm, and drew nigh the group.

"Master Eau-douce," said he, as soon as near enough to be heard, "I have come to inquire if you know any spot near by where this cutter can be beached? The moment has arrived when we are driven to this hard alternative."

That instant of indecision on the part of Cap secured the triumph of Jasper. Looking at the Sergeant, the young man received a nod that assured him of all he asked, and he lost not one of those moments that were getting to be so very precious.

"Shall I take the helm," he inquired of Cap, "and see if we can reach a creek that lies to leeward?"

"Do so, do so," said the other, hemming to clear his throat; for he felt oppressed by a responsibility that weighed all the heavier on his shoulders on account of his ignorance. "Do so, Eau-douce, since, to be frank with you, I can see nothing better to be done. We must beach or swamp."

Jasper required no more; springing aft, he soon had the tiller in his own hands. The pilot was prepared for what was to follow; and, at a sign from his young commander, the rag of sail that had so long been set was taken in. At that moment, Jasper, watching his time, put the helm up; the head of a staysail was loosened forward, and the light cutter, as if conscious she was now under the control of familiar hands, fell off, and was soon in the trough of the sea. This perilous instant was passed in safety, and at the next moment the little vessel appeared flying down toward the breakers at a rate that threatened instant destruction. The distances had become so short, that five or six minutes sufficed for all that Jasper wished, and he put the helm down again, when the bows of the *Scud* came up to the wind, notwithstanding the turbulence of the waters, as gracefully as the duck varies its line of direction on the glassy pond. A sign from Jasper set all in motion on the forecastle, and a kedge was thrown from each bow. The fearful nature of the drift was now apparent even to Mabel's eyes, for the two hawsers ran out like tow-lines. As soon as they straightened to a slight strain, both anchors were let go, and cable was given to each, nearly to the better-ends. It was not a difficult task to snub so light a craft with ground-tackle of a quality better than common; and in less than ten minutes from the moment when Jasper went to the helm, the *Scud* was riding, head to sea, with the two cables stretched ahead in lines that resembled bars of iron.

"This is not well done, Master Jasper!" angrily exclaimed Cap, as soon as he perceived the trick which had been played him; "this is not well done, sir. I order you to cut, and to beach the cutter without a moment's delay."

No one, however, seemed disposed to comply with this order; for so long as Eau-douce saw fit to command, his own people were disposed to obey. Finding that the men remained passive, Cap, who believed they were in the utmost peril, turned fiercely to Jasper, and renewed his remonstrances.

"You did not head for your pretended creek," added he, after dealing in some objurgatory remarks that we do not deem it necessary to record, "but steered for that bluff, where every soul on board would have been drowned, had we gone ashore."

"And you wish to cut, and put every soul ashore at that very spot!" Jasper retorted, a little drily.

"Throw a lead-line overboard, and ascertain the drift!" Cap now roared to the people forward. A sign from Jasper sustaining this order, it was instantly obeyed. All on deck watched, with nearly breathless interest, the result of the experiment. The lead was no sooner on the bottom, than the line tended forward, and in about two minutes it was seen that the cutter had drifted her length dead in towards the bluff. Jasper looked gravely, for he well knew nothing would hold the vessel did she get within the vortex of the breakers, the first line of which was appearing and disappearing about a cable's length directly under their stern.

"Traitor!" exclaimed Cap, shaking a finger at the young commander, though passion choked the rest. "You must answer for this with your life!" he added after a short pause. "If I were at the head of this expedition, Sergeant, I would hang him at the end of the main-boom, lest he escape drowning."

"Moderate your feelings, brother; be more moderate, I beseech you; Jasper appears to have done all for the best, and matters may not be so bad as you believe them."

"Why did he not run for the creek he mentioned?—why has

he brought us here, dead to windward of that bluff, and to a spot where even the breakers are only of half the ordinary width, as if in a hurry to drown all on board?"

"I headed for the bluff, for the precise reason that the breakers are so narrow at this spot," answered Jasper mildly, though his gorge had risen at the language the other held.

"Do you mean to tell an old seaman like me that this cutter could live in those breakers?"

"I do not, sir. I think she would fill and swamp if driven into the first line of them; I am certain she would never reach the shore on her bottom, if fairly entered. I hope to keep her clear of them altogether."

"With a drift of her length in a minute?"

"The backing of the anchors does not yet fairly tell, nor do I even hope that *they* will entirely bring her up."

"On what, then, do you rely? To moor a craft, head and stern, by faith, hope, and charity?"

"No, sir, I trust to the under-tow. I headed for the bluff because I knew that it was stronger at that point than at any other, and because we could get nearer in with the land without entering the breakers."

This was said with spirit, though without any particular show of resentment. Its effect on Cap was marked, the feeling that was uppermost being evidently that of surprise.

"Under-tow!" he repeated; "who the devil ever heard of saving a vessel from going ashore by the under-tow?"

"This may never happen on the ocean, sir," Jasper answered modestly; "but we have known it to happen here."

"The lad is right, brother," put in the Sergeant; "for, though I do not well understand it, I have often heard the sailors of the lake speak of such a thing. We shall do well to trust to Jasper in this strait."

Cap grumbled and swore; but, as there was no remedy, he was compelled to acquiesce. Jasper, being now called on to explain what he meant by the under-tow, gave this account of the matter. The water that was driven up on the shore by the gale was necessarily compelled to find its level by returning to the lake by some secret channels. This could not be done on the surface, where both wind and waves were constantly urging it towards the land, and it necessarily formed a sort of lower eddy, by means of which it flowed back again to its ancient and proper bed. This inferior current had received the name of the under-tow, and, as it would necessarily act on the bottom of a vessel which drew as much water as the *Scud*, Jasper trusted to the aid of this reaction to keep his cables from parting. In short, the upper and lower currents would, in a manner, counteract each other.

Simple and ingenious as was this theory, however, as yet there was little evidence of its being reduced to practice. The drift continued; though, as the kedges and hawsers with which the anchors were backed took the strains, it became sensibly less. At length the man at the lead announced the joyful intelli-gence that the anchors had ceased to drag, and that the vessel had brought up! At this precise moment the first line of breakers was about a hundred feet astern of the *Scud*, even appearing to approach much nearer as the foam vanished and returned on the raging surges. Jasper sprang forward, and, casting a glance over the bows, he smiled in triumph, as he pointed exultingly to the cables. Instead of resembling bars of iron in rigidity, as before, they were curving downwards, and to a seaman's senses it was evident that the cutter rose and fell on the seas as they came in with the ease of a ship in a tides-way, when the power of the wind is relieved by the counteracting pressure of the water.

" 'Tis the under-tow!" he exclaimed with delight, fairly bounding along the deck to steady the helm, in order that the cutter might ride still easier. "Providence has placed us directly in its current, and there is no longer any danger."

"Ay, ay, Providence is a good seaman," growled Cap, "and often helps lubbers out of difficulty. Under-tow or upper-tow, the gale has abated; and, fortunately for us all, the anchors have met with good holding-ground. Then this d—d fresh water has an unnatural way with it."

Men are seldom inclined to quarrel with good fortune, but it is in distress that they grow clamorous and critical. Most on board were disposed to believe that they had been saved from shipwreck by the skill and knowledge of Jasper, without re-garding the opinions of Cap, whose remarks were now little heeded.

There was half an hour of uncertainty and doubt, it is true, during which period the lead was anxiously watched; and then a feeling of security came over all, and the weary slept without dreaming of instant death.

CHAPTER XVIII

It is to be all made of sighs and tears;
It is to be all made of faith and service;
It is to be all made of phantasy;
All made of passion, and all made of wishes;
All adoration, duty, and observance;
All humbleness, all patience, and impatience;
All purity, all trial, all observance.   SHAKESPEARE

IT WAS near noon when the gale broke; and then its force abated as suddenly as its violence had arisen. In less than two hours after the wind fell, the surface of the lake, though still agitated, was no longer glittering with foam; and in double that time, the entire sheet presented the ordinary scene of disturbed water, that was unbroken by the violence of a tempest. Still the waves came rolling incessantly towards the shore, and the lines of breakers remained, though the spray had ceased to fly; the combing of the swells was more moderate, and all that there was of violence proceeded from the impulsion of wind which had abated.

As it was impossible to make head against the sea that was still up, with the light opposing air that blew from the eastward, all thoughts of getting under way that afternoon were abandoned. Jasper, who had now quietly resumed the command of the *Scud*, busied himself, however, in heaving-up the anchors, which were lifted in succession; the kedges that backed them were weighed, and everything was got in readiness for a prompt departure, as soon as the state of the weather would allow. In the meantime, they who had no concern with these duties sought such means of amusement as their peculiar circumstances allowed.

As is common with those who are unused to the confinement of a vessel, Mabel cast wistful eyes towards the shore; nor was it long before she expressed a wish that it were possible to land. The Pathfinder was near her at the time, and he assured her that nothing would be easier, as they had a bark canoe on deck, which was the best possible mode of conveyance to go through a surf. After the usual doubts and misgivings, the Sergeant was appealed to; his opinion proved to be favorable, and preparations to carry the whim into effect were immediately made.

The party which was to land consisted of Sergeant Dunham, his daughter, and the Pathfinder. Accustomed to the canoe, Mabel took her seat in the centre with great steadiness, her father was placed in the bows, while the guide assumed the office of conductor, by steering in the stern. There was little need of impelling the canoe by means of the paddle, for the rollers sent it forward at moments with a violence that set every effort to govern its movements at defiance. More than once, before the shore was reached, Mabel repented of her temerity, but Pathfinder encouraged her, and really manifested so much self-possession, coolness, and strength of arm himself, that even a female might have hesitated about owning all her apprehensions. Our heroine was no coward; and while she felt the novelty of her situation, in landing through a surf, she also experienced a fair proportion of its wild delight. At moments, indeed, her heart was in her mouth, as the bubble of a boat floated on the very crest of a foaming breaker, appearing to skim the water like a swallow, and then she flushed and laughed, as, left by the glancing element, they appeared to linger behind as if ashamed of having been outdone in the headlong race. A few minutes sufficed for this excitement; for though the distance between the cutter and the land considerably exceeded a quarter of a mile, the intermediate space was passed in a very few minutes.

On landing, the Sergeant kissed his daughter kindly, for he was so much of a soldier as always to feel more at home on *terra firma* than when afloat; and, taking his gun, he announced his intention to pass an hour in quest of game.

"Pathfinder will remain near you, girl, and no doubt he will tell you some of the traditions of this part of the world, or some of his own experiences with the Mingos."

The guide laughed, promised to have a care of Mabel, and in a few minutes the father had ascended a steep acclivity and disappeared in the forest. The others took another direction, which, after a few minutes of a sharp ascent also, brought them to a small naked point on the promontory, where the eye overlooked an extensive and very peculiar panorama. Here Mabel seated herself on a fragment of fallen rock to recover her breath and strength, while her companion, on whose sinews no personal exertion seemed to make any impression, stood at her side, leaning in his own and not ungraceful manner on his long rifle. Several minutes passed, and neither spoke; Mabel, in particular, being lost in admiration of the view.

The position the two had obtained was sufficiently elevated to command a wide reach of the lake, which stretched away towards the north-east in a boundless sheet, glittering beneath the rays of an afternoon's sun, and yet betraying the remains of that agitation which it had endured while tossed by the late tempest. The land set bounds to its limits in a huge crescent, disappearing in distance towards the south-east and the north. Far as the eye could reach, nothing but forest was visible, not even a solitary sign of civilization breaking in upon the uniform and grand magnificence of nature. The gale had driven the *Scud* beyond the line of those forts with which the French were then endeavoring to gird the English North American possessions; for, following the channels of communication between the great lakes, their posts were on the banks of the Niagara, while our adventurers had reached a point many leagues westward of that celebrated strait. The cutter rode at single anchor, without the breakers, resembling some well-imagined and accurately-executed toy, intended rather for a glass case than for struggles with the elements which she had so lately gone through, while the canoe lay on the narrow beach, just out of reach of the waves that came booming upon the land, a speck upon the shingles.

"We are very far here from human habitations!" exclaimed Mabel, when, after a long survey of the scene, its principal peculiarities forced themselves on her active and ever brilliant imagination; "this is indeed being on a frontier."

"Have they more sightly scenes than this nearer the sea and around their large towns?" demanded Pathfinder, with an interest he was apt to discover in such a subject.

"I will not say that: there is more to remind one of his fellow-beings there than here; less, perhaps, to remind one of God."

"Ay, Mabel, that is what my own feelings say. I am but a poor hunter, I know, untaught and unlarned; but God is as near me, in this my home, as he is near the king in his royal palace."

"Who can doubt it?" returned Mabel, looking from the view up into the hard-featured but honest face of her companion, though not without surprise at the energy of his manner. "One feels nearer to God in such a spot, I think, than when the mind is distracted by the objects of the towns."

"You say all I wish to say myself, Mabel, but in so much plainer speech, that you make me ashamed of wishing to let others know what I feel on such matters. I have coasted this lake in search of skins afore the war, and have been here already; not at this very spot, for we landed yonder, where you may see the blasted oak that stands above the cluster of hemlocks——"

"How, Pathfinder, can you remember all these trifles so accurately?"

"These are our streets and houses, our churches and palaces. Remember them, indeed! I once made an appointment with the Big Sarpent, to meet at twelve o'clock at noon, near the foot of a certain pine, at the end of six months, when neither of us was within three hundred miles of the spot. The tree stood, and stands still, unless the judgment of Providence has lighted on that too, in the midst of the forest, fifty miles from any settlement, but in a most extraordinary neighborhood for beaver."

"And did you meet at that very spot and hour?"

"Does the sun rise and set? When I reached the tree, I found the Sarpent leaning against its trunk with torn leggings and muddied moccasins. The Delaware had got into a swamp, and it worried him not a little to find his way out of it; but as the sun which comes over the eastern hills in the morning goes down behind the western at night, so was he true to time and place. No fear of Chingachgook when there is either a friend or an enemy in the case. He is equally sartain with each."

"And where is the Delaware now? why is he not with us to-day?"

"He is scouting on the Mingo trail, where I ought to have been too, but for a great human infirmity."

"You seem above, beyond, superior to all infirmity, Pathfinder; I never yet met with a man who appeared to be so little liable to the weaknesses of nature."

"If you mean in the way of health and strength, Mabel, Providence has been kind to me; though I fancy the open air, long hunts, active scoutings, forest fare, and the sleep of a good conscience, may always keep the doctors at a distance. But I am human after all; yes, I find I'm very human in some of my feelings."

Mabel looked surprised, and it would be no more than delineating the character of her sex, if we added that her sweet countenance expressed a good deal of curiosity, too, though her tongue was more discreet.

"There is something bewitching in this wild life of yours, Pathfinder," she exclaimed, a tinge of enthusiasm mantling her cheeks. "I find I'm fast getting to be a frontier girl, and am coming to love all this grand silence of the woods. The towns seem tame to me; and, as my father will probably pass the remainder of his days here, where he has already lived so long, I begin to feel that I should be happy to continue with him, and not to return to the sea-shore."

"The woods are never silent, Mabel, to such as understand their meaning. Days at a time have I travelled them alone, without feeling the want of company; and, as for conversation, for such as can comprehend their language, there is no want of rational and instructive discourse."

"I believe you are happier when alone, Pathfinder, than when mingling with your fellow-creatures."

"I will not say that, I will not say exactly that. I have seen the time when I have thought that God was sufficient for me in the forest, and that I have craved no more than His bounty and His care. But other feelings have got uppermost, and I suppose natur' will have its way. All other creatures mate, Mabel, and it was intended man should do so too."

"And have you never bethought you of seeking a wife, Pathfinder, to share your fortunes?" inquired the girl, with the directness and simplicity that the pure of heart and the undesigning are the most apt to manifest, and with that feeling of affection which is inbred in her sex. "To me it seems you only want a home to return to from your wanderings to render your life completely happy. Were I a man, it would be my delight to roam through these forests at will, or to sail over this beautiful lake."

"I understand you, Mabel; and God bless you for thinking of the welfare of men as humble as we are. We have our pleasures, it is true, as well as our gifts, but we might be happier; yes, I do think we might be happier."

"Happier! in what way, Pathfinder? In this pure air, with these cool and shaded forests to wander through, this lovely lake to gaze at and sail upon, with clear consciences, and abundance for all their real wants, men ought to be nothing less than as perfectly happy as their infirmities will allow."

"Every creatur' has its gifts, Mabel, and men have theirs," answered the guide, looking stealthily at his beautiful companion, whose cheeks had flushed and eyes brightened under the ardor of feelings excited by the novelty of her striking situation; "and all must obey them. Do you see yonder pigeon that is just alightin' on the beach—here in a line with the fallen chestnut?"

"Certainly; it is the only thing stirring with life in it, besides ourselves, that is to be seen in this vast solitude."

"Not so, Mabel, not so; Providence makes nothing that lives to live quite alone. Here is its mate, just rising on the wing; it has been feeding near the other beach, but it will not long be separated from its companion."

"I understand you, Pathfinder," returned Mabel, smiling sweetly, though as calmly as if the discourse was with her father. "But a hunter may find a mate, even in this wild region. The Indian girls are affectionate and true, I know; for such was the wife of Arrowhead, to a husband who oftener frowned than smiled."

"That would never do, Mabel, and good would never come of it. Kind must cling to kind, and country to country, if one would find happiness. If, indeed, I could meet with one like you, who would consent to be a hunter's wife, and who would not scorn my ignorance and rudeness, then, indeed, would all the toil of the past appear like the sporting of the young deer, and all the future like sunshine."

"One like me! A girl of my years and indiscretion would

hardly make a fit companion for the boldest scout and surest hunter on the lines."

"Ah, Mabel! I fear me that I have been improving a red-skin's gifts with a pale-face's natur'? Such a character would insure a wife in an Indian village."

"Surely, surely, Pathfinder, you would not think of choosing one so ignorant, so frivolous, so vain, and so inexperienced as I for your wife?" Mabel would have added, "and as young"; but an instinctive feeling of delicacy repressed the words.

"Any why not, Mabel? If you are ignorant of frontier usages, you know more than all of us of pleasant anecdotes and town customs: as for frivolous, I know not what it means; but if it signifies beauty, ah's me! I fear it is no fault in my eyes. Vain you are not, as is seen by the kind manner in which you listen to all my idle tales about scoutings and trails; and as for experience, that will come with years. Besides, Mabel, I fear men think little of these matters when they are about to take wives: I do."

"Pathfinder, your words—your looks—surely, all this is meant in trifling; you speak in pleasantry?"

"To me it is always agreeable to be near you, Mabel; and I should sleep sounder this blessed night than I have done for a week past, could I think that you find such discourse as pleasant as I do."

We shall not say that Mabel Dunham had not believed herself a favorite with the guide. This her quick feminine sagacity had early discovered; and perhaps she had occasionally thought there had mingled with his regard and friendship some of that manly tenderness which the ruder sex must be coarse, indeed, not to show on occasions to the gentler; but the idea that he seriously sought her for his wife had never before crossed the mind of the spirited and ingenuous girl. Now, however, a gleam of something like the truth broke in upon her imagination, less induced by the words of her companion, perhaps, than by his manner. Looking earnestly into the rugged, honest countenance of the scout, Mabel's own features became concerned and grave; and when she spoke again, it was with a gentleness of manner that attracted him to her even more powerfully than the words themselves were calculated to repel.

"You and I should understand each other, Pathfinder," said she with an earnest sincerity; "nor should there be any cloud between us. You are too upright and frank to meet with anything but sincerity and frankness in return. Surely, surely, all this means nothing—has no other connection with your feelings than such a friendship as one of your wisdom and character would naturally feel for a girl like me?"

"I believe it's all nat'ral, Mabel; yes, I do: the Sergeant tells me he had such feelings towards your own mother, and I think I've seen something like it in the young people I have from time to time guided through the wilderness. Yes, yes, I daresay it's all nat'ral enough, and that makes it come so easy, and is a great comfort to me."

"Pathfinder, your words make me uneasy. Speak plainer, or change the subject for ever. You do not, cannot mean that— you cannot wish me to understand"—even the tongue of the spirited Mabel faltered, and she shrank, with maiden shame, from adding what she wished so earnestly to say. Rallying her courage, however, and determined to know all as soon and as plainly as possible, after a moment's hesitation, she continued— "I mean, Pathfinder, that you do not wish me to understand that you seriously think of me as a wife?"

"I do, Mabel; that's it, that's just it; and you have put the matter in a much better point of view than I with my forest gifts and frontier ways would ever be able to do. The Sergeant and I have concluded on the matter, if it is agreeable to you, as he thinks is likely to be the case; though I doubt my own power to please one who deserves the best husband America can produce."

Mabel's countenance changed from uneasiness to surprise; and then, by a transition still quicker, from surprise to pain.

"My father!" she exclaimed—"my dear father has thought of my becoming your wife, Pathfinder?"

"Yes, he has, Mabel, he has, indeed. He has even thought such a thing might be agreeable to you, and has almost encouraged me to fancy it might be true."

"But you yourself—you certainly can care nothing whether this singular expectation shall ever be realized or not?"

"Anan?"

"I mean, Pathfinder, that you have talked of this match more to oblige my father than anything else; that your feelings are no way concerned, let my answer be what it may?"

The scout looked earnestly into the beautiful face of Mabel, which had flushed with the ardor and novelty of her sensations, and it was not possible to mistake the intense admiration that betrayed itself in every lineament of his ingenuous countenance.

"I have often thought myself happy, Mabel, when ranging the woods on a successful hunt, breathing the pure air of the hills, and filled with vigor and health; but I now know that it has all been idleness and vanity compared with the delight it would give me to know that you thought better of me than you think of most others."

"Better of you!—I do, indeed, think better of you, Pathfinder, than of most others: I am not certain that I do not think better of you than of any other; for your truth, honesty, simplicity, justice, and courage are scarcely equalled by any of earth."

"Ah, Mabel, these are sweet and encouraging words from you! and the Sergeant, after all, was not so near wrong as I feared."

"Nay, Pathfinder, in the name of all that is sacred and just, do not let us misunderstand each other in a matter of so much importance. While I esteem, respect, nay, reverence you, almost as much as I reverence my own dear father, it is impossible that I should ever become your wife—that I   "

The change in her companion's countenance was so sudden and so great, that the moment the effect of what she had uttered became visible in the face of the Pathfinder, Mabel arrested her own words, notwithstanding her strong desire to be explicit, the reluctance with which she could at any time cause pain being sufficient of itself to induce the pause. Neither spoke for some time, the shade of disappointment that crossed the rugged lineaments of the hunter amounting so nearly to anguish as to frighten his companion, while the sensation of choking became so strong in the Pathfinder that he fairly griped his throat, like one who sought physical relief for physical suffering. The convulsive manner in which his fingers worked actually struck the alarmed girl with a feeling of awe.

"Nay, Pathfinder," Mabel eagerly added, the instant she could command her voice—"I may have said more than I mean; for all things of this nature are possible, and women, they say, are never sure of their own minds. What I wish you to understand is, that it is not likely that you and I should ever think of each other as man and wife ought to think of each other."

"I do not—I shall never think in that way again, Mabel," gasped forth the Pathfinder, who appeared to utter his words like one just raised above the pressure of some suffocating substance. "No, no, I shall never think of you, or any one else, again in that way."

"Pathfinder, dear Pathfinder, understand me; do not attach more meaning to my words than I do myself: a match like that would be unwise, unnatural, perhaps."

"Yes, unnat'ral—ag'in natur'; and so I told the Sergeant, but he *would* have it otherwise."

"Pathfinder! oh, this is worse than I could have imagined! Take my hand, excellent Pathfinder, and let me see that you do not hate me. For God's sake, smile upon me again."

"Hate you, Mabel! Smile upon you! Ah's me!"

"Nay, give me your hand; your hardy, true, and manly hand—both, both, Pathfinder! for I shall not be easy until I feel certain that we are friends again, and that all this has been a mistake."

"Mabel!" said the guide, looking wistfully into the face of the generous and impetuous girl, as she held his two hard and sunburnt hands in her own pretty and delicate fingers, and laughing in his own silent and peculiar manner, while anguish gleamed over lineaments which seemed incapable of deception, even while agitated with emotions so conflicting—"Mabel! the Sergeant was wrong."

The pent-up feelings could endure no more, and the tears rolled down the cheeks of the scout like rain. His fingers again worked convulsively at his throat; and his breast heaved, as if it possessed a tenant of which it would be rid, by any effort, however desperate.

"Pathfinder! Pathfinder!" Mabel almost shrieked; "anything but this, anything but this! Speak to me, Pathfinder! smile again, say one kind word, anything to prove you can forgive me."

"The Sergeant was wrong!" exclaimed the guide, laughing amid his agony, in a way to terrify his companion by the unnatural mixture of anguish and light-heartedness. "I knew it, I knew it, and said it; yes, the Sergeant was wrong after all."

"We can be friends, though we cannot be man and wife," continued Mabel, almost as much disturbed as her companion, scarcely knowing what she said; "we can always be friends, and always will."

"I thought the Sergeant was mistaken," resumed the Pathfinder, when a great effort had enabled him to command himself, "for I did not think my gifts were such as would please the fancy of a town-bred girl. It would have been better, Mabel, had he not over-persuaded me into a different notion; and it might have been better, too, had you not been so pleasant and confiding like; yes, it would."

"If I thought any error of mine had raised false expectations in you, Pathfinder, however unintentionally on my part, I should never forgive myself; for, believe me, I would rather endure pain in my own feelings than you should suffer."

"That's just it, Mabel, that's just it. These speeches and opinions, spoken in so soft a voice, and in a way I'm so unused to in the woods, have done the mischief. But I now see plainly, and begin to understand the difference between us better, and will strive to keep down thought, and to go abroad again as I used to do, looking for the game and the inimy. Ah's me, Mabel! I have indeed been on a false trail since we met."

"In a little while you will forget all this, and think of me as a friend, who owes you her life."

"This may be the way in the towns, but I doubt if it's nat'ral to the woods. With us, when the eye sees a lovely sight, it is apt to keep it long in view, or when the mind takes in an upright and proper feeling, it is loath to part with it."

"You will forget it all, when you come seriously to recollect that I am altogether unsuited to be your wife."

"So I told the Sergeant; but he would have it otherwise. I knew you was too young and beautiful for one of middle age, like myself, and who never was comely to look at even in youth; and then your ways have not been my ways; nor would a hunter's cabin be a fitting place for one who was edicated among chiefs, as it were. If I were younger and comelier, though, like Jasper Eau-douce——"

"Never mind Jasper Eau-douce," interrupted Mabel impatiently; "we can talk of something else."

"Jasper is a worthy lad, Mabel; ay, and a comely," returned the guileless guide, looking earnestly at the girl, as if he distrusted her judgment in speaking slightingly of his friend. "Were I only half as comely as Jasper Western, my misgivings in this affair would not have been so great, and they might not have been so true."

"We will not talk of Jasper Western," repeated Mabel, the color mounting to her temples; "he may be good enough in a gale, or on the lake, but he is not good enough to talk of here."

"I fear me, Mabel, he is better than the man who is likely to be your husband, though the Sergeant says that never can take place. But the Sergeant was wrong once, and he may be wrong twice."

"And who is likely to be my husband, Pathfinder! This is scarcely less strange than what has just passed between us."

"I know it is nat'ral for like to seek like, and for them that have consorted much with officers' ladies to wish to be officers' ladies themselves. But, Mabel, I may speak plainly to you, I know; and I hope my words will not give you pain; for, now I understand what it is to be disappointed in such feelings, I wouldn't wish to cause even a Mingo sorrow on this head. But happiness is not always to be found in a marquee, any more than in a tent; and though the officers' quarters may look more tempting than the rest of the barracks, there is often great misery between husband and wife inside of their doors."

"I do not doubt it in the least, Pathfinder; and, did it rest with me to decide, I would sooner follow you to some cabin in the woods, and share your fortune, whether it might be better or worse, than go inside the door of any officer I know, with an intention of remaining there as its master's wife."

"Mabel, this is not what Lundie hopes, or Lundie thinks."

"And what care I for Lundie? He is major of the 55th, and may command his men to wheel and march about as he pleases; but he cannot compel me to wed the greatest or the meanest of his mess. Besides, what can you know of Lundie's wishes on such a subject?"

"From Lundie's own mouth. The Sergeant had told him that he wished me for a son-in-law; and the Major, being an old and a true friend, conversed with me on the subject. He put it to me plainly, whether it would not be more ginerous in me to let an officer succeed, than to strive to make you share a hunter's fortune. I owned the truth, I did; and that was, that I thought it might; but when he told me that the Quartermaster would be his choice, I would not abide by the conditions. No, no, Mabel; I know Davy Muir well, and though he may make you a lady, he can never make you a happy woman, or himself a gentleman."

"My father has been very wrong if he has said or done aught to cause you sorrow, Pathfinder; and so great is my respect for you, so sincere my friendship, that were it not for one—I mean that no person need fear Lieutenant Muir's influence with me—I would rather remain as I am to my dying day than become a lady at the cost of being his wife."

"I do not think you would say that which you do not feel, Mabel," returned Pathfinder earnestly.

"Not at such a moment, on such a subject, and least of all to you. No; Lieutenant Muir may find wives where he can—my name shall never be on his catalogue."

"Thank you, thank you for that, Mabel; for, though there is no longer any hope for me, I could never be happy were you to take to the Quartermaster. I feared the commission might count for something, I did; and I know the man. It is not jealousy that makes me speak in this manner, but truth, for I know the man. Now, were you to fancy a desarving youth, one like Jasper Western, for instance——"

"Why always mention Jasper Eau-douce, Pathfinder? he can have no concern with our friendship; let us talk of yourself, and of the manner in which you intend to pass the winter."

"Ah's me!—I'm little worth at the best, Mabel, unless it may be on a trail or with the rifle; and less worth now that I have discovered the Sergeant's mistake. There is no need, therefore, of talking of me. It has been very pleasant to me to be near you so long, and even to fancy that the Sergeant was right; but that is all over now. I shall go down the lake with Jasper, and then there will be business to occupy us, and that will keep useless thoughts out of the mind."

"And you will forget this—forget me—no, not forget me, either, Pathfinder; but you will resume your old pursuits, and cease to think a girl of sufficient importance to disturb your peace?"

"I never knowed it afore, Mabel; but girls are of more account in this life than I could have believed. Now, afore I knowed you, the new-born babe did not sleep more sweetly than I used; my head was no sooner on the root, or the stone, or mayhap on the skin, than all was lost to the senses, unless it might be to go over in the night the business of the day in a dream like; and there I lay till the moment came to be stirring, and the swallows were not more certain to be on the wing with the light, than I to be afoot at the moment I wished to be. All this seemed a gift, and might be calculated on even in the midst of a Mingo camp; for I've been outlying in my time, in the very villages of the vagabonds."

"And all this will return to you, Pathfinder, for one so upright and sincere will never waste his happiness on a mere fancy. You will dream again of your hunts, of the deer you have slain, and of the beaver you have taken."

"Ah's me, Mabel, I wish never to dream again! Before we met, I had a sort of pleasure in following up the hounds, in fancy, as it might be; and even in striking a trail of the Iroquois —nay, I've been in scrimmages and ambushments, in thought like, and found satisfaction in it, according to my gifts; but all those things have lost their charms since I've made acquaintance with you. Now, I think no longer of anything rude in my dreams; but the very last night we stayed in the garrison I imagined I had a cabin in a grove of sugar maples, and at the root of every tree was a Mabel Dunham, while the birds among the branches sang ballads instead of the notes that natur' gave, and even the deer stopped to listen. I tried to shoot a fa'n, but Killdeer missed fire, and the creatur' laughed in my face, as pleasantly as a young girl laughs in her merriment, and then it bounded away, looking back as if expecting me to follow."

"No more of this, Pathfinder; we'll talk no more of these things," said Mabel, dashing the tears from her eyes; for the simple, earnest manner in which this hardy woodsman betrayed the deep hold she had taken of his feelings nearly proved too much for her own generous heart. "Now, let us look for my father; he cannot be distant, as I heard his gun quite near."

"The Sergeant was wrong—yes, he was wrong, and it's of no avail to attempt to make the dove consort with the wolf."

"Here comes my dear father," interrupted Mabel. "Let us look cheerful and happy, Pathfinder, as such good friends ought to look, and keep each other's secrets."

A pause succeeded; the Sergeant's foot was heard crushing the dried twigs hard by, and then his form appeared shoving aside the bushes of a copse just near. As he issued into the open ground, the old soldier scrutinized his daughter and her companion, and speaking good-naturedly, he said, "Mabel, child, you are young and light of foot—look for a bird that I've shot that fell just beyond the thicket of young hemlocks on the shore; and, as Jasper is showing signs of an intention of getting under way, you need not take the trouble to clamber up this hill again, but we will meet you on the beach in a few minutes."

Mabel obeyed, bounding down the hill with the elastic step of youth and health. But, notwithstanding the lightness of her steps, the heart of the girl was heavy, and no sooner was she hid from observation by the thicket, than she threw herself on the root of a tree and wept as if her heart would break. The Sergeant watched her until she disappeared, with a father's pride, and then turned to his companion with a smile as kind and as familiar as his habits would allow him to use towards any.

"She has her mother's lightness and activity, my friend, with somewhat of her father's force," said he. "Her mother was not quite so handsome, I think myself; but the Dunhams were always thought comely, whether men or women. Well, Pathfinder, I take it for granted you've not overlooked the opportunity, but have spoken plainly to the girl? women like frankness in matters of this sort."

"I believe Mabel and I understand each other at last, Sergeant," returned the other, looking another way to avoid the soldier's face.

"So much the better. Some people fancy that a little doubt and uncertainty makes love all the livelier; but I am one of those who think the plainer the tongue speaks the easier the mind will comprehend. Was Mabel surprised?"

"I fear she was, Sergeant; I fear she was taken quite by surprise—yes, I do."

"Well, well, surprises in love are like an ambush in war, and quite as lawful; though it is not so easy to tell when a woman is surprised, as to tell when it happens to an enemy. Mabel did not run away, my worthy friend, did she?"

"No, Sergeant, Mabel did not try to escape; *that* I can say with a clear conscience."

"I hope the girl was not too willing, neither! Her mother was shy and coy for a month, at least; but frankness, after all, is a recommendation in a man or woman."

"That it is, that it is; and judgment, too."

"You are not to look for too much judgment in a young creature of twenty, Pathfinder, but it will come with experience. A mistake in you or me, for instance, might not be so easily overlooked; but in a girl of Mabel's years, one is not to strain at a gnat lest they swallow a camel."

The reader will remember that Sergeant Dunham was not a Hebrew scholar.

The muscles of the listener's face twitched as the Sergeant was thus delivering his sentiments, though the former had now recovered a portion of that stoicism which formed so large a part of his character, and which he had probably imbibed from long association with the Indians. His eyes rose and fell, and once a gleam shot athwart his hard features as if he were about to indulge in his peculiar laugh; but the joyous feeling, if it really existed, was as quickly lost in a look allied to anguish. It was this unusual mixture of wild and keen mental agony with native, simple joyousness, which had most struck Mabel, who, in the interview just related, had a dozen times been on the point of believing that her suitor's heart was only lightly touched, as images of happiness and humor gleamed over a mind that was almost infantine in its simplicity and nature; an impression, however, which was soon driven away by the discovery of emotions so painful and so deep, that they seemed to harrow the very soul.

"You say true, Sergeant," Pathfinder answered; "a mistake in one like you is a more serious matter."

"You will find Mabel sincere and honest in the end; give her but a little time."

"Ah's me, Sergeant!"

"A man of your merits would make an impression on a rock, give him time, Pathfinder."

"Sergeant Dunham, we are old fellow-campaigners—that is, as campaigns are carried on here in the wilderness; and we have done so many kind acts to each other that we can afford to be candid—what has caused you to believe that a girl like Mabel could ever fancy one so rude as I am?"

"What?—why, a variety of reasons, and good reasons too, my friend. Those same acts of kindness, perhaps, and the campaigns you mention; moreover, you are my sworn and tried comrade."

"All this sounds well, so far as you and I are consarned; but they do not touch the case of your pretty daughter. She may think these very campaigns have destroyed the little comeliness I may once have had; and I am not quite sartain that being an old friend of her father would lead any young maiden's mind into a particular affection for a suitor. Like loves like, I tell you, Sergeant; and my gifts are not altogether the gifts of Mabel Dunham."

"These are some of your old modest qualms, Pathfinder, and will do you no credit with the girl. Women distrust men who distrust themselves, and take to men who distrust nothing. Modesty is a capital thing in a recruit, I grant you; or in a young subaltern who has just joined, for it prevents his railing at the non-commissioned officers before he knows what to rail at; I'm not sure it is out of place in a commissary or a parson, but it's the devil and all when it gets possession of a real soldier or a lover. Have as little to do with it as possible, if you would win a woman's heart. As for your doctrine that like loves like, it is as wrong as possible in matters of this sort. If like loved like, women would love one another, and men also. No, no, like loves dislike"—the Sergeant was merely a scholar of the camp— "and you have nothing to fear from Mabel on that score. Look at Lieutenant Muir; the man has had five wives already, they tell me, and there is no more modesty in him than there is in a cat-o'-nine-tails."

"Lieutenant Muir will never be the husband of Mabel Dunham, let him ruffle his feathers as much as he may."

"That is a sensible remark of yours, Pathfinder; for my mind is made up that you shall be my son-in-law. If I were an officer myself, Mr. Muir might have some chance; but time has placed one door between my child and myself, and I don't intend there shall be that of a marquee also."

"Sergeant, we must let Mabel follow her own fancy; she is young and light of heart, and God forbid that any wish of mine should lay the weight of a feather on a mind that is all gaiety now, or take one note of happiness from her laughter!"

"Have you conversed freely with the girl?" the Sergeant demanded quickly, and with some asperity of manner.

Pathfinder was too honest to deny a truth plain as that which the answer required, and yet too honorable to betray Mabel, and expose her to the resentment of one whom he well knew to be stern in his anger.

"We have laid open our minds," he said; "and though Mabel's is one that any man might love to look at, I find little there, Sergeant, to make me think any better of myself."

"The girl has not dared to refuse you—to refuse her father's best friend?"

Pathfinder turned his face away to conceal the look of anguish that consciousness told him was passing athwart it, but he continued the discourse in his own quiet, manly tones.

"Mabel is too kind to refuse anything, or to utter harsh words to a dog. I have not put the question in a way to be downright refused, Sergeant."

"And did you expect my daughter to jump into your arms before you asked her? She would not have been her mother's child had she done any such thing, nor do I think she would have been mine. The Dunhams like plain dealing as well as the king's majesty; but they are no jumpers. Leave me to manage this matter for you, Pathfinder, and there shall be no unnecessary delay. I'll speak to Mabel myself this very evening, using your name as principal in the affair."

"I'd rather not, I'd rather not, Sergeant. Leave the matter to Mabel and me, and I think all will come right in the ind. Young girls are like timorsome birds; they do not over-relish being hurried or spoken harshly to nither. Leave the matter to Mabel and me."

"On one condition I will, my friend; and that is, that you will promise me, on the honor of a scout, that you will put the matter plainly to Mabel the first suitable opportunity, and no mincing of words."

"I will ask her, Sergeant, on condition that you promise not to meddle in the affair—yes, I will promise to ask Mabel whether she will marry me, even though she laugh in my face at my doing so, on that condition."

Sergeant Dunham gave the desired promise very cheerfully; for he had completely wrought himself up into the belief that the man he so much esteemed himself must be acceptable to his daughter. He had married a woman much younger than himself, and he saw no unfitness in the respective years of the intended couple. Mabel was educated so much above him, too, that he was not aware of the difference which actually existed between the parent and child in this respect. It followed that Sergeant Dunham was not altogether qualified to appreciate his daughter's tastes, or to form a very probable conjecture what would be the direction taken by those feelings which oftener depend on impulses and passion than on reason. Still, the worthy soldier was not so wrong in his estimate of the Pathfinder's chances as might at first appear. Knowing all the sterling qualities of the man, his truth, integrity of purpose, courage, self-devotion, disinterestedness, it was far from unreasonable to suppose that qualities like these would produce a deep impression on any female heart; and the father erred principally in fancying that the daughter might know as it might be by intuition what he himself had acquired by years of intercourse and adventure.

As Pathfinder and his military friend descended the hill to the shore of the lake, the discourse did not flag. The latter continued to persuade the former that his diffidence alone prevented complete success with Mabel, and that he had only to persevere in order to prevail. Pathfinder was much too modest by nature, and had been too plainly, though so delicately, discouraged in the recent interview to believe all he heard; still the father used so many arguments which seemed plausible, and it was so grateful to fancy that the daughter might yet be his, that the reader is not to be surprised when he is told that this unsophisticated being did not view Mabel's recent conduct in precisely the light in which he may be inclined to view it himself. He did not credit all that the Sergeant told him, it is true; but he began to think virgin coyness and ignorance of her own feelings might have induced Mabel to use the language she had.

"The Quartermaster is no favorite," said Pathfinder in answer to one of his companion's remarks. "Mabel will never look on him as more than one who has had four or five wives already."

"Which is more than his share. A man may marry twice without offence to good morals and decency, I allow! but four times is an aggravation."

"I should think even marrying once what Master Cap calls a circumstance," put in Pathfinder, laughing in his quiet way, for by this time his spirits had recovered some of their buoyancy.

"It is, indeed, my friend, and a most solemn circumstance too. If it were not that Mabel is to be your wife, I would advise you to remain single. But here is the girl herself, and discretion is the word."

"Ah's me, Sergeant, I fear you are mistaken!"

CHAPTER XIX

Thus was this place
A happy rural seat of various view. MILTON

MABEL was in waiting on the beach, and the canoe was soon launched. Pathfinder carried the party out through the surf in the same skillful manner that he had brought it in; and though Mabel's color heightened with excitement, and her heart seemed often ready to leap out of her mouth again, they reached the side of the *Scud* without having received even a drop of spray.

Ontario is like a quick-tempered man, sudden to be angered, and as soon appeased. The sea had already fallen; and though the breakers bounded the shore, far as the eye could reach, it was merely in lines of brightness, that appeared and vanished like the returning waves produced by a stone which had been dropped into a pool. The cable of the *Scud* was scarcely seen above the water, and Jasper had already hoisted his sails, in readiness to depart as soon as the expected breeze from the shore should fill the canvas.

It was just sunset as the cutter's mainsail flapped and its stem began to sever the water. The air was light and southerly, and the head of the vessel was kept looking up along the south shore, it being the intention to get to the eastward again as fast as possible. The night that succeeded was quiet; and the rest of those who slept deep and tranquil.

Some difficulty occurred concerning the command of the vessel, but the matter had been finally settled by an amicable compromise. As the distrust of Jasper was far from being appeased, Cap retained a supervisory power, while the young man was allowed to work the craft, subject, at all times, to the control and interference of the old seaman. To this Jasper consented, in preference to exposing Mabel any longer to the dangers of their present situation; for, now that the violence of the elements had ceased, he well knew that the *Montcalm* would be in search of them. He had the discretion, however, not to reveal his apprehensions on this head; for it happened that the very means he deemed the best to escape the enemy were those which would be most likely to awaken new suspicions of his honesty in the minds of those who held the power to defeat his intentions. In other words, Jasper believed that the gallant young Frenchman, who commanded the ship of the enemy, would quit his anchorage under the fort at Niagara, and stand up the lake, as soon as the wind abated, in order to ascertain the fate of the *Scud*, keeping midway between the two shores as the best means of commanding a broad view; and that, on his part, it would be expedient to hug one coast or the other, not only to avoid a meeting, but as affording a chance of passing without detection by blending his sails and spars with objects on the land. He preferred the south because it was the weather shore, and because he thought it was that which the enemy would the least expect him to take, though it necessarily led near his settlements, and in front of one of the strongest posts he held in that part of the world.

Of all this, however, Cap was happily ignorant, and the Sergeant's mind was too much occupied with the details of his military trust to enter into these niceties, which so properly belonged to another profession. No opposition was made, therefore, and before morning Jasper had apparently dropped quietly into all his former authority, issuing his orders freely, and meeting with obedience without hesitation or cavil.

The appearance of day brought all on board on deck again; and, as is usual with adventurers on the water, the opening horizon was curiously examined, as objects started out of the obscurity, and the panorama brightened under the growing light. East, west, and north nothing was visible but water glittering in the rising sun; but southward stretched the endless belt of woods that then held Ontario in a setting of forest verdure. Suddenly an opening appeared ahead, and then the massive walls of a château-looking house, with outworks, bastions, blockhouses, and palisadoes, frowned on a headland that bordered the outlet of a broad stream. Just as the fort became visible, a little cloud rose over it, and the white ensign of France was seen fluttering from a lofty flagstaff.

Cap gave an ejaculation as he witnessed this ungrateful exhibition, and he cast a quick suspicious glance at his brother-in-law.

"The dirty tablecloth hung up to air, as my name is Charles Cap!" he muttered; "and we hugging this d—d shore as if it were our wife and children met on the return from an India v'y'ge! Hark'e, Jasper, are you in search of a cargo of frogs, that you keep so near in to this New France?"

"I hug the land, sir, in the hope of passing the enemy's ship without being seen, for I think she must be somewhere down here to leeward."

"Ay, ay, this sounds well, and I hope it may turn out as you say. I trust there is no under-tow here?"

"We are on a weather shore, now," said Jasper, smiling; "and I think you will admit, Master Cap, that a strong under-tow makes an easy cable: we owe all our lives to the under-tow of this very lake."

"French flummery!" growled Cap, though he did not care to be heard by Jasper. "Give me a fair, honest, English-Yankee-American tow, above board, and above water too, if I must have a tow at all, and none of your sneaking drift that is below the surface, where one can neither see nor feel. I daresay, if the truth could be come at, that this late escape of ours was all a contrived affair."

"We have now a good opportunity, at least, to reconnoitre the enemy's post at Niagara, brother, for such I take this fort to be," put in the Sergeant. "Let us be all eyes in passing, and remember that we are almost in face of the enemy."

This advice of the Sergeant needed nothing to enforce it; for the interest and novelty of passing a spot occupied by human beings were of themselves sufficient to attract deep attention in that scene of a vast but deserted nature. The wind was now fresh enough to urge the *Scud* through the water with considerable velocity, and Jasper eased her helm as she opened the river, and luffed nearly into the mouth of that noble strait, or river, as it is termed. A dull, distant, heavy roar came down through the opening in the banks, swelling on the currents of the air, like the deeper notes of some immense organ, and occasionally seeming to cause the earth itself to tremble.

"That sounds like surf on some long unbroken coast!" exclaimed Cap, as a swell, deeper than common, came to his ears.

"Ay, that is such surf as we have in this quarter of the world," Pathfinder answered. "There is no under-tow there, Master Cap; but all the water that strikes the rocks stays there, so far as going back again is consarned. That is old Niagara that you hear, or this noble stream tumbling down a mountain."

"No one will have the impudence to pretend that this fine broad river falls over yonder hills?"

"It does, Master Cap, it does; and all for the want of stairs, or a road to come down by. This is natur', as we have it up hereaway, though I daresay you beat us down on the ocean. Ah's me, Mabel! a pleasant hour it would be if we could walk on the shore some ten or fifteen miles up this stream, and gaze on all that God has done there."

"You have, then, seen these renowned falls, Pathfinder?" the girl eagerly inquired.

"I have—yes, I have; and an awful sight I witnessed at that same time. The Sarpent and I were out scouting about the garrison there, when he told me that the traditions of his people gave an account of a mighty cataract in this neighborhood, and he asked me to vary from the line of march a little to look at the wonder. I had heard some marvels consarning the spot from the soldiers of the 60th, which is my nat'ral corps like, and not the 55th, with which I have sojourned so much of late; but there are so many terrible liars in all rijiments that I hardly believed half they had told me. Well, we went; and though we expected to be led by our ears, and to hear some of that awful roaring that we hear to-day, we were disappointed, for natur' was not then speaking in thunder, as she is this morning. Thus it is in the forest, Master Cap; there being moments when God seems to be walking abroad in power, and then again, there is a calm over all, as if His spirit lay in quiet along the 'arth. Well, we came suddenly upon the stream, a short distance above the fall, and a young Delaware, who was in our company, found a bark canoe, and he would push into the current to reach an island that lies in the very centre of the confusion and strife. We told him of his folly, we did; and we reasoned with him on the wickedness of tempting Providence by seeking danger that led to no ind; but the youth among the Delawares are very much the same as the youth among the soldiers, risky and vain. All we could say did not change his mind, and the lad had his way. To me it seems, Mabel, that whenever a thing is really grand and potent, it has a quiet majesty about it, altogether unlike the frothy and fluster-ing manner of smaller matters, and so it was with them rapids. The canoe was no sooner fairly in them, than down it went, as it might be, as one sails through the air on the 'arth, and no skill of the young Delaware could resist the stream. And yet he strug-gled manfully for life, using the paddle to the last, like the deer that is swimming to cast the hounds. At first he shot across the current so swiftly, that we thought he would prevail; but he had miscalculated his distance, and when the truth really struck him, he turned the head up-stream, and struggled in a way that was fearful to look at. I could have pitied him even had he been a Mingo. For a few moments his efforts were so frantic that he actually prevailed over the power of the cataract; but natur' has its limits, and one faltering stroke of the paddle set him back, and then he lost ground, foot by foot, inch by inch, until he got near the spot where the river looked even and green, and as if it were made of millions of threads of water, all bent over some huge rock, when he shot backwards like an arrow and disap-peared, the bow of the canoe tipping just enough to let us see what had become of him. I met a Mohawk some years later who had witnessed the whole affair from the bed of the stream below, and he told me that the Delaware continued to paddle in the air until he was lost in the mists of the falls."

"And what became of the poor wretch?" demanded Mabel, who had been strongly interested by the natural eloquence of the speaker.

"He went to the happy hunting-grounds of his people, no doubt; for though he was risky and vain, he was also just and brave. Yes, he died foolishly, but the Manitou of the red-skins has compassion on his creaturs as well as the God of a Christian."

A gun at this moment was discharged from a blockhouse near the fort; and the shot, one of light weight, came whistling over the cutter's mast, an admonition to approach no nearer. Jasper was at the helm, and he kept away, smiling at the same time as if he felt no anger at the rudeness of the salutation. The *Scud* was now in the current, and her outward set soon carried her far enough to leeward to avoid the danger of a repetition of the shot, and then she quietly continued her course along the land. As soon as the river was fairly opened, Jasper ascertained that the *Montcalm* was not at anchor in it; and a man sent aloft came down with the report that the horizon showed no sail. The hope was now strong that the artifice of Jasper had succeeded, and that the French commander had missed them by keeping the middle of the lake as he steered towards its head.

All that day the wind hung to the southward, and the cutter continued her course about a league from the land, running six or eight knots the hour in perfectly smooth water. Although the scene had one feature of monotony, the outline of unbroken forest, it was not without its interest and pleasures. Various headlands presented themselves, and the cutter, in running from one to another, stretched across bays so deep as almost to deserve the name of gulfs. But nowhere did the eye meet with the evidences of civilization; rivers occasionally poured their tribute into the great reservoir of the lake, but their banks could be traced inland for miles by the same outlines of trees; and even large bays, that lay embosomed in woods, communicating with Ontario only by narrow outlets, appeared and disappeared, without bringing with them a single trace of a human habitation.

Of all on board, the Pathfinder viewed the scene with the most unmingled delight. His eyes feasted on the endless line of forest, and more than once that day, notwithstanding he found it so grateful to be near Mabel, listening to her pleasant voice, and echoing, in feelings at least, her joyous laugh, did his soul pine to be wandering beneath the high arches of the maples, oaks, and lindens, where his habits had induced him to fancy lasting and true joys were only to be found. Cap viewed the prospect differently; more than once he expressed his disgust at there being no lighthouses, church-towers, beacons, or roadsteads with their shipping. Such another coast, he protested, the world did not contain; and, taking the Sergeant aside, he gravely assured him that the region could never come to anything, as the havens were neglected, the rivers had a deserted and useless look, and that even the breeze had a smell of the forest about it, which spoke ill of its properties.

But the humors of the different individuals in her did not stay the speed of the *Scud:* when the sun was setting, she was already a hundred miles on her route towards Oswego, into which river Sergeant Dunham now thought it his duty to go, in order to receive any communications that Major Duncan might please to make. With a view to effect this purpose, Jasper continued to hug the shore all night; and though the wind began to fail him towards morning, it lasted long enough to carry the cutter up to a point that was known to be but a league or two from the fort. Here the breeze came out light at the northward, and the cutter hauled a little from the land, in order to obtain a safe offing should it come on to blow, or should the weather again get to be easterly.

When the day dawned, the cutter had the mouth of the Oswego well under the lee, distant about two miles; and just as the morning gun from the fort was fired, Jasper gave the order to ease off the sheets, and to bear up for his port. At that moment a cry from the forecastle drew all eyes towards the point on the eastern side of the outlet, and there, just without the range of shot from the light guns of the works, with her canvas reduced to barely enough to keep her stationary, lay the *Montcalm*, evidently in waiting for their appearance.

To pass her was impossible, for by filling her sails the French ship could have intercepted them in a few minutes; and the circumstances called for a prompt decision. After a short consultation, the Sergeant again changed his plan, determining to make the best of his way towards the station for which he had been originally destined, trusting to the speed of the *Scud* to throw the enemy so far astern as to leave no clue to her movements.

The cutter accordingly hauled upon a wind with the least possible delay, with everything set that would draw. Guns were fired from the fort, ensigns shown, and the ramparts were again crowded. But sympathy was all the aid that Lundie could lend to his party; and the *Montcalm*, also firing four or five guns of defiance, and throwing abroad several of the banners of France, was soon in chase under a cloud of canvas.

For several hours the two vessels were pressing through the water as fast as possible, making short stretches to windward, apparently with a view to keep the port under their lee, the one to enter it if possible, and the other to intercept it in the attempt.

At meridian the French ship was hull down, dead to leeward, the disparity of sailing on a wind being very great, and some islands were near by, behind which Jasper said it would be possible for the cutter to conceal her future movements. Although Cap and the Sergeant, and particularly Lieutenant Muir, to judge by his language, still felt a good deal of distrust of the young man, and Frontenac was not distant, this advice was followed; for time pressed, and the Quartermaster discreetly observed that Jasper could not well betray them without running openly into the enemy's harbor, a step they could at any time prevent, since the only cruiser of force the French possessed at the moment was under their lee and not in a situation to do them any immediate injury.

Left to himself, Jasper Western soon proved how much was really in him. He weathered upon the islands, passed them, and on coming out to the eastward, kept broad away, with nothing in sight in his wake or to leeward. By sunset again the cutter was up with the first of the islands that lie in the outlet of the lake; and ere it was dark she was running through the narrow channels on her way to the long-sought station. At nine o'clock, however, Cap insisted that they should anchor; for the maze of islands became so complicated and obscure, that he feared, at every opening, the party would find themselves under the guns of a French fort. Jasper consented cheerfully, it being a part of his standing instructions to approach the station under such circumstances as would prevent the men from obtaining any very accurate notions of its position, lest a deserter might betray the little garrison to the enemy.

The *Scud* was brought to in a small retired bay, where it would have been difficult to find her by daylight, and where she was perfectly concealed at night, when all but a solitary sentinel on deck sought their rest. Cap had been so harassed during the previous eight-and-forty hours, that his slumbers were long and deep; nor did he awake from his first nap until the day was just beginning to dawn. His eyes were scarcely open, however, when his nautical instinct told him that the cutter was under way. Springing up, he found the *Scud* threading the islands again, with no one on deck but Jasper and the pilot, unless the sentinel be excepted, who had not in the least interfered with movements that he had every reason to believe were as regular as they were necessary.

"How's this, Master Western?" demanded Cap, with sufficient fierceness for the occasion; "are you running us into Frontenac at last, and we all asleep below, like so many mariners waiting for the 'sentry go'?"

"This is according to orders, Master Cap, Major Duncan having commanded me never to approach the station unless at a moment when the people were below; for he does not wish there should be more pilots in those waters than the king has need of."

"Whe—e—e—w! a pretty job I should have made of running down among these bushes and rocks with no one on deck! Why, a regular York branch could make nothing of such a channel."

"I always thought, sir," said Jasper, smiling, "you would have done better had you left the cutter in my hands until she had safely reached her place of destination."

"We should have done it, Jasper, we should have done it, had it not been for a circumstance; these circumstances are serious matters, and no prudent man will overlook them."

"Well, sir, I hope there is now an end of them. We shall arrive in less than an hour if the wind holds, and then you'll be safe from any circumstances that I can contrive."

"Humph!"

Cap was obliged to acquiesce; and, as everything around him had the appearance of Jasper's being sincere, there was not much difficulty in making up his mind to submit. It would not have been easy indeed for a person the most sensitive on the subject

of circumstances to fancy that the *Scud* was anywhere in the
vicinity of a port so long established and so well known on the
frontiers as Frontenac. The islands might not have been literally
a thousand in number, but they were so numerous and small as
to baffle calculation, though occasionally one of larger size than
common was passed. Jasper had quitted what might have been
termed the main channel, and was winding his way, with a good
stiff breeze and a favorable current, through passes that were
sometimes so narrow that there appeared to be barely room sufficient for the *Scud's* spars to clear the trees, while at other moments he shot across little bays, and buried the cutter again amid
rocks, forests, and bushes. The water was so transparent that
there was no occasion for the lead, and being of very equal depth,
little risk was actually run, though Cap, with his maritime habits, was in a constant fever lest they should strike.

"I give it up, I give it up, Pathfinder!" the old seaman at
length exclaimed, when the little vessel emerged in safety from
the twentieth of these narrow inlets through which she had been
so boldly carried; "this is defying the very nature of seamanship,
and sending all its laws and rules to the d——l!"

"Nay, nay, Saltwater, 'tis the perfection of the art. You perceive that Jasper never falters, but, like a hound with a true
nose, he runs with his head high as if he had a strong scent. My
life on it, the lad brings us out right in the ind, as he would have
done in the beginning had we given him leave."

"No pilot, no lead, no beacons, buoys, or lighthouses, no——"

"Trail," interrupted Pathfinder; "for that to me is the most
mysterious part of the business. Water leaves no trail, as every
one knows; and yet here is Jasper moving ahead as boldly as if
he had before his eyes the prints of the moccasins on leaves as
plainly as we can see the sun in the heaven."

"D— me, if I believe there is even any compass!"

"Stand by to haul down the jib," called out Jasper, who merely
smiled at the remarks of his companion. "Haul down—starboard
your helm—starboard hard—so—meet her—gently there with
the helm—touch her lightly—now jump ashore with the fast,
lad—no, heave; there are some of our people ready to take it."

All this passed so quickly as barely to allow the spectator time
to note the different evolutions, ere the *Scud* had been thrown
into the wind until her mainsail shivered, next cast a little by the

use of the rudder only, and then she set bodily alongside of a natural rocky quay, where she was immediately secured by good fasts run to the shore. In a word, the station was reached, and the men of the 55th were greeted by their expecting comrades, with the satisfaction which a relief usually brings.

Mabel sprang upon the shore with a delight which she did not care to express; and her father led his men after her with an alacrity which proved how wearied he had become of the cutter. The station, as the place was familiarly termed by the soldiers of the 55th, was indeed a spot to raise expectations of enjoyment among those who had been cooped up so long in a vessel of the dimensions of the *Scud*. None of the islands were high, though all lay at a sufficient elevation above the water to render them perfectly healthy and secure. Each had more or less of wood; and the greater number at that distant day were clothed with the virgin forest. The one selected by the troops for their purpose was small, containing about twenty acres of land, and by some of the accidents of the wilderness it had been partly stripped of its trees, probably centuries before the period of which we are writing, and a little grassy glade covered nearly half its surface.

The shores of Station Island were completely fringed with bushes, and great care had been taken to preserve them, as they answered as a screen to conceal the persons and things collected within their circle. Favored by this shelter, as well as by that of several thickets of trees and different copses, some six or eight low huts had been erected to be used as quarters for the officer and his men, to contain stores, and to serve the purposes of kitchen, hospital, etc. These huts were built of logs in the usual manner, had been roofed by bark brought from a distance, lest the signs of labor should attract attention, and, as they had now been inhabited some months, were as comfortable as dwellings of that description usually ever get to be.

At the eastern extremity of the island, however, was a small, densely-wooded peninsula, with a thicket of underbrush so closely matted as nearly to prevent the possibility of seeing across it, so long as the leaves remained on the branches. Near the narrow neck that connected this acre with the rest of the island, a small blockhouse had been erected, with some attention to its means of resistance. The logs were bullet-proof, squared and jointed with a care to leave no defenceless points; the windows were loopholes, the door massive and small, and the roof, like the rest of the structure, was framed of hewn timber, covered properly with bark to exclude the rain. The lower apartment as usual contained stores and provisions; here indeed the party kept all their supplies; the second story was intended for a dwelling, as well as for the citadel, and a low garret was subdivided into two or three rooms, and could hold the pallets of some ten or fifteen persons. All the arrangements were exceedingly simple and cheap, but they were sufficient to protect the soldiers against the effects of a surprise. As the whole building was considerably less than forty feet high, its summit was concealed by the tops of the trees, except from the eyes of those who had reached the interior of the island. On that side the view was open from the upper loops, though bushes even there, more or less, concealed the base of the wooden tower.

The object being purely defence, care had been taken to place the blockhouse so near an opening in the limestone rock that formed the base of the island as to admit of a bucket being dropped into the water, in order to obtain that great essential in the event of a siege. In order to facilitate this operation, and to enfilade the base of the building, the upper stories projected several feet beyond the lower, in the manner usual to block-houses, and pieces of wood filled the apertures cut in the log flooring, which were intended as loops and traps. The communications between the different stories were by means of ladders. If we add that these blockhouses were intended as citadels for garrisons or settlements to retreat to, in the cases of attacks, the general reader will obtain a sufficiently correct idea of the arrangements it is our wish to explain.

But the situation of the island itself formed its principal merit as a military position. Lying in the midst of twenty others, it was not an easy matter to find it; since boats might pass quite near, and, by glimpses caught through the openings, this particular island would be taken for a part of some other. Indeed, the channels between the islands which lay around the one we have been describing were so narrow that it was even difficult to say which portions of the land were connected, or which separated, even as one stood in the centre, with the express desire of ascertaining the truth. The little bay in particular, which Jasper used as a harbor, was so embowered with bushes and shut in with islands, that, the sails of the cutter being lowered, her own people on one occasion had searched for hours before they could find the *Scud*, in their return from a short excursion among the adjacent channels in quest of fish. In short, the place was admirably adapted to its present objects, and its natural advantages had been as ingeniously improved as economy and the limited means of a frontier post would very well allow.

The hour which succeeded the arrival of the *Scud* was one of hurried excitement. The party in possession had done nothing worthy of being mentioned, and, wearied with their seclusion, they were all eager to return to Oswego. The Sergeant and the officer he came to relieve had no sooner gone through the little ceremonies of transferring the command, than the latter hurried on board the *Scud* with his whole party; and Jasper, who would gladly have passed the day on the island, was required to get under way forthwith, the wind promising a quick passage up the river and across the lake. Before separating, however, Lieutenant Muir, Cap, and the Sergeant had a private conference with the ensign who had been relieved, in which the last was made acquainted with the suspicions that existed against the fidelity of the young sailor. Promising due caution, the officer embarked, and in less than three hours from the time when she had arrived the cutter was again in motion.

Mabel had taken possession of a hut; and with female readiness and skill she made all the simple little domestic arrangements of which the circumstances would admit, not only for her own comfort, but for that of her father. To save labor, a messtable was prepared in a hut set apart for that purpose, where all the heads of the detachment were to eat, the soldier's wife performing the necessary labor. The hut of the Sergeant, which was the best on the island, being thus freed from any of the vulgar offices of a household, admitted of such a display of womanly taste, that, for the first time since her arrival on the frontier, Mabel felt proud of her home. As soon as these important duties were discharged, she strolled out on the island, taking a path which led through the pretty glade, and which conducted to the only point not covered with bushes. Here she stood gazing at the limpid water, which lay with scarcely a ruffle on it at her feet, musing on the novel situation in which she was placed, and permitting a pleasing and deep excitement to steal over her feelings, as she remembered the scenes through which she had so lately passed, and conjectured those which still lay veiled in the future.

"You're a beautiful fixture, in a beautiful spot, Mistress Mabel," said David Muir, suddenly appearing at her elbow; "and I'll no' engage you're not just the handsomest of the two."

"I will not say, Mr. Muir, that compliments on my person are altogether unwelcome, for I should not gain credit for speaking the truth, perhaps," answered Mabel with spirit; "but I will say that if you would condescend to address to me some remarks of a different nature, I may be led to believe you think I have sufficient faculties to understand them."

"Hoot! your mind, beautiful Mabel, is polished just like the barrel of a soldier's musket, and your conversation is only too discreet and wise for a poor d—l who has been chewing birch up here these four years on the lines, instead of receiving it in an application that has the virtue of imparting knowledge. But you are no' sorry, I take it, young lady, that you've got your pretty foot on *terra firma* once more."

"I thought so two hours since, Mr. Muir; but the *Scud* looks so beautiful, as she sails through these vistas of trees, that I almost regret I am no longer one of her passengers."

As Mabel ceased speaking, she waved her handkerchief in return to a salutation from Jasper, who kept his eyes fastened on her form until the white sails of the cutter had swept round a point, and were nearly lost behind its green fringe of leaves.

"There they go, and I'll no' say 'joy go with them'; but may they have the luck to return safely, for without them we shall be in danger of passing the winter on this island; unless, indeed, we have the alternative of the castle at Quebec. Yon Jasper Eaudouce is a vagrant sort of a lad, and they have reports of him in the garrison that it pains my very heart to hear. Your worthy father, and almost as worthy uncle, have none of the best opinion of him."

"I am sorry to hear it, Mr. Muir; I doubt not that time will remove all their distrust."

"If time would only remove mine, pretty Mabel," rejoined the Quartermaster in a wheedling tone, "I should feel no envy of the commander-in-chief. I think if I were in a condition to retire, the Sergeant would just step into my shoes."

"If my dear father is worthy to step into your shoes, Mr. Muir," returned the girl, with malicious pleasure, "I'm sure that the qualification is mutual, and that you are every way worthy to step into his."

"The deuce is in the child! you would not reduce me to the rank of a non-commissioned officer, Mabel?"

"No, indeed, sir; I was not thinking of the army at all as you spoke of retiring. My thoughts were more egotistical, and I was thinking how much you reminded me of my dear father, by your experience, wisdom, and suitableness to take his place as the head of a family."

"As its bridegroom, pretty Mabel, but not as its parent or natural chief. I see how it is with you, loving your repartee, and brilliant with wit. Well, I like spirit in a young woman, so it be not the spirit of a scold. This Pathfinder is an extraordinair, Mabel, if truth may be said of the man."

"Truth should be said of him or nothing. Pathfinder is my friend—my very particular friend, Mr. Muir, and no evil can be said of him in my presence that I shall not deny."

"I shall say nothing evil of him, I can assure you, Mabel; but, at the same time, I doubt if much good can be said in his favor."

"He is at least expert with the rifle," returned Mabel, smiling. "That *you* cannot deny."

"Let him have all the credit of his exploits in that way if you please; but he is as illiterate as a Mohawk."

"He may not understand Latin, but his knowledge of Iroquois is greater than that of most men, and it is the more useful language of the two in this part of the world."

"If Lundie himself were to call on me for an opinion which I admire more, your person or your wit, beautiful and caustic Mabel, I should be at a loss to answer. My admiration is so nearly divided between them, that I often fancy this is the one that bears off the palm, and then the other! Ah! the late Mrs. Muir was a paragon in that way also."

"The latest Mrs. Muir, did you say, sir?" asked Mabel, looking up innocently at her companion.

"Hoot, hoot! That is some of Pathfinder's scandal. Now I daresay that the fellow has been trying to persuade you, Mabel, that I have had more than one wife already."

"In that case his time would have been thrown away, sir, as everybody knows that you have been so unfortunate as to have had four."

"Only three, as sure as my name is David Muir. The fourth is pure scandal—or rather, pretty Mabel, she is yet *in petto*, as they say at Rome; and that means, in matters of love, in the heart, my dear."

"Well, I'm glad I'm not that fourth person, *in petto*, or in anything else, as I should not like to be a scandal."

"No fear of that, charming Mabel; for were you the fourth, all the others would be forgotten, and your wonderful beauty and merit would at once elevate you to be the first. No fear of your being the fourth in anything."

"There is consolation in that assurance, Mr. Muir," said Mabel, laughing, "whatever there may be in your other assurance; for I confess I should prefer being even a fourth-rate beauty to being a fourth wife."

So saying she tripped away, leaving the Quartermaster to meditate on his success. Mabel had been induced to use her female means of defence thus freely, partly because her suitor had of late been so pointed as to stand in need of a pretty strong repulse, and partly on account of his innuendoes against Jasper and the Pathfinder. Though full of spirit and quick of intellect, she was not naturally pert; but on the present occasion she thought circumstances called for more than usual decision. When she left her companion, therefore, she believed she was now finally released from attentions which she thought as ill-bestowed as they were certainly disagreeable. Not so, however, with David Muir; accustomed to rebuffs, and familiar with the virtue of perseverance, he saw no reason to despair, though the half-menacing, half-self-satisfied manner in which he shook his head towards the retreating girl might have betrayed designs as sinister as they were determined. While he was thus occupied, the Pathfinder approached, and got within a few feet of him unseen.

"'Twill never do, Quartermaster, 'twill never do," commenced the latter, laughing in his noiseless way; "she is young and active, and none but a quick foot can overtake her. They tell me you are her suitor, if you are not her follower."

"And I hear the same of yourself, man, though the presumption would be so great that I scarcely can think it true."

"I fear you're right, I do; yes, I fear you're right;—when I consider myself, what I am, how little I know, and how rude my life has been, I altogether distrust my claim, even to think a moment of one so tutored, and gay, and light of heart, and delicate——"

"You forget handsome," coarsely interrupted Muir.

"And handsome, too, I fear," returned the meek and self-abased guide; "I might have said handsome at once, among her other qualities; for the young fa'n, just as it learns to bound, is not more pleasant to the eye of the hunter than Mabel is lovely in mine. I do indeed fear that all the thoughts I have harbored about her are vain and presumptuous."

"If you think this, my friend, of your own accord and natural modesty, as it might be, my duty to you as an old fellow-campaigner compels me to say——"

"Quartermaster," interrupted the other, regarding his companion keenly, "you and I have lived together much behind the ramparts of forts, but very little in the open woods or in front of the enemy."

"Garrison or tent, it all passes for part of the same campaign, ou know, Pathfinder; and then my duty keeps me much within sight of the storehouses, greatly contrary to my inclinations, as ye may well suppose, having yourself the ardor of battle in your temperament. But had ye heard what Mabel had just been saying of you, ye'd no think another minute of making yourself agreeable to the saucy and uncompromising hussy."

Pathfinder looked earnestly at the lieutenant, for it was impossible he should not feel an interest in what might be Mabel's opinion; but he had too much of the innate and true feeling of a gentleman to ask to hear what another had said of him. Muir, however, was not to be foiled by this self-denial and self-respect; for, believing he had a man of great truth and simplicity to deal with, he determined to practise on his credulity, as one means of getting rid of his rivalry. He therefore pursued the subject, as soon as he perceived that his companion's self-denial was stronger than his curiosity.

"You ought to know her opinion, Pathfinder," he continued;

"and I think every man ought to hear what his friends and acquaintances say of him: and so, by way of proving my own regard for your character and feelings, I'll just tell you in as few words as possible. You know that Mabel has a wicked, malicious way with them eyes of her own, when she has a mind to be hard upon one's feelings."

"To me her eyes, Lieutenant Muir, have always seemed winning and soft, though I will acknowledge that they sometimes laugh; yes, I have known them to laugh, and that right heartily, and with downright goodwill."

"Well, it was just that then; her eyes were laughing with all their might, as it were; and in the midst of all her fun, she broke out with an exclamation to this effect:—I hope 'twill no' hurt your sensibility, Pathfinder?"

"I will not say, Quartermaster, I will not say. Mabel's opinion of me is of more account than that of most others."

"Then I'll no' tell ye, but just keep discretion on the subject; and why should a man be telling another what his friends say of him, especially when they happen to say that which may not be pleasant to hear? I'll not add another word to this present communication."

"I cannot make you speak, Quartermaster, if you are not so minded, and perhaps it is better for me not to know Mabel's opinion, as you seem to think it is not in my favor. Ah's me! if we could be what we wish to be, instead of being only what we are, there would be a great difference in our characters and knowledge and appearance. One may be rude and coarse and ignorant, and yet happy, if he does not know it; but it is hard to see our own failings in the strongest light, just as we wish to hear the least about them."

"That's just the *rationale*, as the French say, of the matter; and so I was telling Mabel, when she ran away and left me. You noticed the manner in which she skipped off as you approached?"

"It was very observable," answered Pathfinder, drawing a long breath and clenching the barrel of his rifle as if the fingers would bury themselves in the iron.

"It was more than observable—it was flagrant; that's just the word, and the dictionary wouldn't supply a better, after an hour's search. Well, you must know, Pathfinder—for I cannot reasonably deny you the gratification of hearing this—so you must know the minx bounded off in that manner in preference to hearing what I had to say in your justification."

"And what could you find to say in my behalf, Quartermaster?"

"Why, d'ye understand, my friend, I was ruled by circumstances, and no' ventured indiscreetly into generalities, but was preparing to meet particulars, as it might be, with particulars. If you were thought wild, half-savage, or of a frontier formation, I could tell her, ye know, that it came of the frontier, wild and half-savage life ye'd led; and all her objections must cease at once, or there would be a sort of a misunderstanding with Providence."

"And did you tell her this, Quartermaster?"

"I'll no' swear to the exact words, but the idea was prevalent in my mind, ye'll understand. The girl was impatient, and would not hear the half I had to say; but away she skipped, as ye saw with your own eyes, Pathfinder, as if her opinion were fully made up, and she cared to listen no longer. I fear her mind may be said to have come to its conclusion?"

"I fear it has indeed, Quartermaster, and her father, after all, is mistaken. Yes, yes; the Sergeant has fallen into a grievous error."

"Well, man, why need ye lament, and undo all the grand reputation ye've been so many weary years making? Shoulder the rifle that ye use so well, and off into the woods with ye, for there's not the female breathing that is worth a heavy heart for a minute, as I know from experience. Tak' the word of one who knows the sax, and has had two wives, that women, after all, are very much the sort of creatures we do not imagine them to be. Now, if you would really mortify Mabel, here is as glorious an occasion as any rejected lover could desire."

"The last wish I have, Lieutenant, would be to mortify Mabel."

"Well, ye'll come to that in the end, notwithstanding; for it's human nature to desire to give unpleasant feelings to them that give unpleasant feelings to us. But a better occasion never offered to make your friends love you, than is to be had at this very moment, and that is the certain means of causing one's enemies to envy us."

"Quartermaster, Mabel is not my inimy; and if she was, the last thing I could desire would be to give her an uneasy moment."

"Ye say so, Pathfinder, ye say so, and I daresay ye think so; but reason and nature are both against you, as ye'll find in the end. Ye've heard the saying of 'love me, love my dog': well, now, that means, read backwards, 'don't love me, don't love my dog.' Now, listen to what is in your power to do. You know we occupy an exceedingly precarious and uncertain position here, almost in the jaws of the lion, as it were?"

"Do you mean the Frenchers by the lion, and this island as his jaws, Lieutenant?"

"Metaphorically only, my friend, for the French are no lions, and this island is not a jaw—unless, indeed, it may prove to be, what I greatly fear may come true, the jawbone of an ass."

Here the Quartermaster indulged in a sneering laugh, that proclaimed anything but respect and admiration for his friend Lundie's sagacity in selecting that particular spot for his operations.

"The post is as well chosen as any I ever put foot in," said Pathfinder, looking around him as one surveys a picture.

"I'll no' deny it, I'll no' deny it. Lundie is a great soldier, in a small way; and his father was a great laird, with the same qualification. I was born on the estate, and have followed the Major so long that I've got to reverence all he says and does: that's just my weakness, ye'll know, Pathfinder. Well, this post may be the post of an ass, or of a Solomon, as men fancy; but it's most critically placed, as is apparent by all Lundie's precautions and injunctions. There are savages out scouting through these Thousand Islands and over the forest, searching for this very spot, as is known to Lundie himself, on certain information; and the greatest service you can render the 55th is to discover their trails and lead them off on a false scent. Unhappily Sergeant Dunham has taken up the notion that the danger is to be apprehended from up-stream, because Frontenac lies above us; whereas all experience tells us that Indians come on the side which is most contrary to reason, and, consequently, are to be expected from below. Take your canoe, therefore, and go down-stream among the islands, that we may have notice if any danger approaches from that quarter."

"The Big Sarpent is on the look-out in that quarter; and as he knows the station well, no doubt he will give us timely notice, should any wish to sarcumvent us in that direction."

"He is but an Indian, after all, Pathfinder; and this is an affair that calls for the knowledge of a white man. Lundie will be eternally grateful to the man who shall help this little enterprise to come off with flying colors. To tell you the truth, my friend, he is conscious it should never have been attempted; but he has too much of the old laird's obstinacy about him to own an error, though it be as manifest as the morning star."

The Quartermaster then continued to reason with his companion, in order to induce him to quit the island without delay, using such arguments as first suggested themselves, sometimes contradicting himself, and not unfrequently urging at one moment a motive that at the next was directly opposed by another. The Pathfinder, simple as he was, detected these flaws in the Lieutenant's philosophy, though he was far from suspecting that they proceeded from a desire to clear the coast of Mabel's suitor. He did not exactly suspect the secret objects of Muir, but he was far from being blind to his sophistry. The result was that the two parted, after a long dialogue, unconvinced, and distrustful of each other's motives, though the distrust of the guide, like all that was connected with the man, partook of his own upright, disinterested, and ingenuous nature.

A conference that took place soon after between Sergeant Dunham and the Lieutenant led to more consequences. When it was ended, secret orders were issued to the men, the blockhouse was taken possession of, the huts were occupied, and one accustomed to the movements of soldiers might have detected that an expedition was in the wind. In fact, just as the sun was setting, the Sergeant, who had been much occupied at what was called the harbor, came into his own hut, followed by Pathfinder and Cap; and as he took his seat at the neat table which Mabel had prepared for him, he opened the budget of his intelligence.

"You are likely to be of some use here, my child," the old soldier commenced, "as this tidy and well-ordered supper can testify; and I trust, when the proper moment arrives, you will show yourself to be the descendant of those who know how to face their enemies."

"You do not expect me, dear father, to play Joan of Arc, and to lead the men to battle?"

"Play whom, child? Did you ever hear of the person Mabel mentions, Pathfinder?"

"Not I, Sergeant; but what of that? I am ignorant and un-edicated, and it is too great a pleasure to me to listen to her voice, and take in her words, to be particular about persons."

"I know her," said Cap decidedly; "she sailed a privateer out of Morlaix in the last war; and good cruises she made of them."

Mabel blushed at having inadvertently made an allusion that went beyond her father's reading, to say nothing of her uncle's dogmatism, and, perhaps, a little at the Pathfinder's simple, ingenuous earnestness; but she did not forbear the less to smile.

"Why, father, I am not expected to fall in with the men, and to help defend the island?"

"And yet women have often done such things in this quarter of the world, girl, as our friend, the Pathfinder here, will tell you. But lest you should be surprised at not seeing us when you awake in the morning, it is proper that I now tell you we intend to march in the course of this very night."

"*We*, father! and leave me and Jennie on this island alone?"

"No, my daughter; not quite as unmilitary as that. We shall leave Lieutenant Muir, brother Cap, Corporal M'Nab, and three men to compose the garrison during our absence. Jennie will remain with you in this hut, and brother Cap will occupy my place."

"And Mr. Muir?" said Mabel, half unconscious of what she uttered, though she foresaw a great deal of unpleasant persecution in the arrangement.

"Why, he can make love to you, if you like it, girl; for he is an amorous youth, and, having already disposed of four wives, is impatient to show how much he honors their memories by taking a fifth."

"The Quartermaster tells me," said Pathfinder innocently, "that when a man's feelings have been harassed by so many losses, there is no wiser way to soothe them than by ploughing up the soil anew, in such a manner as to leave no traces of what have gone over it before."

"Ay, that is just the difference between ploughing and harrowing," returned the Sergeant, with a grim smile. "But let him tell Mabel his mind, and there will be an end of his suit. I very well know that *my* daughter will never be the wife of Lieutenant Muir."

This was said in a way that was tantamount to declaring that no daughter of his ever *should* become the wife of the person in question. Mabel had colored, trembled, half laughed, and looked uneasy; but, rallying her spirit, she said, in a voice so cheerful as completely to conceal her agitation, "But, father, we might better wait until Mr. Muir manifests a wish that your daughter would have him, or rather a wish to have your daughter, lest we get the fable of sour grapes thrown into our faces."

"And what is that fable, Mabel?" eagerly demanded Pathfinder, who was anything but learned in the ordinary lore of white men. "Tell it to us, in your own pretty way; I daresay the Sergeant never heard it."

Mabel repeated the well-known fable, and, as her suitor had desired, in her own pretty way, which was a way to keep his eyes riveted on her face, and the whole of his honest countenance covered with a smile.

"That was like a fox!" cried Pathfinder, when she had ceased; "ay, and like a Mingo, too, cunning and cruel; that is the way with both the riptyles. As to grapes, they are sour enough in this part of the country, even to them that can get at them, though I daresay there are seasons and times and places where they are sourer to them that can't. I should judge, now, my scalp is very sour in Mingo eyes."

"The sour grapes will be the other way, child, and it is Mr. Muir who will make the complaint. You would never marry that man, Mabel?"

"Not she," put in Cap; "a fellow who is only half a soldier after all. The story of them there grapes is quite a circumstance."

"I think little of marrying any one, dear father and dear uncle, and would rather talk about it less, if you please. But, did I think of marrying at all, I do believe a man whose affections have already been tried by three or four wives would scarcely be my choice."

The Sergeant nodded at the guide, as much as to say, You

see how the land lies; and then he had sufficient consideration for his daughter's feelings to change the subject.

"Neither you nor Mabel, brother Cap," he resumed, "can have any legal authority with the little garrison I leave behind on the island; but you may counsel and influence. Strictly speaking, Corporal M'Nab will be the commanding officer, and I have endeavored to impress him with a sense of his dignity, lest he might give way too much to the superior rank of Lieutenant Muir, who, being a volunteer, can have no right to interfere with the duty. I wish you to sustain the Corporal, brother Cap; for should the Quartermaster once break through the regulations of the expedition, he may pretend to command me, as well as M'Nab."

"More particularly, should Mabel really cut him adrift while you are absent. Of course, Sergeant, you'll leave everything that is afloat under my care? The most d—ble confusion has grown out of misunderstandings between commanders-in-chief, ashore and afloat."

"In one sense, brother, though in a general way, the Corporal is commander-in-chief. The Corporal must command; but you can counsel freely, particularly in all matters relating to the boats, of which I shall leave one behind to secure your retreat, should there be occasion. I know the Corporal well; he is a brave man and a good soldier; and one that may be relied on, if the Santa Cruz can be kept from him. But then he is a Scotchman, and will be liable to the Quartermaster's influence, against which I desire both you and Mabel to be on your guard."

"But why leave us behind, dear father? I have come thus far to be a comfort to you, and why not go farther?"

"You are a good girl, Mabel, and very like the Dunhams. But you must halt here. We shall leave the island tomorrow, before the day dawns, in order not to be seen by any prying eyes coming from our cover, and we shall take the two largest boats, leaving you the other and one bark canoe. We are about to go into the channel used by the French, where we shall lie in wait, perhaps a week, to intercept their supply-boats, which are about to pass up on their way to Frontenac, loaded, in particular, with a heavy amount of Indian goods."

"Have you looked well to your papers, brother?" Cap anxiously demanded. "Of course you know a capture on the high seas is piracy, unless your boat is regularly commissioned, either as a public or a private armed cruiser."

"I have the honor to hold the Colonel's appointment as sergeant-major of the 55th," returned the other, drawing himself up with dignity, "and that will be sufficient even for the French king. If not, I have Major Duncan's written orders."

"No papers, then, for a warlike cruiser?"

"They must suffice, brother, as I have no other. It is of vast importance to his Majesty's interests, in this part of the world, that the boats in question should be captured and carried into Oswego. They contain the blankets, trinkets, rifles, ammunition, in short, all the stores with which the French bribe their accursed savage allies to commit their unholy acts, setting at nought our holy religion and its precepts, the laws of humanity, and all that is sacred and dear among men. By cutting off these supplies we shall derange their plans, and gain time on them; for the articles cannot be sent across the ocean again this autumn."

"But, father, does not his Majesty employ Indians also?" asked Mabel, with some curiosity.

"Certainly, girl, and he has a right to employ them—God bless him! It's a very different thing whether an Englishman or a Frenchman employs a savage, as everybody can understand."

"But, father, I cannot see that this alters the case. If it be wrong in a Frenchman to hire savages to fight his enemies, it would seem to be equally wrong in an Englishman. *You* will admit this, Pathfinder?"

"It's reasonable, it's reasonable; and I have never been one of them that has raised a cry ag'in the Frenchers for doing the very thing we do ourselves. Still it is worse to consort with a Mingo than to consort with a Delaware. If any of that just tribe were left, I should think it no sin to send them out ag'in the foe."

"And yet they scalp and slay young and old, women and children!"

"They have their gifts, Mabel, and are not to be blamed for following them; natur' is natur', though the different tribes have different ways of showing it. For my part I am white, and endeavor to maintain white feelings."

"This is all unintelligible to me," answered Mabel. "What is right in King George, it would seem, ought to be right in King Louis."

As all parties, Mabel excepted, seemed satisfied with the course the discussion had taken, no one appeared to think it necessary to pursue the subject. Supper was no sooner ended than the Sergeant dismissed his guests, and then held a long and confidential dialogue with his daughter. He was little addicted to giving way to the gentler emotions, but the novelty of his present situation awakened feelings that he was unused to experience. The soldier or the sailor, so long as he acts under the immediate supervision of a superior, thinks little of the risks he runs, but the moment he feels the responsibility of command, all the hazards of his undertaking begin to associate themselves in his mind with the chances of success or failure. While he dwells less on his own personal danger, perhaps, than when that is the principal consideration, he has more lively general perceptions of all the risks, and submits more to the influence of the feelings which doubt creates. Such was now the case with Sergeant Dunham, who, instead of looking forward to victory as certain, according to his usual habits, began to feel the possibility that he might be parting with his child for ever.

Never before had Mabel struck him as so beautiful as she appeared that night. Possibly she never had displayed so many engaging qualities to her father; for concern on his account had begun to be active in her breast; and then her sympathies met with unusual encouragement through those which had been stirred up in the sterner bosom of the veteran. She had never been entirely at her ease with her parent, the great superiority of her education creating a sort of chasm, which had been widened by the military severity of manner he had acquired by dealing so long with beings who could only be kept in subjection by an unremitted discipline. On the present occasion, however, the conversation between the father and daughter became more confidential than usual, until Mabel rejoiced to find that it was gradually becoming endearing, a state of feeling that the warm-hearted girl had silently pined for in vain ever since her arrival.

"Then mother was about my height?" Mabel said, as she

held one of her father's hands in both her own, looking up into his face with humid eyes. "I had thought her taller."

"That is the way with most children who get a habit of thinking of their parents with respect, until they fancy them larger and more commanding than they actually are. Your mother, Mabel, was as near your height as one woman could be to another."

"And her eyes, father?"

"Her eyes were like thine, child, too; blue and soft, and inviting like, though hardly so laughing."

"Mine will never laugh again, dearest father, if you do not take care of yourself in this expedition."

"Thank you, Mabel—hem—thank you, child; but I must do my duty. I wish I had seen you comfortably married before we left Oswego; my mind would be easier."

"Married!—to whom, father?"

"You know the man I wish you to love. You may meet with many gayer, and many dressed in finer clothes; but with none with so true a heart and just a mind."

"None father?"

"I know of none; in these particulars Pathfinder has few equals at least."

"But I need not marry at all. You are single, and I can remain to take care of you."

"God bless you, Mabel! I know you would, and I do not say that the feeling is not right, for I suppose it is; and yet I believe there is another that is more so."

"What can be more right than to honor one's parents?"

"It is just as right to honor one's husband, my dear child."

"But I have no husband, father."

"Then take one as soon as possible, that you may have a husband to honor. I cannot live for ever, Mabel, but must drop off in the course of nature ere long, if I am not carried off in the course of war. You are young, and may yet live long; and it is proper that you should have a male protector, who can see you safe through life, and take care of you in age, as you now wish to take care of me."

"And do you think, father," said Mabel, playing with his sinewy fingers with her own little hands, and looking down at them, as if they were subjects of intense interest, though her

lips curled in a slight smile as the words came from them—
"and do you think, father, that Pathfinder is just the man to
do this? Is he not, within ten or twelve years, as old as yourself?"

"What of that? His life has been one of moderation and
exercise, and years are less to be counted, girl, than constitution. Do you know another more likely to be your protector?"

Mabel did not; at least another who had expressed a desire
to that effect, whatever might have been her hopes and her
wishes.

"Nay, father, we are not talking of another, but of the Pathfinder," she answered evasively. "If he were younger, I think it
would be more natural for me to think of him for a husband."

"'Tis all in the constitution, I tell you, child; Pathfinder is a
younger man than half our subalterns."

"He is certainly younger than one, sir—Lieutenant Muir."
Mabel's laugh was joyous and light-hearted, as if just then
she felt no care.

"That he is—young enough to be his grandson; he is younger
in years, too. God forbid, Mabel, that you should ever become
an officer's lady, at least until you are an officer's daughter!"

"There will be little fear of that, father, if I marry Pathfinder,"
returned the girl, looking up archly in the Sergeant's face again.

"Not by the king's commission, perhaps, though the man is
even now the friend and companion of generals. I think I could
die happy, Mabel, if you were his wife."

"Father!"

"'Tis a sad thing to go into battle with the weight of an un-
protected daughter laid upon the heart."

"I would give the world to lighten yours of its load, my dear
sir."

"It might be done," said the Sergeant, looking fondly at his
child; "though I could not wish to put a burthen on yours in
order to do so."

The voice was deep and tremulous, and never before had
Mabel witnessed such a show of affection in her parent. The
habitual sternness of the man lent an interest to his emotions
which they might otherwise have wanted, and the daughter's
heart yearned to relieve the father's mind.

"Father, speak plainly!" she cried, almost convulsively.

"Nay, Mabel, it might not be right; your wishes and mine may be very different."

"I have no wishes—know nothing of what you mean. Would you speak of my future marriage?"

"If I could see you promised to Pathfinder—know that you were pledged to become his wife, let my own fate be what it might, I think I could die happy. But I will ask no pledge of you, my child; I will not force you to do what you might repent. Kiss me, Mabel, and go to your bed."

Had Sergeant Dunham exacted of Mabel the pledge that he really so much desired, he would have encountered a resistance that he might have found it difficult to overcome; but, by letting nature have its course, he enlisted a powerful ally on his side, and the warm-hearted, generous-minded Mabel was ready to concede to her affections much more than she would ever have yielded to menace. At that touching moment she thought only of her parent, who was about to quit her, perhaps for ever; and all of that ardent love for him, which had possibly been as much fed by the imagination as by anything else, but which had received a little check by the restrained intercourse of the last fortnight, now returned with a force that was increased by pure and intense feeling. Her father seemed all in all to her, and to render him happy there was no proper sacrifice which she was not ready to make. One painful, rapid, almost wild gleam of thought shot across the brain of the girl, and her resolution wavered; but endeavoring to trace the foundation of the pleasing hope on which it was based, she found nothing positive to support it. Trained like a woman to subdue her most ardent feelings, her thoughts reverted to her father, and to the blessings that awaited the child who yielded to a parent's wishes.

"Father," she said quietly, almost with a holy calm, "God blesses the dutiful daughter."

"He will, Mabel; we have the Good Book for that."

"I will marry whomever you desire."

"Nay, nay, Mabel, you may have a choice of your own——"

"I have no choice; that is, none have asked me to have a choice, but Pathfinder and Mr. Muir; and between *them*, neither of us would hesitate. No, father; I will marry whomever you may choose."

"Thou knowest my choice, beloved child; none other can make thee as happy as the noble-hearted guide."

"Well, then, if he wish it, if he ask me again—for, father, you would not have me offer myself, or that any one should do that office for me," and the blood stole across the pallid cheeks of Mabel as she spoke, for high and generous resolutions had driven back the stream of life to her heart; "no one must speak to him of it; but if he seek me again, and, knowing all that a true girl ought to tell the man she marries, he then wishes to make me his wife, I will be his."

"Bless you, my Mabel! God in heaven bless you, and reward you as a pious daughter deserves to be rewarded!"

"Yes, father, put your mind at peace; go on this expedition with a light heart, and trust in God. For me you will have now no care. In the spring—I must have a little time, father—but in the spring I will marry Pathfinder, if that noble-hearted hunter shall then desire it."

"Mabel, he loves you as I loved your mother. I have seen him weep like a child when speaking of his feelings towards you."

"Yes, I believe it; I've seen enough to satisfy me that he thinks better of me than I deserve; and certainly the man is not living for whom I have more respect than for Pathfinder; not even for you, dear father."

"That is as it should be, child, and the union will be blessed. May I not tell Pathfinder this?"

"I would rather you would not, father. Let it come of itself, come naturally." The smile that illuminated Mabel's handsome face was angelic, as even her parent thought, though one better practised in detecting the passing emotions, as they betray themselves in the countenance, might have traced something wild and unnatural in it. "No, no, *we* must let things take their course; father, you have my solemn promise."

"That will do, that will do, Mabel; now kiss me. God bless and protect you, girl! you are a good daughter."

Mabel threw herself into her father's arms—it was the first time in her life—and sobbed on his bosom like an infant. The stern soldier's heart was melted, and the tears of the two mingled; but Sergeant Dunham soon started, as if ashamed of himself, and, gently forcing his daughter from him, he bade her good-night, and sought his pallet. Mabel went sobbing to the rude corner that had been prepared for her reception; and in a few minutes the hut was undisturbed by any sound, save the heavy breathing of the veteran.

CHAPTER XX

Wandering, I found on my ruinous walk,
By the dial stone, aged and green,
One rose of the wilderness, left on its stalk,
To mark where a garden had been.   CAMPBELL

IT WAS not only broad daylight when Mabel awoke, but the sun had actually been up some time. Her sleep had been tranquil, for she rested on an approving conscience, and fatigue contributed to render it sweet; and no sound of those who had been so early in motion had interfered with her rest. Springing to her feet and rapidly dressing herself, the girl was soon breathing the fragrance of the morning in the open air. For the first time she was sensibly struck with the singular beauties, as well as with the profound retirement, of her present situation. The day proved to be one of those of the autumnal glory, so common to a climate that is more abused than appreciated, and its influence was every way inspiriting and genial. Mabel was benefitted by this circumstance; for, as she fancied, her heart was heavy on account of the dangers to which a father, whom she now began to love as women love when confidence is created, was exposed.

But the island seemed absolutely deserted. The previous night, the bustle of the arrival had given the spot an appearance of life which was now entirely gone; and our heroine had turned her eyes nearly around on every object in sight, before she caught a view of a single human being to remove the sense of utter solitude. Then, indeed, she beheld all who were left behind, collected in a group around a fire which might be said to belong to the camp. The person of her uncle, to whom she was so much accustomed, reassured Mabel; and she examined the remainder with a curiosity natural to her situation. Besides Cap and the Quartermaster, there were the Corporal, the three soldiers, and the woman, who was cooking. The huts were silent and empty; and the low but tower-like summit of the block-house rose above the bushes, by which it was half concealed, in picturesque beauty. The sun was just casting its brightness into the open places of the glade, and the vault over her head was impending in the soft sublimity of the blue void. Not a cloud was visible, and she secretly fancied the circumstance might be taken as a harbinger of peace and security.

Perceiving that all the others were occupied with that great concern of human nature, a breakfast, Mabel walked, unobserved, towards an end of the island where she was completely shut out of view by the trees and bushes. Here she got a stand on the very edge of the water, by forcing aside the low branches, and stood watching the barely perceptible flow and re-flow of the miniature waves which laved the shore; a sort of physical echo to the agitation that prevailed on the lake fifty miles above her. The glimpses of natural scenery that offered were very soft and pleasing; and our heroine, who had a quick eye for all that was lovely in nature, was not slow in selecting the most striking bits of landscape. She gazed through the different vistas formed by the openings between the islands, and thought she had never looked on aught more lovely.

While thus occupied, Mabel was suddenly alarmed by fancying that she caught a glimpse of a human form among the bushes that lined the shore of the island which lay directly before her. The distance across the water was not a hundred yards; and, though she might be mistaken, and her fancy was wandering when the form passed before her sight, still she did not think she could be deceived. Aware that her sex would be no protection against a rifle bullet, should an Iroquois get a view of her, the girl instinctively drew back, taking care to conceal her person as much as possible by the leaves, while she kept her own look riveted on the opposite shore, vainly waiting for some time in the expectation of the stranger. She was about to quit her post in the bushes and hasten to her uncle, in order to acquaint him of her suspicions, when she saw the branch of an alder thrust beyond the fringe of bushes on the other island, and waved towards her significantly, and as she fancied in token of amity. This was a breathless and a trying moment to one as inexperienced in frontier warfare as our heroine; and yet she felt the great necessity that existed for preserving her recollection, and of acting with steadiness and discretion.

It was one of the peculiarities of the exposure to which those who dwelt on the frontiers of America were liable, to bring out the moral qualities of the women to a degree which they must themselves, under other circumstances, have believed they were incapable of manifesting; and Mabel well knew that the borderers loved to dwell in their legends on the presence of mind, fortitude, and spirit that their wives and sisters had displayed under circumstances the most trying. Her emulation had been awakened by what she had heard on such subjects; and it at once struck her that now was the moment for her to show that she was truly Sergeant Dunham's child. The motion of the branch was such as she believed indicated amity; and, after a moment's hesitation, she broke off a twig, fastened it to a stick, and, thrusting it through an opening, waved it in return, imitating as closely as possible the manner of the other.

This dumb show lasted two or three minutes on both sides, when Mabel perceived that the bushes opposite were cautiously pushed aside, and a human face appeared at an opening. A glance sufficed to let Mabel see that it was the countenance of a red-skin, as well as that of a woman. A second and a better look satisfied her that it was the face of the Dew-of-June, the wife of Arrowhead. During the time she had travelled in company with this woman, Mabel had been won by the gentleness of manner, the meek simplicity, and the mingled awe and affection with which she regarded her husband. Once or twice in the course of the journey she fancied the Tuscarora had manifested towards herself an unpleasant degree of attention; and on those occasions it had struck her that his wife exhibited sorrow and mortification. As Mabel, however, had more than compensated for any pain she might in this way unintentionally have caused her companion, by her own kindness of manner and attentions, the woman had shown much attachment to her, and they had parted, with a deep conviction on the mind of our heroine that in the Dew-of-June she had lost a friend.

It is useless to attempt to analyze all the ways by which the human heart is led into confidence. Such a feeling, however, had the young Tuscarora woman awakened in the breast of our heroine; and the latter, under the impression that this extraordinary visit was intended for her own good, felt every disposition to have a closer communication. She no longer hesitated about showing herself clear of the bushes, and was not sorry to see the Dew-of-June imitate her confidence, by stepping fearlessly out of her own cover. The two girls, for the Tuscarora, though married, was even younger than Mabel, now openly exchanged signs of friendship, and the latter beckoned to her friend to approach, though she knew not the manner herself in which this object could be effected. But the Dew-of-June was not slow in letting it be seen that it was in her power; for, disappearing in a moment, she soon showed herself again in the end of a bark canoe, the bows of which she had drawn to the edge of the bushes, and of which the body still lay in a sort of covered creek. Mabel was about to invite her to cross, when her own name was called aloud in the stentorian voice of her uncle. Making a hurried gesture for the Tuscarora girl to conceal herself, Mabel sprang from the bushes and tripped up the glade towards the sound, and perceived that the whole party had just seated themselves at breakfast; Cap having barely put his appetite under sufficient restraint to summon her to join them. That this was the most favorable instant for the interview flashed on the mind of Mabel; and, excusing herself on the plea of not being prepared for the meal, she bounded back to the thicket, and soon renewed her communications with the young Indian woman.

Dew-of-June was quick of comprehension; and with half a dozen noiseless strokes of the paddle, her canoe was concealed in the bushes of Station Island. In another minute, Mabel held her hand, and was leading her through the grove towards her own hut. Fortunately the latter was so placed as to be completely hid from the sight of those at the fire, and they both entered it unseen. Hastily explaining to her guest, in the best manner she could, the necessity of quitting her for a short time, Mabel, first placing the Dew-of-June in her own room, with a full certainty that she would not quit it until told to do so, went to the fire and took her seat among the rest, with all the composure it was in her power to command.

"Late come, late served, Mabel," said her uncle, between mouthfuls of broiled salmon; for though the cookery might be very unsophisticated on that remote frontier, the viands were generally delicious—"late come, late served; it is a good rule, and keeps laggards up to their work."

"I am no laggard, uncle; for I have been stirring nearly an hour, and exploring our island."

"It's little you'll make o' that, Mistress Mabel," put in Muir; "that's little by nature. Lundie—or it might be better to style him Major Duncan in this presence" (this was said in consideration of the corporal and the common men, though they were taking their meal a little apart)—"has not added an empire to his Majesty's dominions in getting possession of this island, which is likely to equal that of the celebrated Sancho in revenues and profits—Sancho, of whom, doubtless, Master Cap, you'll often have been reading in your leisure hours, more especially in calms and moments of inactivity."

"I know the spot you mean, Quartermaster; Sancho's Island—coral rock, of new formation, and as bad a land-fall, in a dark night and blowing weather, as a sinner could wish to keep clear of. It's a famous place for cocoanuts and bitter water, that Sancho's Island."

"It's no' very famous for dinners," returned Muir, repressing the smile which was struggling to his lips out of respect to Mabel; "nor do I think there'll be much to choose between its revenue and that of this spot. In my judgment, Master Cap, this is a very unmilitary position, and I look to some calamity befalling it, sooner or later."

"It is to be hoped not until our turn of duty is over," observed Mabel. "I have no wish to study the French language."

"We might think ourselves happy, did it not prove to be the Iroquois. I have reasoned with Major Duncan on the occupation of this position, but 'a wilfu' man maun ha' his way.' My first object in accompanying this party was to endeavor to make myself acceptable and useful to your beautiful niece, Master Cap; and the second was to take such an account of the stores that belong to my particular department as shall leave no question open to controversy, concerning the manner of expenditure, when they shall have disappeared by means of the enemy."

"Do you look upon matters as so serious?" demanded Cap,

actually suspending his mastication of a bit of venison—for he passed alternately from fish to flesh and back again—in the interest he took in the answer "Is the danger pressing?"

"I'll no' say just that; and I'll no' say just the contrary. There is always danger in war, and there is more of it at the advanced posts than at the main encampment. It ought, therefore, to occasion no surprise were we to be visited by the French at any moment."

"And what the devil is to be done in that case? Six men and two women would make but a poor job in defending such a place as this, should the enemy invade us; as, no doubt, Frenchman-like, they would take very good care to come strong-handed."

"That we may depend on—some very formidable force at the very lowest. A military disposition might be made in defence of the island, out of all question, and according to the art of war, though we would probably fail in the force necessary to carry out the design in any very creditable manner. In the first place, a detachment should be sent off to the shore, with orders to annoy the enemy in landing; a strong party ought instantly to be thrown into the blockhouse, as the citadel, for on that all the different detachments would naturally fall back for support, as the French advanced; and an entrenched camp might be laid out around the stronghold, as it would be very unmilitary indeed to let the foe get near enough to the foot of the walls to mine them. Chevaux-de-frise would keep the cavalry in check; and as for the artillery, redoubts should be thrown up under cover of yon woods. Strong skirmishing parties, moreover, would be exceedingly serviceable in retarding the march of the enemy; and these different huts, if properly piqueted and ditched, would be converted into very eligible positions for that object."

"Whe—e—e—w—, Quartermaster! And who the d—l is to find all the men to carry out such a plan?"

"The king, out of all question, Master Cap. It is his quarrel, and it's just he should bear the burthen o' it."

"And we are only six! This is fine talking, with a vengeance. You could be sent down to the shore to oppose the landing, Mabel might skirmish with her tongue at least, the soldier's wife might act chevaux-de-frise to entangle the cavalry, the

Corporal should command the entrenched camp, his three men could occupy the five huts, and I would take the blockhouse. Whe—e—e—w! you describe well, Lieutenant; and should have been a limner instead of a soldier."

"Na, I've been very literal and upright in my exposition of matters. That there is no greater force here to carry out the plan is a fault of his Majesty's ministers, and none of mine."

"But should our enemy really appear," asked Mabel, with more interest than she might have shown, had she not remembered the guest in the hut, "what course ought we to pursue?"

"My advice would be to attempt to achieve that, pretty Mabel, which rendered Xenophon so justly celebrated."

"I think you mean a retreat, though I half guess at your allusion."

"You've imagined my meaning from the possession of a strong native sense, young lady. I am aware that your worthy father has pointed out to the Corporal certain modes and methods by which he fancies this island could be held, in case the French should discover its position; but the excellent Sergeant, though your father, and as good a man in his duties as ever wielded a spontoon, is not the great Lord Stair, or even the Duke of Marlborough. I'll not deny the Sergeant's merits in his particular sphere; though I cannot exaggerate qualities, however excellent, into those of men who may be in some trifling degree his superiors. Sergeant Dunham has taken counsel of his heart, instead of his head, in resolving to issue such orders; but, if the fort fall, the blame will lie on him that ordered it to be occupied, and not on him whose duty it was to defend it. Whatever may be the determination of the latter, should the French and their allies land, a good commander never neglects the preparations necessary to effect a retreat; and I would advise Master Cap, who is the admiral of our navy, to have a boat in readiness to evacuate the island, if need comes to need. The largest boat that we have left carries a very ample sail; and by hauling it round here, and mooring it under those bushes, there will be a convenient place for a hurried embarkation; and then you'll perceive, pretty Mabel, that it is scarcely fifty yards before we shall be in a channel between two other islands, and hid from the sight of those who may happen to be on this."

"All that you say is very true, Mr. Muir; but may not the

French come from that quarter themselves? If it is so good for a retreat, it is equally good for an advance."

"They'll no' have the sense to do so discreet a thing," returned Muir, looking furtively and a little uneasily around him; "they'll no' have sufficient discretion. Your French are a head-over-heels nation, and usually come forward in a random way; so we may look for them, if they come at all, on the other side of the island."

The discourse now became exceedingly desultory, touching principally, however, on the probabilities of an invasion, and the best means of meeting it.

To most of this Mabel paid but little attention; though she felt some surprise that Lieutenant Muir, an officer whose character for courage stood well, should openly recommend an abandonment of what appeared to her to be doubly a duty, her father's character being connected with the defence of the island. Her mind, however, was so much occupied with her guest, that, seizing the first favorable moment, she left the table, and was soon in her own hut again. Carefully fastening the door, and seeing that the simple curtain was drawn before the single little window, Mabel next led the Dew-of-June, or June, as she was familiarly termed by those who spoke to her in English, into the outer room, making signs of affection and confidence.

"I am glad to see you, June," said Mabel, with one of her sweetest smiles, and in her own winning voice—"very glad to see you. What has brought you hither, and how did you discover the island?"

"Speak slow," said June, returning smile for smile, and pressing the little hand she held with one of her own that was scarcely larger, though it had been hardened by labor; "more slow—too quick."

Mabel repeated her questions, endeavoring to repress the impetuosity of her feelings; and she succeeded in speaking so distinctly as to be understood.

"June, friend," returned the Indian woman.

"I believe you, June—from my soul I believe you; what has this to do with your visit?"

"Friend come to see friend," answered June, again smiling openly in the other's face.

"There is some other reason, June, else would you never run this risk, and alone. You are alone, June?"

"June wid you, no one else. June come alone, paddle canoe."

"I hope so, I think so—nay, I *know so*. You would not be treacherous with me, June?"

"What treacherous?"

"You would not betray me, would not give me to the French, to the Iroquois, to Arrowhead?"

June shook her head earnestly.

"You would not sell my scalp?"

Here June passed her arm fondly around the slender waist of Mabel and pressed her to her heart with a tenderness and affection that brought tears into the eyes of our heroine. It was done in the fond caressing manner of a woman, and it was scarcely possible that it should not obtain credit for sincerity with a young and ingenuous person of the same sex. Mabel returned the pressure, and then held the other off at the length of her arm, looked her steadily in the face, and continued her inquiries.

"If June has something to tell her friend, let her speak plainly," she said. "My ears are open."

"June 'fraid Arrowhead kill her."

"But Arrowhead will never know it." Mabel's blood mounted to her temples as she said this; for she felt that she was urging a wife to be treacherous to her husband. "That is, Mabel will not tell him."

"He bury tomahawk in June's head."

"That must never be, dear June; I would rather you should say no more than run this risk."

"Blockhouse good place to sleep, good place to stay."

"Do you mean that I may save my life by keeping in the blockhouse, June? Surely, surely, Arrowhead will not hurt you for telling me that. He cannot wish me any great harm, for I never injured him."

"Arrowhead wish no harm to handsome pale-face," returned June, averting her face; and, though she always spoke in the soft, gentle voice of an Indian girl, now permitting its notes to fall so low as to cause them to sound melancholy and timid. "Arrowhead love pale-face girl."

Mabel blushed, she knew not why, and for a moment her questions were repressed by a feeling of inherent delicacy. But it was necessary to know more, for her apprehensions had been keenly awakened, and she resumed her inquiries.

"Arrowhead can have no reason to love or to hate *me*," she said. "Is he near you?"

"Husband always near wife, here," said June, laying her hand on her heart.

"Excellent creature! But tell me, June, ought I to keep in the blockhouse to-day—this morning—now?"

"Blockhouse very good; good for women. Blockhouse got no scalp."

"I fear I understand you only too well, June. Do you wish to see my father?"

"No here; gone away."

"You cannot know that, June; you see the island is full of his soldiers."

"No full; gone away"—here June held up four of her fingers —"so many red-coats."

"And Pathfinder? would you not like to see the Pathfinder? He can talk to you in the Iroquois tongue."

"Tongue gone wid him," said June, laughing; "keep tongue in his mout'."

There was something so sweet and contagious in the infantine laugh of an Indian girl, that Mabel could not refrain from joining in it, much as her fears were aroused by all that had passed.

"You appear to know, or to think you know, all about us, June. But if Pathfinder be gone, Eau-douce can speak French too. You know Eau-douce; shall I run and bring *him* to talk with you?"

"Eau-douce gone too, all but heart; that there." As June said this, she laughed again; looked in different directions, as if unwilling to confuse the other, and laid her hand on Mabel's bosom.

Our heroine had often heard of the wonderful sagacity of the Indians, and of the surprising manner in which they noted all things, while they appeared to regard none; but she was scarcely prepared for the direction the discourse had so singularly taken. Willing to change it, and at the same time truly anxious to learn how great the danger that impended over them might really be, she rose from the camp-stool on which she had been seated; and, by assuming an attitude of less affectionate confidence, she hoped to hear more of that she really desired to learn, and to avoid allusions to that which she found so embarrassing.

"You know how much or how little you ought to tell me, June," she said; "and I hope you love me well enough to give me the information I ought to hear. My dear uncle, too, is on the island, and you are, or ought to be, his friend as well as mine; and both of us will remember your conduct when we get back to Oswego."

"Maybe, never get back; who know?" This was said doubtingly, or as one who lays down an uncertain proposition, and not with a taunt, or a desire to alarm.

"No one knows what will happen but God. Our lives are in His hands. Still, I think you are to be His instrument in saving us."

This passed June's comprehension, and she only looked her ignorance; for it was evident she wished to be of use.

"Blockhouse very good," she repeated, as soon as her countenance ceased to express uncertainty, laying strong emphasis on the last two words.

"Well, I understand this, June, and will sleep in it tonight. Of course I am to tell my uncle what you have said?"

The Dew-of-June started, and she discovered a very manifest uneasiness at the interrogatory.

"No, no, no, no!" she answered, with a volubility and vehemence that was imitated from the French of the Canadas; "no good to tell Saltwater. He much talk and long tongue. Thinks woods all water, understand not'ing. Tell Arrowhead, and June die."

"You do my dear uncle injustice, for he would be as little likely to betray you as any one."

"No understand. Saltwater got tongue, but no eyes, no ears, no nose—not'ing but tongue, tongue, tongue!"

Although Mabel did not exactly coincide in this opinion, she saw that Cap had not the confidence of the young Indian woman, and that it was idle to expect she would consent to his being admitted to their interview.

"You appear to think you know our situation pretty well, June," Mabel continued; "have you been on the island before this visit?"

"Just come."

"How then do you know that what you say is true? my father, the Pathfinder, and Eau-douce may all be here within sound of my voice, if I choose to call them."

"All gone," said June positively, smiling good-humoredly at the same time.

"Nay, this is more than you *can* say certainly, not having been over the island to examine it."

"Got good eyes; see boat with men go away—see ship with Eau-douce."

"Then you have been some time watching us. I think, however, you have not counted them that remain."

June laughed, held up her four fingers again, and then pointed to her two thumbs; passing a finger over the first, she repeated the words "red-coats"; and touching the last, she added, "Salt-water," "Quartermaster." All this was being very accurate, and Mabel began to entertain serious doubts as to the propriety of her permitting her visitor to depart without her becoming more explicit. Still it was so repugnant to her feelings to abuse the confidence this gentle and affectionate creature had evidently reposed in her, that Mabel had no sooner admitted the thought of summoning her uncle, than she rejected it as unworthy of herself and unjust to her friend. To aid this good resolution, too, there was the certainty that June would reveal nothing, but take refuge in a stubborn silence, if any attempt were made to coerce her.

"You think, then, June," Mabel continued, as soon as these thoughts had passed through her mind, "that I had better live in the blockhouse?"

"Good place for woman. Blockhouse got no scalp. Logs t'ick."

"You speak confidently, June; as if you had been in it, and had measured its walls."

June laughed; and she looked knowing, though she said nothing.

"Does any one but yourself know how to find this island? have any of the Iroquois seen it?"

June looked sad, and she cast her eyes warily about her, as if distrusting a listener.

"Tuscarora, everywhere—Oswego, here, Frontenac, Mohawk —everywhere. If he see June, kill her."

"But we thought that no one knew of this island, and that we had no reason to fear our enemies while on it."

"Much eye, Iroquois."

"Eyes will not always do, June. This spot is hid from ordinary sight, and few of even our own people know how to find it."

"One man can tell; some Yengeese talk French."

Mabel felt a chill at her heart. All the suspicions against Jasper, which she had hitherto disdained entertaining, crowded in a body on her thoughts; and the sensation that they brought was so sickening, that for an instant she imagined she was about to faint. Arousing herself, and remembering her promise to her father, she arose and walked up and down the hut for a minute, fancying that Jasper's delinquencies were naught to her, though her inmost heart yearned with the desire to think him innocent.

"I understand your meaning, June," she then said; "you wish me to know that some one has treacherously told your people where and how to find the island?"

June laughed, for in her eyes artifice in war was oftener a merit than a crime; but she was too true to her tribe herself to say more than the occasion required. Her object was to save Mabel, and Mabel only; and she saw no sufficient reason for "travelling out of the record," as the lawyers express it, in order to do anything else.

"Pale-face know now," she added. "Blockhouse good for girl, no matter for men and warriors."

"But it is much matter with me, June; for one of these men is my uncle, whom I love, and the others are my countrymen and friends. I must tell them what has passed."

"Then June be kill," returned the young Indian quietly, though she evidently spoke with concern.

"No; they shall not know that you have been here. Still, they must be on their guard, and we can all go into the blockhouse."

"Arrowhead know, see everything, and June be kill. June come to tell young pale-face friend, not to tell men. Every warrior watch his own scalp. June woman, and tell woman; no tell men."

Mabel was greatly distressed at this declaration of her wild friend, for it was now evident the young creature understood that her communication was to go no further. She was ignorant how far these people consider the point of honor interested in her keeping the secret; and most of all was she unable to say how far any indiscretion of her own might actually commit June and endanger her life. All these considerations flashed on her mind, and reflection only rendered their influence more painful. June, too, manifestly viewed the matter gravely; for she began to gather up the different little articles she had dropped in taking Mabel's hand, and was preparing to depart. To attempt detaining her was out of the question; and to part from her, after all she had hazarded to serve her, was repugnant to all the just and kind feelings of our heroine's nature.

"June," said she eagerly, folding her arms round the gentle but uneducated being, "we are friends. From me you have nothing to fear, for no one shall know of your visit. If you could give me some signal just before the danger comes, some sign by which to know when to go into the blockhouse, how to take care of myself."

June paused, for she had been in earnest in her intention to depart; and then she said quietly, "Bring June pigeon."

"A pigeon! Where shall I find a pigeon to bring you?"

"Next hut; bring old one; June go to canoe."

"I think I understand you, June; but had I not better lead you back to the bushes, lest you meet some of the men?"

"Go out first; count men, one, two, t'ree, four, five, six"— here June held up her fingers, and laughed—"all out of the way —good; all but one, call him one side. Then sing, and fetch pigeon."

Mabel smiled at the readiness and ingenuity of the girl, and prepared to execute her requests. At the door, however, she stopped, and looked back entreatingly at the Indian woman. "Is there no hope of your telling me more, June?" she said.

"Know all now, blockhouse good, pigeon tell, Arrowhead kill."

The last words sufficed; for Mabel could not urge further communications, when her companion herself told her that the penalty of her revelations might be death by the hand of her husband. Throwing open the door, she made a sign of adieu to June, and went out of the hut. Mabel resorted to the simple expedient of the young Indian girl to ascertain the situation of the different individuals on the island. Instead of looking about her with the intention of recognizing faces and dresses, she merely counted them; and found that three still remained at the fire, while two had gone to the boat, one of whom was Mr. Muir. The sixth man was her uncle; and he was coolly arranging some fishing-tackle at no great distance from the fire. The woman was just entering her own hut; and this accounted for the whole party. Mabel now, affecting to have dropped something, returned nearly to the hut she had left, warbling an air, stooped as if to pick up some object from the ground, and hurried towards the hut June had mentioned. This was a dilapidated structure, and it had been converted by the soldiers of the last detachment into a sort of storehouse for their live stock. Among other things, it contained a few dozen pigeons, which were regaling on a pile of wheat that had been brought off from one of the farms plundered on the Canada shore. Mabel had not much difficulty in catching one of these pigeons, although they fluttered and flew about the hut with a noise like that of drums; and, concealing it in her dress, she stole back towards her own hut with the prize. It was empty; and, without doing more than cast a glance in at the door, the eager girl hurried down to the shore. She had no difficulty in escaping observation, for the trees and bushes made a complete cover to her person. At the canoe she found June, who took the pigeon, placed it in a basket of her own manufacturing, and, repeating the words, "blockhouse good," she glided out of the bushes and across the narrow passage, as noiselessly as she had come. Mabel waited some time to catch a signal of leave-taking or amity after her friend had landed, but none was given. The adjacent islands, without exception, were as quiet as if no one had ever disturbed the sublime repose of nature, and nowhere could any sign or symptom be discovered, as Mabel then thought, that might denote the proximity of the sort of danger of which June had given notice.

On returning, however, from the shore, Mabel was struck with a little circumstance, that, in an ordinary situation, would have attracted no attention, but which, now that her suspicions had been aroused, did not pass before her uneasy eye unnoticed. A small piece of red bunting, such as is used in the ensigns of ships, was fluttering at the lower branch of a small tree, fastened in a way to permit it to blow out, or to droop like a vessel's pennant.

Now that Mabel's fears were awakened, June herself could not have manifested greater quickness in analyzing facts that she believed might affect the safety of the party. She saw at a glance that this bit of cloth could be observed from an adjacent island; that it lay so near the line between her own hut and the canoe as to leave no doubt that June had passed near it, if not directly under it; and that it might be a signal to communicate some important fact connected with the mode of attack to those who were probably lying in ambush near them. Tearing the little strip of bunting from the tree, Mabel hastened on, scarcely knowing what her duty next required of her. June might be false to her, but her manner, her looks, her affection, and her disposition as Mabel had known it in the journey, forbade the idea. Then came the allusion to Arrowhead's admiration of the pale-face beauties, some dim recollections of the looks of the Tuscarora, and a painful consciousness that few wives could view with kindness one who had estranged a husband's affections. None of these images were distinct and clear, but they rather gleamed over the mind of our heroine than rested in it, and they quickened her pulses, as they did her step, without bringing with them the prompt and clear decisions that usually followed her reflections. She had hurried onwards towards the hut occupied by the soldier's wife, intending to remove at once to the blockhouse with the woman, though she could persuade no other to follow, when her impatient walk was interrupted by the voice of Muir.

"Whither so fast, pretty Mabel?" he cried; "and why so given to solitude? The worthy Sergeant will deride my breeding, if he hear that his daughter passes the mornings alone and unattended to, though he well knows it is my ardent wish to be her slave and companion from the beginning of the year to its end."

"Surely, Mr. Muir, you must have some authority here?" Mabel suddenly arrested her steps to say. "One of your rank would be listened to, at least, by a corporal?"

"I don't know that, I don't know that," interrupted Muir, with an impatience and appearance of alarm that might have excited Mabel's attention at another moment. "Command is command; discipline, discipline; and authority, authority. Your good father would be sore grieved did he find me interfering to sully or carry off the laurels he is about to win; and I cannot command the Corporal without equally commanding the Sergeant. The wisest way will be for me to remain in the obscurity of a private individual in this enterprise; and it is so that all parties, from Lundie down, understand the transaction."

"This I know, and it may be well, nor would I give my dear father any cause of complaint; but you may influence the Corporal to his own good."

"I'll no' say that," returned Muir in his sly Scotch way; "it would be far safer to promise to influence him to his injury. Mankind, pretty Mabel, have their peculiarities; and to influence a fellow-being to his own good is one of the most difficult tasks of human nature, while the opposite is just the easiest. You'll no' forget this, my dear, but bear it in mind for your edification and government. But what is that you're twisting round your slender finger as you may be said to twist hearts?"

"It is nothing but a bit of cloth—a sort of flag—a trifle that is hardly worth our attention at this grave moment. If——"

"A trifle! It's no' so trifling as ye may imagine, Mistress Mabel," taking the bit of bunting from her, and stretching it at full length with both his arms extended, while his face grew grave and his eye watchful. "Ye'll no' ha' been finding this, Mabel Dunham, in the breakfast?"

Mabel simply acquainted him with the spot where and the manner in which she had found the bit of cloth. While she was speaking, the eye of the Quartermaster was not quiet for a moment, glancing from the rag to the face of our heroine, then back again to the rag. That his suspicions were awakened was easy to be seen, nor was he long in letting it be known what direction they had taken.

"We are not in a part of the world where our ensigns and gauds ought to be spread abroad to the wind, Mabel Dunham!" he said, with an ominous shake of the head.

"I thought as much myself, Mr. Muir, and brought away the little flag lest it might be the means of betraying our presence here to the enemy, even though nothing is intended by its display. Ought not my uncle to be made acquainted with the circumstance?"

"I no' see the necessity for that, pretty Mabel; for, as you justly say, it is a circumstance, and circumstances sometimes worry the worthy mariner. But this flag, if flag it can be called, belongs to a seaman's craft. You may perceive that it is made of what is called bunting, and that is a description of cloth used only by vessels for such purposes, *our* colors being of silk, as you may understand, or painted canvas. It's surprisingly like the fly of the *Scud's* ensign. And now I recollect me to have observed that a piece had been cut from that very flag."

Mabel felt her heart sink, but she had sufficient self-command not to attempt an answer.

"It must be looked to," Muir continued, "and, after all, I think it may be well to hold a short consultation with Master Cap, than whom a more loyal subject does not exist in the British empire."

"I have thought the warning so serious," Mabel rejoined, "that I am about to remove to the blockhouse, and to take the woman with me."

"I do not see the prudence of that, Mabel. The blockhouse will be the first spot assailed should there really be an attack; and it's no' well provided for a siege, that must be allowed. If I might advise in so delicate a contingency, I would recommend your taking refuge in the boat, which, as you may now perceive, is most favorably placed to retreat by that channel opposite, where all in it would be hid by the islands in one or two minutes. Water leaves no trail, as Pathfinder well expresses it; and there appears to be so many different passages in that quarter that escape would be more than probable. I've always been of opinion that Lundie hazarded too much in occupying a post so far advanced and so much exposed as this."

"It's too late to regret it now, Mr. Muir, and we have only to consult our own security."

"And the king's honor, pretty Mabel. Yes, his Majesty's arms and his glorious name are not to be overlooked on any occasion."

"Then I think it might be better if we all turned our eyes towards the place that has been built to maintain them instead of the boat," said Mabel, smiling; "and so, Mr. Muir, I am for the blockhouse, intending to await there the return of my father and his party. He would be sadly grieved at finding we had fled when he got back successful himself, and filled with the confidence of our having been as faithful to our duties as he has been to his own."

"Nay, nay, for heaven's sake, do not misunderstand me, Mabel!" Muir interrupted, with some alarm of manner; "I am far from intimating that any but you females ought to take refuge in the boat. The duty of us men is sufficiently plain, no doubt, and my resolution has been formed from the first to stand or fall by the blockhouse."

"And did you imagine, Mr. Muir, that two females could row that heavy boat in a way to escape the bark canoe of an Indian?"

"Ah, my pretty Mabel, love is seldom logical, and its fears and misgivings are apt to warp the faculties! I only saw your sweet person in the possession of the means of safety, and overlooked the want of ability to use them; but you'll not be so cruel, lovely creature, as to impute to me as a fault my intense anxiety on your own account!"

Mabel had heard enough: her mind was too much occupied with what had passed that morning, and with her fears, to wish to linger longer to listen to love speeches, which in her most joyous and buoyant moments she would have found unpleasant. She took a hasty leave of her companion, and was about to trip away towards the hut of the other woman, when Muir arrested the movement by laying a hand on her arm.

"One word, Mabel," said he, "before you leave me. This little flag may, or it may not, have a particular meaning; if it has, now that we are aware of its being shown, may it not be better to put it back again, while we watch vigilantly for some answer that may betray the conspiracy; and if it mean nothing, why, nothing will follow."

"This may be all right, Mr. Muir, though, if the whole is accidental, the flag might be the occasion of the fort's being discovered."

Mabel stayed to utter no more; but she was soon out of sight, running into the hut towards which she had been first proceeding. The Quartermaster remained on the very spot and in the precise attitude in which she had left him for quite a minute, first looking at the bounding figure of the girl and then at the bit of bunting, which he still held before him in a way to denote indecision. His irresolution lasted but for this minute, however; for he was soon beneath the tree, where he fastened the mimic flag to a branch again, though, from his ignorance of the precise spot from which it had been taken by Mabel, he left it fluttering from a part of the oak where it was still more exposed than before to the eyes of any passenger on the river, though less in view from the island itself.

CHAPTER XXI

Each one has had his supping mess,
The cheese is put into the press,
The pans and bowls, clean scalded all,
Reared up against the milk-house wall.   OTTO

IT SEEMED strange to Mabel Dunham, as she passed along on her way to find her female companion, that others should be so composed, while she herself felt as if the responsibilities of life and death rested on her shoulders. It is true that distrust of June's motives mingled with her forebodings; but when she came to recall the affectionate and natural manner of the young Indian girl, and all the evidences of good faith and sincerity she had seen in her conduct during the familiar intercourse of their journey, she rejected the idea with the unwillingness of a generous disposition to believe ill of others. She saw, however, that she could not put her companions properly on their guard without letting them into the secret of her conference with June; and she found herself compelled to act cautiously and with a forethought to which she was unaccustomed, more especially in a matter of so much moment.

The soldier's wife was told to transport the necessaries into the blockhouse, and admonished not to be far from it at any time during the day. Mabel did not explain her reasons. She merely stated that she had detected some signs in walking about the island, which induced her to apprehend that the enemy had more knowledge of its position than had been previously believed, and that they two at least, would do well to be in readiness to seek a refuge at the shortest notice. It was not difficult to arouse the apprehension of this person, who, though a stouthearted Scotchwoman, was ready enough to listen to anything that confirmed her dread of Indian cruelties. As soon as Mabel believed that her companion was sufficiently frightened to make her wary, she threw out some hints touching the inexpediency of letting the soldiers know the extent of their own fears. This was done with a view to prevent discussions and inquiries that might embarrass our heroine: she determining to render her uncle, the Corporal, and his men more cautious, by adopting a different course. Unfortunately, the British army could not have furnished a worse person for the particular duty that he was now required to discharge than Corporal M'Nab, the individual who had been left in command during the absence of Sergeant Dunham. On the one hand, he was resolute, prompt, familiar with all the details of a soldier's life, and used to war; on the other, he was supercilious as regards the provincials, opinionated on every subject connected with the narrow limits of his professional practice, much disposed to fancy the British empire the centre of all that is excellent in the world, and Scotland the focus of, at least, all moral excellence in that empire. In short, he was an epitome, though on a scale suited to his rank, of those very qualities which were so peculiar to the servants of the Crown that were sent into the colonies, as these servants estimated themselves in comparison with the natives of the country; or, in other words, he considered the American as an animal inferior to the parent stock, and viewed all his notions of military service, in particular, as undigested and absurd. A more impracticable subject, therefore, could not well have offered for the purpose of Mabel, and yet she felt obliged to lose no time in putting her plan in execution.

"My father has left you a responsible command, Corporal," she said, as soon as she could catch M'Nab a little apart; "for should the island fall into the hands of the enemy, not only should we be captured, but the party that is now out would in all probability become their prisoners also."

"It needs no journey from Scotland to this place to know the facts needful to be o' that way of thinking," returned M'Nab drily.

"I do not doubt your understanding it as well as myself, Mr.

M'Nab, but I'm fearful that you veterans, accustomed as you are to dangers and battles, are a little apt to overlook some of the precautions that may be necessary in a situation as peculiar as ours."

"They say Scotland is no conquered country, young woman, but I'm thinking there must be some mistak' in the matter, as we, her children, are so drowsy-headed and apt to be o'ertaken when we least expect it."

"Nay, my good friend, you mistake my meaning. In the first place, I'm not thinking of Scotland at all, but of this island; and then I am far from doubting your vigilance when you think it necessary to practise it; but my great fear is that there may be danger to which your courage will make you indifferent."

"My courage, Mistress Dunham, is doubtless of a very poor quality, being nothing but Scottish courage; your father's is Yankee, and were he here amang us we should see different preparations, beyond a doubt. Well, times are getting wrang, when foreigners hold commissions and carry halberds in Scottish corps; and I no' wonder that battles are lost, and campaigns go wrang end foremost."

Mabel was almost in despair; but the quiet warning of June was still too vividly impressed on her mind to allow her to yield the matter. She changed her mode of operating, therefore, still clinging to the hope of getting the whole party within the block-house, without being compelled to betray the source whence she obtained her notices of the necessity of vigilance.

"I daresay you are right, Corporal M'Nab," she observed; "for I've often heard of the heroes of your country, who have been among the first of the civilized world, if what they tell me of them is true."

"Have you read the history of Scotland, Mistress Dunham?" demanded the Corporal, looking up at his pretty companion, for the first time with something like a smile on his hard, repulsive countenance.

"I have read a little of it, Corporal, but I've heard much more. The lady who brought me up had Scottish blood in her veins, and was fond of the subject."

"I'll warrant ye, the Sergeant no' troubled himself to expatiate on the renown of the country where his regiment was raised?"

"My father has other things to think of, and the little I know was got from the lady I have mentioned."

"She'll no' be forgetting to tall ye o' Wallace?"

"Of him I've even read a good deal."

"And o' Bruce, and the affair of Bannockburn?"

"Of that too, as well as of Culloden Muir."

The last of these battles was then a recent event, it having actually been fought within the recollection of our heroine, whose notions of it, however, were so confused that she scarcely appreciated the effect her allusion might produce on her companion. She knew it had been a victory, and had often heard the guests of her patroness mention it with triumph; and she fancied their feelings would find a sympathetic chord in those of every British soldier. Unfortunately, M'Nab had fought throughout that luckless day on the side of the Pretender; and a deep scar that garnished his face had been left there by the sabre of a German soldier in the service of the House of Hanover. He fancied that his wound bled afresh at Mabel's allusion; and it is certain that the blood rushed to his face in a torrent, as if it would pour out of his skin at the cicatrix.

"Hoot! hoot awa'!" he fairly shouted, "with your Culloden and Sherriff muirs, young woman; ye'll no' be understanding the subject at all, and will manifest not only wisdom but modesty in speaking o' your ain country and its many failings. King George has some loyal subjects in the colonies, na doubt, but 'twill be a lang time before he sees or hears any guid of them."

Mabel was surprised at the Corporal's heat, for she had not the smallest idea where the shoe pinched; but she was determined not to give up the point.

"I've always heard that the Scotch had two of the good qualities of soldiers," she said, "courage and circumspection; and I feel persuaded that Corporal M'Nab will sustain the national renown."

"Ask yer own father, Mistress Dunham; he is acquaint' with Corporal M'Nab, and will no' be backward to point out his demerits. We have been in battle thegither, and he is my superior officer, and has a sort o' official right to give the characters of his subordinates."

"My father thinks well of you, M'Nab, or he would not have

left you in charge of this island and all it contains, his own daughter included. Among other things, I well know that he calculates largely on your prudence. He expects the blockhouse in particular to be strictly attended to."

"If he wishes to defend the honor of the 55th behind logs, he ought to have remained in command himsel'; for, to speak frankly, it goes against a Scotchman's bluid and opinions to be beaten out of the field even before he is attacked. We are broadsword men, and love to stand foot to foot with the foe. This American mode of fighting, that is getting into so much favor, will destroy the reputation of his Majesty's army, if it no' destroy its spirit."

"No true soldier despises caution. Even Major Duncan himself, than whom there is none braver, is celebrated for his care of his men."

"Lundie has his weakness, and is fast forgetting the broadsword and open heaths in his tree and rifle practice. But, Mistress Dunham, tak' the word of an old soldier, who has seen his fifty-fifth year, when he talls ye that there is no surer method to encourage your enemy than to seem to fear him; and that there is no danger in this Indian warfare that the fancies and imaginations of your Americans have not enlarged upon, until they see a savage in every bush. We Scots come from a naked region, and have no need and less relish for covers, and so ye'll be seeing, Mistress Dunham——"

The Corporal gave a spring into the air, fell forward on his face, and rolled over on his back, the whole passing so suddenly that Mabel had scarcely heard the sharp crack of the rifle that had sent a bullet through his body. Our heroine did not shriek—did not even tremble; for the occurrence was too sudden, too awful, and too unexpected for that exhibition of weakness; on the contrary, she stepped hastily forward, with a natural impulse to aid her companion. There was just enough of life left in M'Nab to betray his entire consciousness of all that had passed. His countenance had the wild look of one who had been overtaken by death by surprise; and Mabel, in her cooler moments, fancied that it showed the tardy repentance of a willful and obstinate sinner.

"Ye'll be getting into the blockhouse as fast as possible,"

M'Nab whispered, as Mabel leaned over him to catch his dying words.

Then came over our heroine the full consciousness of her situation and of the necessity of exertion. She cast a rapid glance at the body at her feet, saw that it had ceased to breathe, and fled. It was but a few minutes' run to the blockhouse, the door of which Mabel had barely gained when it was closed violently in her face by Jennie, the soldier's wife, who in blind terror thought only of her own safety. The reports of five or six rifles were heard while Mabel was calling out for admittance; and the additional terror they produced prevented the woman within from undoing quickly the very fastenings she had been so expert in applying. After a minute's delay, however, Mabel found the door reluctantly yielding to her constant pressure, and she forced her slender body through the opening the instant it was large enough to allow of its passage. By this time Mabel's heart ceased to beat tumultuously and she gained sufficient self-command to act collectedly. Instead of yielding to the almost convulsive efforts of her companion to close the door again, she held it open long enough to ascertain that none of her own party was in sight, or likely on the instant to endeavor to gain admission: then she allowed the opening to be shut. Her orders and proceedings now became more calm and rational. But a single bar was crossed, and Jennie was directed to stand in readiness to remove even that at any application from a friend. She then ascended the ladder to the room above, where by means of a loophole she was enabled to get as good a view of the island as the surrounding bushes would allow. Admonishing her associate below to be firm and steady, she made as careful an examination of the environs as her situation permitted.

To her great surprise, Mabel could not at first see a living soul on the island, friend or enemy. Neither Frenchman nor Indian was visible, though a small straggling white cloud that was floating before the wind told her in which quarter she ought to look for them. The rifles had been discharged from the direction of the island whence June had come, though whether the enemy were on that island, or had actually landed on her own, Mabel could not say. Going to the loop that commanded a view of the spot where M'Nab lay, her blood curdled at perceiving all three of his soldiers lying apparently lifeless at his side. These men had rushed to a common centre at the first alarm, and had been shot down almost simultaneously by the invisible foe whom the Corporal had affected to despise.

Neither Cap nor Lieutenant Muir was to be seen. With a beating heart, Mabel examined every opening through the trees, and ascended even to the upper story or garret of the blockhouse, where she got a full view of the whole island, so far as its covers would allow, but with no better success. She had expected to see the body of her uncle lying on the grass like those of the soldiers, but it was nowhere visible. Turning towards the spot where the boat lay, Mabel saw that it was still fastened to the shore; and then she supposed that by some accident Muir had been prevented from effecting his retreat in that quarter. In short, the island lay in the quiet of the grave, the bodies of the soldiers rendering the scene as fearful as it was extraordinary.

"For God's holy sake, Mistress Mabel," called out the woman from below; for, though her fear had become too ungovernable to allow her to keep silence, our heroine's superior refinement, more than the regimental station of her father, still controlled her mode of address—"Mistress Mabel, tell me if any of our friends are living! I think I hear groans that grow fainter and fainter, and fear that they will all be tomahawked!"

Mabel now remembered that one of the soldiers was this woman's husband, and she trembled at what might be the immediate effect of her sorrow, should his death become suddenly known to her. The groans, too, gave a little hope, though she feared they might come from her uncle, who lay out of view.

"We are in His holy keeping, Jennie," she answered. "We must trust in Providence, while we neglect none of its benevolent means of protecting ourselves. Be careful with the door; on no account open it without my directions."

"Oh, tell me, Mistress Mabel, if you can anywhere see Sandy! If I could only let him know that I'm in safety, the guid man would be easier in his mind, whether free or a prisoner."

Sandy was Jennie's husband, and he lay dead in plain view of the loop from which our heroine was then looking.

"You no' tell me if you're seeing of Sandy," the woman repeated from below, impatient at Mabel's silence.

"There are some of our people gathered about the body of M'Nab," was the answer; for it seemed sacrilegious in her eyes to tell a direct untruth under the awful circumstances in which she was placed.

"Is Sandy amang them?" demanded the woman, in a voice that sounded appalling by its hoarseness and energy.

"He may be certainly; for I see one, two, three, four, and all in the scarlet coats of the regiment."

"Sandy!" called out the woman frantically; "why d'ye no' care for yoursal', Sandy? Come hither the instant, man, and share your wife's fortunes in weal or woe. It's no' a moment for your silly discipline and vain-glorious notions of honor! Sandy! Sandy!"

Mabel heard the bar turn, and then the door creaked on its hinges. Expectation, not to say terror, held her in suspense at the loop, and she soon beheld Jennie rushing through the bushes in the direction of the cluster of the dead. It took the woman but an instant to reach the fatal spot. So sudden and unexpected had been the blow, that she in her terror did not appear to comprehend its weight. Some wild and half-frantic notion of a deception troubled her fancy, and she imagined that the men were trifling with her fears. She took her husband's hand, and it was still warm, while she thought a covert smile was struggling on his lip.

"Why will ye fool life away, Sandy?" she cried, pulling at the arm. "Ye'll all be murdered by these accursed Indians, and you no' takin' to the block like trusty soldiers! Awa'! awa'! and no' be losing the precious moments."

In her desperate efforts, the woman pulled the body of her husband in a way to cause the head to turn completely over, when the small hole in the temple, caused by the entrance of a rifle bullet, and a few drops of blood trickling over the skin, revealed the meaning of her husband's silence. As the horrid truth flashed in its full extent on her mind, the woman clasped her hands, gave a shriek that pierced the glades of every island near, and fell at length on the dead body of the soldier. Thrilling, heart-reaching, appalling as was that shriek, it was melody to the cry that followed it so quickly as to blend the sounds. The terrific war-whoop arose out of the covers of the island, and some twenty savages, horrible in their paint and the other devices of Indian ingenuity, rushed forward, eager to secure the coveted scalps. Arrowhead was foremost, and it was his tomahawk that brained the insensible Jennie; and her reeking hair was hanging at his girdle as a trophy in less than two minutes after she had quitted the blockhouse. His companions were equally active, and M'Nab and his soldiers no longer presented the quiet aspect of men who slumbered. They were left in their gore, unequivocally butchered corpses.

All this passed in much less time than has been required to relate it, and all this did Mabel witness. She had stood riveted to the spot, gazing on the whole horrible scene, as if enchained by some charm, nor did the idea of self or of her own danger once obtrude itself on her thoughts. But no sooner did she perceive the place where the men had fallen covered with savages, exulting in the success of their surprise, than it occurred to her that Jennie had left the blockhouse door unbarred. Her heart beat violently, for that defence alone stood between her and immediate death, and she sprang toward the ladder with the intention of descending to make sure of it. Her foot had not yet reached the floor of the second story, however, when she heard the door grating on its hinges, and she gave herself up for lost. Sinking on her knees, the terrified but courageous girl endeavored to prepare herself for death, and to raise her thoughts to God. The instinct of life, however, was too strong for prayer, and while her lips moved, the jealous senses watched every sound beneath. When her ears heard the bars, which went on pivots secured to the centre of the door, turning into their fastenings, not one, as she herself had directed, with a view to admit her uncle should he apply, but all three, she started again to her feet, all spiritual contemplations vanishing in her actual temporal condition, and it seemed as if all her faculties were absorbed in the sense of hearing.

The thoughts are active in a moment so fearful. At first Mabel fancied that her uncle had entered the blockhouse, and she was about to descend the ladder and throw herself into his arms; then the idea that it might be an Indian, who had barred the door to shut out intruders while he plundered at leisure, arrested the movement. The profound stillness below was unlike the bold, restless movements of Cap, and it seemed to savor more of the artifices of an enemy. If a friend at all, it could only be her uncle or the Quartermaster; for the horrible conviction now presented itself to our heroine that to these two and herself were the whole party suddenly reduced, if, indeed, the two latter survived. This consideration held Mabel in check, and for full two minutes more a breathless silence reigned in the building. During this time the girl stood at the foot of the upper ladder, the trap which led to the lower opening on the opposite side of the floor; the eyes of Mabel were riveted on this spot, for she now began to expect to see at each instant the horrible sight of a savage face at the hole. This apprehension soon became so intense, that she looked about her for a place of concealment. The procrastination of the catastrophe she now fully expected, though it were only for a moment, afforded a relief. The room contained several barrels; and behind two of these Mabel crouched, placing her eyes at an opening by which she could still watch the trap. She made another effort to pray; but the moment was too horrible for that relief. She thought, too, that she heard a low rustling, as if one were ascending the lower ladder with an effort at caution so great as to betray itself by its own excess; then followed a creaking that she was certain came from one of the steps of the ladder, which had made the same noise under her own light weight as she ascended. This was one of those instants into which are compressed the sensations of years of ordinary existence. Life, death, eternity, and extreme bodily pain were all standing out in bold relief from the plane of every-day occurrences; and she might have been taken at that moment for a beautiful pallid representation of herself, equally without motion and without vitality. But while such was the outward appearance of the form, never had there been a time in her brief career when Mabel heard more acutely, saw more clearly, or felt more vividly. As yet, nothing was visible at the trap, but her ears, rendered exquisitely sensitive by intense feeling, distinctly acquainted her that some one was within a few inches of the opening in the floor. Next followed the evidence of her eyes, which beheld the dark hair of an Indian rising so slowly through the passage that the movements of the head might be likened to that of the minute-hand of a clock; then came the dark skin and wild features, until the whole of the swarthy face had risen above the floor. The human countenance seldom appears to advantage when partially concealed; and Mabel imagined many additional horrors as she first saw the black, roving eyes and the expression of wildness as the savage countenance was revealed, as it might be, inch by inch; but when the entire head was raised above the floor, a second and a better look assured our heroine that she saw the gentle, anxious, and even handsome face of June.

CHAPTER XXII

Spectre though I be,
I am not sent to scare thee or deceive;
But in reward of thy fidelity.   WORDSWORTH

IT WOULD BE difficult to say which evinced the most satisfaction, when Mabel sprang to her feet and appeared in the centre of the room, our heroine, on finding that her visitor was the wife of Arrowhead, and not Arrowhead himself, or June, at discovering that her advice had been followed, and that the blockhouse contained the person she had so anxiously and almost hopelessly sought. They embraced each other, and the unsophisticated Tuscarora woman laughed in her sweet accents as she held her friend at arm's length, and made certain of her presence.

"Blockhouse good," said the young Indian; "got no scalp."

"It is indeed good, June," Mabel answered, with a shudder, veiling her eyes at the same time, as if to shut out a view of the horrors she had so lately witnessed. "Tell me, for God's sake, if you know what has become of my dear uncle! I have looked in all directions without being able to see him."

"No here in blockhouse?" June asked, with some curiosity.

"Indeed he is not: I am quite alone in this place; Jennie, the woman who was with me, having rushed out to join her husband, and perishing for her imprudence."

"June know, June see; very bad, Arrowhead no feel for any wife; no feel for his own."

"Ah, June, your life, at least, is safe!"

"Don't know; Arrowhead kill me, if he know all."

"God bless and protect you, June! He *will* bless and protect you for this humanity. Tell me what is to be done, and if my poor uncle is still living?"

"Don't know. Saltwater has boat; maybe he go on river."

"The boat is still on the shore, but neither my uncle nor the Quartermaster is anywhere to be seen."

"No kill, or June would see. Hide away! Red man hide; no shame for pale-face."

"It is not the shame that I fear for them, but the opportunity. Your attack was awfully sudden, June!"

"Tuscarora!" returned the other, smiling with exultation at the dexterity of her husband. "Arrowhead great warrior!"

"You are too good and gentle for this sort of life, June; you *cannot* be happy in such scenes?"

June's countenance grew clouded, and Mabel fancied there was some of the savage fire of a chief in her frown as she answered—

"Yengeese too greedy, take away all hunting-grounds; chase Six Nation from morning to night; wicked king, wicked people. Pale-face very bad."

Mabel knew that, even in that distant day, there was much truth in this opinion, though she was too well instructed not to understand that the monarch, in this, as in a thousand other cases, was blamed for acts of which he was most probably ignorant. She felt the justice of the rebuke, therefore, too much to attempt an answer, and her thoughts naturally reverted to her own situation.

"And what am I to do, June?" she demanded. "It cannot be long before your people will assault this building."

"Blockhouse good—got no scalp."

"But they will soon discover that it has got no garrison too, if they do not know it already. You yourself told me the number of people that were on the island, and doubtless you learned it from Arrowhead."

"Arrowhead know," answered June, holding up six fingers, to indicate the number of the men. "All red men know. Four lose scalp already; two got 'em yet."

"Do not speak of it, June; the horrid thought curdles my blood. Your people cannot know that I am alone in the blockhouse, but may fancy my uncle and the Quartermaster with me, and may set fire to the building, in order to dislodge them. They tell me that fire is the great danger to such places."

"No burn blockhouse," said June quietly.

"You cannot know that, my good June, and I have no means to keep them off."

"No burn blockhouse. Blockhouse good; got no scalp."

"But tell me why, June; I fear they will burn it."

"Blockhouse wet—much rain—logs green—no burn easy. Red man know it—fine t'ing—then no burn it to tell Yengeese that Iroquois been here. Fader come back, miss blockhouse, no found. No, no; Indian too much cunning; no touch anything."

"I understand you, June, and hope your prediction may be true; for, as regards my dear father, should he escape—perhaps he is already dead or captured, June?"

"No touch fader—don't know where he gone—water got no trail—red man can't follow. No burn blockhouse—blockhouse good; got no scalp."

"Do you think it possible for me to remain here safely until my father returns?"

"Don't know; daughter tell best when fader come back."

Mabel felt uneasy at the glance of June's dark eye as she uttered this; for the unpleasant surmise arose that her companion was endeavoring to discover a fact that might be useful to her own people, while it would lead to the destruction of her parent and his party. She was about to make an evasive answer, when a heavy push at the outer door suddenly drew all her thoughts to the immediate danger.

"They come!" she exclaimed. "Perhaps, June, it is my uncle or the Quartermaster. I cannot keep out even Mr. Muir at a moment like this."

"Why no look? plenty loophole, made purpose."

Mabel took the hint, and, going to one of the downward loops, that had been cut through the logs in the part that overhung the basement, she cautiously raised the little block that ordinarily filled the small hole, and caught a glance at what was passing at the door. The start and changing countenance told her companion that some of her own people were below.

"Red man," said June, lifting a finger in admonition to be prudent.

"Four; and horrible in their paint and bloody trophies. Arrowhead is among them."

June had moved to a corner, where several spare rifles had been deposited, and had already taken one into her hand, when the name of her husband appeared to arrest her movements. It was but for an instant, however, for she immediately went to the loop, and was about to thrust the muzzle of the piece through it, when a feeling of natural aversion induced Mabel to seize her arm.

"No, no, no, June!" said the latter; "not against your own husband, though my life be the penalty."

"No hurt Arrowhead," returned June, with a slight shudder; "no hurt red man at all. No fire at 'em; only scare."

Mabel now comprehended the intention of June, and no longer opposed it. The latter thrust the muzzle of the rifle through the loophole; and, taking care to make noise enough to attract attention, she pulled the trigger. The piece had no sooner been discharged than Mabel reproached her friend for the very act that was intended to serve her.

"You declared it was not your intention to fire," she said, "and you may have destroyed your own husband."

"All run away before I fire," returned June, laughing, and going to another loop to watch the movements of her friends, laughing still heartier. "See! get cover—every warrior. Think Saltwater and Quartermaster here. Take good care now."

"Heaven be praised! And now, June, I may hope for a little time to compose my thoughts to prayer, that I may not die like Jennie, thinking only of life and the things of the world."

June laid aside the rifle, and came and seated herself near the box on which Mabel had sunk, under that physical reaction which accompanies joy as well as sorrow. She looked steadily in our heroine's face, and the latter thought that her countenance had an expression of severity mingled with its concern.

"Arrowhead great warrior," said the Tuscarora's wife. "All the girls of tribe look at him much. The pale-face beauty has eyes too?"

"June!—what do these words—that look—imply? what would you say?"

"Why you so 'fraid June shoot Arrowhead?"

"Would it not have been horrible to see a wife destroy her own husband? No, June, rather would I have died myself."

"Very sure, dat all?"

"That was all, June, as God is my judge!—and surely that was enough. No, no! there have been sufficient horrors to-day, without increasing them by an act like this. What other motive can you suspect?"

"Don't know. Poor Tuscarora girl very foolish. Arrowhead great chief, and look all round him. Talk of pale-face beauty in his sleep. Great chief like many wives."

"Can a chief possess more than one wife, June, among your people?"

"Have as many as he can keep. Great hunter marry often. Arrowhead got only June now; but he look too much, see too much, talk too much of pale-face girl."

Mabel was conscious of this fact, which had distressed her not a little, in the course of their journey; but it shocked her to hear this allusion, coming, as it did, from the mouth of the wife herself. She knew that habit and opinions made great differences in such matters; but, in addition to the pain and mortification she experienced at being the unwilling rival of a wife, she felt an apprehension that jealousy would be but an equivocal guarantee for her personal safety in her present situation. A closer look at June, however, reassured her; for, while it was easy to trace in the unpractised features of this unsophisticated being the pain of blighted affections, no distrust could have tortured the earnest expression of her honest countenance into that of treachery or hate.

"You will not betray me, June?" Mabel said, pressing the other's hand, and yielding to an impulse of generous confidence. "You will not give up one of your own sex to the tomahawk?"

"No tomahawk touch you. Arrowhead no let 'em. If June must have sister-wife, love to have you."

"No, June; my religion, my feelings, both forbid it; and, if I could be the wife of an Indian at all, I would never take the place that is yours in a wigwam."

June made no answer, but she looked gratified, and even grateful. She knew that few, perhaps no Indian girl within the circle of Arrowhead's acquaintance, could compare with herself in personal attractions; and, though it might suit her husband to marry a dozen wives, she knew of no one, beside Mabel, whose influence she could really dread. So keen an interest, however, had she taken in the beauty, winning manners, kindness, and feminine gentleness of our heroine, that when jealousy came to chill these feelings, it had rather lent strength to that interest; and, under its wayward influence, had actually been one of the strongest of the incentives that had induced her to risk so much in order to save her imaginary rival from the consequences of the attack that she so well knew was about to take place. In a word, June, with a wife's keenness of perception, had detected Arrowhead's admiration of Mabel; and, instead of feeling that harrowing jealousy that might have rendered her rival hateful, as would have been apt to be the case with a woman unaccustomed to defer to the superior rights of the lordly sex, she had studied the looks and character of the pale-face beauty, until, meeting with nothing to repel her own feelings, but everything to encourage them, she had got to entertain an admiration and love for her, which, though certainly very different, was scarcely less strong than that of her husband. Arrowhead himself had sent her to warn Mabel of the coming danger, though he was ignorant that she had stolen upon the island in the rear of the assailants, and was now intrenched in the citadel along with the object of their joint care. On the contrary, he supposed, as his wife had said, that Cap and Muir were in the blockhouse with Mabel, and that the attempt to repel him and his companions had been made by the men.

"June sorry the Lily"—for so the Indian, in her poetical language, had named our heroine—"June sorry the Lily no marry Arrowhead. His wigwam big, and a great chief must get wives enough to fill it."

"I thank you, June, for this preference, which is not according to the notion of us white women," returned Mabel, smiling in spite of the fearful situation in which she was placed; "but I may not, probably never shall, marry at all."

"Must have good husband," said June; "marry Eau-douce, if don't like Arrowhead."

"June! this is not a fit subject for a girl who scarcely knows if she is to live another hour or not. I would obtain some signs of my dear uncle's being alive and safe, if possible."

"June go see."

"Can you?—will you?—would it be safe for you to be seen on the island? is your presence known to the warriors, and would they be pleased to find a woman on the warpath with them?"

All this Mabel asked in rapid connection, fearing that the answer might not be as she wished. She had thought it extraordinary that June should be of the party, and, improbable as it seemed, she had fancied that the woman had covertly followed the Iroquois in her own canoe, and had got in their advance, merely to give her the notice which had probably saved her life. But in all this she was mistaken, as June, in her imperfect manner, now found means to let her know.

Arrowhead, though a chief, was in disgrace with his own people, and was acting with the Iroquois temporarily, though with a perfect understanding. He had a wigwam, it is true, but was seldom in it; feigning friendship for the English, he had passed the summer ostensibly in their service, while he was, in truth, acting for the French, and his wife journeyed with him in his many migrations, most of the distances being passed over in canoes. In a word, her presence was no secret, her husband seldom moving without her. Enough of this to embolden Mabel to wish that her friend might go out, to ascertain the fate of her uncle, did June succeed in letting the other know; and it was soon settled between them that the Indian woman should quit the blockhouse with that object the moment a favorable opportunity offered.

They first examined the island, as thoroughly as their position would allow, from the different loops, and found that its conquerors were preparing for a feast, having seized upon the provisions of the English and rifled the huts. Most of the stores were in the blockhouse; but enough were found outside to reward the Indians for an attack that had been attended by so little risk. A party had already removed the dead bodies, and Mabel saw that their arms were collected in a pile near the spot chosen for the banquet. June suggested that, by some signs which she understood, the dead themselves were carried into a thicket and either buried or concealed from view. None of the more prominent objects on the island, however, were disturbed, it being the desire of the conquerors to lure the party of the Sergeant into an ambush on its return. June made her companion observe a man in a tree, a look-out, as she said, to give timely notice of the approach of any boat, although, the departure of the expedition being so recent, nothing but some unexpected event would be likely to bring it back so soon. There did not appear to be any intention to attack the blockhouse immediately; but every indication, as understood by June, rather showed that it was the intention of the Indians to keep it besieged until the return of the Sergeant's party, lest the signs of an assault should give a warning to eyes as practised as those of Pathfinder. The boat, however, had been secured, and was removed to the spot where the canoes of the Indians were hid in the bushes.

June now announced her intention to join her friends, the moment being particularly favorable for her to quit the blockhouse. Mabel felt some distrust as they descended the ladder; but at the next instant she was ashamed of the feeling, as unjust to her companion and unworthy of herself, and by the time they both stood on the ground her confidence was restored. The process of unbarring the door was conducted with the utmost caution, and when the last bar was ready to be turned June took her station near the spot where the opening must necessarily be. The bar was just turned free of the brackets, the door was opened merely wide enough to allow her body to pass, and June glided through the space. Mabel closed the door again, with a convulsive movement; and as the bar turned into its place, her heart beat audibly. She then felt secure; and the two other bars were turned down in a more deliberate manner. When all was fast again, she ascended to the first floor, where alone she could get a glimpse of what was going on without.

Long and painfully melancholy hours passed, during which Mabel had no intelligence from June. She heard the yells of the savages, for liquor had carried them beyond the bounds of precaution; occasionally caught glimpses of their mad orgies through the loops; and at all times was conscious of their fearful presence by sounds and sights that would have chilled the blood of one who had not so lately witnessed scenes so much more terrible. Toward the middle of the day, she fancied she saw a white man on the island, though his dress and wild appearance at first made her take him for a newly-arrived savage. A view of his face, although it was swarthy naturally, and much darkened by exposure, left no doubt that her conjecture was true; and she felt as if there was now one of a species more like her own present, and one to whom she might appeal for succor in the last emergency. Mabel little knew, alas! how small was the influence exercised by the whites over their savage allies, when the latter had begun to taste of blood; or how slight, indeed, was the disposition to divert them from their cruelties.

The day seemed a month by Mabel's computation, and the only part of it that did not drag were the minutes spent in prayer. She had recourse to this relief from time to time; and at each effort she found her spirit firmer, her mind more tranquil, and her resignation more confirmed. She understood the reasoning of June, and believed it highly probable that the blockhouse would be left unmolested until the return of her father, in order to entice him into an ambuscade, and she felt much less apprehension of immediate danger in consequence; but the future offered little ground of hope, and her thoughts had already begun to calculate the chances of her captivity. At such moments, Arrowhead and his offensive admiration filled a prominent place in the background: for our heroine well knew that the Indians usually carried off to their villages, for the purposes of adoption, such captives as they did not slay; and that many instances had occurred in which individuals of her sex had passed the remainder of their lives in the wigwams of their conquerors. Such thoughts as these invariably drove her to her knees and to her prayers.

While the light lasted the situation of our heroine was sufficiently alarming; but as the shades of evening gradually gathered over the island, it became fearfully appalling. By this time the savages had wrought themselves up to the point of fury, for they had possessed themselves of all the liquor of the English; and their outcries and gesticulations were those of men truly possessed by evil spirits. All the efforts of their French leader to restrain them were entirely fruitless, and he had wisely withdrawn to an adjacent island, where he had a sort of bivouac, that he might keep at a safe distance from friends so apt to run into excesses. Before quitting the spot, however, this officer, at great risk to his own life, had succeeded in extinguishing the fire, and in securing the ordinary means to relight it. This precaution he took lest the Indians should burn the blockhouse, the preservation of which was necessary to the success of his future plans. He would gladly have removed all the arms also, but this he found impracticable, the warriors clinging to their knives and tomahawks with the tenacity of men who regarded a point of honor as long as a faculty was left; and to carry off the rifles, and leave behind him the very weapons that were generally used on such occasions, would have been an idle expedient. The extinguishing of the fire proved to be the most prudent measure; for no sooner was the officer's back turned than one of the warriors in fact proposed to fire the blockhouse. Arrowhead had also withdrawn from the group of drunkards, as soon as he found that they were losing their senses, and had taken possession of a hut, where he had thrown himself on the straw, and sought the rest that two wakeful and watchful nights had rendered necessary. It followed that no one was left among the Indians to care for Mabel, if, indeed, any knew of her existence at all; and the proposal of the drunkard was received with yells of delight by eight or ten more as much intoxicated and habitually as brutal as himself.

This was the fearful moment for Mabel. The Indians, in their present condition, were reckless of any rifles that the blockhouse might hold, though they did retain dim recollections of its containing living beings, an additional incentive to their enterprise; and they approached its base whooping and leaping like demons. As yet they were excited, not overcome, by the liquor they had drunk. The first attempt was made at the door, against which they ran in a body; but the solid structure, which was built entirely of logs, defied their efforts. The rush of a hundred men with the same object would have been useless. This Mabel, however, did not know; and her heart seemed to leap into her mouth as she heard the heavy shock at each renewed effort. At length when she found that the door resisted these assaults as if it were of stone, neither trembling nor yielding, and only betraying its not being a part of the wall by rattling a little on its heavy hinges, her courage revived, and she seized the first moment of a cessation to look down through the loop, in order, if possible, to learn the extent of her danger. A silence, for which it was not easy to account, stimulated her curiosity:

for nothing is so alarming to those who are conscious of the
presence of imminent danger, as to be unable to trace its
approach.

Mabel found that two or three of the Iroquois had been
raking the embers, where they had found a few small coals,
and with these they were endeavoring to light a fire. The interest with which they labored, the hope of destroying, and the
force of habit, enabled them to act intelligently and in unison,
so long as their fell object was kept in view. A white man would
have abandoned the attempt to light a fire in despair, with
coals that came out of the ashes resembling sparks; but these
children of the forest had many expedients that were unknown
to civilization. By the aid of a few dry leaves, which they alone
knew where to seek, a blaze was finally kindled, and then the
addition of a few light sticks made sure of the advantage that
had been obtained. When Mabel stooped down over the loop,
the Indians were making a pile of brush against the door, and
as she remained gazing at their proceedings, she saw the twigs
ignite, the flame dart from branch to branch, until the whole
pile was cracking and snapping under a bright blaze. The
Indians now gave a yell of triumph, and returned to their
companions, well assured that the work of destruction was
commenced. Mabel remained looking down, scarcely able to
tear herself away from the spot, so intense and engrossing was
the interest she felt in the progress of the fire. As the pile kindled
throughout, however, the flames mounted, until they flashed
so near her eyes as to compel her to retreat. Just as she reached
the opposite side of the room, to which she had retired in her
alarm, a forked stream shot up through the loophole, the lid
of which she had left open, and illuminated the rude apartment,
with Mabel and her desolation. Our heroine now naturally
enough supposed that her hour was come; for the door, the only
means of retreat, had been blocked up by the brush and fire,
with hellish ingenuity, and she addressed herself, as she believed,
for the last time to her Maker in prayer. Her eyes were closed,
and for more than a minute her spirit was abstracted; but the
interests of the world too strongly divided her feelings to be
altogether suppressed; and when they involuntarily opened
again, she perceived that the streak of flame was no longer
flaring in the room, though the wood around the little aperture

had kindled, and the blaze was slowly mounting under the impulsion of a current of air that sucked inward. A barrel of water stood in a corner; and Mabel, acting more by instinct than by reason, caught up a vessel, filled it, and, pouring it on the wood with a trembling hand, succeeded in extinguishing the fire at that particular spot. The smoke prevented her from looking down again for a couple of minutes; but when she did her heart beat high with delight and hope at finding that the pile of blazing brush had been overturned and scattered, and that water had been thrown on the logs of the door, which were still smoking though no longer burning.

"Who is there?" said Mabel, with her mouth at the loop. "What friendly hand has a merciful Providence sent to my succor?"

A light footstep was audible below, and one of those gentle pushes at the door was heard, which just moved the massive beams on the hinges.

"Who wishes to enter? Is it you, dear, dear uncle?"

"Saltwater no here. St. Lawrence sweet water," was the answer. "Open quick; want to come in."

The step of Mabel was never lighter, or her movements more quick and natural, than while she was descending the ladder and turning the bars, for all her motions were earnest and active. This time she thought only of her escape, and she opened the door with a rapidity which did not admit of caution. Her first impulse was to rush into the open air, in the blind hope of quitting the blockhouse; but June repulsed the attempt, and entering, she coolly barred the door again before she would notice Mabel's eager efforts to embrace her.

"Bless you! bless you, June!" cried our heroine most fervently; "you are sent by Providence to be my guardian angel!"

"No hug so tight," answered the Tuscarora woman. "Pale-face woman all cry, or all laugh. Let June fasten door."

Mabel became more rational, and in a few minutes the two were again in the upper room, seated as before, hand in hand, all feeling of distrust between them being banished.

"Now tell me, June," Mabel commenced as soon as she had given and received one warm embrace, "have you seen or heard aught of my poor uncle?"

"Don't know. No one see him; no one hear him; no one know

anyt'ing. Saltwater run into river, I t'ink, for I no find him. Quartermaster gone too. I look, and look, and look; but no see 'em, one, t'other, nowhere.''

"Blessed be God! They must have escaped, though the means are not known to us. I thought I saw a Frenchman on the island, June.''

"Yes: French captain come, but he go away too. Plenty of Indian on island.''

"Oh, June, June, are there no means to prevent my beloved father from falling into the hands of his enemies?''

"Don't know; t'ink dat warriors wait in ambush, and Yengeese must lose scalp.''

"Surely, surely, June, you, who have done so much for the daughter, will not refuse to help the father?''

"Don't know fader, don't love fader. June help her own people, help Arrowhead—husband love scalp.''

"June, this is not yourself. I cannot, will not believe that you wish to see our men murdered!''

June turned her dark eyes quietly on Mabel; and for a moment her look was stern, though it was soon changed into one of melancholy compassion.

"Lily, Yengeese girl?'' she said, as one asks a question.

"Certainly, and as a Yengeese girl I would save my countrymen from slaughter.''

"Very good, if can. June no Yengeese; June Tuscarora—got Tuscarora husband—Tuscarora heart—Tuscarora feeling—all over Tuscarora. Lily wouldn't run and tell French that her fader was coming to gain victory?''

"Perhaps not,'' returned Mabel, pressing a hand on a brain that felt bewildered—"perhaps not; but you serve me, aid me— have saved me, June! Why have you done this, if you only feel as a Tuscarora?''

"Don't only feel as Tuscarora; feel as girl, feel as squaw. Love pretty Lily, and put it in my bosom.''

Mabel melted into tears, and she pressed the affectionate creature to her heart. It was near a minute before she could renew the discourse, but then she succeeded in speaking more calmly and with greater coherence.

"Let me know the worst, June,'' said she. "To-night your people are feasting; what do they intend to do to-morrow?''

"Don't know; afraid to see Arrowhead, afraid to ask question; t'ink hide away till Yengeese come back."

"Will they not attempt anything against the blockhouse? You have seen what they can threaten if they will."

"Too much rum. Arrowhead sleep, or no dare; French captain gone away, or no dare. All go to sleep now."

"And you think I am safe for this night, at least?"

"Too much rum. If Lily like June, might do much for her people."

"I am like you, June, if a wish to serve my countrymen can make a resemblance with one as courageous as yourself."

"No, no, no!" muttered June in a low voice; "no got heart, and June no let you, if had. June's moder prisoner once, and warriors got drunk; moder tomahawked 'em all. Such de way red skin women do when people in danger and want scalp."

"You say what is true," returned Mabel, shuddering, and unconsciously dropping June's hand. "I cannot do that. I have neither the strength, the courage, nor the will to dip my hands in blood."

"T'ink that too; then stay where you be—blockhouse good—got no scalp."

"You believe, then, that I am safe here, at least until my father and his people return?"

"Know so. No dare touch blockhouse in morning. Hark! all still now—drink rum till head fall down, and sleep like log."

"Might I not escape? Are there not several canoes on the island? Might I not get one, and go and give my father notice of what has happened?"

"Know how to paddle?" demanded June, glancing her eye furtively at her companion.

"Not so well as yourself, perhaps; but enough to get out of sight before morning."

"What do then?—couldn't paddle six—ten—eight mile!"

"I do not know; I would do much to warn my father, and the excellent Pathfinder, and all the rest, of the danger they are in."

"Like Pathfinder?"

"All like him who know him—you would like him, nay, love him, if you only knew his heart!"

"No like him at all. Too good rifle—too good eye—too much

shoot Iroquois and June's people. Must get his scalp if can."

"And I must save it if I can, June. In this respect, then, we are opposed to each other. I will go and find a canoe the instant they are all asleep, and quit the island."

"No can—June won't let you. Call Arrowhead."

"June! you would not betray me—you could not give me up after all you have done for me?"

"Just so," returned June, making a backward gesture with her hand, and speaking with a warmth and earnestness Mabel had never witnessed in her before. "Call Arrowhead in loud voice. One call from wife wake a warrior up. June no let Lily help enemy—no let Indian hurt Lily."

"I understand you, June, and feel the nature and justice of your sentiments; and, after all, it were better that I should remain here, for I have most probably overrated my strength. But tell me one thing: if my uncle comes in the night, and asks to be admitted, you will let me open the door of the blockhouse that he may enter?"

"Sartain—he prisoner here, and June like prisoner better than scalp; scalp good for honor, prisoner good for feeling. But Saltwater hide so close, he don't know where he be himself."

Here June laughed in her girlish, mirthful way, for to her scenes of violence were too familiar to leave impressions sufficiently deep to change her natural character. A long and discursive dialogue now followed, in which Mabel endeavored to obtain clearer notions of her actual situation, under a faint hope that she might possibly be enabled to turn some of the facts she thus learned to advantage. June answered all her interrogatories simply, but with a caution which showed she fully distinguished between that which was immaterial and that which might endanger the safety or embarrass the future operations of her friends. The substance of the information she gave may be summed up as follows.

Arrowhead had long been in communication with the French, though this was the first occasion on which he had entirely thrown aside the mask. He no longer intended to trust himself among the English, for he had discovered traces of distrust, particularly in Pathfinder; and, with Indian bravado, he now rather wished to blazon than to conceal his treachery. He had led the party of warriors in the attack on the island, subject, however, to the supervision of the Frenchman who has been mentioned, though June declined saying whether he had been the means of discovering the position of a place which had been thought to be so concealed from the enemy or not. On this point she would say nothing; but she admitted that she and her husband had been watching the departure of the *Scud* at the time they were overtaken and captured by the cutter. The French had obtained their information of the precise position of the station but very recently; and Mabel felt a pang when she thought that there were covert allusions of the Indian woman which would convey the meaning that the intelligence had come from a pale-face in the employment of Duncan of Lundie. This was intimated, however, rather than said; and when Mabel had time to reflect on her companion's words, she found room to hope that she had misunderstood her, and that Jasper Western would yet come out of the affair freed from every injurious imputation.

June did not hesitate to confess that she had been sent to the island to ascertain the precise number and the occupations of those who had been left on it, though she also betrayed in her *naïve* way that the wish to serve Mabel had induced her principally to consent to come. In consequence of her report, and information otherwise obtained, the enemy was aware of precisely the force that could be brought against them. They also knew the number of men who had gone with Sergeant Dunham, and were acquainted with the object he had in view, though they were ignorant of the spot where he expected to meet the French boats. It would have been a pleasant sight to witness the eager desire of each of these two sincere females to ascertain all that might be of consequence to their respective friends; and yet the native delicacy with which each refrained from pressing the other to make revelations which would have been improper, as well as the sensitive, almost intuitive, feeling with which each avoided saying aught that might prove injurious to her own nation. As respects each other, there was perfect confidence; as regarded their respective people, entire fidelity. June was quite as anxious as Mabel could be on any other point to know where the Sergeant had gone and when he was expected to return; but she abstained from putting the question, with a delicacy that would have done honor to the highest civilization; nor did she once frame any other inquiry in a way to lead indirectly to a betrayal of the much-desired information on that particular point: though when Mabel of her own accord touched on any matter that might by possibility throw a light on the subject, she listened with an intentness which almost suspended respiration.

In this manner the hours passed away unheeded, for both were too much interested to think of rest. Nature asserted her rights, however, towards morning; and Mabel was persuaded to lie down on one of the straw beds provided for the soldiers, where she soon fell into a deep sleep. June lay near her, and a quiet reigned on the whole island as profound as if the dominion of the forest had never been invaded by man.

When Mabel awoke the light of the sun was streaming in through the loopholes, and she found that the day was considerably advanced. June still lay near her, sleeping as tranquilly as if she reposed on—we will not say "down," for the superior civilization of our own times repudiates the simile—but on a French mattress, and as profoundly as if she had never experienced concern. The movements of Mabel, notwithstanding, soon awakened one so accustomed to vigilance; and then the two took a survey of what was passing around them by means of the friendly apertures.

CHAPTER XXIII

What had the Eternall Maker need of thee,
The world in his continuall course to keepe,
That doest all things deface? ne lettest see
The beautie of his worke? Indeede in sleepe,
The slouthfull body that doth love to steepe
His lustlesse limbs, and drowne his baser mind,
Doth praise thee oft, and oft from Stygian deepe,
Calles thee his goddesse, in his errour blind,
And great dame Nature's hand-maide, chearing every kind.

Faerie Queene

THE tranquillity of the previous night was not contradicted by the movements of the day. Although Mabel and June went to every loophole, not a sign of the presence of a living being on the island was at first to be seen, themselves excepted. There was a smothered fire on the spot where M'Nab and his comrades had cooked, as if the smoke which curled upwards from it was intended as a lure to the absent; and all around the huts had been restored to former order and arrangement. Mabel started involuntarily when her eye at length fell on a group of three men, dressed in the scarlet of the 55th, seated on the grass in lounging attitudes, as if they chatted in listless security; and her blood curdled as, on a second look, she traced the bloodless faces and glassy eyes of the dead. They were very near the blockhouse, so near indeed as to have been overlooked at the first eager inquiry, and there was a mocking levity in their postures and gestures, for their limbs were stiffening in different attitudes, intended to resemble life, at which the soul revolted. Still, horrible as these objects were to those near enough to discover the frightful discrepancy between their assumed and their real characters, the arrangement had been made with so much art that it would have deceived a negligent observer at the distance of a hundred yards. After carefully examining the shores of the island, June pointed out to her companion the fourth soldier, seated, with his feet hanging over the water, his back fastened to a sapling, and holding a fishing-rod in his hand. The scalpless heads were covered with the caps, and all appearance of blood had been carefully washed from each countenance.

Mabel sickened at this sight, which not only did so much violence to all her notions of propriety, but which was in itself so revolting and so opposed to natural feeling. She withdrew to a seat, and hid her face in her apron for several minutes, until a low call from June again drew her to a loophole. The latter then pointed out the body of Jennie, seemingly standing in the door of a hut, leaning forward as if to look at the group of men, her cap fluttering in the wind, and her hand grasping a broom. The distance was too great to distinguish the features very accurately; but Mabel fancied that the jaw had been depressed, as if to distort the mouth into a sort of horrible laugh.

"June! June!" she exclaimed; "this exceeds all I have ever heard, or imagined as possible, in the treachery and artifices of your people."

"Tuscarora very cunning," said June, in a way to show that

she rather approved of than condemned the uses to which the dead bodies had been applied. "Do soldier no harm now; do Iroquois good; got the scalp first; now make bodies work. By and by, burn 'em."

This speech told Mabel how far she was separated from her friend in character; and it was several minutes before she could again address her. But this temporary aversion was lost on June, who set about preparing their simple breakfast, in a way to show how insensible she was to feelings in others which her own habits taught her to discard. Mabel ate sparingly, and her companion as if nothing had happened. Then they had leisure again for their thoughts, and for further surveys of the island. Our heroine, though devoured with a feverish desire to be always at the loops, seldom went that she did not immediately quit them in disgust, though compelled by her apprehensions to return again in a few minutes, called by the rustling of leaves, or the sighing of the wind. It was, indeed, a solemn thing to look out upon that deserted spot, peopled by the dead in the panoply of the living, and thrown into the attitudes and acts of careless merriment and rude enjoyment. The effect on our heroine was much as if she had found herself an observer of the revelries of demons.

Throughout the livelong day not an Indian nor a Frenchman was to be seen, and night closed over the frightful but silent masquerade, with the steady and unalterable progress with which the earth obeys her laws, indifferent to the petty actors and petty scenes that are in daily bustle and daily occurrence on her bosom. The night was far more quiet than that which had preceded it, and Mabel slept with an increasing confidence; for she now felt satisfied that her own fate would not be decided until the return of her father. The following day he was expected, however, and when our heroine awoke, she ran eagerly to the loops in order to ascertain the state of the weather and the aspect of the skies, as well as the condition of the island. There lounged the fearful group on the grass; the fisherman still hung over the water, seemingly intent on his sport; and the distorted countenance of Jennie glared from out the hut in horrible contortions. But the weather had changed; the wind blew fresh from the southward, and though the air was bland, it was filled with the elements of storm.

"This grows more and more difficult to bear, June," Mabel said, when she left the window. "I could even prefer to see the enemy than to look any longer on this fearful array of the dead."

"Hush! here they come. June thought hear a cry like a warrior's shout when he take a scalp."

"What mean you? There is no more butchery!—there *can* be no more."

"Saltwater!" exclaimed June, laughing, as she stood peeping through a loophole.

"My dear uncle! Thank God! he then lives! Oh, June, June, *you* will not let them harm *him?*"

"June, poor squaw. What warrior t'ink of what she say? Arrowhead bring him here."

By this time Mabel was at a loop; and, sure enough, there were Cap and the Quartermaster in the hands of the Indians, eight or ten of whom were conducting them to the foot of the block, for, by this capture, the enemy now well knew that there could be no man in the building. Mabel scarcely breathed until the whole party stood ranged directly before the door, when she was rejoiced to see that the French officer was among them. A low conversation followed, in which both the white leader and Arrowhead spoke earnestly to their captives, when the Quartermaster called out to her in a voice loud enough to be heard.

"Pretty Mabel! pretty Mabel!" said he; "look out of one of the loopholes, and pity our condition. We are threatened with instant death unless you open the door to the conquerors. Relent, then, or we'll no' be wearing our scalps half an hour from this blessed moment."

Mabel thought there were mockery and levity in this appeal, and its manner rather fortified than weakened her resolution to hold the place as long as possible.

"Speak to me, uncle," said she, with her mouth at a loop, "and tell me what I ought to do."

"Thank God! thank God!" ejaculated Cap; "the sound of your sweet voice, Magnet, lightens my heart of a heavy load, for I feared you had shared the fate of poor Jennie. My breast has felt the last four-and-twenty hours as if a ton of kentledge had been stowed in it. You ask me what you ought to do, child, and I do not know how to advise you, though you are my own sister's daughter! The most I can say just now, my poor girl, is most heartily to curse the day you or I ever saw this bit of fresh water."

"But, uncle, is your life in danger—do *you* think I ought to open the door?"

"A round turn and two half-hitches make a fast belay; and I would counsel no one who is out of the hands of these devils to unbar or unfasten anything in order to fall into them. As to the Quartermaster and myself, we are both elderly men, and not of much account to mankind in general, as honest Pathfinder would say; and it can make no great odds to him whether he balances the purser's books this year or the next; and as for myself, why, if I were on the seaboard, I should know what to do, but up here, in this watery wilderness, I can only say, that if I wcrc bchind that bit of a bulwark, it would take a good deal of Indian logic to rouse me out of it."

"You'll no' be minding all your uncle says, pretty Mabel," put in Muir, "for distress is obviously fast unsettling his faculties, and he is far from calculating all the necessities of the emergency. We are in the hands here of very considerate and gentlemanly pairsons, it must be acknowledged, and one has little occasion to apprehend disagreeable violence. The casualties that have occurred are the common incidents of war, and can no' change our sentiments of the enemy, for they are far from indicating that any injustice will be done the prisoners. I'm sure that neither Master Cap nor myself has any cause of complaint since we have given ourselves up to Master Arrowhead, who reminds me of a Roman or a Spartan by his virtues and moderation; but ye'll be remembering that usages differ, and that our scalps may be lawful sacrifices to appease the manes of fallen foes, unless you save them by capitulation."

"I shall do wiser to keep within the blockhouse until the fate of the island is settled," returned Mabel. "Our enemies can feel no concern on account of one like me, knowing that I can do them no harm, and I greatly prefer to remain here as more befitting my sex and years."

"If nothing but your convenience were concerned, Mabel, we should all cheerfully acquiesce in your wishes, but these gentlemen fancy that the work will aid their operations, and they have a strong desire to possess it. To be frank with you, finding myself and your uncle in a very peculiar situation, I acknowledge that, to avert consequences, I have assumed the power that belongs to his Majesty's commission, and entered into a verbal capitulation, by which I have engaged to give up the blockhouse and the whole island. It is the fortune of war, and must be submitted to; so open the door, pretty Mabel, forthwith, and confide yourself to the care of those who know how to treat beauty and virtue in distress. There's no courtier in Scotland more complaisant than this chief, or who is more familiar with the laws of decorum."

"No leave blockhouse," muttered June, who stood at Mabel's side, attentive to all that passed. "Blockhouse good—got no scalp."

Our heroine might have yielded but for this appeal; for it began to appear to her that the wisest course would be to conciliate the enemy by concessions instead of exasperating them by resistance. They must know that Muir and her uncle were in their power; that there was no man in the building, and she fancied they might proceed to batter down the door, or cut their way through the logs with axes, if she obstinately refused to give them peaceable admission, since there was no longer any reason to dread the rifle. But the words of June induced her to hesitate, and the earnest pressure of the hand and entreating looks of her companion strengthened a resolution that was faltering.

"No prisoner yet," whispered June; "let 'em make prisoner before 'ey take prisoner—talk big; June manage 'em."

Mabel now began to parley more resolutely with Muir, for her uncle seemed disposed to quiet his conscience by holding his tongue, and she plainly intimated that it was not her intention to yield the building.

"You forget the capitulation, Mistress Mabel," said Muir; "the honor of one of his Majesty's servants is concerned, and the honor of his Majesty through his servant. You will remember the finesse and delicacy that belong to military honor?"

"I know enough, Mr. Muir, to understand that you have no command in this expedition, and therefore can have no right to yield the blockhouse; and I remember, moreover, to have heard my dear father say that a prisoner loses all his authority for the time being."

"Rank sophistry, pretty Mabel, and treason to the king, as well as dishonoring his commission and discrediting his name. You'll no' be persevering in your intentions, when your better judgment has had leisure to reflect and to make conclusions on matters and circumstances."

"Ay," put in Cap, "this *is* a circumstance, and be d—d to it!"

"No mind what'e uncle say," ejaculated June, who was occupied in a far corner of the room. "Blockhouse good—got no scalp."

"I shall remain as I am, Mr. Muir, until I get some tidings of my father. He will return in the course of the next ten days."

"Ah, Mabel, this artifice will no' deceive the enemy, who, by means that would be unintelligible, did not our suspicions rest on an unhappy young man with too much plausibility, are familiar with all our doings and plans, and well know that the sun will not set before the worthy Sergeant and his companions will be in their power. Aweel! Submission to Providence is truly a Christian virtue!"

"Mr. Muir, you appear to be deceived in the strength of this work, and to fancy it weaker than it is. Do you desire to see what I can do in the way of defence, if so disposed?"

"I dinna mind if I do," answered the Quartermaster, who always grew Scotch as he grew interested.

"What do you think of that, then? Look at the loop of the upper story?"

As soon as Mabel had spoken, all eyes were turned upward, and beheld the muzzle of a rifle cautiously thrust through a hole, June having resorted again to a *ruse* which had already proved so successful. The result did not disappoint expectation. No sooner did the Indians catch a sight of the fatal weapon than they leaped aside, and in less than a minute every man among them had sought a cover. The French officer kept his eye on the barrel of the piece in order to ascertain that it was not pointed in his particular direction, and he coolly took a pinch of snuff. As neither Muir nor Cap had anything to apprehend from the quarter in which the others were menaced, they kept their ground.

"Be wise, my pretty Mabel, be wise!" exclaimed the former; "and no' be provoking useless contention. In the name of all the kings of Albion, who have ye closeted with you in that wooden tower that seemeth so bloody-minded? There is necromancy about this matter, and all our characters may be involved in the explanation."

"What do you think of the Pathfinder, Master Muir, for a garrison to so strong a post?" cried Mabel, resorting to an equivocation which the circumstances rendered very excusable. "What will your French and Indian companions think of the aim of the Pathfinder's rifle?"

"Bear gently on the unfortunate, pretty Mabel, and do not confound the king's servants—may Heaven bless him and all his royal lineage!—with the king's enemies. If Pathfinder be indeed in the blockhouse, let him speak, and we will hold our negotiations directly with him. He knows us as friends, and we fear no evil at his hands, and least of all to myself; for a generous mind is apt to render rivalry in a certain interest a sure ground of respect and amity, since admiration of the same woman proves a community of feeling and tastes."

The reliance on Pathfinder's friendship did not extend beyond the Quartermaster and Cap, however, for even the French officer, who had hitherto stood his ground so well, shrank back at the sound of the terrible name. So unwilling, indeed, did this individual, a man of iron nerves, and one long accustomed to the dangers of the peculiar warfare in which he was engaged, appear to remain exposed to the assaults of Killdeer, whose reputation throughout all that frontier was as well established as that of Marlborough in Europe, that he did not disdain to seek a cover, insisting that his two prisoners should follow him. Mabel was too glad to be rid of her enemies to lament the departure of her friends, though she kissed her hand to Cap through the loop, and called out to him in terms of affection as he moved slowly and unwillingly away.

The enemy now seemed disposed to abandon all attempts on the blockhouse for the present; and June, who had ascended to a trap in the roof, whence the best view was to be obtained, reported that the whole party had assembled to eat, on a distant and sheltered part of the island, where Muir and Cap were quietly sharing in the good things which were going, as if they had no concern on their minds. This information greatly relieved Mabel, and she began to turn her thoughts again to the means of effecting her own escape, or at least of letting her father know of the danger that awaited him. The Sergeant was expected to return that afternoon, and she knew that a moment gained or lost might decide his fate.

Three or four hours flew by. The island was again buried in a profound quiet, the day was wearing away, and yet Mabel had decided on nothing. June was in the basement, preparing their frugal meal, and Mabel herself had ascended to the roof, which was provided with a trap that allowed her to go out on the top of the building, whence she commanded the best view of surrounding objects that the island possessed; still it was limited, and much obstructed by the tops of trees. The anxious girl did not dare to trust her person in sight, knowing well that the unrestrained passions of some savage might induce him to send a bullet through her brain. She merely kept her head out of the trap, therefore, whence, in the course of the afternoon, she made as many surveys of the different channels about the island as "Anne, sister Anne," took of the environs of the castle of Blue Beard.

The sun had actually set; no intelligence had been received from the boats, and Mabel ascended to the roof to take a last look, hoping that the party would arrive in the darkness; which would at least prevent the Indians from rendering their ambuscade so fatal as it might otherwise prove, and which possibly might enable her to give some more intelligible signal, by means of fire, than it would otherwise be in her power to do. Her eye had turned carefully round the whole horizon, and she was just on the point of drawing in her person, when an object that struck her as new caught her attention. The islands lay grouped so closely, that six or eight different channels or passages between them were in view; and in one of the most covered, concealed in a great measure by the bushes of the shore, lay what a second look assured her was a bark canoe. It contained a human being beyond a question. Confident that if an enemy her signal could do no harm, and, if a friend, that it might do good, the eager girl waved a little flag towards the stranger, which she had prepared for her father, taking care that it should not be seen from the island.

Mabel had repeated her signal eight or ten times in vain, and she began to despair of its being noticed, when a sign was given in return by the wave of a paddle, and the man so far discovered himself as to let her see it was Chingachgook. Here, then, at last, was a friend; one, too, who was able, and she doubted not would be willing, to aid her. From that instant her courage and her spirits revived. The Mohican had seen her; must have recognized her, as he knew that she was of the party; and no doubt, as soon as it was sufficiently dark, he would take the steps necessary to release her. That he was aware of the presence of the enemy was apparent by the great caution he observed, and she had every reliance on his prudence and address. The principal difficulty now existed with June; for Mabel had seen too much of her fidelity to her own people, relieved as it was by sympathy for herself, to believe she would consent to a hostile Indian's entering the blockhouse, or indeed to her leaving it, with a view to defeat Arrowhead's plans. The half-hour which succeeded the discovery of the presence of the Great Serpent was the most painful of Mabel Dunham's life. She saw the means of effecting all she wished, as it might be within reach of her hand, and yet it eluded her grasp. She knew June's decision and coolness, notwithstanding all her gentleness and womanly feeling; and at last she came reluctantly to the conclusion that there was no other way of attaining her end than by deceiving her tried companion and protector. It was revolting to one so sincere and natural, so pure of heart, and so much disposed to ingenuousness as Mabel Dunham, to practise deception on a friend like June; but her own father's life was at stake, her companion would receive no positive injury, and she had feelings and interests directly touching herself which would have removed greater scruples.

As soon as it was dark, Mabel's heart began to beat with increased violence; and she adopted and changed her plan of proceeding at least a dozen times in a single hour. June was always the source of her greatest embarrassment; for she did not well see, first, how she was to ascertain when Chingachgook was at the door, where she doubted not he would soon appear; and, secondly, how she was to admit him, without giving the alarm to her watchful companion. Time pressed, however; for the Mohican might come and go away again, unless she was ready to receive him. It would be too hazardous to the Delaware to remain long on the island; and it became absolutely necessary to determine on some course, even at the risk of choosing one that was indiscreet. After running over various projects in her mind, therefore, Mabel came to her companion, and said, with as much calmness as she could assume—

"Are you not afraid, June, now your people believe Pathfinder is in the blockhouse, that they will come and try to set it on fire?"

"No t'ink such t'ing. No burn blockhouse. Blockhouse good; got no scalp."

"June, we cannot know. They hid because they believed what I told them of Pathfinder's being with us."

"Believe fear. Fear come quick, go quick. Fear make run away; wit make come back. Fear make warrior fool, as well as young girl."

Here June laughed, as her sex is apt to laugh when anything particularly ludicrous crosses their youthful fancies.

"I feel uneasy, June; and wish you yourself would go up again to the roof and look out upon the island, to make certain that nothing is plotting against us; you know the signs of what your people intend to do better than I."

"June go, Lily wish; but very well know that Indian sleep; wait for 'e fader. Warrior eat, drink, sleep, all time, when don't fight and go on war-trail. Den never sleep, eat, drink—never feel. Warrior sleep now."

"God send it may be so! but go up, dear June, and look well about you. Danger may come when we least expect it."

June arose, and prepared to ascend to the roof; but she paused, with her foot on the first round of the ladder. Mabel's heart beat so violently that she was fearful its throbs would be heard; and she fancied that some gleamings of her real intentions had crossed the mind of her friend. She was right in part, the Indian woman having actually stopped to consider whether there was any indiscretion in what she was about to do. At first the suspicion that Mabel intended to escape flashed across her mind; then she rejected it, on the ground that the pale-face had no means of getting off the island, and that the blockhouse was much the most secure place she could find. The next thought was, that Mabel had detected some sign of the near approach of her father. This idea, too, lasted but an instant; for June entertained some such opinion of her companion's ability to understand symptoms of this sort—symptoms that had escaped her own sagacity—as a woman of high fashion entertains of the accomplishments of her maid. Nothing else in the same way offering, she began slowly to mount the ladder.

Just as she reached the upper floor, a lucky thought suggested itself to our heroine; and, by expressing it in a hurried but natural manner, she gained a great advantage in executing her projected scheme.

"I will go down," she said, "and listen by the door, June, while you are on the roof; and we will thus be on our guard, at the same time, above and below."

Though June thought this savored of unnecessary caution, well knowing that no one could enter the building unless aided from within, nor any serious danger menace them from the exterior without giving sufficient warning, she attributed the proposition to Mabel's ignorance and alarm; and, as it was made apparently with frankness, it was received without distrust. By these means our heroine was enabled to descend to the door, as her friend ascended to the roof. The distance between the two was now too great to admit of conversation; and for three or four minutes one was occupied in looking about her as well as the darkness would allow, and the other in listening at the door with as much intentness as if all her senses were absorbed in the single faculty of hearing.

June discovered nothing from her elevated stand; the obscurity indeed almost forbade the hope of such a result; but it would not be easy to describe the sensation with which Mabel thought she perceived a slight and guarded push against the door. Fearful that all might not be as she wished, and anxious to let Chingachgook know that she was near, she began, though in tremulous and low notes, to sing. So profound was the stillness of the moment that the sound of the unsteady warbling ascended to the roof, and in a minute June began to descend. A slight tap at the door was heard immediately after. Mabel was bewildered, for there was no time to lose. Hope proved stronger than fear; and with unsteady hands she commenced unbarring the door. The moccasin of June was heard on the floor above her when only a single bar was turned. The second was released as her form reached half-way down the lower ladder.

"What you do?" exclaimed June angrily. "Run away—mad—leave blockhouse; blockhouse good." The hands of both were on the last bar, and it would have been cleared from the fastenings but for a vigorous shove from without, which jammed the wood. A short struggle ensued, though both were disinclined to violence. June would probably have prevailed, had not another and a more vigorous push from without forced the bar past the trifling impediment that held it, when the door opened. The form of a man was seen to enter; and both the females rushed up the ladder, as if equally afraid of the consequences. The stranger secured the door; and, first examining the lower room with great care, he cautiously ascended the ladder. June, as soon as it became dark, had closed the loops of the principal floor, and lighted a candle. By means of this dim taper, then, the two females stood in expectation, waiting to ascertain the person of their visitor, whose wary ascent of the ladder was distinctly audible, though sufficiently deliberate. It would not be easy to say which was the more astonished on finding, when the stranger had got through the trap, that Pathfinder stood before them.

"God be praised!" Mabel exclaimed, for the idea that the blockhouse would be impregnable with such a garrison at once crossed her mind. "O Pathfinder! what has become of my father?"

"The Sergeant is safe as yet, and victorious; though it is not in the gift of man to say what will be the ind of it. Is not that the wife of Arrowhead skulking in the corner there?"

"Speak not of her reproachfully, Pathfinder; I owe her my life, my present security. Tell me what has happened to my father's party—why you are here; and I will relate all the horrible events that have passed upon this island."

"Few words will do the last, Mabel; for one used to Indian devilries needs but little explanations on such a subject. Everything turned out as we had hoped with the expedition; for the Sarpent was on the look-out, and he met us with all the information heart could desire. We ambushed three boats, druv' the Frenchers out of them, got possession and sunk them, according to orders, in the deepest part of the channel; and the savages of Upper Canada will fare badly for Indian goods this winter. Both powder and ball, too, will be scarcer among them than keen hunters and active warriors may relish. We did not lose a man or have even a skin barked; nor do I think the inimy suffered to speak of. In short, Mabel, it has been just such an expedition as Lundie likes; much harm to the foe, and little harm to ourselves."

"Ah, Pathfinder, I fear, when Major Duncan comes to hear the whole of the sad tale, he will find reason to regret he ever undertook the affair."

"I know what you mean, I know what you mean; but by telling my story straight you will understand it better. As soon as the Sergeant found himself successful, he sent me and the Sarpent off in canoes to tell you how matters had turned out, and he is following with the two boats, which, being so much heavier, cannot arrive before morning. I parted from Chingachgook this forenoon, it being agreed that he should come up one set of channels, and I another, to see that the path was clear. I've not seen the chief since."

Mabel now explained the manner in which she had discovered the Mohican, and her expectation that he would yet come to the blockhouse.

"Not he, not he! A regular scout will never get behind walls or logs so long as he can keep the open air and find useful employment. I should not have come myself, Mabel, but I promised the Sergeant to comfort you and to look after your safety. Ah's me! I reconnoitred the island with a heavy heart this forenoon; and there was a bitter hour when I fancied you might be among the slain."

"By what lucky accident were you prevented from paddling up boldly to the island and from falling into the hands of the enemy?"

"By such an accident, Mabel, as Providence employs to tell the hound where to find the deer and the deer how to throw off the hound. No, no! these artifices and devilries with dead bodies may deceive the soldiers of the 55th and the king's officers; but they are all lost upon men who have passed their days in the forest. I came down the channel in face of the pretended fisherman; and, though the riptyles have set up the poor wretch with art, it was not ingenious enough to take in a practysed eye. The rod was held too high, for the 55th have learned to fish at Oswego, if they never knew how before; and then the man was too quiet for one who got neither prey nor bite. But we never come in upon a post blindly; and I have lain outside a garrison a whole night, because they had changed their sentries and their mode of standing guard. Neither the Sarpent nor myself would be likely to be taken in by these clumsy contrivances, which were most probably intended for the Scotch, who are cunning enough in some particulars, though anything but witches when Indian sarcumventions are in the wind."

"Do you think my father and his men may yet be deceived?" said Mabel quickly.

"Not if I can prevent it, Mabel. You say the Sarpent is on the look-out too; so there is a double chance of our succeeding in letting him know his danger; though it is by no means sartain by which channel the party may come."

"Pathfinder," said our heroine solemnly, for the frightful scenes she had witnessed had clothed death with unusual horrors—"Pathfinder, you have professed love for me, a wish to make me your wife?"

"I did ventur' to speak on that subject, Mabel, and the Sergeant has even lately said that you are kindly disposed; but I am not a man to persecute the thing I love."

"Hear me, Pathfinder, I respect you, honor you, revere you; save my father from this dreadful death, and I can worship you. Here is my hand, as a solemn pledge for my faith, when you come to claim it."

"Bless you, bless you, Mabel; this is more than I desarve—more, I fear, than I shall know how to profit by as I ought. It was not wanting, however, to make me sarve the Sergeant. We are old comrades, and owe each other a life; though I fear me, Mabel, being a father's comrade is not always the best recommendation with a daughter."

"You want no other recommendation than your own acts—your courage, your fidelity. All that you do and say, Pathfinder, my reason approves, and the heart will, nay, it *shall* follow."

"This is a happiness I little expected this night; but we are in God's hands, and He will protect us in His own way. These are sweet words, Mabel; but they were not wanting to make me do all that man can do in the present circumstances; they will not lessen my endeavors, neither."

"Now we understand each other, Pathfinder," Mabel added hoarsely, "let us not lose one of the precious moments, which may be of incalculable value. Can we not get into your canoe and go and meet my father?"

"That is not the course I advise. I don't know by which channel the Sergeant will come, and there are twenty; rely on it, the Sarpent will be winding his way through them all. No, no! my advice is to remain here. The logs of this blockhouse are still green, and it will not be easy to set them on fire; and I can make good the place, bating a burning, ag'in a tribe. The Iroquois nation cannot dislodge me from this fortress, so long as we can keep the flames off it. The Sergeant is now 'camped on some island, and will not come in until morning. If we hold the block, we can give him timely warning, by firing rifles, for instance; and should he determine to attack the savages, as a man of his temper will be very likely to do, the possession of this building will be of great acccunt in the affair. No, no! my judgment says remain, if the object be to sarve the Sergeant, though escape for our two selves will be no very difficult matter."

"Stay," murmured Mabel, "stay, for God's sake, Pathfinder! Anything, everything to save my father!"

"Yes, that is natur'. I am glad to hear you say this, Mabel, for I own a wish to see the Sergeant fairly supported. As the matter now stands, he has gained himself credit; and, could he once drive off these miscreants, and make an honorable retreat, laying the huts and block in ashes, no doubt, Lundie would remember it and sarve him accordingly. Yes, yes, Mabel, we must not only save the Sergeant's life, but we must save his reputation."

"No blame can rest on my father on account of the surprise of this island."

"There's no telling, there's no telling; military glory is a most unsartain thing. I've seen the Delawares routed, when they desarved more credit than at other times when they've carried the day. A man is wrong to set his head on success of any sort, and worst of all on success in war. I know little of the settlements, or of the notions that men hold in them; but up here—

away even the Indians rate a warrior's character according to his luck. The principal thing with a soldier is never to be whipt; nor do I think mankind stops long to consider how the day was won or lost. For my part, Mabel, I make it a rule when facing the inimy to give him as good as I can send, and to try to be moderate as I can when we get the better. As for feeling moderate after a defeat, little need be said on that score, as a flogging is one of the most humbling things in natur'. The parsons preach about humility in the garrison; but if humility would make Christians, the king's troops ought to be saints, for they've done little as yet this war but take lessons from the French, beginning at Fort du Quesne and ending at Ty."

"My father could not have suspected that the position of the island was known to the enemy," resumed Mabel, whose thoughts were running on the probable effect of the recent events on the Sergeant.

"That is true; nor do I well see how the Frenchers found it out. The spot is well chosen, and it is not an easy matter, even for one who has travelled the road to and from it, to find it again. There has been treachery, I fear; yes, yes, there must have been treachery."

"Oh, Pathfinder! can this be?"

"Nothing is easier, Mabel, for treachery comes as nat'ral to some men as eating. Now when I find a man all fair words I look close to his deeds; for when the heart is right, and really intends to do good, it is generally satisfied to let the conduct speak instead of the tongue."

"Jasper Western is not one of these," said Mabel impetuously. "No youth can be more sincere in his manner, or less apt to make the tongue act for the head."

"Jasper Western! tongue and heart are both right with that lad, depend on it, Mabel; and the notion taken up by Lundie, and the Quartermaster, and the Sergeant, and your uncle too, is as wrong as it would be to think that the sun shone by night and the stars shone by day. No, no; I'll answer for Eau-douce's honesty with my own scalp, or, at need, with my own rifle."

"Bless you, bless you, Pathfinder!" exclaimed Mabel, extending her own hand and pressing the iron fingers of her companion, under a state of feeling that far surpassed her own consciousness of its strength. "You are all that is generous, all that is noble! God will reward you for it."

"Ah, Mabel, I fear me, if this be true, I should not covet such a wife as yourself; but would leave you to be sued for by some gentleman of the garrison, as your desarts require."

"We will not talk of this any more to-night," Mabel answered in a voice so smothered as to seem nearly choked. "We must think less of ourselves just now, Pathfinder, and more of our friends. But I rejoice from my soul that you believe Jasper innocent. Now let us talk of other things—ought we not to release June?"

"I've been thinking about the woman; for it will not be safe to shut our eyes and leave hers open, on this side of the blockhouse door. It we put her in the upper room, and take away the ladder, she'll be a prisoner at least."

"I cannot treat one thus who has saved my life. It would be better to let her depart, for I think she is too much my friend to do anything to harm me."

"You do not know the race, Mabel, you do not know the race. It's true she's not a full-blooded Mingo, but she consorts with the vagabonds, and must have larned some of their tricks. What is that?"

"It sounds like oars; some boat is passing through the channel."

Pathfinder closed the trap that led to the lower room, to prevent June from escaping, extinguished the candle, and went hastily to a loop, Mabel looking over his shoulder in breathless curiosity. These several movements consumed a minute or two; and by the time the eye of the scout had got a dim view of things without, two boats had swept past and shot up to the shore, at a spot some fifty yards beyond the block, where there was a regular landing. The obscurity prevented more from being seen; and Pathfinder whispered to Mabel that the new-comers were as likely to be foes as friends, for he did not think her father could possibly have arrived so soon. A number of men were now seen to quit the boats, and then followed three hearty English cheers, leaving no further doubts of the character of the party. Pathfinder sprang to the trap, raised it, glided down the ladder, and began to unbar the door, with an earnestness that proved how critical he deemed the moment. Mabel had followed, but she rather impeded than aided his exertions, and but a single bar was turned when a heavy discharge of rifles was heard. They were still standing in breathless suspense, as the war-whoop rang in all the surrounding thickets. The door now opened, and both Pathfinder and Mabel rushed into the open air. All human sounds had ceased. After listening half a minute, however, Pathfinder thought he heard a few stifled groans near the boats; but the wind blew so fresh, and the rustling of the leaves mingled so much with the murmurs of the passing air, that he was far from certain. But Mabel was borne away by her feelings, and she rushed by him, taking the way towards the boats.

"This will not do, Mabel," said the scout in an earnest but low voice, seizing her by an arm; "this will never do. Sartain death would follow, and that without sarving any one. We must return to the block."

"Father! my poor, dear, murdered father!" said the girl wildly, though habitual caution, even at that trying moment, induced her to speak low. "Pathfinder, if you love me, let me go to my dear father."

"This will not do, Mabel. It is singular that no one speaks; no one returns the fire from the boats; and I have left Killdeer in the block! But of what use would a rifle be when no one is to be seen?"

At that moment the quick eye of Pathfinder, which, while he held Mabel firmly in his grasp, had never ceased to roam over the dim scene, caught an indistinct view of five or six dark crouching forms, endeavoring to steal past him, doubtless with the intention of intercepting the retreat to the blockhouse. Catching up Mabel, and putting her under an arm, as if she were an infant, the sinewy frame of the woodsman was exerted to the utmost, and he succeeded in entering the building. The tramp of his pursuers seemed immediately at his heels. Dropping his burden, he turned, closed the door, and had fastened one bar, as a rush against the solid mass threatened to force it from the hinges. To secure the other bars was the work of an instant.

Mabel now ascended to the first floor, while Pathfinder remained as a sentinel below. Our heroine was in that state in which the body exerts itself, apparently without the control of the mind. She relighted the candle mechanically, as her companion had desired, and returned with it below, where he was waiting her reappearance. No sooner was Pathfinder in possession of the light than he examined the place carefully, to make certain no one was concealed in the fortress, ascending to each floor in succession, after assuring himself that he left no enemy in his rear. The result was the conviction that the blockhouse now contained no one but Mabel and himself, June having escaped. When perfectly convinced on this material point, Pathfinder rejoined our heroine in the principal apartment, setting down the light and examining the priming of Killdeer before he seated himself.

"Our worst fears are realized!" said Mabel, to whom the hurry and excitement of the last five minutes appeared to contain the emotions of a life. "My beloved father and all his party are slain or captured!"

"We don't know that—morning will tell us all. I do not think the affair so settled as that, or we should hear the vagabond Mingos yelling out their triumph around the blockhouse. Of one thing we may be sartain; if the inimy has really got the better, he will not be long in calling upon us to surrender. The squaw will let him into the secret of our situation; and, as they well know the place cannot be fired by daylight, so long as Killdeer continues to desarve his reputation, you may depend on it that they will not be backward in making their attempt while darkness helps them."

"Surely I hear a groan!"

" 'Tis fancy, Mabel; when the mind gets to be skeary, especially a woman's mind, she often concaits things that have no reality. I've known them that imagined there was truth in dreams."

"Nay, I am *not* deceived; there is surely one below, and in pain."

Pathfinder was compelled to own that the quick senses of Mabel had not deceived her. He cautioned her, however, to repress her feelings; and reminded her that the savages were in the practice of resorting to every artifice to attain their ends, and that nothing was more likely than that the groans were feigned with a view to lure them from the blockhouse, or, at least, to induce them to open the door.

"No, no, no!" said Mabel hurriedly; "there is no artifice in those sounds, and they come from anguish of body, if not of spirit. They are fearfully natural."

"Well, we shall soon know whether a friend is there or not. Hide the light again, Mabel, and I will speak the person from a loop."

Not a little precaution was necessary, according to Pathfinder's judgment and experience, in performing even this simple act; for he had known the careless slain by their want of proper attention to what might have seemed to the ignorant supererogatory means of safety. He did not place his mouth to the loop itself, but so near it that he could be heard without raising his voice, and the same precaution was observed as regards his ear.

"Who is below?" Pathfinder demanded, when his arrangements were made to his mind. "Is any one in suffering? If a friend, speak boldly, and depend on our aid."

"Pathfinder!" answered a voice that both Mabel and the person addressed at once knew to be the Sergeant's—"Pathfinder, in the name of God, tell me what has become of my daughter."

"Father, I am here, unhurt, safe! and oh that I could think the same of you!"

The ejaculation of thanksgiving that followed was distinctly audible to the two, but it was clearly mingled with a groan of pain.

"My worst forebodings are realized!" said Mabel with a sort of desperate calmness. "Pathfinder, my father must be brought within the block, though we hazard everything to do it."

"This is natur', and it is the law of God. But, Mabel, be calm, and endivor to be cool. All that can be effected for the Sergeant by human invention shall be done. I only ask you to be cool."

"I am, I am, Pathfinder. Never in my life was I more calm, more collected, than at this moment. But remember how perilous may be every instant; for Heaven's sake, what we do, let us do without delay."

Pathfinder was struck with the firmness of Mabel's tones, and perhaps he was a little deceived by the forced tranquillity and self-possession she had assumed. At all events, he did not deem any further explanations necessary, but descended forthwith, and began to unbar the door. This delicate process was conducted with the usual caution, but, as he warily permitted the mass of timber to swing back on the hinges, he felt a pressure against it, that had nearly induced him to close it again. But, catching a glimpse of the cause through the crack, the door was permitted to swing back, when the body of Sergeant Dunham, which was propped against it, fell partly within the block. To draw in the legs and secure the fastenings occupied the Path‧finder but a moment. Then there existed no obstacle to their giving their undivided care to the wounded man.

Mabel, in this trying scene, conducted herself with the sort of unnatural energy that her sex, when aroused, is apt to mani-fest. She got the light, administered water to the parched lips of her father, and assisted Pathfinder in forming a bed of straw for his body and a pillow of clothes for his head. All this was done earnestly, and almost without speaking; nor did Mabel shed a tear, until she heard the blessings of her father mur-mured on her head for this tenderness and care. All this time Mabel had merely conjectured the condition of her parent. Pathfinder, however, had shown greater attention to the physi-cal danger of the Sergeant. He had ascertained that a rifle-ball had passed through the body of the wounded man; and he was sufficiently familiar with injuries of this nature to be certain that the chances of his surviving the hurt were very trifling, if any.

CHAPTER XXIV

Then drink my tears, while yet they fall—
    Would that my bosom's blood were balm;
And—well thou knowest—I'd shed it all,
    To give thy brow one minute's calm.   MOORE

THE eyes of Sergeant Dunham had not ceased to follow the form of his beautiful daughter from the moment that the light appeared. He next examined the door of the block, to ascertain its security; for he was left on the ground below, there being no available means of raising him to the upper floor. Then he sought the face of Mabel; for as life wanes fast the affections resume their force, and we begin to value that most which we feel we are about to lose for ever.

"God be praised, my child! you, at least, have escaped their murderous rifles," he said; for he spoke with strength, and seemingly with no additional pain. "Give me the history of this sad business, Pathfinder."

"Ah's me, Sergeant! it *has* been sad, as you say. That there has been treachery, and the position of the island has been betrayed, is now as sartain, in my judgment, as that we still hold the block. But——"

"Major Duncan was right," interrupted Dunham, laying a hand on the other's arm.

"Not in the sense you mean, Sergeant—no, not in that p'int of view; never! At least, not in my opinion. I know that natur' is weak—human natur', I mean—and that we should none of us vaunt of our gifts, whether red or white; but I do not think a truer-hearted lad lives on the lines than Jasper Western."

"Bless you! bless you for that, Pathfinder!" burst forth from Mabel's very soul, while a flood of tears gave vent to emotions that were so varied while they were so violent. "Oh, bless you, Pathfinder, bless you! The brave should never desert the brave —the honest should sustain the honest."

The father's eyes were fastened anxiously on the face of his daughter, until the latter hid her countenance in her apron to conceal her tears; and then they turned with inquiry to the hard features of the guide. The latter merely wore their usual expression of frankness, sincerity, and uprightness; and the Sergeant motioned to him to proceed.

"You know the spot where the Sarpent and I left you, Sergeant," Pathfinder resumed; "and I need say nothing of all that happened afore. It is now too late to regret what is gone and passed; but I do think if I had stayed with the boats this would not have come to pass. Other men may be as good guides—I make no doubt they are; but then natur' bestows its gifts, and some must be better than other some. I daresay poor Gilbert, who took my place, has suffered for his mistake."

"He fell at my elbow," the Sergeant answered in a low melancholy tone. "We have, indeed, all suffered for our mistakes."

"No, no, Sergeant, I meant no condemnation on you; for

men were never better commanded than yourn, in this very expedition. I never beheld a prettier flanking; and the way in which you carried your own boat up ag'in their howitzer might have teached Lundie himself a lesson."

The eyes of the Sergeant brightened, and his face even wore an expression of military triumph, though it was of a degree that suited the humble sphere in which he had been an actor.

" 'Twas not badly done, my friend," said he; "and we carried their log breastwork by storm."

" 'Twas nobly done, Sergeant; though, I fear, when all the truth comes to be known, it will be found that these vagabonds have got their howitzer back ag'in. Well, well, put a stout heart upon it, and try to forget all that is disagreeable, and to remember only the pleasant part of the matter. That is your truest philosophy; ay, and truest religion too. If the inimy has got the howitzer ag'in, they've only got what belonged to them afore, and what we couldn't help. They haven't got the blockhouse yet, nor are they likely to get it, unless they fire it in the dark. Well, Sergeant, the Sarpent and I separated about ten miles down the river; for we thought it wisest not to come upon even a friendly camp without the usual caution. What has become of Chingachgook I cannot say; though Mabel tells me he is not far off, and I make no question the noble-hearted Delaware is doing his duty, although he is not now visible to our eyes. Mark my word, Sergeant, before this matter is over we shall hear of him at some critical time and that in a discreet and creditable manner. Ah, the Sarpent is indeed a wise and virtuous chief! and any white man might covet his gifts, though his rifle is not quite as sure as Killdeer, it must be owned. Well, as I came near the island I missed the smoke, and that put me on my guard; for I knew that the men of the 55th were not cunning enough to conceal that sign, notwithstanding all that has been told them of its danger. This made me more careful, until I came in sight of this mock-fisherman, as I've just told Mabel; and then the whole of their infernal arts was as plain before me as if I saw it on a map. I need not tell you, Sergeant, that my first thoughts were of Mabel; and that, finding she was in the block, I came here, in order to live or die in her company."

The father turned a gratified look upon his child; and Mabel felt a sinking of the heart that at such a moment she could not have thought possible, when she wished to believe all her concern centred in the situation of her parent. As the latter held out his hand, she took it in her own and kissed it. Then, kneeling at his side, she wept as if her heart would break.

"Mabel," said he steadily, "the will of God must be done. It is useless to attempt deceiving either you or myself; my time has come, and it is a consolation to me to die like a soldier. Lundie will do me justice; for our good friend Pathfinder will tell him what has been done, and how all came to pass. You do not forget our last conversation?"

"Nay, father, my time has probably come too," exclaimed Mabel, who felt just then as if it would be a relief to die. "I cannot hope to escape; and Pathfinder would do well to leave us, and return to the garrison with the sad news while he can."

"Mabel Dunham," said Pathfinder reproachfully, though he took her hand with kindness, "I have not desarved this. I know I am wild, and uncouth, and ungainly——"

"Pathfinder!"

"Well, well, we'll forget it; you did not mean it, you could not think it. It is useless now to talk of escaping, for the Sergeant cannot be moved; and the blockhouse must be defended, cost what it will. Maybe Lundie will get the tidings of our disaster, and send a party to raise the siege."

"Pathfinder—Mabel!" said the Sergeant, who had been writhing with pain until the cold sweat stood on his forehead; "come both to my side. You understand each other, I hope?"

"Father, say nothing of that; it is all as you wish."

"Thank God! Give me your hand, Mabel—here, Pathfinder, take it. I can do no more than give you the girl in this way. I know you will make her a kind husband. Do not wait on account of my death; but there will be a chaplain in the fort before the season closes, and let him marry you at once. My brother, if living, will wish to go back to his vessel, and then the child will have no protector. Mabel, your husband will have been my friend, and that will be some consolation to you, I hope."

"Trust this matter to me, Sergeant," put in Pathfinder; "leave it all in my hands as your dying request; and, depend on it, all will go as it should."

"I do, I do put all confidence in you, my trusty friend, and empower you to act as I could act myself in every particular. Mabel, child—hand me the water—you will never repent this night. Bless you, my daughter! God bless, and have you in His holy keeping!"

This tenderness was inexpressibly touching to one of Mabel's feelings; and she felt at that moment as if her future union with Pathfinder had received a solemnization that no ceremony of the Church could render more holy. Still, a weight, as that of a mountain, lay upon her heart, and she thought it would be happiness to die. Then followed a short pause, when the Sergeant, in broken sentences, briefly related what had passed since he parted with Pathfinder and the Delaware. The wind had come more favorable; and, instead of encamping on an island agreeably to the original intention, he had determined to continue, and reach the station that night. Their approach would have been unseen, and a portion of the calamity avoided, he thought, had they not grounded on the point of a neighboring island, where, no doubt, the noise made by the men in getting off the boat gave notice of their approach, and enabled the enemy to be in readiness to receive them. They had landed without the slightest suspicion of danger, though surprised at not finding a sentinel, and had actually left their arms in the boat, with the intention of first securing their knapsacks and provisions. The fire had been so close, that, notwithstanding the obscurity, it was very deadly. Every man had fallen, though two or three subsequently arose and disappeared. Four or five of the soldiers had been killed, or so nearly so as to survive but a few minutes; though, for some unknown reason, the enemy did not make the usual rush for the scalps. Sergeant Dunham fell with the others; and he had heard the voice of Mabel, as she rushed from the blockhouse. This frantic appeal aroused all his parental feelings, and had enabled him to crawl as far as the door of the building, where he had raised himself against the logs in the manner already mentioned.

After this simple explanation was made, the Sergeant was so weak as to need repose, and his companions, while they minis·tered to his wants, suffered some time to pass in silence. Pathfinder took the occasion to reconnoitre from the loops and the roof, and he examined the condition of the rifles, of which there were a dozen kept in the building, the soldiers having used their regimental muskets in the expedition. But Mabel never left her father's side for an instant; and when, by his breathing, she fancied he slept, she bent her knees and prayed.

The half-hour that succeeded was awfully solemn and still. The moccasin of Pathfinder was barely heard overhead, and occasionally the sound of the breech of a rifle fell upon the floor, for he was busied in examining the pieces, with a view to ascertain the state of their charges and their primings. Beyond this, nothing was so loud as the breathing of the wounded man. Mabel's heart yearned to be in communication with the father she was so soon to lose, and yet she would not disturb his apparent repose. But Dunham slept not; he was in that state when the world suddenly loses its attractions, its illusions, and its power; and the unknown future fills the mind with its conjectures, its revelations, and its immensity. He had been a moral man for one of his mode of life, but he had thought little of this all-important moment. Had the din of battle been ringing in his ears, his martial ardor might have endured to the end; but there, in the silence of that nearly untenanted blockhouse, with no sound to enliven him, no appeal to keep alive factitious sentiment, no hope of victory to impel, things began to appear in their true colors, and this state of being to be estimated at its just value. He would have given treasures for religious consolation, and yet he knew not where to turn to seek it. He thought of Pathfinder, but he distrusted his knowledge. He thought of Mabel, but for the parent to appeal to the child for such succor appeared like reversing the order of nature. Then it was that he felt the full responsibility of the parental character, and had some clear glimpse of the manner in which he himself had discharged the trust towards an orphan child. While thoughts like these were rising in his mind, Mabel, who watched the slightest change in his breathing, heard a guarded knock at the door. Supposing it might be Chingachgook, she rose, undid two of the bars, and held the third in her hand, as she asked who was there. The answer was in her uncle's voice, and he implored her to give him instant admission. Without an instant of hesitation, she turned the bar, and Cap entered. He had barely passed the opening, when Mabel closed the door again, and secured it as before, for practice had rendered her expert in this portion of her duties.

The sturdy seaman, when he had made sure of the state of his brother-in-law, and that Mabel, as well as himself, was safe, was softened nearly to tears. His own appearance he explained by saying that he had been carelessly guarded, under the impression that he and the Quartermaster were sleeping under the fumes of liquor with which they had been plied with a view to keep them quiet in the expected engagement. Muir had been left asleep, or seeming to sleep; but Cap had run into the bushes on the alarm of the attack, and having found Pathfinder's canoe, had only succeeded, at that moment, in getting to the block-house, whither he had come with the kind intent of escaping with his niece by water. It is scarcely necessary to say that he changed his plan when he ascertained the state of the Sergeant, and the apparent security of his present quarters.

"If the worst comes to the worst, Master Pathfinder," said he, "we must strike, and that will entitle us to receive quarter. We owe it to our manhood to hold out a reasonable time, and to ourselves to haul down the ensign in season to make saving conditions. I wished Master Muir to do the same thing when we were captured by these chaps you call vagabonds—and rightly are they named, for viler vagabonds do not walk the earth——"

"You've found out their characters?" interrupted Pathfinder, who was always as ready to chime in with abuse of the Mingos as with the praises of his friends. "Now, had you fallen into the hands of the Delawares, you would have learned the difference."

"Well, to me they seem much of a muchness; blackguards fore and aft, always excepting our friend the Serpent, who is a gentleman for an Indian. But, when these savages made the assault on us, killing Corporal M'Nab and his men as if they had been so many rabbits, Lieutenant Muir and myself took refuge in one of the holes of this here island, of which there are so many among the rocks, and there we remained stowed away like two leaguers in a ship's hold, until we gave out for want of grub. A man may say that grub is the foundation of human nature. I desired the Quartermaster to make terms, for we could have defended ourselves for an hour or two in the place, bad as it was; but he declined, on the ground that the knaves wouldn't keep faith if any of them were hurt, and so there was no use in asking them to. I consented to strike, on two principles; one, that we might be said to have struck already, for running below is generally thought to be giving up the ship; and the other, that we had an enemy in our stomachs that was more formidable in his attacks than the enemy on deck. Hunger is a d——ble circumstance, as any man who has lived on it eight-and-forty hours will acknowledge."

"Uncle," said Mabel in a mournful voice and with an expostulatory manner, "my poor father is sadly, sadly hurt!"

"True, Magnet, true; I will sit by him, and do my best at consolation. Are the bars well fastened, girl? for on such an occasion the mind should be tranquil and undisturbed."

"We are safe, I believe, from all but this heavy blow of Providence."

"Well, then, Magnet, do you go up to the floor above and try to compose yourself, while Pathfinder runs aloft and takes a look-out from the cross-trees. Your father may wish to say something to me in private, and it may be well to leave us alone. These are solemn scenes, and inexperienced people, like myself, do not always wish what they say to be overheard."

Although the idea of her uncle's affording religious consolation by the side of a death-bed certainly never obtruded itself on the imagination of Mabel, she thought there might be a propriety in the request with which she was unacquainted, and she complied accordingly. Pathfinder had already ascended to the roof to make his survey, and the brothers-in-law were left alone. Cap took a seat by the side of the Sergeant, and bethought him seriously of the grave duty he had before him. A silence of several minutes succeeded, during which brief space the mariner was digesting the substance of his intended discourse.

"I must say, Sergeant Dunham," Cap at length commenced in his peculiar manner, "that there has been mismanagement somewhere in this unhappy expedition; and, the present being an occasion when truth ought to be spoken, and nothing but the truth, I feel it my duty to say as much in plain language. In short, Sergeant, on this point there cannot well be two opinions; for, seaman as I am, and no soldier, I can see several errors myself, that it needs no great education to detect."

"What would you have, brother Cap?" returned the other in a feeble voice; "what is done is done; and it is now too late to remedy it."

"Very true, brother Dunham, but not to repent of it; the Good Book tells us it is never too late to repent; and I've always heard that this is the precious moment. If you've anything on your mind, Sergeant, hoist it out freely; for, you know, you trust it to a friend. You were my own sister's husband, and poor little Magnet is my own sister's daughter; and, living or dead, I shall always look upon you as a brother. It's a thousand pities that you didn't lie off and on with the boats, and send a canoe ahead to reconnoitre; in which case your command would have been saved, and this disaster would not have befallen us all. Well, Sergeant, we are *all* mortal; that is some consolation, I make no doubt; and if you go before a little, why, we must follow. Yes, that *must* give you consolation."

"I know all this, brother Cap; and hope I'm prepared to meet a soldier's fate—there is poor Mabel——"

"Ay, ay, that's a heavy drag, I know; but you wouldn't take her with you if you could, Sergeant; and so the better way is to make as light of the separation as you can. Mabel is a good girl, and so was her mother before her; she was my sister, and it shall be my care to see that her daughter gets a good husband, if our lives and scalps are spared; for I suppose no one would care about entering into a family that has no scalps."

"Brother, my child is betrothed; she will become the wife of Pathfinder."

"Well, brother Dunham, every man has his opinions and his manner of viewing things; and, to my notion, this match will be anything but agreeable to Mabel. I have no objection to the age of the man; I'm not one of them that thinks it necessary to be a boy to make a girl happy, but, on the whole, I prefer a man of about fifty for a husband; still there ought not to be any circumstance between the parties to make them unhappy. Circumstances play the devil with matrimony, and I set it down as one that Pathfinder don't know as much as my niece. You've seen but little of the girl, Sergeant, and have not got the run of her knowledge; but let her pay it out freely, as she will do when she gets to be thoroughly acquainted, and you'll fall in with but few schoolmasters that can keep their luffs in her company."

"She's a good child—a dear, good child," muttered the Sergeant, his eyes filling with tears; "and it is my misfortune that I have seen so little of her."

"She is indeed a good girl, and knows altogether too much for poor Pathfinder, who is a reasonable man and an experienced man in his own way; but who has no more idea of the main chance than you have of spherical trigonometry, Sergeant."

"Ah, brother Cap, had Pathfinder been with us in the boats, this sad affair might not have happened!"

"That is quite likely; for his worst enemy will allow that the man is a good guide; but then, Sergeant, if the truth must be spoken, you have managed this expedition in a loose way altogether. You should have hove-to off your haven, and sent in a boat to reconnoitre, as I told you before. That is a matter to be repented of? and I tell it to you, because truth, in such a case, ought to be spoken."

"My errors are dearly paid for, brother; and poor Mabel, I fear, will be the sufferer. I think, however, that the calamity would not have happened had there not been treason. I fear me, brother, that Jasper Eau-douce has played us false."

"That is just my notion; for this fresh-water life must sooner or later undermine any man's morals. Lieutenant Muir and myself talked this matter over while we lay in a bit of a hole out here, on this island; and we both came to the conclusion that nothing short of Jasper's treachery could have brought us all into this infernal scrape. Well, Sergeant, you had better compose your mind, and think of other matters; for, when a vessel is about to enter a strange port, it is more prudent to think of the anchorage inside than to be under-running all the events that have turned up during the v'y'ge. There's the log-book expressly to note all these matters in; and what stands there must form the column of figures that's to be posted up for or against us. How now, Pathfinder! is there anything in the wind, that you come down the ladder like an Indian in the wake of a scalp?"

The guide raised a finger for silence, and then beckoned to Cap to ascend the first ladder, and to allow Mabel to take his place at the side of the Sergeant.

"We must be prudent, and we must be bold too," said he in a low voice. "The riptyles are in earnest in their intention to fire the block; for they know there is now nothing to be gained by letting it stand. I hear the voice of that vagabond Arrowhead among them, and he is urging them to set about their devilry this very night. We must be stirring, Saltwater, and doing too. Luckily there are four or five barrels of water in the block, and these are something towards a siege. My reckoning is wrong, too, or we shall yet reap some advantage from that honest fellow's, the Sarpent, being at liberty."

Cap did not wait for a second invitation; but, stealing away, he was soon in the upper room with Pathfinder, while Mabel took his post at the side of her father's humble bed. Pathfinder had opened a loop, having so far concealed the light that it would not expose him to a treacherous shot; and, expecting a summons, he stood with his face near the hole, ready to answer. The stillness that succeeded was at length broken by the voice of Muir.

"Master Pathfinder," called out the Scotchman, "a friend summons you to a parley. Come freely to one of the loops; for you've nothing to fear so long as you are in converse with an officer of the 55th."

"What is your will, Quartermaster? what is your will? I know the 55th, and believe it to be a brave regiment; though I rather incline to the 60th as my favorite, and to the Delawares more than to either; but what would you have, Quartermaster? It must be a pressing errand that brings you under the loops of a blockhouse at this hour of the night, with the sartainty of Killdeer being inside of it."

"Oh, you'll no' harm a friend, Pathfinder, I'm certain; and that's my security. You're a man of judgment, and have gained too great a name on this frontier for bravery to feel the necessity of foolhardiness to obtain a character. You'll very well understand, my good friend, there is as much credit to be gained by submitting gracefully, when resistance becomes impossible, as by obstinately holding out contrary to the rules of war. The enemy is too strong for us, my brave comrade, and I come to counsel you to give up the block, on condition of being treated as a prisoner of war."

"I thank you for this advice, Quartermaster, which is the more acceptable as it costs nothing; but I do not think it belongs to my gifts to yield a place like this while food and water last."

"Well, I'd be the last, Pathfinder, to recommend anything against so brave a resolution, did I see the means of maintaining it. But ye'll remember that Master Cap has fallen."

"Not he, not he!" roared the individual in question through another loop; "and so far from that, Lieutenant, he has risen to the height of this here fortification, and has no mind to put his head of hair into the hands of such barbers again, so long as he can help it. I look upon this blockhouse as a circumstance, and have no mind to throw it away."

"If that is a living voice," returned Muir, "I am glad to hear it; for we all thought the man had fallen in the late fearful confusion. But, Master Pathfinder, although ye're enjoying the society of our friend Cap—and a great pleasure do I know it to be, by the experience of two days and a night passed in a hole in the earth—we've lost that of Sergeant Dunham, who has fallen, with all the brave men he led in the late expedition. Lundie would have it so, though it would have been more discreet and becoming to send a commissioned officer in command. Dunham was a brave man, notwithstanding, and shall have justice done his memory. In short, we have all acted for the best, and that is as much as could be said in favor of Prince Eugene, the Duke of Marlborough, or the great Earl of Stair himself."

"You're wrong ag'in, Quartermaster, you're wrong ag'in," answered Pathfinder, resorting to a ruse to magnify his force. "The Sergeant is safe in the block too, where one might say the whole family is collected."

"Well, I rejoice to hear it, for we had certainly counted the Sergeant among the slain. If pretty Mabel is in the block still, let her not delay an instant, for heaven's sake, in quitting it, for the enemy is about to put it to the trial by fire. Ye know the potency of that dread element, and will be acting more like the discreet and experienced warrior ye're universally allowed to be, in yielding a place you canna' defend, than in drawing down ruin on yourself and companions."

"I know the potency of fire, as you call it, Quartermaster; and am not to be told, at this late hour, that it can be used for something else besides cooking a dinner. But I make no doubt you've heard of the potency of Killdeer, and the man who attempts to lay a pile of brush against these logs will get a taste of his power. As for arrows, it is not in their gift to set this building on fire, for we've no shingles on our roof, but good solid logs and green bark, and plenty of water besides. The roof is so flat, too, as you know yourself, Quartermaster, that we can walk on it, and so no danger on that score while water lasts. I'm peaceable enough if let alone; but he who endivors to burn this block over my head will find the fire squinched in his own blood."

"This is idle and romantic talk, Pathfinder, and ye'll no' maintain it yourself when ye come to meditate on the realities. I hope ye'll no' gainsay the loyalty or the courage of the 55th, and I feel convinced that a council of war would decide on the propriety of a surrender forthwith. Na, na, Pathfinder, foolhardiness is na mair like the bravery o' Wallace or Bruce than Albany on the Hudson is like the old town of Edinbro'."

"As each of us seems to have made up his mind, Quartermaster, more words are useless. If the riptyles near you are disposed to set about their hellish job, let them begin at once. They can burn wood, and I'll burn powder. If I were an Indian at the stake, I suppose I could brag as well as the rest of them; but, my gifts and natur' being both white, my turn is rather for doing than talking. You've said quite enough, considering you carry the king's commission; and should we all be consumed, none of us will bear *you* any malice."

"Pathfinder, ye'll no' be exposing Mabel, pretty Mabel Dunham, to sic' a calamity!"

"Mabel Dunham is by the side of her wounded father, and God will care for the safety of a pious child. Not a hair of her head shall fall, while my arm and sight remain true; and though *you* may trust the Mingos, Master Muir, I put no faith in them. You've a knavish Tuscarora in your company there, who has art and malice enough to spoil the character of any tribe with which he consorts, though he found the Mingos ready ruined to his hands, I fear. But enough said; now let each party go to the use of his means and his gifts."

Throughout this dialogue Pathfinder had kept his body covered, lest a treacherous shot should be aimed at the loop; and he now directed Cap to ascend to the roof in order to be in readiness to meet the first assault. Although the latter used sufficient diligence, he found no less than ten blazing arrows sticking to the bark, while the air was filled with the yells and whoops of the enemy. A rapid discharge of rifles followed, and the bullets came pattering against the logs, in a way to show that the struggle had indeed seriously commenced.

These were sounds, however, that appalled neither Pathfinder nor Cap, while Mabel was too much absorbed in her affliction to feel alarm. She had good sense enough, too, to understand the nature of the defences, and fully to appreciate their importance. As for her father, the familiar noises revived him; and it pained his child, at such a moment, to see that his glassy eye began to kindle, and that the blood returned to a cheek it had deserted, as he listened to the uproar. It was now Mabel first perceived that his reason began slightly to wander.

"Order up the light companies," he muttered, "and let the grenadiers charge! Do they dare to attack us in our fort? Why does not the artillery open on them?"

At that instant the heavy report of a gun burst on the night; and the crashing of rending wood was heard, as a heavy shot tore the logs in the room above, and the whole block shook with the force of a shell that lodged in the work. The Pathfinder narrowly escaped the passage of this formidable missile as it entered; but when it exploded, Mabel could not suppress a shriek, for she supposed all over her head, whether animate or inanimate, destroyed. To increase her horror, her father shouted in a frantic voice to "charge!"

"Mabel," said Pathfinder, with his head at the trap, "this is true Mingo work—more noise than injury. The vagabonds have got the howitzer we took from the French, and have discharged it ag'in the block; but fortunately they have fired off the only shell we had, and there is an ind of its use for the present. There is some confusion among the stores up in this loft, but no one is hurt. Your uncle is still on the roof; and, as for myself, I've run the gauntlet of too many rifles to be skeary about such a thing as a howitzer, and that in Indian hands."

Mabel murmured her thanks, and tried to give all her attention to her father, whose efforts to rise were only counteracted by his debility. During the fearful minutes that succeeded, she was so much occupied with the care of the invalid that she scarcely heeded the clamor that reigned around her. Indeed, the uproar was so great, that, had not her thoughts been otherwise employed, confusion of faculties rather than alarm would probably have been the consequence.

Cap preserved his coolness admirably. He had a profound and increasing respect for the power of the savages, and even for the majesty of fresh water, it is true; but his apprehensions of the former proceeded more from his dread of being scalped and tortured than from any unmanly fear of death; and, as he was now on the deck of a house, if not on the deck of a ship, and knew that there was little danger of boarders, he moved about with a fearlessness and a rash exposure of his person that Pathfinder, had he been aware of the fact, would have been the first to condemn. Instead of keeping his body covered, agreeably to the usages of Indian warfare, he was seen on every part of the roof, dashing the water right and left, with the apparent steadiness and unconcern he would have manifested had he been a sail trimmer exercising his art in a battle afloat. His appearance was one of the causes of the extraordinary clamor among the assailants; who, unused to see their enemies so reckless, opened upon him with their tongues, like a pack that has the fox in view. Still he appeared to possess a charmed life; for, though the bullets whistled around him on every side, and his clothes were several times torn, nothing cut his skin. When the shell passed through the logs below, the old sailor dropped his bucket, waved his hat, and gave three cheers; in which heroic act he was employed as the dangerous missile exploded. This characteristic feat probably saved his life; for from that instant the Indians ceased to fire at him, and even to shoot their flaming arrows at the block, having taken up the notion simultaneously, and by common consent, that the "Saltwater" was mad; and it was a singular effect of their magnanimity never to lift a hand against those whom they imagined devoid of reason.

The conduct of Pathfinder was very different. Everything he did was regulated by the most exact calculation, the result of long experience and habitual thoughtfulness. His person was kept carefully out of a line with the loops, and the spot that he selected for his look-out was one quite removed from danger. This celebrated guide had often been known to lead forlorn hopes: he had once stood at the stake, suffering under the cruelties and taunts of savage ingenuity and savage ferocity without quailing; and legends of his exploits, coolness, and daring were

to be heard all along that extensive frontier, or wherever men
dwelt and men contended. But on this occasion, one who did
not know his history and character might have thought his
exceeding care and studied attention to self-preservation proceeded from an unworthy motive. But such a judge would not
have understood his subject; the Pathfinder bethought him of
Mabel, and of what might possibly be the consequences to that
poor girl should any casualty befall himself. But the recollection
rather quickened his intellect than changed his customary prudence. He was, in fact, one of those who was so unaccustomed
to fear, that he never bethought him of the constructions others
might put upon his conduct. But while in moments of danger
he acted with the wisdom of the serpent, it was also with the
simplicity of a child.

For the first ten minutes of the assault, Pathfinder never
raised the breech of his rifle from the floor, except when he
changed his own position, for he well knew that the bullets of
the enemy were thrown away upon the massive logs of the work;
and, as he had been at the capture of the howitzer, he felt certain that the savages had no other shell than the one found in
it when the piece was taken. There existed no reason, therefore,
to dread the fire of the assailants, except as a casual bullet
might find a passage through a loophole. One or two of these
accidents did occur, but the balls entered at an angle that deprived them of all chance of doing any injury so long as the
Indians kept near the block; and if discharged from a distance,
there was scarcely the possibility of one in a hundred's striking
the apertures. But when Pathfinder heard the sound of moccasined feet and the rustling of brush at the foot of the building,
he knew that the attempt to build a fire against the logs was
about to be renewed. He now summoned Cap from the roof,
where, indeed, all the danger had ceased, and directed him to
stand in readiness with his water at a hole immediately over the
spot assailed.

One less trained than our hero would have been in a hurry to
repel this dangerous attempt also, and might have resorted to
his means prematurely; not so with Pathfinder. His aim was
not only to extinguish the fire, about which he felt little apprehension, but to give the enemy a lesson that would render him
wary during the remainder of the night. In order to effect the

latter purpose, it became necessary to wait until the light of the intended conflagration should direct his aim, when he well knew that a very slight effort of his skill would suffice. The Iroquois were permitted to collect their heap of dried brush, to pile it against the block, to light it, and to return to their covers without molestation. All that Pathfinder would suffer Cap to do, was to roll a barrel filled with water to the hole immediately over the spot, in readiness to be used at the proper instant. That moment, however, did not arrive, in his judgment, until the blaze illuminated the surrounding bushes, and there had been time for his quick and practised eye to detect the forms of three or four lurking savages, who were watching the progress of the flames, with the cool indifference of men accustomed to look on human misery with apathy. Then, indeed, he spoke.

"Are you ready, friend Cap?" he asked. "The heat begins to strike through the crevices; and although these green logs are not of the fiery natur' of an ill-tempered man, they may be kindled into a blaze if one provokes them too much. Are you ready with the barrel? See that it has the right cut, and that none of the water is wasted."

"All ready!" answered Cap, in the manner in which a seaman replies to such a demand.

"Then wait for the word. Never be over-impatient in a critical time, nor fool-risky in a battle. Wait for the word."

While the Pathfinder was giving these directions, he was also making his own preparations; for he saw it was time to act. Killdeer was deliberately raised, pointed, and discharged. The whole process occupied about half a minute, and as the rifle was drawn in the eye of the marksman was applied to the hole.

"There is one riptyle the less," Pathfinder muttered to himself; "I've seen that vagabond afore, and know him to be a marciless devil. Well, well! the man acted according to his gifts, and he has been rewarded according to his gifts. One more of the knaves, and that will sarve the turn for to-night. When daylight appears, we may have hotter work."

All this time another rifle was being got ready; and as Pathfinder ceased, a second savage fell. This indeed sufficed; for, indisposed to wait for a third visitation from the same hand, the whole band, which had been crouching in the bushes around the block, ignorant of who was and who was not exposed to view, leaped from their covers and fled to different places for safety.

"Now, pour away, Master Cap," said Pathfinder; "I've made my mark on the blackguards; and we shall have no more fires lighted to-night."

"Scaldings!" cried Cap, upsetting the barrel, with a care that at once and completely extinguished the flames.

This ended the singular conflict; and the remainder of the night passed in peace. Pathfinder and Cap watched alternately, though neither can be said to have slept. Sleep indeed scarcely seemed necessary to them, for both were accustomed to protracted watchings; and there were seasons and times when the former appeared to be literally insensible to the demands of hunger and thirst and callous to the effects of fatigue.

Mabel watched by her father's pallet, and began to feel how much our happiness in this world depends even on things that are imaginary. Hitherto she had virtually lived without a father, the connection with her remaining parent being ideal rather than positive; but now that she was about to lose him, she thought for the moment that the world would be a void after his death, and that she could never be acquainted with happiness again.

CHAPTER XXV

There was a roaring in the wind all night;
  The rain came heavily, and fell in floods;
But now the sun is rising calm and bright;
  The birds are singing in the distant woods.
                                        WORDSWORTH

As THE light returned, Pathfinder and Cap ascended again to the roof, with a view to reconnoitre the state of things once more on the island. This part of the blockhouse had a low battlement around it, which afforded a considerable protection to those who stood in its centre; the intention having been to enable marksmen to lie behind it and to fire over its top. By making proper use, therefore, of these slight defences—slight as to height, though abundantly ample as far as they went—

the two look-outs commanded a pretty good view of the island, its covers excepted, and of most of the channels that led to the spot.

The gale was still blowing very fresh at south; and there were places in the river where its surface looked green and angry, though the wind had hardly sweep enough to raise the water into foam. The shape of the little island was nearly oval, and its greater length was from east to west. By keeping in the channels that washed it, in consequence of their several courses and of the direction of the gale, it would have been possible for a vessel to range past the island on either of its principal sides, and always to keep the wind very nearly abeam. These were the facts first noticed by Cap, and explained to his companion; for the hopes of both now rested on the chances of relief sent from Oswego. At this instant, while they stood gazing anxiously about them, Cap cried out, in his lusty, hearty manner,

"Sail, ho!"

Pathfinder turned quickly in the direction of his companion's face; and there, sure enough, was just visible the object of the old sailor's exclamation. The elevation enabled the two to overlook the low land of several of the adjacent islands; and the canvas of a vessel was seen through the bushes that fringed the shore of one that lay to the southward and westward. The stranger was under what seamen call low sail; but so great was the power of the wind, that her white outlines were seen flying past the openings of the verdure with the velocity of a fast-travelling horse—resembling a cloud driving in the heavens.

"That cannot be Jasper," said Pathfinder in disappointment; for he did not recognize the cutter of his friend in the swift-passing object. "No, no, the lad is behind the hour; and that is some craft which the Frenchers have sent to aid their friends, the accursed Mingos."

"This time you are out in your reckoning, friend Pathfinder, if you never were before," returned Cap in a manner that had lost none of its dogmatism by the critical circumstances in which they were placed. "Fresh water or salt, that is the head of the *Scud's* mainsail, for it is cut with a smaller gore than common; and then you can see that the gaff has been fished— quite neatly done, I admit, but fished."

"I can see none of this, I confess," answered Pathfinder, to whom even the terms of his companion were Greek.

"No! Well, I own that surprises me, for I thought *your* eyes could see anything! Now to me nothing is plainer than that gore and that fish; and I must say, my honest friend, that in your place I should apprehend that my sight was beginning to fail."

"If Jasper is truly coming, I shall apprehend but little. We can make good the block against the whole Mingo nation for the next eight or ten hours; and with Eau-douce to cover the retreat, I shall despair of nothing. God send that the lad may not run alongside of the bank, and fall into an ambushment, as befell the Sergeant!"

"Ay, there's the danger. There ought to have been signals concerted, and an anchorage-ground buoyed out, and even a quarantine station or a lazaretto would have been useful, could we have made these Minks-ho respect the laws. If the lad fetches up, as you say, anywhere in the neighborhood of this island, we may look upon the cutter as lost. And, after all, Master Pathfinder, ought we not to set down this same Jasper as a secret ally of the French, rather than as a friend of our own? I know the Sergeant views the matter in that light; and I must say this whole affair looks like treason."

"We shall soon know, we shall soon know, Master Cap; for there, indeed, comes the cutter clear of the other island, and five minutes must settle the matter. It would be no more than fair, however, if we could give the boy some sign in the way of warning. It is not right that he should fall into the trap without a notice that it has been laid."

Anxiety and suspense, notwithstanding, prevented either from attempting to make any signal. It was not easy, truly, to see how it could be done; for the *Scud* came foaming through the channel, on the weather side of the island, at a rate that scarcely admitted of the necessary time. Nor was any one visible on her deck to make signs to; even her helm seemed deserted, though her course was as steady as her progress was rapid.

Cap stood in silent admiration of a spectacle so unusual. But, as the *Scud* drew nearer, his practised eye detected the helm in play by means of tiller-ropes, though the person who steered was concealed. As the cutter had weatherboards of some little height, the mystery was explained, no doubt remaining that her people lay behind the latter, in order to be protected from the rifles of the enemy. As this fact showed that no force beyond that of the small crew could be on board, Pathfinder received his companion's explanation with an ominous shake of the head.

"This proves that the Sarpent has not reached Oswego," said he, "and that we are not to expect succor from the garrison. I hope Lundie has not taken it into his head to displace the lad, for Jasper Western would be a host of himself in such a strait. We three, Master Cap, ought to make a manful warfare: you, as a seaman, to keep up the intercourse with the cutter; Jasper, as a laker who knows all that is necessary to be done on the water; and I, with gifts that are as good as any among the Mingos, let me be what I may in other particulars. I say we ought to make a manful fight in Mabel's behalf."

"That we ought, and that we will," answered Cap heartily; for he began to have more confidence in the security of his scalp now that he saw the sun again. "I set down the arrival of the *Scud* as one circumstance, and the chances of Oh-deuce's honesty as another. This Jasper is a young man of prudence, you find; for he keeps a good offing, and seems determined to know how matters stand on the island before he ventures to bring up."

"I have it! I have it!" exclaimed Pathfinder, with exultation. "There lies the canoe of the Sarpent on the cutter's deck; and the chief has got on board, and no doubt has given a true account of our condition; for, unlike a Mingo, a Delaware is sartain to get a story right, or to hold his tongue."

"That canoe may not belong to the cutter," said the captious seaman. "Oh-deuce had one on board when he sailed."

"Very true, friend Cap; but if you know your sails and masts by your gores and fishes, I know my canoes and my paths by frontier knowledge. If you can see new cloth in a sail, I can see new bark in a canoe. That is the boat of the Sarpent, and the noble fellow has struck off for the garrison as soon as he found the block beseiged, has fallen in with the *Scud*, and, after telling his story, has brought the cutter down here to see what can be done. The Lord grant that Jasper Western be still on board her!"

"Yes, yes; it might not be amiss; for, traitor or loyal, the lad has a handy way with him in a gale, it must be owned."

"And in coming over waterfalls!" said Pathfinder, nudging the ribs of his companion with an elbow, and laughing in his silent but hearty manner. "We will give the boy his due, though he scalps us all with his own hand."

The *Scud* was now so near, that Cap made no reply. The scene, just at that instant, was so peculiar, that it merits a particular description, which may also aid the reader in forming a more accurate notion of the picture we wish to draw.

The gale was still blowing violently. Many of the smaller trees bowed their tops, as if ready to descend to the earth, while the rushing of the wind through the branches of the groves resembled the roar of distant chariots.

The air was filled with leaves, which, at that late season, were readily driven from their stems, and flew from island to island like flights of birds. With this exception, the spot seemed silent as the grave. That the savages still remained, was to be inferred from the fact that their canoes, together with the boats of the 55th, lay in a group in the little cove that had been selected as a harbor. Otherwise, not a sign of their presence was to be detected. Though taken entirely by surprise by the cutter, the sudden return of which was altogether unlooked-for, so uniform and inbred were their habits of caution while on the war-path, that the instant an alarm was given every màn had taken to his cover with the instinct and cunning of a fox seeking his hole. The same stillness reigned in the blockhouse; for though Pathfinder and Cap could command a view of the channel, they took the precaution necessary to lie concealed. The unusual absence of anything like animal life on board the *Scud*, too, was still more remarkable. As the Indians witnessed her apparently undirected movements, a feeling of awe gained a footing among them, and some of the boldest of their party began to distrust the issue of an expedition that had commenced so prosperously. Even Arrowhead, accustomed as he was to intercourse with the whites on both sides of the lakes, fancied there was something ominous in the appearance of this unmanned vessel, and he would gladly at that moment have been landed again on the main.

In the meantime the progress of the cutter was steady and rapid. She held her way mid-channel, now inclining to the gusts, and now rising again, like the philosopher that bends to the calamities of life to resume his erect attitude as they pass away, but always piling the water beneath her bows in foam. Although she was under so very short canvas, her velocity was great, and there could not have elapsed ten minutes between the time when her sails were first seen glancing past the trees and bushes in the distance and the moment when she was abreast of the blockhouse. Cap and Pathfinder leaned forward, as the cutter came beneath their eyrie, eager to get a better view of her deck, when, to the delight of both, Jasper Eau-douce sprang upon his feet and gave three hearty cheers. Regardless of all risk, Cap leaped upon the rampart of logs and returned the greeting, cheer for cheer. Happily, the policy of the enemy saved the latter; for they still lay quiet, not a rifle being discharged. On the other hand, Pathfinder kept in view the useful, utterly disregarding the mere dramatic part of warfare. The moment he beheld his friend Jasper, he called out to him with stentorian lungs—

"Stand by us, lad, and the day's our own! Give 'em a grist in yonder bushes, and you'll put 'em up like partridges."

Part of this reached Jasper's ears, but most was borne off to leeward on the wings of the wind. By the time this was said, the *Scud* had driven past, and in the next moment she was hid from view by the grove in which the blockhouse was partially concealed.

Two anxious minutes succeeded; but, at the expiration of that brief space, the sails were again gleaming through the trees, Jasper having wore, jibed, and hauled up under the lee of the island on the other tack. The wind was free enough, as has been already explained, to admit of this manœuvre; and the cutter, catching the current under her lee bow, was breasted up to her course in a way that showed she would come out to windward of the island again without any difficulty. This whole evolution was made with the greatest facility, not a sheet being touched, the sails trimming themselves, the rudder alone controlling the admirable machine. The object appeared to be a reconnoissance. When, however, the *Scud* had made the circuit of the entire island, and had again got her weatherly position in the channel by which she had first approached, her helm was put down, and she tacked. The noise of the mainsail flapping when it filled, close-reefed as it was, sounded like the report of a gun, and Cap trembled lest the seams should open.

"His Majesty gives good canvas, it must be owned," muttered the old seaman; "and it must be owned, too, that boy handles his boat as if he were thoroughly bred! D— me, Master Pathfinder, if I believe, after all that has been reported in the matter, that this Mister Oh-deuce got his trade on this bit of fresh water."

"He did; yes, he did. He never saw the ocean, and has come by his calling altogether up here on Ontario. I have often thought he has a nat'ral gift in the way of schooners and sloops, and have respected him accordingly. As for treason and lying and black-hearted vices, friend Cap, Jasper Western is as free as the most virtuousest of the Delaware warriors; and if you crave to see a truly honest man, you must go among that tribe to discover him."

"There he comes round!" exclaimed the delighted Cap, the *Scud* at this moment filling on her original tack; "and now we shall see what the boy would be at; he cannot mean to keep running up and down these passages, like a girl footing it through a country-dance."

The *Scud* now kept so much away, that for a moment the two observers on the blockhouse feared Jasper meant to come-to; and the savages, in their lairs, gleamed out upon her with the sort of exultation that the crouching tiger may be supposed to feel as he sees his unconscious victim approach his bed. But Jasper had no such intention: familiar with the shore, and acquainted with the depth of water on every part of the island, he well knew that the *Scud* might be run against the bank with impunity, and he ventured fearlessly so near, that, as he passed through the little cove, he swept the two boats of the soldiers from their fastenings and forced them out into the channel, towing them with the cutter. As all the canoes were fastened to the two Dunham boats, by this bold and successful attempt the savages were at once deprived of the means of quitting the island, unless by swimming, and they appeared to be instantly aware of the very important fact. Rising in a body, they filled the air with yells, and poured in a harmless fire. While up in this unguarded manner, two rifles were discharged by their adversaries. One came from the summit of the block, and an Iroquois fell dead in his tracks, shot through the brain. The other came from the *Scud*. The last was the piece of the Delaware, but, less true than that of his friend, it only maimed an enemy for life. The people of the *Scud* shouted, and the savages sank again, to a man, as if it might be into the earth.

"That was the Sarpent's voice," said Pathfinder, as soon as the second piece was discharged. "I know the crack of his rifle as well as I do that of Killdeer. 'Tis a good barrel, though not sartain death. Well, well, with Chingachgook and Jasper on the water, and you and I in the block, friend Cap, it will be hard if we don't teach these Mingo scamps the rationality of a fight."

All this time the *Scud* was in motion. As soon as she had reached the end of the island, Jasper sent his prizes adrift; and they went down before the wind until they stranded on a point half a mile to leeward. He then wore, and came stemming the current again, through the other passage. Those on the summit of the block could now perceive that something was in agitation on the deck of the *Scud;* and, to their great delight, just as the cutter came abreast of the principal cove, on the spot where most of the enemy lay, the howitzer which composed her sole armament was unmasked, and a shower of case-shot was sent hissing into the bushes. A bevy of quail would not have risen quicker than this unexpected discharge of iron hail put up the Iroquois; when a second savage fell by a messenger sent from Killdeer, and another went limping away by a visit from the rifle of Chingachgook. New covers were immediately found, however; and each party seemed to prepare for the renewal of the strife in another form. But the appearance of June, bearing a white flag, and accompanied by the French officer and Muir, stayed the hands of all, and was the forerunner of another parley.

The negotiation that followed was held beneath the blockhouse; and so near it as at once to put those who were uncovered completely at the mercy of Pathfinder's unerring aim. Jasper anchored directly abeam; and the howitzer, too, was kept trained upon the negotiators: so that the besieged and their friends, with the exception of the man who held the match, had no hesitation about exposing their persons. Chingachgook alone lay in ambush; more, however, from habit than distrust.

"You've triumphed, Pathfinder," called out the Quartermaster, "and Captain Sanglier has come himself to offer terms. You'll no' be denying a brave enemy honorable retreat, when he has fought ye fairly, and done all the credit he could to king and country. Ye are too loyal a subject yourself to visit loyalty and fidelity with a heavy judgment. I am authorized to offer, on the part of the enemy, an evacuation of the island, a mutual exchange of prisoners, and a restoration of scalps. In the absence of baggage and artillery, little more can be done."

As the conversation was necessarily carried on in a high key, both on account of the wind and of the distance, all that was said was heard equally by those in the block and those in the cutter.

"What do you say to that, Jasper?" called out Pathfinder. "You hear the proposal. Shall we let the vagabonds go? or shall we mark them, as they mark their sheep in the settlements, that we may know them again?"

"What has befallen Mabel Dunham?" demanded the young man, with a frown on his handsome face, that was visible even to those on the block. "If a hair of her head has been touched, it will go hard with the whole Iroquois tribe."

"Nay, nay, she is safe below, nursing a dying parent, as becomes her sex. We owe no grudge on account of the Sergeant's hurt, which comes of lawful warfare; and as for Mabel——"

"She is here!" exclaimed the girl herself, who had mounted to the roof the moment she found the direction things were taking—"she is here! and, in the name of our holy religion, and of that God whom we profess to worship in common, let there be no more bloodshed! Enough has been spilt already; and if these men will go away, Pathfinder—if they will depart peaceably, Jasper—oh, do not detain one of them! My poor father is approaching his end, and it were better that he should draw his last breath in peace with the world. Go, go, Frenchmen and Indians! we are no longer your enemies, and will harm none of you."

"Tut, tut, Magnet!" put in Cap; "this sounds religious, perhaps, or like a book of poetry; but it does not sound like common sense. The enemy is just ready to strike; Jasper is anchored with his broadside to bear, and, no doubt, with springs on his cables; Pathfinder's eye and hand are as true as the needle; and we shall get prize-money, head-money, and honor in the bargain, if you will not interfere for the next half-hour."

"Well," said Pathfinder, "I incline to Mabel's way of thinking. There *has* been enough blood shed to answer our purpose and to sarve the king; and as for honor, in that meaning, it will do better for young ensigns and recruits than for cool-headed, obsarvant Christian men. There is honor in doing what's right, and unhonor in doing what's wrong; and I think it wrong to take the life even of a Mingo, without a useful end in view, I do; and right to hear reason at all times. So, Lieutenant Muir, let us know what your friends the Frenchers and Indians have to say for themselves."

"My friends!" said Muir, starting; "you'll no' be calling the king's enemies my friends, Pathfinder, because the fortune of war has thrown me into their hands? Some of the greatest warriors, both of ancient and modern times, have been prisoners of war; and yon is Master Cap, who can testify whether we did not do all that men could devise to escape the calamity."

"Ay, ay," drily answered Cap; "escape is the proper word. We ran below and hid ourselves, and so discreetly, that we might have remained in the hole to this hour, had it not been for the necessity of re-stowing the bread lockers. You burrowed on that occasion, Quartermaster, as handily as a fox; and how the d—l you knew so well where to find the spot is a matter of wonder to me. A regular skulk on board ship does not trail aft more readily when the jib is to be stowed, than you went into that same hole."

"And did ye no' follow? There are moments in a man's life when reason ascends to instinct——"

"And men descend into holes," interrupted Cap, laughing in his boisterous way, while Pathfinder chimed in, in his peculiar manner. Even Jasper, though still filled with concern for Mabel, was obliged to smile. "They say the d—l wouldn't make a sailor if he didn't look aloft; and now it seems he'll not make a soldier if he doesn't look below!"

This burst of merriment, though it was anything but agreeable to Muir, contributed largely towards keeping the peace. Cap fancied he had said a thing much better than common; and that disposed him to yield his own opinion on the main point, so long as he got the good opinion of his companions on his novel claim to be a wit. After a short discussion, all the savages on the island were collected in a body, without arms, at the distance of a hundred yards from the block, and under the gun of the *Scud;* while Pathfinder descended to the door of the blockhouse and settled the terms on which the island was to be finally evacuated by the enemy. Considering all the circumstances, the conditions were not very discreditable to either party. The Indians were compelled to give up all their arms, even to their knives and tomahawks, as a measure of precaution, their force being still quadruple that of their foes. The French officer, Monsieur Sanglier, as he was usually styled, and chose to call himself, remonstrated against this act as one likely to reflect more discredit on his command than any other part of the affair; but Pathfinder, who had witnessed one or two Indian massacres, and knew how valueless pledges became when put in opposition to interest where a savage was concerned, was obdurate. The second stipulation was of nearly the same importance. It compelled Captain Sanglier to give up all his prisoners, who had been kept well guarded in the very hole or cave in which Cap and Muir had taken refuge. When these men were produced, four of them were found to be unhurt; they had fallen merely to save their lives, a common artifice in that species of warfare; and of the remainder, two were so slightly injured as not to be unfit for service. As they brought their muskets with them, this addition to his force immediately put Pathfinder at his ease; for, having collected all the arms of the enemy in the blockhouse, he directed these men to take possession of the building, stationing a regular sentinel at the door. The remainder of the soldiers were dead, the badly wounded having been instantly despatched in order to obtain the much-coveted scalps.

As soon as Jasper was made acquainted with the terms, and the preliminaries had been so far observed as to render it safe for him to be absent, he got the *Scud* under way; and, running down to the point where the boats had stranded, he took them in tow again, and, making a few stretches, brought them into the leeward passage. Here all the savages instantly embarked, when Jasper took the boats in tow a third time, and, running off before the wind, he soon set them adrift full a mile to leeward of the island. The Indians were furnished with but a single oar in each boat to steer with, the young sailor well knowing that by keeping before the wind they would land on the shores of Canada in the course of the morning.

Captain Sanglier, Arrowhead, and June alone remained, when this disposition had been made of the rest of the party: the former having certain papers to draw up and sign with Lieutenant Muir, who in his eyes possessed the virtues which are attached to a commission; and the latter preferring, for reasons of his own, not to depart in company with his late friends, the Iroquois. Canoes were detained for the departure of these three, when the proper moment should arrive.

In the meantime, or while the *Scud* was running down with the boats in tow, Pathfinder and Cap, aided by proper assistants, busied themselves with preparing a breakfast; most of the party not having eaten for four-and-twenty hours. The brief space that passed in this manner before the *Scud* came-to again was little interrupted by discourse, though Pathfinder found leisure to pay a visit to the Sergeant, to say a few friendly words to Mabel, and to give such directions as he thought might smooth the passage of the dying man. As for Mabel herself, he insisted on her taking some light refreshment; and, there no longer existing any motive for keeping it there, he had the guard removed from the block, in order that the daughter might have no impediment to her attentions to her father. These little arrangements completed, our hero returned to the fire, around which he found all the remainder of the party assembled, including Jasper.

CHAPTER XXVI

> You saw but sorrow in its waning form;
> A working sea remaining from a storm,
> Where now the weary waves roll o'er the deep,
> And faintly murmur ere they fall asleep.   DRYDEN

MEN accustomed to a warfare like that we have been describing are not apt to be much under the influence of the tender feelings while still in the field. Notwithstanding their habits, however, more than one heart was with Mabel in the block, while the incidents we are about to relate were in the course of occurrence; and even the indispensable meal was less relished by the hardiest of the soldiers than it might have been had not the Sergeant been so near his end.

As Pathfinder returned from the block, he was met by Muir, who led him aside in order to hold a private discourse. The manner of the Quartermaster had that air of supererogatory courtesy about it which almost invariably denotes artifice; for, while physiognomy and phrenology are but lame sciences at the best, and perhaps lead to as many false as right conclusions, we hold that there is no more infallible evidence of insincerity of purpose, short of overt acts, than a face that smiles when there is no occasion, and the tongue that is out of measure smooth. Muir had much of this manner in common, mingled with an apparent frankness that his Scottish intonation of voice, Scottish accent, and Scottish modes of expression were singularly adapted to sustain. He owed his preferment, indeed, to a long-exercised deference to Lundie and his family; for, while the Major himself was much too acute to be the dupe of one so much his inferior in real talents and attainments, most persons are accustomed to make liberal concessions to the flatterer, even while they distrust his truth and are perfectly aware of his motives. On the present occasion, the contest in skill was between two men as completely the opposites of each other in all the leading essentials of character as very well could be. Pathfinder was as simple as the Quartermaster was practised; he was as sincere as the other was false, and as direct as the last was tortuous. Both were cool and calculating, and both were brave, though in different modes and degrees; Muir never exposing his person except for effect, while the guide included fear among the rational passions, or as a sensation to be deferred to only when good might come of it.

"My dearest friend," Muir commenced—"for ye'll be dearer to us all, by seventy and sevenfold, after your late conduct than ever ye were—ye've just established yourself in this late transaction. It's true that they'll not be making ye a commissioned officer, for that species of prefairment is not much in your line, nor much in your wishes, I'm thinking; but as a guide, and a counsellor, and a loyal subject, and an expert marksman, yer renown may be said to be full. I doubt if the commander-in-chief will carry away with him from America as much credit as will fall to yer share, and ye ought just to set down in content and enjoy yoursal' for the remainder of yer days. Get married, man, without delay, and look to your precious happiness; for ye've no occasion to look any longer to your glory. Take Mabel Dunham, for Heaven's sake, to your bosom, and ye'll have both a bonnie bride and a bonnie reputation."

"Why, Quartermaster, this is a new piece of advice to come from your mouth. They've told me I had a rival in you."

"And ye had, man; and a formidable one, too, I can tell you —one that has never yet courted in vain, and yet one that has courted five times. Lundie twits me with four, and I deny the charge; but he little thinks the truth would outdo even his arithmetic. Yes, yes, ye had a rival, Pathfinder; but ye've one no longer in me. Ye've my hearty wishes for yer success with Mabel; and were the honest Sergeant likely to survive, ye might rely on my good word with him, too, for a certainty."

"I feel your friendship, Quartermaster, I feel your friendship, though I have no great need of any favor with Sergeant Dunham, who has long been my friend. I believe we may look upon the matter to be as sartain as most things in war-time; for, Mabel and her father consenting, the whole 55th couldn't very well put a stop to it. Ah's me! the poor father will scarcely live to see what his heart has so long been set upon."

"But he'll have the consolation of knowing it will come to pass, in dying. Oh, it's a great relief, Pathfinder, for the parting spirit to feel certain that the beloved ones left behind will be well provided for after its departure. All the Mistress Muirs have duly expressed that sentiment with their dying breaths."

"All your wives, Quartermaster, have been likely to feel this consolation."

"Out upon ye, man! I'd no' thought ye such a wag. Well, well; pleasant words make no heart-burnings between auld fri'nds. If I cannot espouse Mabel, ye'll no object to my esteeming her, and speaking well of her, and of yoursal', too, on all suitable occasions and in all companies. But, Pathfinder, ye'll easily understan' that a poor deevil who loses such a bride will probably stand in need of some consolation?"

"Quite likely, quite likely, Quartermaster," returned the simple-minded guide; "I know the loss of Mabel would be found heavy to be borne by myself. It may bear hard on your feelings to see us married; but the death of the Sergeant will be likely to put it off, and you'll have time to think more manfully of it, you will."

"I'll bear up against it; yes, I'll bear up against it, though my heart-strings crack! and ye might help me, man, by giving me something to do. Ye'll understand that this expedition has been of a very peculiar nature; for here am I, bearing the king's commission, just a volunteer, as it might be; while a mere orderly has had the command. I've submitted for various reasons, though my blood has boiled to be in authority, while ye war' battling for the honor of the country and his Majesty's rights——"

"Quartermaster," interrupted the guide, "you fell so early into the enemy's hands that your conscience ought to be easily satisfied on that score; so take my advice, and say nothing about it."

"That's just my opinion, Pathfinder; we'll all say nothing about it. Sergeant Dunham is *hors de combat*——"

"Anan?" said the guide.

"Why, the Sergeant can command no longer, and it will hardly do to leave a corporal at the head of a victorious party like this; for flowers that will bloom in a garden will die on a heath; and I was just thinking I would claim the authority that belongs to one who holds a lieutenant's commission. As for the men, they'll no dare to raise any objection; and as for yoursal', my dear friend, now that ye've so much honor, and Mabel, and the consciousness of having done yer duty, which is more precious than all, I expect to find an ally rather than one to oppose the plan."

"As for commanding the soldiers of the 55th, Lieutenant, it is your right, I suppose, and no one here will be likely to gainsay it; though you've been a prisoner of war, and there are men who might stand out ag'in giving up their authority to a prisoner released by their own deeds. Still no one here will be likely to say anything hostile to your wishes."

"That's just it, Pathfinder; and when I come to draw up the report of our success against the boats, and the defence of the block, together with the general operations, including the capitulation, ye'll no' find any omission of your claims and merits."

"Tut for my claims and merits, Quartermaster! Lundie knows what I am in the forest and what I am in the fort; and the General knows better than he. No fear of me; tell your own story, only taking care to do justice by Mabel's father, who, in one sense, is the commanding officer at this very moment."

Muir expressed his entire satisfaction with this arrangement, as well as his determination to do justice by all, when the two went to the group assembled round the fire. Here the Quartermaster began, for the first time since leaving Oswego, to assume some of the authority that might properly be supposed to belong to his rank. Taking the remaining corporal aside, he distinctly told that functionary that he must in future be regarded as one holding the king's commission, and directed him to acquaint his subordinates with the new state of things. This change in the dynasty was effected without any of the usual symptoms of a revolution; for, as all well understood the Lieutenant's legal claims to command, no one felt disposed to dispute his orders. For reasons best known to themselves, Lundie and the Quartermaster had originally made a different disposition; and now, for reasons of his own, the latter had seen fit to change it. This was reasoning enough for soldiers, though the hurt received by Sergeant Dunham would have sufficiently explained the circumstance had an explanation been required.

All this time Captain Sanglier was looking after his own breakfast with the resignation of a philosopher, the coolness of a veteran, the ingenuity and science of a Frenchman, and the voracity of an ostrich. This person had now been in the colony some thirty years, having left France in some such situation in his own army as Muir filled in the 55th. An iron constitution, perfect obduracy of feeling, a certain address well suited to manage savages, and an indomitable courage, had early pointed him out to the commander-in-chief as a suitable agent to be employed in directing the military operations of his Indian allies. In this capacity, then, he had risen to the titular rank of captain; and with his promotion had acquired a portion of the habits and opinions of his associates with a facility and an adaptation of self which are thought in America to be peculiar to his countrymen. He had often led parties of the Iroquois in their predatory expeditions; and his conduct on such occasions exhibited the contradictory results of both alleviating the misery produced by this species of warfare, and of augmenting it by the broader views and greater resources of civilization. In other words, he planned enterprises that, in their importance and consequences, much exceeded the usual policy of the Indians, and then stepped in to lessen some of the evils of his own creating. In short, he was an adventurer whom circumstances had thrown into a situation where the callous qualities of men of his class might readily show themselves for good or for evil; and he was not of a character to baffle fortune by any ill-timed squeamishness on the score of early impressions, or to trifle with her liberality by unnecessarily provoking her frowns through wanton cruelty. Still, as his name was unavoidably connected with many of the excesses committed by his parties, he was generally considered in the American provinces a wretch who delighted in bloodshed, and who found his greatest happiness in tormenting the helpless and the innocent; and the name of Sanglier, which was a sobriquet of his own adopting, or of Flint Heart, as he was usually termed on the borders, had got to be as terrible to the women and children of that part of the country as those of Butler and Brandt became at a later day.

The meeting between Pathfinder and Sanglier bore some resemblance to that celebrated interview between Wellington and Blucher which has been so often and graphically told. It took place at the fire; and the parties stood earnestly regarding each other for more than a minute without speaking. Each felt that in the other he saw a formidable foe; and each felt, while he ought to treat the other with the manly liberality due to a warrior, that there was little in common between them in the way of character as well as of interests. One served for money and preferment; the other, because his life had been cast in the wilderness, and the land of his birth needed his arm and experience. The desire of rising above his present situation never disturbed the tranquillity of Pathfinder; nor had he ever known an ambitious thought, as ambition usually betrays itself, until he became acquainted with Mabel. Since then, indeed, distrust of himself, reverence for her, and the wish to place her in a situation above that which he then filled, had caused him some uneasy moments; but the directness and simplicity of his character had early afforded the required relief; and he soon came to feel that the woman who would not hesitate to accept him for her husband would not scruple to share his fortunes, however humble. He respected Sanglier as a brave warrior; and he had far too much of that liberality which is the result of practical knowledge to believe half of what he had heard to his prejudice, for the most bigoted and illiberal on every subject are usually those who know nothing about it; but he could not approve of his selfishness, cold-blooded calculations, and least of all of the manner in which he forgot his "white gifts," to adopt those that were purely "red." On the other hand, Pathfinder was a riddle to Captain Sanglier. The latter could not comprehend the other's motives; he had often heard of his disinterestedness, justice, and truth; and in several instances they had led him into grave errors, on that principle by which a frank and open-mouthed diplomatist is said to keep his secrets better than one that is close-mouthed and wily.

After the two heroes had gazed at each other in the manner mentioned, Monsieur Sanglier touched his cap; for the rudeness of a border life had not entirely destroyed the courtesy of manner he had acquired in youth, nor extinguished that appearance of *bonhomie* which seems inbred in a Frenchman.

"Monsieur le Pathfinder," said he, with a very decided accent, though with a friendly smile, "*un militaire* honor *le courage, et la loyauté.* You speak Iroquois?"

"Ay, I understand the language of the riptyles, and can get along with it if there's occasion," returned the literal and truth-telling guide; "but it's neither a tongue nor a tribe to my taste. Wherever you find the Mingo blood, in my opinion, Master Flinty-heart, you find a knave. Well, I've seen you often, though it was in battle; and I must say it was always in the van. You must know most of our bullets by sight?"

"Nevvair, sair, your own; *une balle* from your honorable hand be sairtaine deat'. You kill my best warrior on some island."

"That may be, that may be; though I daresay, if the truth

was known, they would turn out to be great rascals. No offence to you, Master Flinty-heart, but you keep desperate evil company."

"Yes, sair," returned the Frenchman, who, bent on saying that which was courteous himself, and comprehending with difficulty, was disposed to think he received a compliment, "you too good. But *un brave* always *comme çà*. What that mean? ha! what that *jeune homme* do?"

The hand and eye of Captain Sanglier directed the look of Pathfinder to the opposite side of the fire, where Jasper, just at that moment, had been rudely seized by two of the soldiers, who were binding his arms under the direction of Muir.

"What does that mean, indeed?" cried the guide, stepping forward and shoving the two subordinates away with a power of muscle that would not be denied. "Who has the heart to do this to Jasper Eau-douce? and who has the boldness to do it before my eyes?"

"It is by my orders, Pathfinder," answered the Quartermaster, "and I command it on my own responsibility. Ye'll no' tak' on yourself to dispute the legality of orders given by one who bears the king's commission to the king's soldiers?"

"I'd dispute the king's words, if they came from the king's own mouth, did he say that Jasper desarves this. Has not the lad just saved all our scalps, taken us from defeat, and given us victory? No, no, Lieutenant; if this is the first use that you make of your authority, I, for one, will not respect it."

"This savors a little of insubordination," answered Muir; "but we can bear much from Pathfinder. It is true this Jasper has *seemed* to serve us in this affair, but we ought not to overlook past transactions. Did not Major Duncan himself denounce him to Sergeant Dunham before we left the post? Have we not seen sufficient with our own eyes to make sure of having been betrayed? and is it not natural, and almost necessary, to believe that this young man has been the traitor? Ah, Pathfinder! ye'll no' be making yourself a great statesman or a great captain if you put too much faith in appearances. Lord bless me! Lord bless me! if I do not believe, could the truth be come at, as you often say yourself, Pathfinder, that hypocrisy is a more common vice than even envy, and that's the bane of human nature."

Captain Sanglier shrugged his shoulders; then he looked earnestly from Jasper towards the Quartermaster, and from the Quartermaster towards Jasper.

"I care not for your envy, or your hypocrisy, or even 'for your human natur'," returned Pathfinder. "Jasper Eau-douce is my friend; Jasper Eau-douce is a brave lad, and an honest lad, and a loyal lad; and no man of the 55th shall lay hands on him, short of Lundie's own orders, while I'm in the way to prevent it. You may have authority over your soldiers; but you have none over Jasper and me, Master Muir."

"*Bon!*" ejaculated Sanglier, the sound partaking equally of the energies of the throat and of the nose.

"Will ye no' hearken to reason, Pathfinder? Ye'll no' be forgetting our suspicions and judgments; and here is another circumstance to augment and aggravate them all. Ye can see this little bit of bunting; well, where should it be found but by Mabel Dunham, on the branch of a tree on this very island, just an hour or so before the attack of the enemy; and if ye'll be at the trouble to look at the fly of the *Scud's* ensign, ye'll just say that the cloth has been cut from out it. Circumstantial evidence was never stronger."

"*Ma foi, c'est un peu fort, ceci,*" growled Sanglier between his teeth.

"Talk to me of no ensigns and signals when I know the heart," continued the Pathfinder. "Jasper has the gift of honesty; and it is too rare a gift to be trifled with, like a Mingo's conscience. No, no; off hands, or we shall see which can make the stoutest battle; you and your men of the 55th, or the Serpent here, and Killdeer, with Jasper and his crew. You overrate your force, Lieutenant Muir, as much as you underrate Eau-douce's truth."

"*Très bon!*"

"Well, if I must speak plainly, Pathfinder, I e'en must. Captain Sanglier here and Arrowhead, this brave Tuscarora, have both informed me that this unfortunate boy is the traitor. After such testimony you can no longer oppose my right to correct him, as well as the necessity of the act."

"*Scélérat,*" muttered the Frenchman.

"Captain Sanglier is a brave soldier, and will not gainsay the

conduct of an honest sailor," put in Jasper. "Is there any
traitor here, Captain Flinty-heart?"

"Ay," added Muir, "let him speak out then, since ye wish it,
unhappy youth! that the truth may be known. I only hope
that ye may escape the last punishment when a court will be
sitting on your misdeeds. How is it, Captain; do ye, or do ye
not, see a traitor amang us?"

"*Oui*—yes, sair—*bien sûr*."

"Too much lie!" said Arrowhead in a voice of thunder, striking the breast of Muir with the back of his own hand in a sort
of ungovernable gesture; "where my warriors?—where Yengeese scalp? Too much lie!"

Muir wanted not for personal courage, nor for a certain sense
of personal honor. The violence which had been intended only
for a gesture he mistook for a blow; for conscience was suddenly aroused within him, and he stepped back a pace, extending his hand towards a gun. His face was livid with rage, and
his countenance expressed the fell intention of his heart. But
Arrowhead was too quick for him; with a wild glance of the eye
the Tuscarora looked about him; then thrust a hand beneath
his own girdle, drew forth a concealed knife, and, in the twin-
kling of an eye, buried it in the body of the Quartermaster to
the handle. As the latter fell at his feet, gazing into his face
with the vacant stare of one surprised by death, Sanglier took
a pinch of snuff, and said in a calm voice—

"*Voilà l'affaire finie; mais,*" shrugging his shoulders, "*ce
n'est qu'un scélérat de moins.*"

The act was too sudden to be prevented; and when Arrowhead, uttering a yell, bounded into the bushes, the white men
were too confounded to follow. Chingachgook, however, was
more collected; and the bushes had scarcely closed on the passing body of the Tuscarora than they were again opened by
that of the Delaware in full pursuit.

Jasper Western spoke French fluently, and the words and
manner of Sanglier struck him.

"Speak, Monsieur," said he in English; "*am* I the traitor?"

"*Le voilà,*" answered the cool Frenchman, "dat is our *espion*
—our *agent*—our friend—*ma foi—c'était un grand scélérat—
voici.*"

While speaking, Sanglier bent over the dead body, and thrust his hand into a pocket of the Quartermaster, out of which he drew a purse. Emptying the contents on the ground, several double-louis rolled towards the soldiers, who were not slow in picking them up. Casting the purse from him in contempt, the soldier of fortune turned towards the soup he had been preparing with so much care, and, finding it to his liking, he began to break his fast with an air of indifference that the most stoical Indian warrior might have envied.

CHAPTER XXVII

The only amaranthian flower on earth
Is virtue; the only lasting treasure, truth.   COWPER

THE reader must imagine some of the occurrences that followed the sudden death of Muir. While his body was in the hands of his soldiers, who laid it decently aside, and covered it with a greatcoat, Chingachgook silently resumed his place at the fire, and both Sanglier and Pathfinder remarked that he carried a fresh and bleeding scalp at his girdle. No one asked any questions; and the former, although perfectly satisfied that Arrowhead had fallen, manifested neither curiosity nor feeling. He continued calmly eating his soup, as if the meal had been tranquil as usual. There was something of pride and of an assumed indifference to fate, imitated from the Indians, in all this; but there was more that really resulted from practice, habitual self-command, and constitutional hardihood. With Pathfinder the case was a little different in feeling, though much the same in appearance. He disliked Muir, whose smooth-tongued courtesy was little in accordance with his own frank and ingenuous nature; but he had been shocked at his unexpected and violent death, though accustomed to similar scenes, and he had been surprised at the exposure of his treachery. With a view to ascertain the extent of the latter, as soon as the body was removed, he began to question the Captain on the subject. The latter, having no particular motive for secrecy now that his agent was dead, in the course of the breakfast revealed the following circumstances, which will serve to clear up some of the minor incidents of our tale.

Soon after the 55th appeared on the frontiers, Muir had volunteered his services to the enemy. In making his offers, he boasted of his intimacy with Lundie, and of the means it afforded of furnishing more accurate and important information than usual. His terms had been accepted, and Monsieur Sanglier had several interviews with him in the vicinity of the fort at Oswego, and had actually passed one entire night secreted in the garrison. Arrowhead, however, was the usual channel of communication; and the anonymous letter to Major Duncan had been originally written by Muir, transmitted to Frontenac, copied, and sent back by the Tuscarora, who was returning from that errand when captured by the *Scud*. It is scarcely necessary to add that Jasper was to be sacrificed in order to conceal the Quartermaster's treason, and that the position of the island had been betrayed to the enemy by the latter. An extraordinary compensation—that which was found in his purse—had induced him to accompany the party under Sergeant Dunham, in order to give the signals that were to bring on the attack. The disposition of Muir towards the sex was a natural weakness, and he would have married Mabel, or any one else who would accept his hand; but his admiration of her was in a great degree feigned, in order that he might have an excuse for accompanying the party without sharing in the responsibility of its defeat, or incurring the risk of having no other strong and seemingly sufficient motive. Much of this was known to Captain Sanglier, particularly the part in connection with Mabel, and he did not fail to let his auditors into the whole secret, frequently laughing in a sarcastic manner, as he revealed the different expedients of the luckless Quartermaster.

"*Touchez-la*," said the cold-blooded partisan, holding out his sinewy hand to Pathfinder, when he ended his explanations; "you be *honnête*, and dat is *beaucoup*. We tak' de·spy as we tak' *la médecine*, for de good; *mais, je les déteste! Touchez-la*."

"I'll shake your hand, Captain, I will; for you're a lawful and nat'ral inimy," returned Pathfinder, "and a manful one; but the body of the Quartermaster shall never disgrace English ground. I did intend to carry it back to Lundie, that he might play his bagpipes over it, but now it shall lie here on the spot where he acted his villainy, and have his own treason for a headstone. Captain Flinty-heart, I suppose this consorting with traitors is a part of a soldier's regular business; but, I tell you honestly, it is not to my liking, and I'd rather it should be you than I who had this affair on his conscience. What an awful sinner! To plot, right and left, ag'in country, friends, and the Lord! Jasper, boy, a word with you aside, for a single minute."

Pathfinder now led the young man apart; and, squeezing his hand, with the tears in his own eyes, he continued:

"You know me, Eau-douce, and I know you," said he, "and this news has not changed my opinion of you in any manner. I never believed their tales, though it looked solemn at one minute, I will own; yes, it did look solemn, and it made me feel solemn too. I never suspected you for a minute, for I know your gifts don't lie that-a-way; but, I must own, I didn't suspect the Quartermaster neither."

"And he holding his Majesty's commission, Pathfinder!"

"It isn't so much that, Jasper Western, it isn't so much that. He held a commission from God to act right, and to deal fairly with his fellow-creatures, and he has failed awfully in his duty."

"To think of his pretending love for one like Mabel, too, when he felt none."

"That was bad, sartainly; the fellow must have had Mingo blood in his veins. The man that deals unfairly by a woman can be but a mongrel, lad; for the Lord has made them helpless on purpose that we may gain their love by kindness and sarvices. Here is the Sergeant, poor man, on his dying bed; he has given me his daughter for a wife, and Mabel, dear girl, she has consented to it; and it makes me feel that I have two welfares to look after, two naturs to care for, and two hearts to gladden. Ah's me, Jasper! I sometimes feel that I'm not good enough for that sweet child!"

Eau-douce had nearly gasped for breath when he first heard this intelligence; and, though he succeeded in suppressing any other outward signs of agitation, his cheek was blanched nearly to the paleness of death. Still he found means to answer not only with firmness, but with energy—

"Say not so, Pathfinder; you are good enough for a queen."

"Ay, ay, boy, according to your idees of my goodness; that is to say, I can kill a deer, or even a Mingo at need, with any man on the lines; or I can follow a forest-path with as true an eye, or read the stars, when others do not understand them.

No doubt, no doubt, Mabel will have venison enough, and fish enough, and pigeons enough; but will she have knowledge enough, and will she have idees enough, and pleasant conversation enough, when life comes to drag a little, and each of us begins to pass for our true value?"

"If you pass for your value, Pathfinder, the greatest lady in the land would be happy with you. On that head you have no reason to feel afraid."

"Now, Jasper, I dare to say *you* think so, nay, I *know* you do; for it is nat'ral, and according to friendship, for people to look over-favorably at them they love. Yes, yes; if I had to marry you, boy, I should give myself no consarn about my being well looked upon, for you have always shown a disposition to see me and all I do with friendly eyes. But a young gal, after all, must wish to marry a man that is nearer to her own age and fancies, than to have one old enough to be her father, and rude enough to frighten her. I wonder, Jasper, that Mabel never took a fancy to you, now, rather than setting her mind on me."

"Take a fancy to me, Pathfinder!" returned the young man, endeavoring to clear his voice without betraying himself; "what is there about me to please such a girl as Mabel Dunham? I have all that you find fault with in yourself, with none of that excellence that makes even the generals respect you."

"Well, well, it's all chance, say what we will about it. Here have I journeyed and guided through the woods female after female, and consorted with them in the garrisons, and never have I even felt an inclination for any, until I saw Mabel Dunham. It's true the poor Sergeant first set me to thinking about his daughter; but after we got a little acquainted like, I'd no need of being spoken to, to think of her night and day. I'm tough, Jasper; yes, I'm very tough; and I'm risolute enough, as you all know; and yet I do think it would quite break me down, now, to lose Mabel Dunham!"

"We will talk no more of it, Pathfinder," said Jasper, returning his friend's squeeze of the hand, and moving back towards the fire, though slowly, and in the manner of one who cared little where he went; "we will talk no more of it. You are worthy of Mabel, and Mabel is worthy of you—you like Mabel, and Mabel likes you—her father has chosen you for her husband, and no one has a right to interfere. As for the Quartermaster, his feigning love for Mabel is worse even than his treason to the king."

By this time they were so near the fire that it was necessary to change the conversation. Luckily, at that instant, Cap, who had been in the block in company with his dying brother-in-law, and who knew nothing of what had passed since the capitulation, now appeared, walking with a meditative and melancholy air towards the group. Much of that hearty dogmatism, that imparted even to his ordinary air and demeanor an appearance of something like contempt for all around him, had disappeared, and he seemed thoughtful, if not meek.

"This death, gentlemen," said he, when he had got sufficiently near, "is a melancholy business, make the best of it. Now, here is Sergeant Dunham, a very good soldier, I make no question, about to slip his cable; and yet he holds on to the better end of it, as if he was determined it should never run out of the hawse-hole; and all because he loves his daughter, it seems to me. For my part, when a friend is really under the necessity of making a long journey, I always wish him well and happily off."

"You wouldn't kill the Sergeant before his time?" Pathfinder reproachfully answered. "Life is sweet, even to the aged; and, for that matter, I've known some that seemed to set much store by it when it got to be of the least value."

Nothing had been further from Cap's real thoughts than the wish to hasten his brother-in-law's end. He had found himself embarrassed with the duties of smoothing a deathbed, and all he had meant was to express a sincere desire that the Sergeant were happily rid of doubt and suffering. A little shocked, therefore, at the interpretation that had been put on his words, he rejoined with some of the asperity of the man, though rebuked by a consciousness of not having done his own wishes justice. "You are too old and too sensible a person, Pathfinder," said he, "to fetch a man up with a surge, when he is paying out his ideas in distress, as it might be. Sergeant Dunham is both my brother-in-law and my friend—that is to say, as intimate a friend as a soldier well can be with a seafaring man—and I respect and honor him accordingly. I make no doubt, moreover, that he has lived such a life as becomes a man, and there can be no great harm, after all, in wishing any one well berthed in heaven. Well! we are mortal, the best of us, that you'll not deny; and it ought to be a lesson not to feel pride in our strength and beauty. Where is the Quartermaster, Pathfinder? It is proper he should come and have a parting word with the poor Sergeant, who is only going a little before us."

"You have spoken more truth, Master Cap, than you've been knowing to, all this time. You might have gone further, notwithstanding, and said that we are mortal, the *worst* of us; which is quite as true, and a good deal more wholesome, than saying that we are mortal, the *best* of us. As for the Quartermaster's coming to speak a parting word to the Sergeant, it is quite out of the question, seeing that he has gone ahead, and that too with little parting notice to himself, or to any one else."

"You are not quite so clear as common in your language, Pathfinder. I know that we ought all to have solemn thoughts on these occasions, but I see no use in speaking in parables."

"If my words are not plain, the idee is. In short, Master Cap, while Sergeant Dunham has been preparing himself for a long journey, like a conscientious and honest man as he is, deliberately, the Quartermaster has started, in a hurry, before him; and, although it is a matter on which it does not become me to be very positive, I give it as my opinion that they travel such different roads that they will never meet."

"Explain yourself, my friend," said the bewildered seaman, looking around him in search of Muir, whose absence began to excite his distrust. "I see nothing of the Quartermaster; but I think him too much of a man to run away, now that the victory is gained. If the fight were ahead, instead of in our wake, the case would be altered."

"There lies all that is left of him, beneath that greatcoat," returned the guide, who then briefly related the manner of the Lieutenant's death. "The Tuscarora was as venomous in his blow as a rattler, though he failed to give the warning," continued Pathfinder. "I've seen many a desperate fight, and several of these sudden outbreaks of savage temper; but never before did I see a human soul quit the body more unexpectedly, or at a worse moment for the hopes of the dying man. His breath was stopped with the lie on his lips, and the spirit might be said to have passed away in the very ardor of wickedness."

Cap listened with a gaping mouth; and he gave two or three violent hems, as the other concluded, like one who distrusted his own respiration.

"This is an uncertain and uncomfortable life of yours, Master Pathfinder, what between the fresh water and the savages," said he; "and the sooner I get quit of it, the higher will be my opinion of myself. Now you mention it, I will say that the man ran for that berth in the rocks, when the enemy first bore down upon us, with a sort of instinct that I thought surprising in an officer; but I was in too great a hurry to follow, to log the whole matter accurately. God bless me! God bless me!—a traitor, do you say, and ready to sell his country, and to a rascally Frenchman too?"

"To sell anything; country, soul, body, Mabel, and all our scalps; and no ways particular, I'll engage, as to the purchaser. The countrymen of Captain Flinty-heart here were the paymasters this time."

"Just like 'em; ever ready to buy when they can't thrash, and to run when they can do neither."

Monsieur Sanglier lifted his cap with ironical gravity, and acknowledged the compliment with an expression of polite contempt that was altogether lost on its insensible subject. But Pathfinder had too much native courtesy, and was far too just-minded, to allow the attack to go unnoticed.

"Well, well," he interposed, "to my mind there is no great difference 'atween an Englishman and a Frenchman, after all. They talk different tongues, and live under different kings, I will allow; but both are human, and feel like human beings, when there is occasion for it."

Captain Flinty-heart, as Pathfinder called him, made another obeisance; but this time the smile was friendly, and not ironical; for he felt that the intention was good, whatever might have been the mode of expressing it. Too philosophical, however, to heed what a man like Cap might say or think, he finished his breakfast, without allowing his attention to be again diverted from that important pursuit.

"My business here was principally with the Quartermaster," Cap continued, as soon as he had done regarding the prisoner's pantomime. "The Sergeant must be near his end, and I have thought he might wish to say something to his successor in authority before he finally departed. It is too late, it would seem; and, as you say, Pathfinder, the Lieutenant has truly gone before."

"That he has, though on a different path. As for authority, I suppose the Corporal has now a right to command what's left of the 55th; though a small and worried, not to say frightened, party it is. But, if anything needs to be done, the chances are greatly in favor of my being called on to do it. I suppose, however, we have only to bury our dead; set fire to the block and the huts, for they stand in the inimy's territory by position, if not by law, and must not be left for their convenience. Our using them again is out of the question; for, now the Frenchers know where the island is to be found, it would be like thrusting the hand into a wolf-trap with our eyes wide open. This part of the work the Sarpent and I will see to, for we are as practysed in retreats as in advances."

"All that is very well, my good friend. And now for my poor brother-in-law: though he is a soldier, we cannot let him slip without a word of consolation and a leave-taking, in my judgment. This has been an unlucky affair on every tack; though I suppose it is what one had a right to expect, considering the state of the times and the nature of the navigation. We must make the best of it, and try to help the worthy man to unmoor, without straining his messengers. Death is a circumstance, after all, Master Pathfinder, and one of a very general character too, seeing that we must all submit to it, sooner or later."

"You say truth, you say truth; and for that reason I hold it to be wise to be always ready. I've often thought, Saltwater, that he is the happiest who has the least to leave behind him when the summons comes. Now, here am I, a hunter and a scout and a guide, although I do not own a foot of land on 'arth, yet do I enjoy and possess more than the great Albany Patroon. With the heavens over my head to keep me in mind of the last great hunt, and the dried leaves beneath my feet, I tramp over the ground as freely as if I was its lord and owner; and what more need heart desire? I do not say that I love nothing that belongs to 'arth; for I do, though not much, unless it might be Mabel Dunham, that I can't carry with me. I have some pups at the higher fort that I vally considerable, though they are too noisy for warfare, and so we are compelled to live separate for awhile; and then I think it would grieve me to part with Killdeer; but I see no reason why we should not be buried in the same grave, for we are as near as can be of the same length —six feet to a hair's breadth; but, bating these, and a pipe that the Sarpent gave me, and a few tokens received from travellers, all of which might be put in a pouch and laid under my head, when the order comes to march I shall be ready at a minute's warning; and, let me tell you, Master Cap, that's what I call a circumstance too."

" 'Tis just so with me," answered the sailor, as the two walked towards the block, too much occupied with their respective morality to remember at the moment the melancholy errand they were on; "that's just my way of feeling and reasoning. How often have I felt, when near shipwreck, the relief of not owning the craft! 'If she goes,' I have said to myself, 'why, my life goes with her, but not my property, and there's great comfort in that.' I've discovered, in the course of boxing about the world from the Horn to Cape North, not to speak of this run on a bit of fresh water, that if a man has a few dollars, and puts them in a chest under lock and key, he is pretty certain to fasten up his heart in the same till; and so I carry pretty much all I own in a belt round my body, in order, as I say, to keep the vitals in the right place. D— me, Pathfinder, if I think a man without a heart any better than a fish with a hole in his air-bag."

"I don't know how that may be, Master Cap; but a man without a conscience is but a poor creatur', take my word for it, as any one will discover who has to do with a Mingo. I trouble myself but little with dollars or half-joes, for these are the favoryte coin in this part of the world; but I can easily believe, by what I've seen of mankind, that if a man *has* a chest filled with either, he may be said to lock up his heart in the same box. I once hunted for two summers, during the last peace, and I collected so much peltry that I found my right feelings giving way to a craving after property; and if I have consarn in marrying Mabel, it is that I may get to love such things too well, in order to make her comfortable."

"You're a philosopher, that's clear, Pathfinder; and I don't know but you're a Christian."

"I should be out of humor with the man that gainsayed the

last, Master Cap. I have not been Christianized by the Moravians, like so many of the Delawares, it is true; but I hold to Christianity and white gifts. With me, it is as on-creditable for a white man not to be a Christian as it is for a red-skin not to believe in his happy hunting-grounds; indeed, after allowing for difference in traditions, and in some variations about the manner in which the spirit will be occupied after death, I hold that a good Delaware is a good Christian, though he never saw a Moravian; and a good Christian a good Delaware, so far as natur' is consarned. The Sarpent and I talk these matters over often, for he has a hankerin' after Christianity——"

"The d—l he has!" interrupted Cap. "And what does he intend to do in a church with all the scalps he takes?"

"Don't run away with a false idee, friend Cap, don't run away with a false idee. These things are only skin-deep, and all depend on edication and nat'ral gifts. Look around you at mankind, and tell me why you see a red warrior here, a black one there, and white armies in another place? All this, and a great deal more of the same kind that I could point out, has been ordered for some special purpose; and it is not for us to fly in the face of facts and deny their truth. No, no; each color has its gifts, and its laws, and its traditions; and one is not to condemn another because he does not exactly comprehend it."

"You must have read a great deal, Pathfinder, to see things so clear as this," returned Cap, not a little mystified by his companion's simple creed. "It's all as plain as day to me now, though I must say I never fell in with these opinions before. What denomination do you belong to, my friend?"

"Anan?"

"What sect do you hold out for? What particular church do you fetch up in?"

"Look about you, and judge for yourself. I'm in church now; I eat in church, drink in church, sleep in church. The 'arth is the temple of the Lord, and I wait on Him hourly, daily, without ceasing, I humbly hope. No, no, I'll not deny my blood and color; but am Christian born, and shall die in the same faith. The Moravians tried me hard; and one of the King's chaplains has had his say too, though that's a class no ways strenuous on such matters; and a missionary sent from Rome talked much with me, as I guided him through the forest, during the last

CHAPTER XXVIII

Thou barraine ground, whom winter's wrath hath wasted,
  Art made a mirror to behold my plight:
Whilome thy fresh spring flower'd: and after hasted
  Thy summer proude, with daffodillies dight;
And now is come thy winter's stormy state,
  Thy mantle mar'd wherein thou maskedst late.   SPENSER

ALTHOUGH the soldier may regard danger and even death with indifference in the tumult of battle, when the passage of the soul is delayed to moments of tranquillity and reflection the change commonly brings with it the usual train of solemn reflections; of regrets for the past, and of doubts and anticipations for the future. Many a man has died with a heroic expression on his lips, but with heaviness and distrust at his heart; for, whatever may be the varieties of our religious creeds, let us depend on the mediation of Christ, the dogmas of Mahomet, or the elaborated allegories of the East, there is a conviction, common to all men, that death is but the stepping-stone between this and a more elevated state of being. Sergeant Dunham was a brave man; but he was departing for a country in which resolution could avail him nothing; and as he felt himself gradually loosened from the grasp of the world, his thoughts and feelings took the natural direction; for if it be true that death is the great leveller, in nothing is it more true than that it reduces all to the same views of the vanity of life.

Pathfinder, though a man of peculiar habits and opinions, was always thoughtful, and disposed to view the things around him with a shade of philosophy, as well as with seriousness. In him, therefore, the scene in the blockhouse awakened no very novel feelings. But the case was different with Cap: rude, opinionated, dogmatical, and boisterous, the old sailor was little accustomed to view even death with any approach to the gravity which its importance demands; and notwithstanding all that had passed, and his real regard for his brother-in-law, he now entered the room of the dying man with much of that callous unconcern which was the fruit of long training in a

peace; but I've had one answer for them all—I'm a Christian already, and want to be neither Moravian, nor Churchman, nor Papist. No, no, I'll not deny my birth and blood."

"I think a word from you might lighten the Sergeant over the shoals of death, Master Pathfinder. He has no one with him but poor Mabel; and she, you know, besides being his daughter, is but a girl and a child after all."

"Mabel is feeble in body, friend Cap; but in matters of this natur' I doubt if she may not be stronger than most men. But Sergeant Dunham is my friend, and he is your brother-in-law; so, now the press of fighting and maintaining our rights is over, it is fitting we should both go and witness his departure. I've stood by many a dying man, Master Cap," continued Pathfinder, who had a besetting propensity to enlarge on his experience, stopping and holding his companion by a button—"I've stood by many a dying man's side, and seen his last gasp, and heard his last breath; for, when the hurry and tumult of the battle is over, it is good to bethink us of the misfortunate, and it is remarkable to witness how differently human natur' feels at such solemn moments. Some go their way as stupid and ignorant as if God had never given them reason and an accountable state; while others quit us rejoicing, like men who leave heavy burthens behind them. I think that the mind sees clearly at such moments, my friend, and that past deeds stand thick before the recollection."

"I'll engage they do, Pathfinder. I have witnessed something of this myself, and hope I'm the better man for it. I remember once that I thought my own time had come, and the log was overhauled with a diligence I did not think myself capable of until that moment. I've not been a very great sinner, friend Pathfinder; that is to say, never on a large scale; though I daresay, if the truth were spoken, a considerable amount of small matters might be raked up against me, as well as against another man; but then, I've never committed piracy, nor high treason, nor arson, nor any of them sort of things. As to smuggling, and the like of that, why, I'm a seafaring man, and I suppose all callings have their weak spots. I daresay your trade is not altogether without blemish, honorable and useful as it seems to be?"

"Many of the scouts and guides are desperate knaves; and,

like the Quartermaster here, some of them take pay of both sides. I hope I'm not one of them, though all occupations lead to temptations Thrice have I been sorely tried in my life, and once I yielded a little, though I hope it was not in a matter to disturb a man's conscience in his last moments. The first time was when I found in the woods a pack of skins that I knowed belonged to a Frencher who was hunting on our side of the lines, where he had no business to be; twenty-six as handsome beavers as ever gladdened human eyes. Well, that was a sore temptation; for I thought the law would have been almost with me, although it was in peace times. But then, I remembered that such laws wasn't made for us hunters, and bethought me that the poor man might have built great expectations for the next winter on the sale of his skins; and I left them where they lay. Most of our people said I did wrong; but the manner in which I slept that night convinced me that I had done right. The next trial was when I found the rifle that is sartainly the only one in this part of the world that can be calculated on as surely as Killdeer, and knowed that by taking it, or even hiding it, I might at once rise to be the first shot in all these parts. I was then young, and by no means so expart as I have since got to be, and youth is ambitious and striving; but, God be praised! I mastered that feeling; and, friend Cap, what is almost as good, I mastered my rival in as fair a shooting-match as was ever witnessed in a garrison; he with his piece, and I with Killdeer, and before the General in person too!" Here Pathfinder stopped to laugh, his triumph still glittering in his eyes and glowing on his sunburnt and browned cheek. "Well, the next conflict with the devil was the hardest of them all; and that was when I came suddenly upon a camp of six Mingos asleep in the woods, with their guns and horns piled in a way that enabled me to get possession of them without waking a miscreant of them all. What an opportunity that would have been for the Sarpent, who would have despatched them, one after another, with his knife, and had their six scalps at his girdle, in about the time it takes me to tell you the story. Oh, he's a valiant warrior, that Chingachgook, and as honest as he's brave, and as good as he's honest!"

"And what may *you* have done in this matter, Master Pathfinder?" demanded Cap, who began to be interested in the re-

sult; "it seems to me you had made either a very lucky, or a very unlucky land-fall."

"'Twas lucky, and 'twas unlucky, if you can understand that. 'Twas unlucky, for it proved a desperate trial; and yet 'twas lucky, all things considered, in the ind. I did not touch a hair of their heads, for a white man has no nat'ral gifts to take scalps; nor did I even make sure of one of their rifles. I distrusted myself, knowing that a Mingo is no favorite in my own eyes."

"As for the scalps, I think you were right enough, my worthy friend; but as for the armament and the stores, they would have been condemned by any prize-court in Christendom."

"That they would, that they would; but then the Mingos would have gone clear, seeing that a white man can no more attack an unarmed than a sleeping inimy. No, no, I did myself, and my color, and my religion too, greater justice. I waited till their nap was over, and they well on their war-path again; and, by ambushing them here and flanking them there, I peppered the blackguards intrinsically like" (Pathfinder occasionally caught a fine word from his associates, and used it a little vaguely), "that only one ever got back to his village, and he came into his wigwam limping. Luckily, as it turned out, the great Delaware had only halted to jerk some venison, and was following on my trail; and when he got up he had five of the scoundrels' scalps hanging where they ought to be; so, you see, nothing was lost by doing right, either in the way of honor or in that of profit."

Cap grunted an assent, though the distinctions in his companion's morality, it must be owned, were not exactly clear to his understanding. The two had occasionally moved toward the block as they conversed, and then stopped again as som matter of more interest than common brought them to a ha They were now so near the building, however, that neith thought of pursuing the subject any further; but each prepa himself for the final scene with Sergeant Dunham.

school that, while it gives so many lessons in the sublimest truths, generally wastes its admonitions on scholars who are little disposed to profit by them.

The first proof that Cap gave of his not entering so fully as those around him into the solemnity of the moment, was by commencing a narration of the events which had just led to the deaths of Muir and Arrowhead. "Both tripped their anchors in a hurry, brother Dunham," he concluded; "and you have the consolation of knowing that others have gone before you in the great journey, and they, too, men whom you've no particular reason to love; which to me, were I placed in your situation, would be a source of very great satisfaction. My mother always said, Master Pathfinder, that dying people's spirits should not be damped, but that they ought to be encouraged by all proper and prudent means; and this news will give the poor fellow a great lift, if he feels towards them savages any way as I feel myself."

June arose at this intelligence, and stole from the blockhouse with a noiseless step. Dunham listened with a vacant stare, for life had already lost so many of its ties that he had really forgotten Arrowhead, and cared nothing for Muir; but he inquired, in a feeble voice, for Eau-douce. The young man was immediately summoned, and soon made his appearance. The Sergeant gazed at him kindly, and the expression of his eyes was that of regret for the injury he had done him in thought. The party in the blockhouse now consisted of Pathfinder, Cap, Mabel, Jasper, and the dying man. With the exception of the daughter, all stood around the Sergeant's pallet, in attendance on his last moments. Mabel kneeled at his side, now pressing a clammy hand to her head, now applying moisture to the parched lips of her father.

"Your case will shortly be ourn, Sergeant," said Pathfinder, who could hardly be said to be awestruck by the scene, for he had witnessed the approach and victories of death too often for that; but who felt the full difference between his triumphs in the excitement of battle and in the quiet of the domestic circle; "and I make no question we shall meet ag'in hereafter. Arrowhead has gone his way, 'tis true; but it can never be the way of a just Indian. You've seen the last of him, for his path cannot be the path of the just. Reason is ag'in the thought in his case, as it is also, in my judgment, ag'in it too in the case of Lieutenant Muir. You have done your duty in life; and when a man does that, he may start on the longest journey with a light heart and an actyve foot."

"I hope so, my friend: I've tried to do my duty."

"Ay, ay," put in Cap; "intention is half the battle; and though you would have done better had you hove-to in the offing and sent a craft in to feel how the land lay, things might have turned out differently: no one here doubts that you meant all for the best, and no one anywhere else, I should think, from what I've seen of this world and read of t'other."

"I did; yes. I meant all for the best."

"Father! Oh, my beloved father!"

"Magnet is taken aback by this blow, Master Pathfinder, and can say or do but little to carry her father over the shoals; so we must try all the harder to serve him a friendly turn ourselves."

"Did you speak, Mabel?" Dunham asked, turning his eyes in the direction of his daughter, for he was already too feeble to turn his body.

"Yes, father; rely on nothing you have done yourself for mercy and salvation; trust altogether in the blessed mediation of the Son of God!"

"The chaplain has told us something like this, brother. The dear child may be right."

"Ay, ay, that's doctrine, out of question. He will be our Judge, and keeps the log-book of our acts, and will foot them all up at the last day, and then say who has done well and who has done ill. I do believe Mabel is right; but then you need not be concerned, as no doubt the account has been fairly kept."

"Uncle!—dearest father! this is a vain illusion! Oh, place all your trust in the mediation of our Holy Redeemer! Have you not often felt your own insufficiency to effect your own wishes in the commonest things? and how can you imagine yourself, by your own acts, equal to raise up a frail and sinful nature sufficiently to be received into the presence of perfect purity? There is no hope for any but in the mediation of Christ!"

"This is what the Moravians used to tell us," said Pathfinder to Cap in a low voice; "rely on it, Mabel is right."

"Right enough, friend Pathfinder, in the distances, but

wrong in the course. I'm afraid the child will get the Sergeant adrift, at the very moment when we had him in the best of the water and in the plainest part of the channel."

"Leave it to Mabel, leave it to Mabel; she knows better than any of us, and can do no harm."

"I have heard this before," Dunham at length replied. "Ah, Mabel! it is strange for the parent to lean on the child at a moment like this!"

"Put your trust in God, father; lean on His holy and compassionate Son. Pray, dearest, dearest father; pray for His omnipotent support."

"I am not used to prayer. Brother, Pathfinder—Jasper, can you help me to words?"

Cap scarcely knew what prayer meant, and he had no answer to give. Pathfinder prayed often, daily, if not hourly; but it was mentally, in his own simple modes of thinking, and without the aid of words at all. In this strait, therefore, he was as useless as the mariner, and had no reply to make. As for Jasper Eaudouce, though he would gladly have endeavored to move a mountain to relieve Mabel, this was asking assistance it exceeded his power to give; and he shrank back with the shame that is only too apt to overcome the young and vigorous, when called on to perform an act that tacitly confesses their real weakness and dependence on a superior power.

"Father," said Mabel, wiping her eyes, and endeavoring to compose features that were pallid, and actually quivering with emotion, "*I* will pray with you, *for* you, for *myself*, for us *all*. The petition of the feeblest and humblest is never unheeded."

There was something sublime, as well as much that was supremely touching, in this act of filial piety. The quiet but earnest manner in which this young creature prepared herself to perform the duty; the self-abandonment with which she forgot her sex's timidity and sex's shame, in order to sustain her parent at that trying moment; the loftiness of purpose with which she directed all her powers to the immense object before her, with a woman's devotion and a woman's superiority to trifles, when her affections make the appeal; and the holy calm into which her grief was compressed, rendered her, for the moment, an object of something very like awe and veneration to her companions.

Mabel had been religiously educated; equally without exaggeration and without self-sufficiency. Her reliance on God was cheerful and full of hope, while it was of the humblest and most dependent nature. She had been accustomed from childhood to address herself to the Deity in prayer; taking example from the Divine mandate of Christ Himself, who commanded His followers to abstain from vain repetitions, and who has left behind Him a petition which is unequalled for sublimity, as if expressly to rebuke the disposition of man to set up his own loose and random thoughts as the most acceptable sacrifice. The sect in which she had been reared has furnished to its followers some of the most beautiful compositions in the language, as a suitable vehicle for its devotion and solicitations. Accustomed to this mode of public and even private prayer, the mind of our heroine had naturally fallen into its train of lofty thought; her task had become improved by its study, and her language elevated and enriched by its phrases. When she kneeled at the bedside of her father, the very reverence of her attitude and manner prepared the spectators for what was to come; and as her affectionate heart prompted her tongue, and memory came in aid of both, the petition and praises that she offered up were of a character which might have worthily led the spirits of angels. Although the words were not slavishly borrowed, the expressions partook of the simple dignity of the liturgy to which she had been accustomed, and was probably as worthy of the Being to whom they were addressed as they could well be made by human powers. They produced their full impression on the hearers; for it is worthy of remark, that, notwithstanding the pernicious effects of a false taste when long submitted to, real sublimity and beauty are so closely allied to nature that they generally find an echo in every heart.

But when our heroine came to touch upon the situation of the dying man, she became the most truly persuasive, for then she was the most truly zealous and natural. The beauty of the language was preserved, but it was sustained by the simple power of love; and her words were warmed by a holy zeal, that approached to the grandeur of true eloquence. We might record some of her expressions, but doubt the propriety of subjecting such sacred themes to a too familiar analysis, and refrain.

The effect of this singular but solemn scene was different on the different individuals present. Dunham himself was soon lost in the subject of the prayer; and he felt some such relief as one who finds himself staggering on the edge of a precipice, under a burthen difficult to be borne, might be supposed to experience when he unexpectedly feels the weight removed, in order to be placed on the shoulders of another better able to sustain it. Cap was surprised, as well as awed; though the effects on his mind were not very deep or very lasting. He wondered a little at his own sensations, and had his doubts whether they were so manly and heroic as they ought to be; but he was far too sensible of the influence of truth, humility, religious submission, and human dependency, to think of interposing with any of his crude objections. Jasper knelt opposite to Mabel, covered his face, and followed her words, with an earnest wish to aid her prayers with his own; though it may be questioned if his thoughts did not dwell quite as much on the soft, gentle accents of the petitioner as on the subject of her petition.

The effect on Pathfinder was striking and visible: visible, because he stood erect, also opposite to Mabel; and the workings of his countenance, as usual, betrayed the workings of the spirit within. He leaned on his rifle, and at moments the sinewy fingers grasped the barrel with a force that seemed to compress the weapon; while, once or twice, as Mabel's language rose in intimate association with her thoughts, he lifted his eyes to the floor above him, as if he expected to find some visible evidence of the presence of the dread Being to whom the words were addressed. Then again his feelings reverted to the fair creature who was thus pouring out her spirit, in fervent but calm petitions, in behalf of a dying parent; for Mabel's cheek was no longer pallid, but was flushed with a holy enthusiasm, while her blue eyes were upturned in the light, in a way to resemble a picture by Guido. At these moments all the honest and manly attachment of Pathfinder glowed in his ingenuous features, and his gaze at our heroine was such as the fondest parent might fasten on the child of his love.

Sergeant Dunham laid his hand feebly on the head of Mabel as she ceased praying, and buried her face in his blanket.

"Bless you, my beloved child! bless you!" he rather whispered than uttered aloud; "this is truly consolation: would that I too could pray!"

"Father, you know the Lord's Prayer; you taught it to me yourself while I was yet an infant."

The Sergeant's face gleamed with a smile, for he *did* remember to have discharged that portion at least of the paternal duty, and the consciousness of it gave him inconceivable gratification at that solemn moment. He was then silent for several minutes, and all present believed that he was communing with God.

"Mabel, my child!" he at length uttered, in a voice which seemed to be reviving—"Mabel, I'm quitting you." The spirit at its great and final passage appears ever to consider the body as nothing. "I'm quitting you, my child; where is your hand?"

"Here, dearest father—here are both—oh, take both!"

"Pathfinder," added the Sergeant, feeling on the opposite side of the bed, where Jasper still knelt, and getting one of the hands of the young man by mistake, "take it—I leave you as her father—as you and she may please—bless you—bless you both!"

At that awful instant, no one would rudely apprise the Sergeant of his mistake; and he died a minute or two later, holding Jasper's and Mabel's hands covered by both his own. Our heroine was ignorant of the fact until an exclamation of Cap's announced the death of her father; when, raising her face, she saw the eyes of Jasper riveted on her own, and felt the warm pressure of his hand. But a single feeling was predominant at that instant, and Mabel withdrew to weep, scarcely conscious of what had occurred. The Pathfinder took the arm of Eau-douce, and he left the block.

The two friends walked in silence past the fire, along the glade, and nearly reached the opposite shore of the island in profound silence. Here they stopped, and Pathfinder spoke.

"'Tis all over, Jasper," said he—"'tis all over. Ah's me! Poor Sergeant Dunham has finished his march, and that, too, by the hand of a venomous Mingo. Well, we never know what is to happen, and his luck may be yourn or mine to-morrow or next day!"

"And Mabel? What is to become of Mabel, Pathfinder?"

"You heard the Sergeant's dying words; he has left his child in my care, Jasper; and it is a most solemn trust, it is; yes—it is a most solemn trust."

"It's a trust, Pathfinder, of which any man would be glad to relieve you," returned the youth, with a bitter smile.

"I've often thought it has fallen into wrong hands. I'm not consaited, Jasper; I'm not consaited, I do think I'm not; but if Mabel Dunham is willing to overlook all my imperfections and ignorances like, I should be wrong to gainsay it, on account of any sartainty I may have myself about my own want of merit."

"No one will blame you, Pathfinder, for marrying Mabel Dunham, any more than they will blame you for wearing a precious jewel in your bosom that a friend had freely given you."

"Do you think they'll blame Mabel, lad? I've had my misgivings about that, too; for all persons may not be so disposed to look at me with the same eyes as you and the Sergeant's daughter."

Jasper Eau-douce started as a man flinches at sudden bodily pain; but he otherwise maintained his self-command. "And mankind is envious and ill-natured, more particularly in and about the garrisons. I sometimes wish, Jasper, that Mabel could have taken a fancy to you—I do; and that you had taken a fancy to her; for it often seems to me that one like you, after all, might make her happier than I ever can."

"We will not talk about this, Pathfinder," interrupted Jasper hoarsely and impatiently; "you will be Mabel's husband, and it is not right to speak of any one else in that character. As for me, I shall take Master Cap's advice, and try and make a man of myself by seeing what is to be done on the salt water."

"You, Jasper Western!—you quit the lakes, the forests, and the lines; and this, too, for the towns and wasty ways of the settlements, and a little difference in the taste of the water. Haven't we the salt-licks, if salt is necessary to you? and oughtn't man to be satisfied with what contents the other creatures of God? I counted on you, Jasper, I counted on you, I did; and thought, now that Mabel and I intend to dwell in a cabin of our own, that some day you might be tempted to choose a companion too, and come and settle in our neighborhood. There is a beautiful spot, about fifty miles west of the garrison, that I had chosen in my mind for my own place of abode; and there is an excellent harbor about ten leagues this side of it where you could run in and out with the cutter at any leisure minute; and I'd even fancied you and your wife in possession of the one place, and Mabel and I in possession of t'other. We should be just a healthy hunt apart; and if the Lord ever intends any of His creaturs to be happy on 'arth, none could be happier than we four."

"You forget, my friend," answered Jasper, taking the guide's hand and forcing a friendly smile, "that I have no fourth person to love and cherish; and I much doubt if I ever shall love any other as I love you and Mabel."

"Thank'e, boy; I thank you with all my heart; but what you call love for Mabel is only friendship like, and a very different thing from what I feel. Now, instead of sleeping as sound as natur' at midnight, as I used to could, I dream nightly of Mabel Dunham. The young does sport before me; and when I raise Killdeer, in order to take a little venison, the animals look back, and it seems as if they all had Mabel's sweet countenance, laughing in my face, and looking as if they said, 'Shoot me if you dare!' Then I hear her soft voice calling out among the birds as they sing; and no later than the last nap I took, I bethought me, in fancy, of going over the Niagara, holding Mabel in my arms, rather than part from her. The bitterest moments I've ever known were them in which the devil, or some Mingo conjuror, perhaps, has just put into my head to fancy in dreams that Mabel is lost to me by some unaccountable calamity—either by changefulness or by violence."

"Oh, Pathfinder! if you think this so bitter in a dream, what must it be to one who feels its reality, and knows it all to be true, true, true? So true as to leave no hope; to leave nothing but despair!"

These words burst from Jasper as a fluid pours from the vessel that has been suddenly broken. They were uttered involuntarily, almost unconsciously, but with a truth and feeling that carried with them the instant conviction of their deep sincerity. Pathfinder started, gazed at his friend for full a minute like one bewildered, and then it was that, in despite of all his simplicity, the truth gleamed upon him. All know how corroborating proofs crowd upon the mind as soon as it catches a direct clue to any hitherto unsuspected fact; how rapidly the thoughts flow and premises tend to their just conclusions under such circumstances. Our hero was so confiding by nature, so just, and so much disposed to imagine that all his friends wished him the same happiness as he wished them, that, until this unfortunate moment, a suspicion of Jasper's attachment for Mabel had never been awakened in his bosom. He was, however, now too experienced in the emotions which characterize the passion; and the burst of feeling in his companion was too violent and too natural to leave any further doubt on the subject. The feeling that first followed this change of opinion was one of deep humility and exquisite pain. He bethought him of Jasper's youth, his higher claims to personal appearance, and all the general probabilities that such a suitor would be more agreeable to Mabel than he could possibly be himself. Then the noble rectitude of mind, for which the man was so distinguished, asserted its power; it was sustained by his rebuked manner of thinking of himself, and all that habitual deference for the rights and feelings of others which appeared to be inbred in his very nature. Taking the arm of Jasper, he led him to a log, where he compelled the young man to seat himself by a sort of irresistible exercise of his iron muscles, and where he placed himself at his side.

The instant his feelings had found vent, Eau-douce was both alarmed at, and ashamed of, their violence. He would have given all he possessed on earth could the last three minutes be recalled; but he was too frank by disposition and too much accustomed to deal ingenuously by his friend to think a moment of attempting further concealment, or of any evasion of the explanation that he knew was about to be demanded. Even while he trembled in anticipation of what was about to follow, he never contemplated equivocation.

"Jasper," Pathfinder commenced, in a tone so solemn as to thrill on every nerve in his listener's body, "this *has* surprised me! You have kinder feelings towards Mabel than I had thought; and, unless my own mistaken vanity and consait have cruelly deceived me, I pity you, boy, from my soul I do! Yes, I think I know how to pity any one who has set his heart on a creature like Mabel, unless he sees a prospect of her regarding him as he regards her. This matter must be cleared up, Eau-douce, as the Delawares say, until there shall not be a cloud 'atween us."

"What clearing up can it want, Pathfinder? I love Mabel Dunham, and Mabel Dunham does not love me; she prefers you for a husband; and the wisest thing I can do is to go off at once to the salt water, and try to forget you both."

"Forget me, Jasper! that would be a punishment I don't desarve. But how do you know that Mabel prefars *me?* how do you know it, lad? To me it seems impossible like!"

"Is she not to marry you, and would Mabel marry a man she does not love?"

"She has been hard urged by the Sergeant, she has; and a dutiful child may have found it difficult to withstand the wishes of a dying parent. Have you ever told Mabel that you prefarred her, Jasper—that you bore her these feelings?"

"Never, Pathfinder. I would not do you that wrong."

"I believe you, lad, I do believe you; and I think you would now go off to the salt water, and let the scent die with you. But this must not be. Mabel shall hear all, and she shall have her own way, if my heart breaks in the trial, she shall. No words have ever passed 'atween you, then, Jasper?"

"Nothing of account, nothing direct. Still, I will own all my foolishness, Pathfinder; for I ought to own it to a generous friend like you, and there will be an end of it. You know how young people understand each other, or think they understand each other, without always speaking out in plain speech, and get to know each other's thoughts, or to think they know them, by means of a hundred little ways."

"Not I, Jasper, not I," truly answered the guide; for, sooth to say, his advances had never been met with any of that sweet and precious encouragement which silently marks the course of sympathy united to passion. "Not I, Jasper; I know nothing of all this. Mabel has always treated me fairly, and said what she has had to say in speech as plain as tongue could tell it."

"You have had the pleasure of hearing her say that she loved you, Pathfinder?"

"Why, no, Jasper, not just that in words. She has told me that we never could, never ought to be married; that *she* was not good enough for *me*, though she *did* say that she honored me and respected me. But then the Sergeant said it was always so with the youthful and timid; that her mother did so and said so afore her; and that I ought to be satisfied if she would consent on any terms to marry me, and therefore I have concluded that all was right, I have."

In spite of all his friendship for the successful wooer, in spite of all his honest, sincere wishes for his happiness, we should be unfaithful chroniclers did we not own that Jasper felt his heart bound with an uncontrollable feeling of delight at this admission. It was not that he saw or felt any hope connected with the circumstance; but it was grateful to the jealous covetousness of unlimited love thus to learn that no other ears had heard the sweet confessions that were denied its own.

"Tell me more of this manner of talking without the use of the tongue," continued Pathfinder, whose countenance was becoming grave, and who now questioned his companion like one who seemed to anticipate evil in the reply. "I can and have conversed with Chingachgook, and with his son Uncas too, in that mode, afore the latter fell; but I didn't know that young girls practysed this art, and, least of all, Mabel Dunham."

" 'Tis nothing, Pathfinder. I mean only a look, or a smile, or a glance of the eye, or the trembling of an arm or a hand when the young woman has had occasion to touch me; and because I have been weak enough to tremble even at Mabel's breath, or her brushing me with her clothes, my vain thoughts have misled me. I never spoke plainly to Mabel myself, and now there is no use for it, since there is clearly no hope."

"Jasper," returned Pathfinder simply, but with a dignity that precluded further remarks at the moment, "we will talk of the Sergeant's funeral and of our own departure from this island. After these things are disposed of, it will be time enough to say more of the Sergeant's daughter. This matter must be looked into, for the father left me the care of his child."

Jasper was glad enough to change the subject, and the friends separated, each charged with the duty most peculiar to his own station and habits.

That afternoon all the dead were interred, the grave of Sergeant Dunham being dug in the centre of the glade, beneath the shade of a huge elm. Mabel wept bitterly at the ceremony, and she found relief in thus disburthening her sorrow. The night passed tranquilly, as did the whole of the following day, Jasper declaring that the gale was too severe to venture on the lake. This circumstance detained Captain Sanglier also, who did not quit the island until the morning of the third day after the death of Dunham, when the weather had moderated, and the wind had become fair. Then, indeed, he departed, after taking leave of the Pathfinder, in the manner of one who believed he was in company of a distinguished character for the last time. The two separated like those who respect one another, while each felt that the other was an enigma to himself.

CHAPTER XXIX

Playful she turn'd that he might see
The passing smile her cheek put on;
But when she mark'd how mournfully
His eyes met hers, that smile was gone.   *Lalla Rookh*

THE occurrences of the last few days had been too exciting, and had made too many demands on the fortitude of our heroine, to leave her in the helplessness of grief. She mourned for her father, and she occasionally shuddered as she recalled the sudden death of Jennie, and all the horrible scenes she had witnessed; but on the whole she had aroused herself, and was no longer in the deep depression which usually accompanies grief. Perhaps the overwhelming, almost stupefying sorrow that crushed poor June, and left her for nearly twenty-four hours in a state of stupor, assisted Mabel in conquering her own feelings, for she had felt called on to administer consolation to the young Indian woman. This she had done in the quiet, soothing, insinuating way in which her sex usually exerts its influence on such occasions.

The morning of the third day was set for that on which the *Scud* was to sail. Jasper had made all his preparations; the different effects were embarked, and Mabel had taken leave of June, a painful and affectionate parting. In a word, all was ready, and every soul had left the island but the Indian woman, Pathfinder, Jasper, and our heroine. The former had gone into a thicket to weep, and the three last were approaching the spot where three canoes lay, one of which was the property of June, and the other two were in waiting to carry the others off to the *Scud*. Pathfinder led the way, but, when he drew near the shore, instead of taking the direction to the boats, he motioned to his companions to follow, and proceeded to a fallen tree, which lay on the margin of the glade and out of view of those in the cutter. Seating himself on the trunk, he signed to Mabel to take her place on one side of him and to Jasper to occupy the other.

"Sit down here, Mabel; sit down there, Eau-douce," he commenced, as soon as he had taken his own seat. "I've something that lies heavy on my mind, and now is the time to take it off, if it's ever to be done. Sit down, Mabel, and let me lighten my heart, if not my conscience, while I've the strength to do it."

The pause that succeeded lasted two or three minutes, and both the young people wondered what was to come next; the idea that Pathfinder could have any weight on his conscience seeming equally improbable to each.

"Mabel," our hero at length resumed, "we must talk plainly to each other afore we join your uncle in the cutter, where the Saltwater has slept every night since the last rally, for he says it's the only place in which a man can be sure of keeping the hair on his head, he does. Ah's me! what have I to do with these follies and sayings now? I try to be pleasant, and to feel light-hearted, but the power of man can't make water run up stream. Mabel, you know that the Sergeant, afore he left us, had settled it 'atween us two that we were to become man and wife, and that we were to live together and to love one another as long as the Lord was pleased to keep us both on 'arth; yes, and afterwards too?"

Mabel's cheeks had regained a little of their ancient bloom in the fresh air of the morning; but at this unlooked-for address they blanched again, nearly to the pallid hue which grief had imprinted there. Still, she looked kindly, though seriously, at Pathfinder, and even endeavored to force a smile.

"Very true, my excellent friend," she answered; "this was my poor father's wish, and I feel certain that a whole life devoted to your welfare and comforts could scarcely repay you for all you have done for us."

"I fear me, Mabel, that man and wife needs be bound together by a stronger tie than such feelings, I do. You have done nothing for me, or nothing of any account, and yet my very heart yearns towards you, it does; and therefore it seems likely that these feelings come from something besides saving scalps and guiding through woods."

Mabel's cheek had begun to glow again; and though she

struggled hard to smile, her voice trembled a little as she answered.

"Had we not better postpone this conversation, Pathfinder?" she said; "we are not alone; and nothing is so unpleasant to a listener, they say, as family matters in which he feels no interest."

"It's because we are not alone, Mabel, or rather because Jasper is with us, that I wish to talk of this matter. The Sergeant believed I might make a suitable companion for you, and, though I had misgivings about it—yes, I had many misgivings—he finally persuaded me into the idee, and things came round 'atween us, as you know. But, when you promised your father to marry me, Mabel, and gave me your hand so modestly, but so prettily, there was one circumstance, as your uncle called it, that you didn't know; and I've thought it right to tell you what it is, before matters are finally settled. I've often taken a poor deer for my dinner when good venison was not to be found; but it's as nat'ral not to take up with the worst when the best may be had."

"You speak in a way, Pathfinder, that is difficult to be understood. If this conversation is really necessary, I trust you will be more plain."

"Well then, Mabel, I've been thinking it was quite likely, when you gave in to the Sergeant's wishes, that you did not know the natur' of Jasper Western's feelings towards you?"

"Pathfinder!" and Mabel's cheek now paled to the livid hue of death; then it flushed to the tint of crimson; and her whole frame shuddered. Pathfinder, however, was too intent on his own object to notice this agitation; and Eau-douce had hidden his face in his hands in time to shut out its view.

"I've been talking with the lad; and, on comparing his dreams with my dreams, his feelings with my feelings, and his wishes with my wishes, I fear we think too much alike consarning you for both of us to be very happy."

"Pathfinder, you forget; you should remember that we are betrothed!" said Mabel hastily, and in a voice so low that it required acute attention in the listeners to catch the syllables. Indeed the last word was not quite intelligible to the guide, and he confessed his ignorance by the usual—

"Anan?"

"You forget that we are to be married; and such allusions are improper as well as painful."

"Everything is proper that is right, Mabel; and everything is right that leads to justice and fair dealing; though it *is painful* enough, as you say, as I find on trial, I do. Now, Mabel, had you known that Eau-douce thinks of you in this way, maybe you never would have consented to be married to one as old and as uncomely as I am."

"Why this cruel trial, Pathfinder? To what can all this lead? Jasper Western thinks no such thing: he says nothing, he feels nothing."

"Mabel!" burst from out of the young man's lips, in a way to betray the uncontrollable nature of his emotions, though he uttered not another syllable.

Mabel buried her face in both her hands; and the two sat like a pair of guilty beings, suddenly detected in the commission of some crime which involved the happiness of a common patron. At that instant, perhaps, Jasper himself was inclined to deny his passion, through an extreme unwillingness to grieve his friend; while Mabel, on whom this positive announcement of a fact that she had rather unconsciously hoped than believed, came so unexpectedly, felt her mind momentarily bewildered; and she scarcely knew whether to weep or to rejoice. Still she was the first to speak; since Eau-douce could utter naught that would be disingenuous, or that would pain his friend.

"Pathfinder," said she, "you talk wildly. Why mention this at all?"

"Well, Mabel, if I talk wildly, I *am* half wild, you know, by natur', I fear, as well as by habit." As he said this, he endeavored to laugh in his usual noiseless way, but the effect produced a strange and discordant sound; and it appeared nearly to choke him. "Yes, I *must* be wild; I'll not attempt to deny it."

"Dearest Pathfinder! my best, almost my only friend! you *cannot, do not* think I intended to say that!" interrupted Mabel, almost breathless in her haste to relieve his mortification. "If courage, truth, nobleness of soul and conduct, unyielding principles, and a hundred other excellent qualities can render any man respectable, esteemed, or beloved, your claims are inferior to those of no other human being."

"What tender and bewitching voices they have, Jasper!"

resumed the guide, now laughing freely and naturally. "Yes, natur' seems to have made them on purpose to sing in our ears, when the music of the woods is silent. But we must come to a right understanding, we must. I ask you again, Mabel, if you had known that Jasper Western loves you as well as I do, or better perhaps, though that is scarcely possible; that in his dreams he sees your face in the water of the lake; that he talks to you, and of you, in his sleep; fancies all that is beautiful like Mabel Dunham, and all that is good and virtuous; believes he never knowed happiness until he knowed you; could kiss the ground on which you have trod, and forgets all the joys of his calling to think of you and the delight of gazing at your beauty and in listening to your voice, would you then have consented to marry me?"

Mabel could not have answered this question if she would; but, though her face was buried in her hands, the tint of the rushing blood was visible between the openings, and the suffusion seemed to impart itself to her very fingers. Still nature asserted her power, for there was a single instant when the astonished, almost terrified girl stole a glance at Jasper, as if distrusting Pathfinder's history of his feelings, read the truth of all he said in that furtive look, and instantly concealed her face again, as if she would hide it from observation for ever.

"Take time to think, Mabel," the guide continued, "for it is a solemn thing to accept one man for a husband while the thoughts and wishes lead to another. Jasper and I have talked this matter over, freely and like old friends, and, though I always knowed that we viewed most things pretty much alike, I couldn't have thought that we regarded any particular object with the very same eyes, as it might be, until we opened our minds to each other about you. Now Jasper owns that the very first time he beheld you, he thought you the sweetest and winningestest creatur' he had ever met; that your voice sounded like murmuring water in his ears; that he fancied his sails were your garments fluttering in the wind; that your laugh haunted him in his sleep; and that ag'in and ag'in has he started up affrighted, because he has fancied some one wanted to force you out of the *Scud*, where he imagined you had taken up your abode. Nay, the lad has even acknowledged that he often weeps at the thought that you are likely to spend your days with another, and not with him."

"Jasper!"

"It's solemn truth, Mabel, and it's right you should know it. Now stand up, and choose 'atween us. I do believe Eau-douce loves you as well as I do myself; he has tried to persuade me that he loves you better, but that I will not allow, for I do not think it possible; but I will own the boy loves you, heart and soul, and he has a good right to be heard. The Sergeant left me your protector, and not your tyrant. I told him that I would be a father to you as well as a husband, and it seems to me no feeling father would deny his child this small privilege. Stand up, Mabel, therefore, and speak your thoughts as freely as if I were the Sergeant himself, seeking your good, and nothing else."

Mabel dropped her hands, arose, and stood face to face with her two suitors, though the flush that was on her cheeks was feverish, the evidence of excitement rather than of shame.

"What would you have, Pathfinder?" she asked; "have I not already promised my poor father to do all you desire?"

"Then I desire this. Here I stand, a man of the forest and of little larning, though I fear with an ambition beyond my desarts, and I'll do my endivors to do justice to both sides. In the first place, it is allowed that, so far as feelings in your behalf are consarned, we love you just the same; Jasper thinks his feelings *must* be the strongest, but this I cannot say in honesty, for it doesn't seem to me that it *can* be true, else I would frankly and freely confess it, I would. So in this particular, Mabel, we are here before you on equal tarms. As for myself, being the oldest, I'll first say what little can be produced in my favor, as well as ag'in it. As a hunter, I do think there is no man near the lines that can outdo me. If venison, or bear's meat, or even birds and fish, should ever be scarce in our cabin, it would be more likely to be owing to natur' and Providence than to any fault of mine. In short, it does seem to me that the woman who depended on me would never be likely to want for food. But I'm fearful ignorant! It's true I speak several tongues, such as they be, while I'm very far from being expart at my own. Then, my years are greater than your own, Mabel; and the circumstance that I was so long the Sergeant's comrade can be no great merit in your eyes. I wish, too, I was more comely, I do; but we are all as natur' made us, and the last thing that a man ought to lament, except on very special occasions, is his looks. When all is remembered, age, looks, learning, and habits, Mabel, conscience tells me I ought to confess that I'm altogether unfit for you, if not downright unworthy; and I would give up the hope this minute, I would, if I didn't feel something pulling at my heart-strings which seems hard to undo."

"Pathfinder! noble, generous Pathfinder!" cried our heroine, seizing his hand and kissing it with a species of holy reverence; "you do yourself injustice—you forget my poor father and your promise—you do not know *me!*"

"Now, here's Jasper," continued the guide, without allowing the girl's caresses to win him from his purpose, "with *him* the case is different. In the way of providing, as in that of loving, there's not much to choose 'atween us; for the lad is frugal, industrious, and careful. Then he is quite a scholar, knows the tongue of the Frenchers, reads many books, and some, I know, that you like to read yourself, can understand you at all times, which, perhaps, is more than I can say for myself."

"What of all this?" interrupted Mabel impatiently; "why speak of it now—why speak of it at all?"

"Then the lad has a manner of letting his thoughts be known, that I fear I can never equal. If there's anything on 'arth that would make my tongue bold and persuading, Mabel, I do think it's yourself; and yet in our late conversations Jasper has out-done me, even on this point, in a way to make me ashamed of myself. He has told me how simple you were, and how true-hearted, and kind-hearted; and how you looked down upon vanities, for though you might be the wife of more than one officer, as he thinks, that you cling to feeling, and would rather be true to yourself and natur' than a colonel's lady. He fairly made my blood warm, he did, when he spoke of your having beauty without seeming ever to have looked upon it, and the manner in which you moved about like a young fa'n, so nat'ral and graceful like, without knowing it; and the truth and justice of your idees, and the warmth and generosity of your heart——"

"Jasper!" interrupted Mabel, giving way to feelings that had gathered an ungovernable force by being so long pent, and falling into the young man's willing arms, weeping like a child, and almost as helpless. "Jasper! Jasper! why have you kept this from me?"

The answer of Eau-douce was not very intelligible, nor was the murmured dialogue that followed remarkable for coherency. But the language of affection is easily understood. The hour that succeeded passed like a very few minutes of ordinary life, so far as a computation of time was concerned; and when Mabel recollected herself, and bethought her of the existence of others, her uncle was pacing the cutter's deck in great impatience, and wondering why Jasper should be losing so much of a favorable wind. Her first thought was of him, who was so likely to feel the recent betrayal of her real emotions.

"Oh, Jasper," she exclaimed, like one suddenly self-convicted, "the Pathfinder!"

Eau-douce fairly trembled, not with unmanly apprehension, but with the painful conviction of the pang he had given his friend; and he looked in all directions in the expectation of seeing his person. But Pathfinder had withdrawn, with a tact and a delicacy that might have done credit to the sensibility and breeding of a courtier. For several minutes the two lovers sat, silently waiting his return, uncertain what propriety required of them under circumstances so marked and so peculiar. At length they beheld their friend advancing slowly towards them, with a thoughtful and even pensive air.

"I now understand what you meant, Jasper, by speaking without a tongue and hearing without an ear," he said when close enough to the tree to be heard. "Yes, I understand it now, I do; and a very pleasant sort of discourse it is, when one can hold it with Mabel Dunham. Ah's me! I told the Sergeant I wasn't fit for her; that I was too old, too ignorant, and too wild like; but he *would* have it otherwise."

Jasper and Mabel sat, resembling Milton's picture of our first parents, when the consciousness of sin first laid its leaden weight on their souls. Neither spoke, neither even moved; though both at that moment fancied they could part with their new-found happiness in order to restore their friend to his peace of mind. Jasper was pale as death, but, in Mabel, maiden modesty had caused the blood to mantle on her cheeks, until their bloom was heightened to a richness that was scarcely equalled in her hours of light-hearted buoyancy and joy. As the feeling which, in her

sex, always accompanies the security of love returned, threw
its softness and tenderness over her countenance, she was singularly beautiful. Pathfinder gazed at her with an intentness he
did not endeavor to conceal, and then he fairly laughed in his
own way, and with a sort of wild exultation, as men that are
untutored are wont to express their delight. This momentary
indulgence, however, was expiated by the pang which followed
the sudden consciousness that this glorious young creature was
lost to him for ever. It required a full minute for this simple-
minded being to recover from the shock of this conviction; and
then he recovered his dignity of manner, speaking with gravity,
almost with solemnity.

"I have always known, Mabel Dunham, that men have their
gifts," said he; "but I'd forgotten that it did not belong to mine
to please the young, the beautiful, and l'arned. I hope the mistake has been no very heavy sin; and if it was, I've been heavily
punished for it, I have. Nay, Mabel, I know what you'd say,
but it's unnecessary; I *feel* it all, and that is as good as if I
heard it all. I've had a bitter hour, Mabel. I've had a very bitter
hour, lad."

"Hour!" echoed Mabel, as the other first used the word; the
tell-tale blood, which had begun to ebb towards her heart, rushing again tumultuously to her very temples; "surely not an
hour, Pathfinder?"

"Hour!" exclaimed Jasper at the same instant; "no, no, my
worthy friend, it is not ten minutes since you left us!"

"Well, it may be so; though to me it has seemed to be a day.
I begin to think, however, that the happy count time by minutes, and the miserable count it by months. But we will talk
no more of this; it is all over now, and many words about it
will make you no happier, while they will only tell me what I've
lost; and quite likely how much I desarved to lose her. No, no,
Mabel, 'tis useless to interrupt me; I admit it all, and your
gainsaying it, though it be so well meant, cannot change my
mind. Well, Jasper, she is yours; and, though it's hard to think
it, I do believe you'll make her happier than I could, for your
gifts are better suited to do so, though I would have strived
hard to do as much, if I know myself, I would. I ought to have
known better than to believe the Sergeant; and I ought to have

put faith in what Mabel told me at the head of the lake, for reason and judgment might have shown me its truth; but it is so pleasant to think what we wish, and mankind so easily over-persuade us, when we over-persuade ourselves. But what's the use in talking of it, as I said afore? It's true, Mabel seemed to be consenting, though it all came from a wish to please her father, and from being skeary about the savages——"

"Pathfinder!"

"I understand you, Mabel, and have no hard feelings, I haven't. I sometimes think I should like to live in your neighbor-hood, that I might look at your happiness; but, on the whole, it's better I should quit the 55th altogether, and go back to the 60th, which is my natyve rigiment, as it might be. It would have been better, perhaps, had I never left it, though my sarvices were much wanted in this quarter, and I'd been with some of the 55th years agone; Sergeant Dunham, for instance, when he was in another corps. Still, Jasper, I do not regret that I've known you——"

"And me, Pathfinder!" impetuously interrupted Mabel; "do you regret having known *me?* Could I think so, I should never be at peace with myself."

"You, Mabel!" returned the guide, taking the hand of our heroine, and looking up into her countenance with guileless simplicity, but earnest affection; "how could I be sorry that a ray of the sun came across the gloom of a cheerless day—that light has broken in upon darkness, though it remained so short a time? I do not flatter myself with being able to march quite so light-hearted as I once used to could, or to sleep as sound, for some time to come; but I shall always remember how near I was to being undeservedly happy, I shall. So far from blaming you, Mabel, I only blame myself for being so vain as to think it possible I could please such a creatur'; for sartainly you told me how it was, when we talked it over on the mountain, and I ought to have believed you then; for I do suppose it's nat'ral that young women should know their own minds better than their fathers. Ah's me! It's settled now, and nothing remains but for me to take leave of you, that you may depart; I feel that Master Cap must be impatient, and there is danger of his coming on shore to look for us all."

"To take leave!" exclaimed Mabel.

"Leave!" echoed Jasper; "you do not mean to quit us, my friend?"

" 'Tis best, Mabel, 'tis altogether best, Eau-douce; and it's wisest. I could live and die in your company, if I only followed feeling; but, if I follow reason, I shall quit you here. You will go back to Oswego, and become man and wife as soon as you arrive—for all that is determined with Master Cap, who hankers after the sea again, and who knows what is to happen—while I shall return to the wilderness and my Maker. Come, Mabel," continued Pathfinder, rising and drawing nearer to our heroine, with grave decorum, "kiss me; Jasper will not grudge me one kiss; then we'll part."

"Oh, Pathfinder!" exclaimed Mabel, falling into the arms of the guide, and kissing his cheeks again and again, with a freedom and warmth she had been far from manifesting while held to the bosom of Jasper; "God bless you, dearest Pathfinder! You'll come to us hereafter. We shall see you again. When old, you will come to our dwelling, and let me be a daughter to you?"

"Yes, that's it," returned the guide, almost gasping for breath; "I'll try to think of it in that way. You're more befitting to be my daughter than to be my wife, you are. Farewell, Jasper. Now we'll go to the canoe; it's time you were on board."

The manner in which Pathfinder led the way to the shore was solemn and calm. As soon as he reached the canoe, he again took Mabel by the hands, held her at the length of his own arms, and gazed wistfully into her face, until the unbidden tears rolled out of the fountains of feeling and trickled down his rugged cheeks in streams.

"Bless me, Pathfinder," said Mabel, kneeling reverently at his feet. "Oh, at least bless me before we part!"

That untutored but noble-minded being did as she desired; and, aiding her to enter the canoe, seemed to tear himself away as one snaps a strong and obstinate cord. Before he retired, however, he took Jasper by the arm and led him a little aside, when he spoke as follows:—

"You're kind of heart and gentle by natur', Jasper; but we are both rough and wild in comparison with that dear creatur'. Be careful of her, and never show the roughness of man's natur' to her soft disposition. You'll get to understand her in time;

and the Lord, who governs the lake and the forest alike, who looks upon virtue with a smile and upon vice with a frown, keep you happy and worthy to be so!''

Pathfinder made a sign for his friend to depart, and he stood leaning on his rifle until the canoe had reached the side of the *Scud*. Mabel wept as if her heart would break; nor did her eyes once turn from the open spot in the glade, where the form of the Pathfinder was to be seen, until the cutter had passed a point that completely shut out the island. When last in view, the sinewy frame of this extraordinary man was as motionless as if it were a statue set up in that solitary place to commemorate the scenes of which it had so lately been the witness.

CHAPTER XXX

Oh! let me only breathe the air,
  The blessed air that's breath'd by thee;
And, whether on its wings it bear
  Healing or death, 'tis sweet to me!   MOORE

PATHFINDER was accustomed to solitude; but, when the *Scud* had actually disappeared, he was almost overcome with a sense of his loneliness. Never before had he been conscious of his isolated condition in the world; for his feelings had gradually been accustoming themselves to the blandishments and wants of social life; particularly as the last were connected with the domestic affections. Now, all had vanished, as it might be, in one moment; and he was left equally without companions and without hope. Even Chingachgook had left him, though it was but temporarily; still his presence was missed at the precise instant which might be termed the most critical in our hero's life.

Pathfinder stood leaning on his rifle, in the attitude described in the last chapter, a long time after the *Scud* had disappeared. The rigidity of his limbs seemed permanent; and none but a man accustomed to put his muscles to the severest proof could have maintained that posture, with its marble-like inflexibility for so great a length of time. At length he moved away from the spot; the motion of the body being preceded by a sigh that seemed to heave up from the very depths of his bosom.

It was a peculiarity of this extraordinary being that his senses and his limbs, for all practical purposes, were never at fault, let the mind be preoccupied with other interests as much as it might. On the present occasion neither of these great auxiliaries failed him; but, though his thoughts were exclusively occupied with Mabel, her beauty, her preference of Jasper, her tears, and her departure, he moved in a direct line to the spot where June still remained, which was the grave of her husband. The conversation that followed passed in the language of the Tuscaroras, which Pathfinder spoke fluently; but, as that tongue is understood only by the extremely learned, we shall translate it freely into the English; preserving, as far as possible, the tone of thought of each interlocutor, as well as the peculiarities of manner. June had suffered her hair to fall about her face, had taken a seat on a stone which had been dug from the excavation made by the grave, and was hanging over the spot which contained the body of Arrowhead, unconscious of the presence of any other. She believed, indeed, that all had left the island but herself, and the tread of the guide's moccasined foot was too noiseless rudely to undeceive her.

Pathfinder stood gazing at the woman for several minutes in mute attention. The contemplation of her grief, the recollection of her irreparable loss, and the view of her desolation produced a healthful influence on his own feelings; his reason telling him how much deeper lay the sources of grief in a young wife, who was suddenly and violently deprived of her husband, than in himself.

"Dew-of-June," he said solemnly, but with an earnestness which denoted the strength of his sympathy, "you are not alone in your sorrow. Turn, and let your eyes look upon a friend."

"June has no longer any friend!" the woman answered. "Arrowhead has gone to the happy hunting-grounds, and there is no one left to care for June. The Tuscaroras would chase her from their wigwams; the Iroquois are hateful in her eyes, and she could not look at them. No! leave June to starve over the grave of her husband."

"This will never do—this will never do. 'Tis ag'in reason and right. You believe in the Manitou, June?"

"He has hid his face from June because he is angry. He has left her alone to die."

"Listen to one who has had a long acquaintance with red natur', though he has a white birth and white gifts. When the Manitou of a pale-face wishes to produce good in a pale-face heart He strikes it with grief; for it is in our sorrows, June, that we look with the truest eyes into ourselves, and with the farthest-sighted eyes too, as respects right. The Great Spirit wishes you well, and He has taken away the chief, lest you should be led astray by his wily tongue, and get to be a Mingo in your disposition, as you were already in your company."

"Arrowhead was a great chief," returned the woman proudly.

"He had his merits, he had; and he had his demerits, too. But, June, you are not desarted, nor will you be soon. Let your grief out—let it out, according to natur', and when the proper time comes I shall have more to say to you."

Pathfinder now went to his own canoe, and he left the island. In the course of the day June heard the crack of his rifle once or twice; and as the sun was setting he reappeared, bringing her birds ready cooked, and of a delicacy and flavor that might have tempted the appetite of an epicure. This species of intercourse lasted a month, June obstinately refusing to abandon the grave of her husband all that time, though she still accepted the friendly offerings of her protector. Occasionally they met and conversed, Pathfinder sounding the state of the woman's feelings; but the interviews were short, and far from frequent. June slept in one of the huts, and she laid down her head in security, for she was conscious of the protection of a friend, though Pathfinder invariably retired at night to an adjacent island, where he had built himself a hut.

At the end of the month, however, the season was getting to be too far advanced to render her situation pleasant to June. The trees had lost their leaves, and the nights were becoming cold and wintry. It was time to depart.

At this moment Chingachgook reappeared. He had a long and confidential interview on the island with his friend. June witnessed their movements, and she saw that her guardian was distressed. Stealing to his side, she endeavored to soothe his sorrow with a woman's gentleness and with a woman's instinct.

"Thank you, June, thank you!" he said; " 'tis well meant, though it's useless. But it is time to quit this place. To-morrow we shall depart. You will go with us, for now you've got to feel reason."

June assented in the meek manner of an Indian woman, and she withdrew to pass the remainder of her time near the grave of Arrowhead. Regardless of the hour and the season, the young widow did not pillow her head during the whole of that autumnal night. She sat near the spot that held the remains of her husband, and prayed, in the manner of her people, for his success on the endless path on which he had so lately gone, and for their reunion in the land of the just. Humble and degraded as she would have seemed in the eyes of the sophisticated and unreflecting, the image of God was on her soul, and it vindicated its divine origin by aspirations and feelings that would have surprised those who, feigning more, feel less.

In the morning the three departed, Pathfinder earnest and intelligent in all he did, the Great Serpent silent and imitative, and June meek, resigned, but sorrowful. They went in two canoes, that of the woman being abandoned: Chingachgook led the way, and Pathfinder followed, the course being up stream. Two days they paddled westward, and as many nights they encamped on islands. Fortunately the weather became mild, and when they reached the lake it was found smooth and glassy as a pond. It was the Indian summer, and the calms, and almost the blandness of June, slept in the hazy atmosphere.

On the morning of the third day they passed the mouth of the Oswego, where the fort and the sleeping ensign invited them in vain to enter. Without casting a look aside, Chingachgook paddled past the dark waters of the river, and Pathfinder still followed in silent industry. The ramparts were crowded with spectators; but Lundie, who knew the persons of his old friends, refused to allow them to be even hailed.

It was noon when Chingachgook entered a little bay where the *Scud* lay at anchor, in a sort of roadstead. A small ancient clearing was on the shore; and near the margin of the lake was a log dwelling, recently and completely, though rudely, fitted up. There was an air of frontier comfort and of frontier abundance around the place, though it was necessarily wild and solitary. Jasper stood on the shore; and when Pathfinder landed, he was the first to take him by the hand. The meeting was simple, but very cordial. No questions were asked, it being apparent that Chingachgook had made the necessary explanations. Pathfinder never squeezed his friend's hand more cordially than in this interview; and he even laughed cordially in his face as he told him how happy and well he appeared.

"Where is she, Jasper? where is she?" the guide at length whispered, for at first he had seemed to be afraid to trust himself with the question.

"She is waiting for us in the house, my dear friend, where you see that June has already hastened before us."

"June may use a lighter step to meet Mabel, but she cannot carry a lighter heart. And so, lad, you found the chaplain at the garrison, and all was soon settled?"

"We were married within a week after we left you, and Master Cap departed next day. You have forgotten to inquire about your friend Saltwater."

"Not I, not I; the Sarpent has told me all that: and then I love to hear so much of Mabel and her happiness, I do. Did the child smile or did she weep when the ceremony was over?"

"She did both, my friend; but——"

"Yes, that's their natur', tearful and cheerful. Ah's me! they are very pleasant to us of the woods; and I do believe I should think all right, whatever Mabel might do. And do you think, Jasper, that she thought of me at all on that joyful occasion?"

"I know she did, Pathfinder; and she thinks of you and talks of you daily, almost hourly. None love you as we do."

"I know few love me better than yourself, Jasper: Chingachgook is perhaps, now, the only creatur' of whom I can say that. Well, there's no use in putting it off any longer; it must be done, and may as well be done at once; so, Jasper, lead the way, and I'll endivor to look upon her sweet countenance once more."

Jasper did lead the way, and they were soon in the presence of Mabel. The latter met her late suitor with a bright blush, and her limbs trembled so, she could hardly stand; still her manner was affectionate and frank. During the hour of Pathfinder's visit (for it lasted no longer, though he ate in the dwelling of his friends), one who was expert in tracing the working of the human mind might have seen a faithful index to the feelings of Mabel in her manner to Pathfinder and her husband. With the latter she still had a little of the reserve that usually accompanies young wedlock; but the tones of her voice were kinder even than common; the glance of her eye was tender, and she seldom looked at him without the glow that tinged her cheeks betraying the existence of feelings that habit and time had not yet soothed into absolute tranquillity. With Pathfinder, all was earnest, sincere, even anxious; but the tones never trembled, the eye never fell; and if the cheek flushed, it was with the emotions that are connected with concern.

At length the moment came when Pathfinder must go his way. Chingachgook had already abandoned the canoes, and was posted on the margin of the woods, where a path led into the forest. Here he calmly waited to be joined by his friend. As soon as the latter was aware of this fact, he rose in a solemn manner and took his leave.

"I've sometimes thought that my own fate has been a little hard," he said; "but that of this woman, Mabel, has shamed me into reason."

"June remains, and lives with me," eagerly interrupted our heroine.

"So I comprehend it. If anybody can bring her back from her grief, and make her wish to live, you can do it, Mabel; though I've misgivings about even your success. The poor creatur' is without a tribe, as well as without a husband, and it's not easy to reconcile the feelings to both losses. Ah's me!—what have I to do with other people's miseries and marriages, as if I hadn't affliction enough of my own? Don't speak to me, Mabel—don't speak to me, Jasper—let me go my way in peace, and like a man. I've seen your happiness, and that is a great deal, and I shall be able to bear my own sorrow all the better for it. No— I'll never kiss you ag'in, Mabel, I'll never kiss you ag'in. Here's my hand, Jasper—squeeze it, boy, squeeze it; no fear of its giving way, for it's the hand of a man;—and now, Mabel, do you take it—nay, you must not do this,"—preventing Mabel from kissing it and bathing it in her tears—"you must not do this——"

"Pathfinder," asked Mabel, "when shall we see you again?"

"I've thought of that, too; yes, I've thought of that, I have. If the time should ever come when I can look upon you alto- gether as a sister, Mabel, or a child—it might be better to say a child, since you're young enough to be my daughter—depend on it I'll come back; for it would lighten my very heart to witness your gladness. But if I cannot—farewell—farewell—the Sergeant was wrong—yes, the Sergeant was wrong!"

This was the last the Pathfinder ever uttered to the ears of Jasper Western and Mabel Dunham. He turned away, as if the words choked him, and was quickly at the side of his friend. As soon as the latter saw him approach, he shouldered his own burthen, and glided in among the trees, without waiting to be spoken to. Mabel, her husband, and June all watched the form of the Pathfinder, in the hope of receiving a parting gesture, or a stolen glance of the eye; but he did not look back. Once or twice they thought they saw his head shake, as one trembles in bitterness of spirit; and a toss of the hand was given, as if he knew that he was watched; but a tread, whose vigor no sorrow could enfeeble, soon bore him out of view, and he was lost in the depths of the forest.

Neither Jasper nor his wife ever beheld the Pathfinder again. They remained for another year on the banks of Ontario; and then the pressing solicitations of Cap induced them to join him in New York, where Jasper eventually became a successful and respected merchant. Thrice Mabel received valuable presents of furs at intervals of years; and her feelings told her whence they came, though no name accompanied the gift. Later in life still, when the mother of several youths, she had occasion to visit the interior; and found herself on the banks of the Mohawk, accompanied by her sons, the eldest of whom was capable of being her protector. On that occasion she observed a man in a singular guise, watching her in the distance, with an intentness that induced her to inquire into his pursuits and character. She was told he was the most renowned hunter of that portion of the State—it was after the Revolution—a being of great purity of character and of as marked peculiarities; and that he was known in that region of country by the name of the Leather-stocking. Further than this Mrs. Western could not ascertain; though the distant glimpse and singular deportment of this unknown hunter gave her a sleepless night, and cast a shade of melancholy over her still lovely face, that lasted many a day.

As for June, the double loss of husband and tribe produced the effect that Pathfinder had foreseen. She died in the cottage of Mabel, on the shores of the lake; and Jasper conveyed her body to the island, where he interred it by the side of that of Arrowhead.

Lundie lived to marry his ancient love, and retired a war-worn and battered veteran; but his name has been rendered illustrious in our own time by the deeds of a younger brother, who succeeded to his territorial title, which, however, was shortly after merged in one earned by his valor on the ocean.